SWINDLE

HOW A MAN NAMED JOHN GRAMBLING, JR., CHEATED BANKS OUT OF MILLIONS

SWINDLE

HOW A MAN NAMED JOHN GRAMBLING, JR., CHEATED BANKS OUT OF MILLIONS

Brian Rosner

BUSINESS ONE IRWIN
Homewood, Illinois 60430

Project editor: Gladys True
Production manager: Diane Palmer
Jacket design: Image House
Compositor: Precision Typographers
Typeface: 11/13 Century Schoolbook
Printer: The Book Press, Inc.

Library of Congress Cataloging-in-Publication Data

Rosner, Brian
    Swindle: how a man named John Grambling, Jr., cheated banks out of
millions / by Brian Rosner.
    p.   cm.
    ISBN 1-55623-291-8
    1. Commercial crimes—New York (N.Y.)—Case studies.
2. Grambling, John. 1950– . 3. Banks and banking—New York (N.Y.)—Case
studies. 4. Fraud—New York (N.Y.)—Case studies. I. Title.
HV6770.N7R67 1990
364.1'63'097471—dc20   90–30965
                                                      CIP

Printed in the United States of America

1 2 3 4 5 6 7 8 9 0 BP 7 6 5 4 3 2 1 0

To Alfred I. Rosner (1902–1987), who taught me
to love and respect Justice and the Law, and
whose skills as a trial attorney I will be forever trying to equal.

PREFACE

Criminal law touches profound issues of right and wrong and people's lives. I was appointed a New York County Assistant District Attorney in January 1976. In 1980, after working almost exclusively on violent crime cases, I joined the Frauds Bureau, where I investigated and prosecuted cases of business fraud.

This book is the story of one of those business fraud cases; specifically that of John A. Grambling, Jr. Between 1984 and 1986, he defrauded a dozen banks in an equal number of states out of millions of dollars. The book recounts the commission of the crimes, the investigation by the Manhattan District Attorney's Office, and the process by which the culprits were, and were not, brought to justice. The book is written from my prospective as the trial attorney who prosecuted the criminals. If criminal prosecution is akin to warfare, then this is a memoir from the front lines, written not by a general, but by a soldier.

The John Grambling story is about bankers and business people; it is an object lesson for both. The bankers who were victimized were dealing with a man they believed had unimpeachable integrity. A former investment banker himself, Grambling spoke the bankers' language: He knew how to obtain a high-level introduction to a bank and how to present himself and his assets so as to appear to be a rising young entrepreneur, an obvious catch for any reasonably aggressive bank. Of course, the bankers did, as goes the phrase in the business world, their "due diligence": background checks, financial verifications, the rest. In response, the bankers were confronted by a ballet arranged by Grambling; the presentation of forged documents, and imposters convincingly vouching for the authenticity of these forged documents. As a result, the bankers were deceived—phenomenally so.

I wish I could say that this book reveals the five, or six, or whatever, secret lessons of "How to Avoid Being Defrauded," whether the reader is a banker or a spouse. This is not that book. Of course, there are cardinal rules of lending and precaution. The rules may be located in numerous training manuals and books, though not this one.

The Grambling story is one of experienced bankers who did their due diligence, and were swindled anyway. The moral? If the swindler is skillful, fraud can be done to anyone, however careful. The lesson of this work is more humble than my attempting to dictate principles of prevention. One of the book's purposes is to sensitize the reader to the possibilities of fraud. The message to the reader who is amused or frightened by what Grambling did to others is: There but for the grace of God, go I. Perhaps something in the book will stick in the reader's memory so that, when he is confronted by a Grambling, he will experience a shock of recognition. Better that than the subsequent, and ill-timed, shock of victimization.

In the end, this is a story about people. There are the too numerous victims, both the bankers and their families and, as will be seen, other victims and their families. And there are the people in the criminal justice system: The prosecutors, detectives, defense counsel, judges, and psychiatric experts, who, each doing what he thought right, worked at odds, and together, to produce an end result that our society calls *justice*.

Though, as will become apparent, the story has not ended for the most helpless victims of this crime, it did end for the defendant. He received the lengthiest prison sentence ever imposed on a white-collar criminal in the history of New York State. In part, the magnitude of the sentence imposed is a reflection of society's recently changed attitude toward white-collar crime, its newfound acknowledgment that money frauds do hurt victims and merit other than a light sentence.

That the writing of this book may prevent such future crimes is my hope, however much I know it will be largely unfulfilled.

Brian Rosner

ACKNOWLEDGMENTS

This book recounts numerous instances in which I exercise my judgment. I am the product of my parents, teachers, and professional colleagues: Insofar as this judgment is flawed or adequate, you may blame or praise them.

Among my practical inadequacies is an inability to type; my aversion to writing machines is total. This book would never have seen daylight but for the long hours and devotion of my secretary Bonni Aptaker.

I wrote this book during my first year of practice at Porter & Travers. I had been instructed in law school that law is a harsh mistress leaving no time for life other than professional work. I thank my partners for tolerating my allotment of time to matters other than billable hours.

And I thank my wife Barbara and our children, Ilana Gabrielle (three and a half years old) and David Abraham (seven). As well as my writing late into the evenings, it was from their time, on weekends and vacations, that I took the hours to author this book. My wife spent the time with Ilana and David, and the children, for the most part, understood. Though demanding to be in the room while I wrote (writing their own books, they said) they often even allowed me to work. Ultimately, this book is for them. I wrote it so they can understand how their father spent the beginning portion of his legal career.

CONTENTS

PART THREE
JUDGMENT

PEOPLE AND INSTITUTIONS

Grambling Energy, Inc.

John A. Grambling, Jr., President and Chairman of the Board

George S. Dibble, Jr., Vice Chairman

Robert Zobel, Chief Operating Officer

Robert Brewer, of counsel (to Grambling personally)

Alan Kaufman, of counsel (to Grambling personally), Buchwald & Kaufman

Joe Kelly, of counsel (to Grambling personally), Curtis, Mallet-Prevost, Colt & Mosle

Barry Kingham, of counsel (to Grambling personally), Curtis, Mallet-Prevost, Colt & Mosle

Peter Fleming, of counsel (to Grambling personally), Curtis, Mallet-Prevost, Colt & Mosle

The Bank of Montreal

Scott Hean, loan officer, Corporate and Government Banking Group

Ivor Hopkyns, loan officer, Corporate and Government Banking Group

Blair Mullin, loan officer, Corporate and Government Banking Group

James Busuttil, of counsel, Shearman & Sterling
Arthur Norman Field, of counsel, Shearman & Sterling
Jonathan Greenblatt, of counsel, Shearman & Sterling

Husky Oil Ltd.

William Miller, Vice President
Arthur R. Price, President

Lazard Freres & Co.

Thomas F. X. Mullarkey, in-house counsel
Robert M. Wilkis, Vice President
Martin Flumenbaum, of counsel, Paul, Weiss, Rifkind, Wharton & Garrison

Colorado National Bank of Denver

Thomas Foncannon, Vice President
Ken Hansen, Vice President
Bruce Rockwell, Chairman

Coronado Bank (El Paso, Texas)

Ronald Keenan, President
Jennie, Keenan's secretary

First Security Bank of Utah

James Conover, Senior Commercial Loan Officer
Spencer F. Eccles, Chairman of Executive Committee
Scott Clark, of counsel, Ray, Quinney & Nebeker

Cumberland Village Mining (West Virginia)
Southern Management (Miami, Florida)

Robert Libman, mine manager

Cecilia Rudd, secretary
Lawrence Goldman, of counsel (to Libman personally), Goldman & Hafetz

Jackson Savings and Loan Association
(Jackson, Mississippi)

Ken Warren, Executive Vice President
John Shows, of counsel, Young, Scanlon and Shows, P.A.

Great American First Savings Bank
(San Diego, California)

Carol Cortez, Vice President
Cynthia Fatica, Senior Counsel
Darwin Olsen, Chief Counsel

Department of Justice

Judith Feigen, Assistant United States Attorney,
San Diego, California

The Office of the District Attorney,
New York County

Robert M. Morgenthau, District Attorney
Peter Benitez, Chief, Frauds Bureau
James Kindler, Executive Assistant District Attorney
John Moscow, Assistant District Attorney (later Chief), Frauds
Bureau
Warren Reiss, Assistant District Attorney, Frauds
Bureau
Brian Rosner, Assistant District Attorney, Frauds
Bureau
Edward Collins, Detective, District Attorney's Office Squad
Ronald Moss, Detective, District Attorney's Office Squad
Martin Small, Detective, District Attorney's Office Squad

Psychiatric Expert

Hillel Bodek, psychiatric social worker retained by the District
Attorney's Office

The Judiciary

Herman Cahn, Acting Justice, Supreme Court, State of New
York

SWINDLE

HOW A MAN NAMED
JOHN GRAMBLING, JR., CHEATED
BANKS OUT OF MILLIONS

PROLOGUE

SUNSET

He sat in the rear of the bus by a window seat. A wire mesh covered the windows, partially obscuring the view, and steel bars separated the passengers from the armed driver and two guards in the front. His departure had been delayed by his sentencing. Finally, he had been placed in one of the late afternoon buses. The prisoners were chained together. He was one of the few white passengers.

The bus halted by the guardhouse at the foot of the bridge. Uniformed officers with guns unholstered at their sides positioned themselves on each side of the vehicle. They waved it on. With a jerk, the bus started the last leg of the journey. The engine groaned as the bus strained to reach the peak of the sharply arching bridge.

As the bus ascended, he looked behind and saw the Manhattan skyline. The skyscraper with the slanted roof, where his journey had begun 29 months before, glistened in the last rays of the setting sun, and then was dark. Abruptly, the driver shifted gears, and the prisoners descended to the island penitentiary.

PART 1

CRIME

CHAPTER 1

SKIING IN MIAMI

It was December 28, the Friday before New Year's Day 1985. John A. Grambling, Jr. rode the elevator to the Citicorp building's 33rd floor, one of several occupied by Shearman & Sterling, a prominent international law firm. A century-old institution, the firm had offices both on Wall Street and in the stylish mid-town skyscraper whose slanted roof was the symbol of Citicorp, the building's owner and the firm's main client.

Grambling presented himself to the receptionist. After a hushed phone call, she asked him to wait: The Shearman & Sterling lawyers were not ready for the closing. The receptionist escorted Grambling, attaché case in hand, to the waiting area. The spongy, low-seated chairs were an invitation to stand and enjoy the panoramic view of mid-Manhattan and the East River sparkling below.

This was Grambling's first visit to the firm. Since October, the young investment banker had been negotiating two loans with the Bank of Montreal, one of the law firm's bank clients. One loan was for $100 million; the other for $7.5 million. On December 28, 1984, Grambling was at Shearman & Sterling to close on the smaller loan.

Grambling's route to the Bank of Montreal, and its New York counsel, had begun three months earlier. In the summer of 1984, Husky Oil Ltd., the Canadian oil giant, had put its American subsidiary, R.M.T. Properties, on the market. The subsidiary owned and operated oil wells and refineries in several mountain states of the American West, where it also distributed petroleum products through 800 gas stations. R.M.T., an entity with yearly revenues of several hundred million dollars, employed thousands. Grambling put in a $30 million bid.

Grambling was a likely purchaser. Living in Connecticut, with a business with offices in Greenwich and on Manhattan's Park Avenue, Grambling's roots were in oil and gas. He was a Texan, born and raised in El Paso. His grandfather and uncles had been oil and gas pioneers whose success had made them millionaires. Grambling was a respected name in Texas, and the family wealth, in money and reputation, was John A. Grambling, Jr.'s inheritance.

After undergraduate work at Southern Methodist University, and a stint in the navy, Grambling had traveled East to Wharton, the business school of the University of Pennsylvania. In 1977, he graduated with an MBA in Finance and Accounting, and then cut his teeth in the world of investment banking. From graduation to 1983, he was employed in the Mergers and Acquisitions departments of, in succession, Citicorp Venture Capital, Lazard Freres & Co., and Dean Witter Reynolds, Inc. But Grambling was uncomfortable at those jobs. He did not want to be a bean-counter, a drone for the projects of other bankers. He wanted to make his own decisions, and take his own profits. In 1983, he established Grambling & Company, the vehicle for his purchase of R.M.T.

In the summer of 1984, Grambling emerged as the likely buyer of R.M.T. Before he could enter the pantheon of petro-businessmen, however, he had to overcome one obstacle: financing. Though a multimillionaire on paper, Grambling's cash flow and liquid assets were insufficient to purchase the multimillion dollar company. He needed $30 million for the purchase of R.M.T., and another $70 million in working capital to operate the company. It was an even $100 million, of which he had none.

But Grambling had learned from his training as an investment banker that the absence of cash is no obstacle to the entrepreneur. In a variation on the Golden Rule, Grambling planned to do for himself what he had done for others as an investment banker at Citicorp, Dean Witter, and Lazard Freres: He would finance the $100 million R.M.T. purchase by a leveraged buyout.

A leveraged buyout is simplicity itself. To pay for R.M.T., Grambling would borrow 100 percent of the purchase price. He would borrow the money from banks. He would borrow the money from Husky itself. The debts so incurred would be repaid from the future cash flow of R.M.T., the purchased company. Except for its relative modesty, Grambling's plan to mortgage R.M.T.'s future was no different from thousands of similar leveraged buyouts financed during the 1980s.

In September 1984, a funding problem jerked Grambling's plans to a halt. General Electric Credit Corporation (GECC), from whom Grambling had expected the bulk of funding, pulled out of the deal. GECC had concluded that Grambling was paying too much for R.M.T. Husky had made its own conclusions, and was eager to sell to Grambling. To save the sale, Husky introduced Grambling to one of its primary bankers, the venerable Bank of Montreal. To sweeten Grambling's financing request and minimize the bank's risk of nonpayment, Husky offered to guarantee repayment of the loan.

Experts at the bank's Calgary unit quickly studied the proposed purchase. They concluded it was a good deal—the purchase price was fair and could be repaid out of the company's future cash flow; and, in light of the Husky guarantee, it was risk-free. The bank agreed to lend $100 million to Grambling; $30 million to purchase R.M.T. and $70 million for working capital.

Mostly face-to-face in Manhattan, and occasionally over the phone between Calgary and New York, teams of attorneys, bankers, and business people negotiated and renegotiated the details of the financing so as to meet a January 1 deadline. By the end of November 1984, with the transaction close but not quite resolved, Husky authorized Grambling to operate R.M.T. as of January 1, 1985. The funding itself would close later in January. As Grambling waited in the Manhattan law firm on December 28, 1984, he was 72 hours short of fulfilling his acquisition dream.

The $100 million loan was the indirect reason for Grambling's presence at Shearman & Sterling that day. On December 7, Grambling had asked a "small" favor of Blair Mullin, one of the Bank's several Calgary officers putting together the

$100 million funding. Grambling needed a personal loan. He had hired accountants, lawyers, and consultants to evaluate the viability of R.M.T. and draft the buy-out documents, and he had assembled a staff of experienced professionals to operate R.M.T. as of the January 1 takeover date. Though the purchase would be leveraged, the debts incurred in order to make the buyout a reality were not. As Grambling explained to Mullin, he had incurred these prepurchase debts with "provincial" banks—lending institutions which, for their own narrow-minded accounting reasons, wanted to close their books on Grambling's debts by year end. Grambling asked Mullin for a $7.5 million personal loan. Mullin referred the request to his Calgary superiors. They assigned the personal loan application to Ivor Hopkyns, a member of the Corporate and Government Unit which was working on the $100 million funding.

In evaluating the request, Hopkyns and his colleagues asked themselves the basic credit question: Is this borrower capable of repaying the requested debt? Grambling's general creditworthiness and credibility were presumed: The bankers in Calgary were about to entrust Grambling with the operation of a major company, financed with the bank's money. Once sufficient collateral for the new loan was identified—this bank, keeping faith with its depositors and stockholders, required collateral from every borrower—the only obstacle to approving the personal loan would be whether the documentation for the collateral could be completed, as Grambling required, by the end of the year. Working weekends and evenings, the bankers and their attorneys had accomplished the task.

Grambling was in the Citicorp building on December 28 to close on the $7.5 million personal loan. As he munched on a bran muffin and jam, and sipped a Coke, Grambling kept close watch on his attaché case. In it was the collateral document essential to the closing.

As Grambling waited, James Busuttil, a Shearman & Sterling associate, feverishly organized the documents for the first closing in which he had primary responsibility. Medium height, and built stoutly like a football player, Busuttil was dark complected, with raven black hair and a thick full beard: He looked more like a Chassid or an ayatollah than a Wall

Street bank attorney. Of Maltese descent, he had been educated at Manhattan's Regis High School, the premier Jesuit
school in the United States. After Regis, he graduated from
Harvard College, and New York University Law School. His
mind had been trained to be sensitive to details.

Two-and-a-half years out of law school, Busuttil had arrived recently at Shearman & Sterling. Such firms are a training ground for corporate attorneys. After several years of representing corporations in their financings, mergers, and
disputes, the Shearman & Sterling associate is as accomplished a corporate counsel as the legal system can produce,
and is prepared to use his or her skills anywhere, whether at
another firm or as corporate in-house counsel.

Busuttil's preparation for the loan's final act testified to
the meticulousness in which he had been schooled. The closing
was scheduled to occur in one of the firm's 33rd floor conference
rooms, wood-paneled and windowless. The room was filled by a
rectangular wooden table, which Busuttil had set for action.

Spaced at even intervals around the table were 40 manila
folders, each folder containing a closing document which,
taken together, was the loan. Some documents were originals
to be signed by Grambling; some were copies to be replaced by
originals. The first folder was on the edge of the table closest to
the door. By moving around the table clockwise, signing (or re-
placing) the documents one by one, Grambling would ultimately return to the door, and the 40th folder, and complete the
loan. It was like a Monopoly game: Moving one folder at a time,
Grambling would, so long as his papers were in order, land on
Park Place, and collect $7.5 million. Busuttil invited Gram-
bling into the room.

The document in the first folder was basic; the promissory
note evidencing that Grambling had borrowed $7.5 million. It
was a legally binding commitment to repay. Grambling signed
the note, and Busuttil notarized the signature. They moved a
step to the second folder.

Resolving the terms and conditions of the loan had been
Hopkyns' job: The second document was his work, the eight-
page loan agreement spelling out the interest rate, period of
the loan, and collateral. The latter was critical. Contrary to

popular suspicion, banks do not print money: They lend the money entrusted to them by depositors and shareholders. The collateral was the guarantee of repayment. In the event of default, the bank could sell specific Grambling assets to repay the loan and make the bank's depositors whole. Grambling signed the loan agreement, and moved to the left.

The next folder contained a guarantee received from Florida two days earlier. An important document, it had been discussed in letters and phone calls between the signatory, Busuttil, and Mullin. By this guarantee, Robert H. Libman of Miami Beach, Florida, committed himself to pay Grambling's $7.5 million loan "with interest" should Grambling himself not pay. Libman had signed the document under oath in the presence of a notary, whose embossed seal clearly rose from the face of the paper in front of Grambling and Busuttil.

A guarantee is only as good as the person who signs it, and Libman, according to the balance sheet submitted to the bank in early December, had a net worth in excess of $23 million. His primary assets were holdings of the nation's most trustworthy blue-chip stocks: AT&T: 100,779 shares—$1,877,512; Disney: 22,212 shares—$1,266,081; IBM: 8,821 shares—$1,109,241; McGraw Hill: 55,893 shares—$2,429,336. In a December 1984 letter to Mullin, Libman had confirmed that "none of the securities listed in my personal statement have been pledged, hypothecated, or otherwise encumbered." The assets were as good as cash.

Libman had not expected the bank to accept his statement of personal creditworthiness without question. In mid-December, he forwarded to Mullin a list of bank and business references in West Virginia, Florida, Texas, Arizona, and Alberta, and encouraged Mullin and his colleagues to confirm Libman's reputation and wealth. The bank references, contacted by Ivor Hopkyns, had declined to state the precise amounts in Libman's accounts, and Hopkyns, an experienced banker, had not thought that they would. Bank information is confidential, and both bankers and their clients prize the secrecy with which account information is treated. When requesting or giving a bank reference, bankers speak in code; statements, often evasive on their face, from which the trained ear can infer the status of the account relationship.

To Hopkyns' trained ear, Libman's bank references had been superlative. Each banker confirmed that his bank's relationship with Libman was long-standing and satisfactory, and several confirmed the accuracy of Libman's balance sheet. Since Libman's net worth could repay the Grambling loan three times over, the guarantee was a compelling statement to the bankers in Calgary that the Grambling loan bore the most minimal risk of nonpayment.

Unknown to the bank officers, Libman had already committed his wealth to the success of the R.M.T. purchase. As with the seller of a house, the seller of a company requires the buyer put down a deposit, a financial commitment to the success of the sale. To buy R.M.T., Husky had required Grambling to put down a $7 million deposit, in cash and nonrefundable. Since this was a leveraged buyout, and not the purchase of a home, Husky did not expect Grambling to commit $7 million of his own money to the purchase. The premise of a leveraged buyout is that the buyer does not have, or does not want to risk, his own funds. To grease the sale, Husky agreed to lend Grambling the $7 million deposit required to buy the Husky subsidiary.

Husky had imposed one condition on the interest-bearing loan: The interest payments had to be guaranteed by a creditworthy third party.

Grambling had proposed Libman as guarantor. As Hopkyns would do later, senior Husky financial officers had scrutinized Libman's $23 million net worth. Arthur Price, Husky president, and William Miller, the vice president responsible for finance, interrogated Libman about his assets. They even flew to Miami and were wined and dined at the posh Jockey Club, where Libman was a member. "I'm an experienced operator of coal mines," Libman assured the Husky people. "When John takes over, I'll assist him in a managerial role." Persuaded, Price and Miller accepted Libman's guarantee, and Husky made the $7 million loan.

Busuttil closed the folder containing the signed, notarized Libman guarantee, and Grambling and Busuttil continued around the table. Grambling's financial statement had listed his ownership of over $10 million of stock; including 20,190 shares in Biosystems, Inc., which owned and operated colleges for rehabilitation therapy in Arizona, and 27,927 shares in the Cumberland Village Mining Group, Inc., the West Virginia coal mine managed by Libman. Grambling leaned over the conference room table to sign various documents transferring the Biosystems and Cumberland Village shares to the bank.

Without more, the assignment of the shares was of limited value. From a credit viewpoint, the problem with Biosystems and Cumberland Village was that they were closely held companies: Grambling owned 100 percent of Biosystems and 18.5 percent of Cumberland. Since the shares were not publicly traded, they had no ready market or ascertainable value. Grambling's guess as to their value ($3.5 million for Biosystems, and $8.5 million for Cumberland Village Mining) was just that—a guess.

But, as Busuttil and the bankers knew, the assignments did not stand alone. In December, Grambling had sent the Calgary bankers a stock purchase agreement for the Biosystems shares. The agreement, a December 14, 1984 letter on the stationery of Datavision, Inc., a Colorado-based computer company, bore the signature of "Richard S. Crawford, Chairman." It read: "Datavision agrees to extend to John Grambling or his lender the option of selling his stock in Biosystems to the Datavision Company for $3.5 million." The letter, a legally enforceable commitment to buy at a set price, gave the stock a set price and ascertainable value: $3.5 million.

The next folder on the table contained the document transferring that value to the Bank of Montreal. In a December letter, Grambling had informed Datavision that he had "assigned to the Bank of Montreal all of my right, title and interest in and to the letter agreement dated December 14, 1984 from you to me whereby you agreed to purchase the stock of Biosystems, Inc. owned by me for $3.5 million." Crawford had been asked to execute a "Consent and Agreement," drafted by Busuttil, which acknowledged that the bank could compel Datavision to pay it $3.5 million for the Biosystems stock.

In the folder in front of Grambling and Busuttil was the original Consent and Agreement, dated December 24, and bearing the signature "Richard Crawford." Busuttil compared the "Richard Crawford" signature on the Consent with the

"Richard Crawford" signature on the December 14 promise to buy. The signatures were identical. Its authenticity established, Busuttil returned the Datavision consent to the file. The document was an additional $3.5 million of collateral for the loan.

Busuttil and Grambling moved to the next document, a stock purchase agreement for the Cumberland Village Mining stock. In a December 3 letter on the stationery of the Cumberland Village Mining Group, Inc., Libman had committed Cumberland to purchase Grambling's shares: "In order to assist you in obtaining financing for your acquisition of Husky–R.M.T. Properties, Cumberland Village Mining Group, Inc. wishes to extend the option to you or to your lender of selling your stock to the company for $8.5 million." As he had done with Crawford, Grambling had notified Libman that Grambling had assigned to the Bank of Montreal his "right, title and interest in and to the letter agreement . . . to purchase my Cumberland Village Mining Group stock for $8.5 million." Libman had been asked to sign a "Consent and Agreement acknowledging such assignment and the rights of the bank."

As Busuttil watched, Grambling opened his attaché case and withdrew the signed Cumberland Consent and Agreement. Dated December 24, 1984, the consent bore the signature "Robert Libman, President." As on all the Libman documents and letters, Libman's signature was an ideogram, a wavy line which bore a greater resemblance to a Chinese block symbol than to a recognizable letter of the English language. Busuttil compared the Libman ideogram on the consent with the signatures on the December purchase agreement and the notarized Libman guarantee, documents that had been signed by Libman and mailed by Libman to the bank. The Libman ideograms—the signatures—were identical. The Cumberland consent was an additional $8.5 million of collateral. Grambling and Busuttil moved another step to the left.

After several more folders, Grambling and Busuttil had made a full circuit of the table and, as when they had begun, were opposite the door. They were at the folder for the document without which the loan would not be made.

Busuttil opened the folder. In it was an unsigned copy of the final Consent and Agreement he had drafted in the frantic days preceding the closing. Grambling's financial statement had listed one major liquid asset—375,136 common shares of the Dr Pepper company, then listed on the New York Stock Exchange. The market value for Grambling's shares was $8,252,992. Shortly after receiving the loan request, Hopkyns and his colleagues analyzed Grambling's statement and agreed that, no matter what other collateral and guarantees were offered, the assignment of the Dr Pepper stock would be the necessary collateral for the loan.

Hopkyns quickly realized that the assignment of the Dr Pepper stock would not be accomplished simply. In a 1984 leveraged buyout, Grambling told Hopkyns, Dr Pepper had been taken private, converted from a publicly held to a closely held corporation. The new owners had obligated themselves to purchase each outstanding Dr Pepper share for $22 cash, payable no later than January 22, 1985, a month away.

For Hopkyns, an expert in oil and gas financing, the Dr Pepper buyout was not a transaction with which he was or should have been familiar. In mid-December, he questioned Grambling about the mechanism by which the stock would be converted to cash, and Grambling suggested that he talk to Bob Wilkis, an investment banker at Lazard Freres & Co., the Manhattan banking firm that had put together the financing on the Dr Pepper buyout.

Grambling's suggestion resulted in several December 1984 conversations between Hopkyns and Wilkis. On each occasion, Hopkyns and Wilkis spoke over the phone, between the Rockefeller Center office of Lazard Freres and the bank office in Calgary. Hopkyns did not have Wilkis' direct line so, to reach him, Hopkyns called the main Lazard number.

Wilkis had been expecting Hopkyns's first call in the middle of December 1984. After polite preliminaries—Wilkis said that he and Grambling had been colleagues at Lazard, they even had shared the same secretary—Wilkis discussed the Dr Pepper buyout. Although he had not worked on the transaction, everyone in the firm knew about the Dr Pepper deal and was proud of it. Cradling the phone on his shoulder, Wilkis reached for his copy of the public documentation on the buy-out. He explained to Hopkyns the process by which each Dr Pepper share would be purchased at $22 a share by January 22, 1985.

Having confirmed the conversion details, Hopkyns phoned Grambling to question him about other details of the stock ownership: where were the physical shares held; in whose name; what Lazard Freres officer was authorized to assign the shares to the bank? Busuttil needed this detailed information to prepare the legal document transferring the stock from Lazard Freres, or whoever held it, to the bank. When Hopkyns asked Grambling for this information, he said, "Ivor, call Bob Wilkis again. The stock is in my Lazard Freres account, and Bob can give you the necessary details."

A few days after his first call to Lazard, Hopkyns called Lazard again and, passing through the switchboard, reached Wilkis. Hopkyns asked for the stock details.

"I can't give you that information. I'm not John's account officer," Wilkis protested. "For the details on John's stock, you have to ask someone in the back office," Wilkis said, referring to the recordkeeping area of the firm.

Hopkyns had an additional question.

"Bob, even if you are not the account officer, are you authorized to sign the document transferring John's stock to the bank?"

Wilkis responded with an emphatic "No."

"I'm an associate, not a member of the firm. Only a partner can sign such a transfer. You're going to have to get a firm member to sign any kind of transfer document."

Hopkyns was annoyed. He needed the ownership details to prepare the assignment, and he needed the assignment to complete the loan that Grambling wanted expedited. The signatory problem was not an immediate problem since, presumably, Wilkis would ask the appropriate person to sign the final document.

After the second Wilkis call, Hopkyns called Grambling to complain about the delay in obtaining the ownership information. "John, we can't close the loan until we have the ownership facts for the assignment."

Grambling apologized. "Everything has been straightened out at Lazard, Ivor. Bob just needed to get the numbers. He has them now waiting for you. Just give him a call."

For the third time in seven days, Hopkyns called Wilkis in New York. Grambling had been correct. The specifics regarding Grambling's Lazard Freres account were now available.

"I just received a call from the recordkeeper at Continental Illinois Bank," Wilkis explained. As Hopkyns knew, Continental Illinois Bank was the transfer agent, the recordkeeper, for the Dr Pepper stock.

"This is how John holds his stock," Wilkis continued. "There's 181,000 shares of stock in his own name, certificate number DX67144. He owns another 194,036 shares in the name of E.F. Hutton and Company, certificate number DX24618." Hopkyns scribbled the numbers down, and thanked Wilkis.

The same day, Hopkyns called Busuttil in New York to give him the figures. The attorney incorporated the numbers into the Consent and Agreement to be signed by Lazard:

> The undersigned hereby acknowledges notice of, and consents to, the assignment from John A. Grambling, Jr. (the "Grantor") to the Bank of Montreal (the "Bank") of all right, title and interest of the Grantor in and to the 181,100 shares of Common Stock of Dr Pepper Company ("DP") registered in the name of the Grantor and the 194,036 shares of Common Stock of DP held in the name of E.F. Hutton and Company, Inc., all held by the undersigned for the account of the Grantor (the 375,136 shares of Common Stock of DP collectively being the "Shares"). As you know, the Shares have been tendered by us and payment of U.S. $8,252,992.00 therefore is due on or about January 22, 1985.

Ever careful, Busuttil himself called Wilkis to double-check the details: The number of shares, the account names, the January purchase date, and the $8,252,992 buyout price. Wilkis confirmed the information. Busuttil also asked Wilkis if he would be signing the Consent and Agreement; Busuttil wanted to know whose name to draft for the signature lines on the Consent.

Irked, Wilkis again explained that only a partner's signature could bind the firm. "I can't sign, and I don't know who

John is going to get to sign the consent." Busuttil told Wilkis that he would send him the transfer document, which would have a space for a Lazard Freres & Co. signature, but no typed identification of the signatory. Busuttil had the Consent and Agreement hand-delivered to Lazard on the 24th.

In the Shearman & Sterling conference room on December 28, Busuttil examined the copy of the Lazard Freres consent, the product of the half dozen phone calls of the preceding two weeks. How and when will I be receiving the signed original, he thought.

Grambling withdrew a document from his attaché case and handed it to Busuttil. The attorney recognized it. It was his work product, the original Consent and Agreement.

Busuttil turned to the the signature page. "In witness hereof, the undersigned has duly executed this Consent and Agreement." Above the typed name "Lazard Freres & Co." was the signature "Lazard Freres & Co." in handwriting. Underneath, in the same handwriting, was the signature of a general partner. Underneath that signature was a second signature, "Robert W. Wilkis, Vice President." Busuttil took the Xerox copy of the Consent and Agreement out of the 40th folder. Into the folder, he placed the signed original. The $7.5 million loan closing was complete—almost.

As he and Hopkyns had agreed, Busuttil called Hopkyns from the conference room phone. Until the Lazard Freres document had been presented, Hopkyns and Busuttil did not know which Lazard Freres partner would sign on behalf of the firm. All they knew was that Wilkis, as he had said more than once, could not bind the firm with his signature. With Grambling on the line, Busuttil told Hopkyns in Calgary, that a general partner had signed. The letters on the partner's signature were crammed together, so Grambling interpreted: "It's Peter Corcoran who signed for Lazard Freres." Hopkyns told Grambling that he wanted to speak to Corcoran. Since Wilkis had raised the issue of whose signature could, and could not, bind Lazard, Hopkyns wanted to confirm with Corcoran that he was empowered to sign for the firm.

"Reaching Corcoran might be a problem," Grambling said. "I think Corcoran may already have left for vacation." A call by Hopkyns to Lazard Freres confirmed Grambling's suspicion: With the three-day weekend ahead, Corcoran had already departed.

Grambling volunteered that one of his Lazard Freres acquaintances might have Corcoran's vacation phone number. Busuttil turned to Grambling and said, "use my office to make the phone calls, John." After a few minutes, his feet resting comfortably on Busuttil's desk, Grambling was again on the line with Hopkyns in Calgary.

"I've gotten the number, Ivor," Grambling said. "Corcoran's already in Miami. He's at 305-940-7536."

From Calgary, Hopkyns dialed the Miami number. A male voice answered.

"Peter Corcoran?" Hopkyns asked.

"Yes, this is he."

Hopkyns identified himself as a Bank of Montreal officer, and Corcoran immediately replied that he understood what the call was about. "You're calling about that consent form I signed for John."

"I'm a general partner at Lazard Freres, and have been for years," Corcoran explained. He had known Grambling when "John" had worked at Lazard Freres. Grambling's departure had not ended his ties to the firm, however. "I anticipate that Lazard Freres will be doing a great deal of business with John's companies in the coming year." Corcoran confirmed that he was a signatory for the firm and, after six minutes, the conversation ended.

Hopkyns was satisfied. Under enormous time pressures, he had completed the $7.5 million loan. He had satisfied the client, a rising star on the American business scene, and he had satisfied his bank's depositors and stockholders. The loan was secured by stock to be converted to cash within a month. The transaction was risk free. Hopkyns called New York. He authorized Busuttil to complete the loan.

Busuttil was satisfied. As had Hopkyns, Busuttil had worked feverishly to complete the transaction by January 1. The task had been accomplished, with every "t" crossed and "i" dotted. The loan was 100 percent collateralized. Busuttil called the Bank of Montreal's Park Avenue branch, and informed the loan department that Grambling could receive his $7.5 million.

Grambling was satisfied. Under pressure to complete the R.M.T. buyout, with constant harassment from those petty-minded "provincial" lenders, pestering him about their little loans when he was so close to his dreamed-of oil company purchase, Grambling had obtained the $7.5 million, and the breathing space it provided. That afternoon, he drafted a letter to James Burgoyne, an account officer at the Park Avenue Bank of Montreal office. The letter directed Burgoyne to disburse the $7.5 million to several of Grambling's most pressing creditors, banks in Kansas, Texas, Arizona, Connecticut, and Tennessee. The money, now Grambling's money, was wire-transferred from the Bank of Montreal's New York branch on December 31.

And Peter Corcoran was satisfied. As with most investment bankers, Corcoran worked long hours. He deserved this vacation. After the five-hour drive from New York, Corcoran got out of his car and stretched. It was good to be in Vermont. The snow was deep, and he looked forward to a weekend of family skiing.

And in Miami, the other "Peter Corcoran," the "Peter Corcoran" with whom Ivor Hopkyns had spoken, was also satisfied. He had helped Grambling close the $7.5 million loan, and put off, for a while, Grambling's creditors. Rather than these prior loans being thrown into work-out, bad debt collection, and litigation, and the inevitable discovery of the forgeries and deceptions by which Grambling had financed his entrepeneurship, the "problem loans" had been paid, and the files on them mercifully closed.

Of course, the work of "Peter Corcoran" in Miami was not done. There was a new $7.5 million loan that would come due eventually, and have to be repaid. But, as long as there were banks in America, there would be some lender somewhere who could be cajoled into parting with his depositors' money.

For now, the Miami "Corcoran" could sit back and enjoy the warm ocean breeze. After all, within a month, the Bank of Montreal would be handing him and Grambling another $100 million, of which $70 million would be discretionary "working capital."

CHAPTER 2

HOPKYNS HAS A PROBLEM

On January 1, 1985, Grambling strutted into the Denver headquarters of R.M.T. It was not just a physical entry into the premises. He was there to take possession: While the bankers in Calgary and New York haggled over the final details of the $100
million Bank of Montreal financing, Grambling and Husky had
agreed that Grambling would act as R.M.T.'s owner with the
New Year. Husky had imposed only one constraint: Grambling
was not to saddle R.M.T. with non-R.M.T. indebtedness.

This restriction was essential: Neither the bank nor Husky
wanted Grambling to fritter away R.M.T.'s assets. The bank
looked to R.M.T.'s already encumbered assets as its primary
source of repayment for the $100 million financing, and Husky,
having agreed to guarantee repayment of Grambling's debt,
wanted those assets preserved. The Term Sheet, which stated
the principal conditions of the $100 million financing, reflected
this concern for preservation. Negative covenants three and
eight stated plainly that Grambling could not "make any loan
or investment or give any guarantee" with R.M.T. assets, or
"incur, create, or otherwise assume any further indebtedness"
on R.M.T.'s behalf.

Bound by this minimal restriction, Grambling took over
the company. His elevation to the control of R.M.T., now called
Grambling Energy, was duly communicated to the business
and financial world. In its first edition after the New Year, *The
Wall Street Journal* reported, "Husky Sells U.S. Refineries to
Grambling Energy, Inc." Among the readers of this announce-
ment was a keenly interested Robert Wilkis, the investment
banker at Lazard Freres in Manhattan.

"Damn!" Wilkis muttered to himself. "Grambling pulled it off. And I helped him." Wilkis made an entry in his mental book of favors: Grambling owes me.

In his new offices halfway across the continent from Manhattan, Grambling knew that any pleasure at his success was woefully premature. A diversified oil company was not a corner candy store, and Grambling had hired a dozen experienced industry professionals to cope with the complex daily problems of such a business. But as he sat alone on Sunday, January 6, looking at the mountains recede into the night, it was not the humdrum affairs of business management that troubled him. It was the disaster about to happen. "What if," he thought, "the Bank of Montreal learns how I bankrolled this purchase?"

Grambling pulled the letter from his attaché case. He scanned the litany of broken promises and unreturned phone calls to locate the only sentence that mattered: "By copy of this letter, I am requesting our corporate counsel to proceed with any collection procedures that are necessary." Dated November 12, 1984, the letter was signed by Carroll Lindsay, vice president and treasurer of the U.S. Shelter corporation, a publicly owned real estate company in Greenville, South Carolina.

Grambling returned the letter to a file thick with similar correspondence from frustrated and angered creditors. He knew from experience that the threat to go to the law set a clock ticking, though the clock ticked differently with each institution. To some lenders, "immediately" meant just that—pay up, or the lawsuit starts tomorrow. These institutions had to be paid quickly. Other creditors, willing to listen to fresh promises of repayment, could be stalled for weeks—even months.

U.S. Shelter had been accommodating, and Grambling had put them off since October. Initially, he had promised to repay with his large receivables, fees from his leveraged buyouts and management contracts. But, as he had sadly explained to Lindsay in November, "the receivables have been slow in being collected." When they failed to appear at all, Grambling strung U.S. Shelter along through December with the promise that "I'll be repaying with a $7.5 million financing from the Bank of Montreal." Grambling had even mailed Lindsay copies of the Bank of Montreal loan documentation, a credible set of papers that Grambling had also mailed to other threatening creditors holding, in total, well over $10 million of Grambling debt. Not every boat would rise with this incoming tide.

And not every boat did. Creditors' demands exceeded the finally approved and disbursed $7.5 million loan. U.S. Shelter had been left in the cold, again. If Grambling judged Lindsay correctly, after not being paid with the Bank of Montreal proceeds, U.S. Shelter would finally do something other than letter writing to collect its $2.2 million. Once it did, the Bank of Montreal $100 million loan was dead. With a single phone inquiry, U.S. Shelter would discover that it was the victim of a $2.2 million fraud that Grambling had accomplished with a Lazard Freres forgery.

Grambling rose and walked around his office. His office, he thought. And he couldn't have gotten there, he knew, but by defrauding U.S. Shelter.

It was a brilliant money-obtaining device. It had begun in Grambling's friendship with Barton Tuck, the president of U.S. Shelter. In the spring of 1984, Grambling had approached Tuck with a business proposition. Grambling had learned that U.S. Shelter wanted to enter the cable TV business, and he also had learned of the opportunity to purchase several Maryland cable TV properties, owned by seven Lazard Freres partners in their individual capacities. Grambling proposed a joint venture to purchase the properties.

He had already worked out the plan with the owners. In exchange for an interest-bearing loan of $2.2 million, the Lazard partners would give Grambling an exclusive option for six months, sufficient time for Grambling to determine the fairness of the Lazard partners' $8.8 million asking price. If the systems were not purchased, the $2.2 million loan would be repaid, with interest, and no one would be worse for the deal. In the joint venture Grambling proposed, he would contribute his expertise, developed in his years at Lazard Freres, to evaluate the system; U.S. Shelter would contribute the $2.2 million for the loan; should the purchase be made, subsequent costs would be split evenly.

However, Grambling had advised Tuck and Lindsay, the final transaction would require discretion. As Grambling had explained, "the Lazard partners told me that they don't want to deal directly with a publicly held corporation such as U.S. Shelter. It's a matter of client relations. They know you're going to fund the loan and be my partner in the transaction, but all the documentation has to be between the Lazard partners and myself." The principals at U.S. Shelter understood the need for discretion: Publicly held corporations are required to disclose their business affairs, and the investment bankers, members of a profession accustomed to secrecy, would not want publicity about their private investments. U.S. Shelter signed on for the deal.

Grambling prepared the paperwork. He contracted with the Lazard partners for a six-month exclusive right to buy the Maryland cable properties, and loaned the partners $2.2 million, to be repaid with interest in six months. Simultaneously, he and U.S. Shelter entered a joint venture. As part of the joint venture agreement, U.S. Shelter lent Grambling the money which he, in turn, lent to the Lazard partners. By using Grambling as middleman, U.S. Shelter had made the loan to the Lazard partners without having to appear on a single document with the partners.

The distancing between U.S. Shelter and the Lazard partners ran even deeper. No one from U.S. Shelter had met or even spoken to any of the Lazard partners, although Lindsay had asked for a copy of the $2.2 million promissory note signed by the partners, and, promptly, a copy had been mailed to Greenville by Grambling's New York counsel. Two columns listing the seven financiers marched down the left- and right-hand side of the note's signature page. Each was a person of wealth who, U.S. Shelter could presume, would repay their debt when due. The first signatory on the $2.2 million note was Lazard Freres partner Peter E. Corcoran.

In November 1984, the six-month exclusive period for Grambling to investigate the systems had ended and the notes—Grambling's note to U. S. Shelter, and the Lazard partners' note to Grambling—had come due. Lindsay told Grambling that U.S. Shelter did not want to make the purchase. Lindsay expected repayment. That it was not forthcoming was inexplicable, Lindsay thought. Why couldn't Grambling just return to U.S. Shelter the $2.2 million he had just received from the Lazard partners on the repayment of their debt?

This was the $2.2 million debt bedeviling Grambling in his Denver headquarters on January 6. The cable transaction had been a sham. He had needed the $2.2 million to fund his purchase of R.M.T. The Lazard Freres story—the cable systems, the $2.2 million loan, the partners' signatures on the note—was as authentic as the Peter Corcoran signature on the assignment Grambling had given to Busuttil.

Grambling realized that the falsity of the transaction in general, and the Lazard Freres forgery in particular, threatened his $100 million loan. What if, in following through on their collection threat, U.S. Shelter actually called one of the Lazard Freres partners to inquire about the underlying cable "deal" or the partners' repayment of the $2.2 million loan? Grambling would be exposed as a forger and a thief. He could imagine the headlines, and the consequences.

Though risky, the solution to the dilemma was only a checkbook and a fountain pen away. Tens of millions of dollars ran through R.M.T.'s checking accounts every month, and Grambling was running R.M.T. He reached for the phone and dialed the Cody, Wyoming office of R.M.T. Though it was Sunday evening, Grambling knew that Paul Gutneckt would answer the call. An accountant, Gutneckt had been a consultant to Grambling since November 1984 and, as of January 1, was Grambling Energy's chief financial officer. That Sunday evening, Gutneckt was working around the clock to move the company's accounting department from Cody to Denver.

"I'm glad I caught you in, Paul. I have an important expense you must pay first thing tomorrow. It's for an appraisal I had done, and payment is overdue. I'll give you the invoice next time I see you in Denver." Grambling paused, and then continued.

"Husky knows about the U.S. Shelter appraisal," Grambling assured Gutneckt. "It's an approved expense."

The next morning, Monday, January 7, Gutneckt asked a subordinate to transfer the $2.2 million. The money was not sent. Though now Grambling Energy employees, the members of the accounting staff had been employed by Husky for years, and they retained feelings of loyalty to their former employer. The transfer ordered by Gutneckt appeared to conflict with the parting instructions of the Husky officers: Grambling was to manage R.M.T. until he owned it outright but, until that time, R.M.T. money was to be used only for R.M.T. debt and expenses. Is this expense allowed, a holdover employee wondered. He figured that he would let his bosses, both the old and the new, resolve the issue among themselves. The employee called his former supervisor, now at Husky in Calgary, and told him of the proposed $2.2 million payment to U.S. Shelter. The Husky supervisor explained that the proposed payment was not allowed. With that explanation, he thought the issue was closed.

Later that morning, however, Gutneckt called Husky to ask about the proposed transfer. "Is the bill payable?" he inquired of Miller. The financial vice president explained that it was not. It was an amicable conversation that ended with the understanding that the $2.2 million would not be sent.

Grambling called Miller at 10:30 that evening. He insisted that the $2.2 million was a valid R.M.T. expense which had to be paid. Miller was not persuaded, but he agreed with Grambling to discuss the issue again in the morning.

In accordance with previously arranged plans, Miller flew to Denver the next day, Tuesday, January 8: He was to visit R.M.T. to monitor its transition to Grambling Energy. Prior to Miller's arrival at R.M.T., Grambling ordered a subordinate to wire transfer the $2.2 million to U.S. Shelter. The employee was told to pay it or be fired. The payment was made.

Miller learned of the transfer when he arrived at R.M.T. He was enraged. He stormed into Grambling's office with a blunt message: "You put that money back by the end of the week, or the whole deal is off." Grambling tried to soothe the Husky vice president for finance. "Bill, the U.S. Shelter debt was a valid R.M.T. debt, and I have the documents to prove it," Grambling explained. Miller would have none of it: This was a man who meant "immediately" when he said it. Calmly, Grambling explained that the money would be returned in a day or two. He had quenched the U.S. Shelter fire only to pour gasoline on the R.M.T. purchase itself.

Rescue would come from the business meeting Grambling had attended in downtown Denver that Monday. A Denver-based entrepreneur with pipelines, refineries, and 800 service stations is a prize business catch for a local bank. At the opening of the banking day on Monday, January 7, Grambling and George S. Dibble, Jr., a former R.M.T. officer and now vice chairman of Grambling Energy, arrived at the Colorado National Bank Building to test the fishing. Known and respected in the Denver business community, Dibble had arranged for Grambling to meet Bruce M. Rockwell, Dibble's friend of 20 years. Rockwell was the Chairman of the Board of Colorado National Bank of Denver. A regional commercial bank with a respectable 1984 net income of $21 million, Colorado National was heavily invested in agriculture, real estate, and oil and gas.

Dibble brought Grambling to the 70-year old bank building at 17th and Champa. They entered the magnificent central hall, four stories tall and flanked by fluted columns. Ringing the hall were tastefully decorated service areas where business was being conducted with a respectful hush. Dibble knew the way. He and Grambling took an elevator to the third floor wood-paneled office of the chairman. Rockwell was there to meet them, as was Senior Vice President Robert Kropf. Broad-shouldered, with white hair and a square jaw, Rockwell was the central casting image of the no-nonsense bank chairman. He was also a real-life example of the businessman as a good citizen. A long-time Denver resident, Rockwell had served as the first Chairman of the Denver Urban Renewal Authority. In that role, he had midwifed the redevelopment of downtown Denver from dilapidated, often vacant buildings to the modern, vibrant skyscrapers of Denver today. He was also a trustee of various philanthropic and cultural organizations. A banker's purpose, in Rockwell's view, was to bring jobs and the good life to his community.

Rockwell guided his guests to his office's subdued but elegant working area, an upholstered couch facing a table and two soft, winged chairs. Paintings of western scenes were on the wall. Rockwell motioned his guests to the couch, as he and Kropf pulled the chairs in a semicircle. Grambling, in his soft voice, explained how he had purchased R.M.T., and his plans for expansion and job creation.

After only a few minutes, and based in part on what they had learned previously from Dibble, Rockwell and Kropf knew how the meeting would end. Kropf telephoned Vice President Thomas Foncannon to join them in the chairman's office. A thin man in his 30s, married with two children, Foncannon was a career banker with 14 years in the industry. His father had been a banker in Missouri, and Foncannon had spent the first five years of his career as a bank examiner for the Federal Reserve Bank in Kansas City. Now a loan officer, he had been summoned to the chairman's office because the bankers had decided that Colorado National wanted to make a loan.

After Foncannon's arrival, Grambling again explained his needs. The Bank of Montreal's $100 million funding was to be interim financing, to last for eight months beginning January 31, 1985, the scheduled closing date.

"I expect that I'll have to replace the $100 million. And, with my expansion plans, I'll probably need more. Would Colorado National," Grambling asked, "be interested in replacing Bank of Montreal as Grambling Energy's major creditor?"

Although interested in working with Grambling and his companies, Rockwell explained that a $100 million loan to a single entity exceeded Colorado National's legal lending limit, and, although Colorado National could try to put together a group of banks to lend the $100 million, neither he nor his colleagues were sure that that could be done. No, the bankers conceded, Colorado National could not replace the Bank of Montreal as Grambling Energy's primary creditor. What Colorado National could do, Rockwell and Foncannon explained, was to participate in any refinancing of the $100 million credit and, of course, be available to finance the smaller needs of Grambling's business.

Grambling was satisfied. He'd be happy to have Colorado National participate in future large-scale fundings. He then began to explain his smaller but still significant needs.

"I'll want a local bank with the capacity to service my credit card business. It's a fair-sized operation, over 800 service stations in all.

"But my most immediate concern is the costs I need to meet this month. There's general operating costs, plus the expense of consolidating the business in Denver. I also have over $4 million of closing costs for the Bank of Montreal funding." Grambling counted off on his fingers the expenses—lawyers' fees, accountants' fees, bank's fee, U.S. Shelter real estate appraisal.

Without hesitation, he moved to the request.

"The company needs $6 million of short-term funding to get it through the month."

Grambling proposed an unsecured loan to Grambling Energy, guaranteed personally by himself. The source of repayment would be the $100 million coming from the Bank of Montreal at month's end. Rockwell asked Foncannon to evaluate the request.

The meeting in the chairman's office ended, and Foncannon invited Grambling and Dibble to his office in the Colorado Bank Tower, the sleek modern skyscraper next to the old bank building. Foncannon's eighth floor office overlooked 17th Street and downtown Denver. Its uninspiring view of buildings and street traffic could have been of any of a hundred American cities. The office was a working environment: foot-tall stacks of documents hid his desk, and business manuals filled the bookcase. The walls, barren of artwork or diplomas, displayed a bulletin board and a multicolored map of the Rocky Mountain area; the oil deposits were highlighted in green, the gas in red. A small, potted plant drooped isolated in a corner. On the credenza behind Foncannon's desk was the one personal touch, a picture of his children.

Foncannon, Dibble and Grambling each took one of the three chairs at the relatively uncluttered round table in front of Foncannon's desk. Balanced on little metal wheels, each rust-colored chair leaned backward with the weight of its occupant. Now the real work on the loan would begin.

Foncannon's assignment was clear; determine if Grambling could repay $6 million in unsecured credit. As they sat two feet away from one another, Foncannon asked Grambling for a financial statement, which he took immediately from his attaché case. Foncannon studied the pages: assets totaled over $40 million; annual income in excess of $900,000. What most interested Foncannon was Schedule C, Grambling's estimated value of his closely held companies. Included in the $26.4 million total was an entry for the R.M.T. purchase: "Husky Oil–Grambling Energy; value—$11.5 million."

Foncannon leaned across his table and pointed to the entry. "What's this $11.5 million figure, John?"

"That's my deposit on the R.M.T. purchase. $2.5 million of the total is earnest money held by Husky. If the R.M.T. purchase doesn't close on January 31, Husky keeps the $2.5 million."

"What about the other $9 million?"

"Oh, that's being held in an escrow account by Husky's New York counsel, Paul, Weiss, Rifkind, Wharton & Garrison. If the deal doesn't close, Husky returns that $9 million to me."

Foncannon thought through the implications of that comment. Though he and Colorado National only wished Grambling well, failure of the R.M.T. purchase guaranteed a $9 million cash pool to repay the $6 million Colorado National loan. That makes the loan risk-free, Foncannon thought. It was a correct conclusion had the assumption been honest. But Grambling had not told Foncannon the truth: The deposit was wholly nonrefundable except for $7 million, the Husky loan which, whether or not the buyout was consummated, would never leave the escrow account controlled by Husky's counsel.

Familiar with bankers' desire to lend without risk, Grambling assured Foncannon that the buyout would provide a cash pool for repayment as secure as the escrow account. Grambling handed Foncannon a copy of the 11-page Bank of Montreal Term Sheet signed a week earlier by Grambling Energy and Husky.

"$70 million of the financing is for working capital, money for the kinds of expenses I'll be paying with my Colorado National loan," Grambling said. "When I get the Bank of Montreal funding at the end of January, I'll repay Colorado National's $6 million out of the $70 million of working capital."

As Grambling watched, Foncannon skimmed the Term Sheet. His pace slowed as he examined the six negative covenants on page nine. These would be the restrictions on the working capital use, Foncannon mused to himself. Although he would want to study the whole document more scrupulously, as would each member of Colorado National's Senior Loan Committee, Foncannon saw nothing in the six negative covenants that prevented Grambling from using the $70 million of working capital to repay Colorado National. Grambling had intended that Foncannon see no such obstacle to repayment. To that end, Grambling had deleted the two covenants that precluded him from burdening Grambling Energy with further debt.

Foncannon's mind was made up. Barring the unearthing of derogatory information, he would recommend that Grambling receive the $6 million credit. Of course, the review process was not over. As he rose, Foncannon said, "I want to speak with your bank references. Also, I'd like to spend a little time studying the Term Sheet." Having noted those qualifications, Foncannon handed Grambling signature cards as well as a corporate borrowing resolution. He invited Grambling to return to the bank the next day, Tuesday, January 8, to sign the $6 million promissory note, which, Foncannon explained, the bank would hold pending the Senior Loan Committee's actual approval of the loan.

As he walked Grambling and Dibble to the elevators, Foncannon mentioned one last point.

"John, I want to discuss the $100 million loan with someone knowledgeable from the Bank of Montreal."

"You should speak to Blair Mullin," Grambling suggested. "He's the officer most familiar with the transaction. Blair's on vacation now, Tom. But I'll locate him, and have him call you."

They shook hands again, and Grambling left.

Foncannon returned to his office to call Grambling's bank references. First, he called Ron Keenan, President of the Coronado Bank in El Paso, Texas, Grambling's hometown. Keenan was enthusiastic about Grambling. Although Keenan had known Grambling only two years, Keenan knew the family well. The Gramblings were long-time residents of El Paso, Keenan said, and Grambling's father was a highly regarded attorney in the most respected law firm in town. Keenan told Foncannon that Grambling Jr.'s financial statement was legitimate. "Coronado has relied on it in making its loans to John."

To the most critical inquiry, Keenan said, "John pays his debts." The enthusiasm was unfeigned. It had been barely a week since Grambling had paid over $1.5 million of his Coronado Bank obligations.

Could not have been more positive, Foncannon thought, as he proceeded down his list: Texas Commerce Bank, Dallas; Bank of New York, New York; American Bank of Commerce, El Paso; First Financial, El Paso; Bank of Scottsdale, Phoenix. One banker offered only general information about his institution's relation with Grambling; another was out of the office. But the bankers who were willing to talk spoke as enthusiastically about Grambling's character and financial capacity as had Keenan: "Excellent reputation" and "highly regarded" were some of the remarks Foncannon noted. Charles Wirth, the Bank of Scottsdale officer whose institution had received in the past week over $700,000 in full payment of Grambling's debt, described his bank's relationship with Grambling as "super." Each banker who spoke with Foncannon had been recently repaid. Not one knew that the loan repaid had itself been obtained by fraud, as had been the Bank of Montreal loan used to make the repayment.

On Tuesday, Grambling went to Foncannon's office to sign the promissory note. On Wednesday, January 9, he called Foncannon twice to ask if he had spoken yet to Blair Mullin of the Bank of Montreal. Foncannon had not. A short while after Grambling's second call, Blair Mullin phoned Foncannon.

"Sorry, I've had trouble reaching you," Mullin began. "I'm on holiday."

Appropriate use of words, Foncannon thought. Mullin, the Canadian banker, uses the English expression for vacation.

Mullin and Foncannon spoke at length.

"Blair, Colorado National is considering John's request for $6 million of interim funding for January," Foncannon began. "John's going to use the money to pay some Grambling Energy expenses until your $100 million loan is in place. The way I read the Term Sheet, Colorado National can look to your $100 million for repayment of its $6 million. Am I reading it correctly, or are there restrictions on the use of that money?"

"Do you have the Term Sheet, Tom?" Mullin responded.

Foncannon located the document in his piles of paper, and Mullin directed him to the Term Sheet's first page. Mullin read the paragraph authorizing use of the Bank of Montreal proceeds for "operating and general corporate purchases."

"Those are the expenses you're talking about, Tom," Mullin said.

"Another concern, Blair, is whether the $100 million loan is going to close on time."

"The financing and the purchase will close as planned on January 31," Mullin replied.

Foncannon raised a last point which he knew would be of concern to the Colorado National lending committee. Page 10 of the Term Sheet authorized the Bank of Montreal to syndicate the Grambling Energy debt.

"Blair, will Colorado National have an opportunity to participate in the syndication?" Foncannon asked.

"Colorado National's participation would be welcomed," Mullin replied. Foncannon had reached the end of his list of questions for Mullin. The responses could not have been more affirmative.

The next morning, Thursday, January 10, Foncannon was at his desk early. The Grambling application was on the agenda for that day's Loan Committee meeting. Before nine o'clock, he received the call: the committee is ready for your presentation. With butterflies in his stomach—Foncannon would be speaking to the nine most senior lenders in the bank— he walked quickly to the third floor committee room, and, with a last deep breath, entered. The committee's members sat around the oval table: The Committee Chair, Robert Kropf, was positioned at the table's head, with four members sitting along each of the table's sides. The secretary distributed copies of the memorandum prepared by Foncannon, who took the seat at the table's far end, opposite from Kropf.

At the nod from Kropf, Foncannon began. Rockwell, the Committee's 10th member, was absent—he had a meeting elsewhere—so Foncannon started with the circumstances of Grambling's arrival at the bank. Grambling had been introduced by Dibble, Foncannon said. The Committee members nodded. They knew Dibble. His introduction meant that Grambling was legitimate.

With that initial presumption, Foncannon guided the members through his memorandum. He began with the purpose of the loan, the reason that the request was being expedited, and the guaranteed sources of repayment. A committee person asked for a copy of the Term Sheet. Foncannon directed the members' attention to the applicable sections and recounted his conversations with Mullin.

"Let's double-check that the expenses are reimbursable," a member suggested.

"Recent due diligence efforts have revealed that Grambling is a legitimate businessman," Foncannon continued, "highly regarded by those contacted, who also corroborated his rather impressive financial statement." He related the responses to his credit inquiries.

After several nonchallenging questions, Foncannon moved to the business opportunity Grambling represented.

"Colorado National is in a position to handle Grambling Energy's cash management, and perhaps more significantly, the credit card services of their 100 wholly owned stations and 700 franchise stations. Also, we have been assured that Colorado National will get an opportunity to participate in the Bank of Montreal's $100 million funding package." And, Foncannon emphasized, Grambling's plans to expand in the Denver area would aid the local economy.

"This requested facility," Foncannon concluded, "appears to be the beginning of a significant new relationship, benefiting both the bank and the community." The presentation, with questions, took 20 minutes.

Kropf passed the original application counterclockwise for each member to initial his vote. The form was returned to the chairman, who wrote his initials and announced the result: unanimous approval. Foncannon rose, and, as he left, several members complimented him on the presentation. He was also reminded to verify again that the working capital expenses were reimbursable from the Bank of Montreal loan.

Within minutes of the committee's vote, Foncannon conferred with Ken Hansen, his immediate supervisor in the Energy Department. They decided to disburse the funds as soon as the Bank of Montreal confirmed by telex that the expenses being paid with Colorado National funds could be repaid with the $100 million funding. Grambling was informed of Colorado National's requirement. That afternoon, a telex arrived at Foncannon's office: "Pursuant to my conversation with John Grambling today, this telex is to verify that upon release of the Bank of Montreal funds currently scheduled for 1/31/85, the Bank of Montreal agrees to repay the working capital loan of U.S. $6 million from Colorado National Bank to Grambling Energy. Blair Mullen, Bank of Montreal." Foncannon took the telex to Hansen's office. It was the necessary confirmation, they concluded.

Foncannon returned to his office; on his desk, was a message to call Ivor Hopkyns at the Bank of Montreal. Foncannon had expected Hopkyns' call. Between meeting Grambling on Monday, and speaking with Mullin on Wednesday, Foncannon had learned from colleagues in the banking industry that Hopkyns was involved in the Grambling loan. Foncannon had called Hopkyns, who had not been in. This message must be his return call, Foncannon thought.

Foncannon called Calgary, but Hopkyns was again not available. Thinking that Hopkyns was responsible for the Bank of Montreal telex which he and Hansen had examined, Foncannon left a message thanking Hopkyns for the telex.

The innocuous message to Hopkyns almost derailed Colorado National's loan to Grambling. Hopkyns called Foncannon early in the morning on Friday, January 11. He was disturbed and, to Foncannon's perception, confused.

"I never sent you a telex, Tom. And this is the first we've heard that Grambling has applied for a loan from Colorado National."

When questioned by Foncannon about the Bank of Montreal funding, however, Hopkyns gave the same responses as Mullin had given on Wednesday: The loan was scheduled to close on January 31; and, pursuant to the limitations of the Term Sheet, the $100 million could be used to pay operating and general corporate expenses.

Unlike Mullin, however, Hopkyns adamantly opposed any participation by Colorado National in the $100 million credit. Foncannon said that Mullin had thought otherwise about participation. Hopkyns continued to disagree, but promised to locate the vacationing Mullin to find out what had been said. Before noon, Hopkyns called again.

"I've spoken to Blair, Tom. He says that he's never spoken to you. He didn't know what I was talking about when I asked him about a conversation with you and a telex." Hopkyns hesitated, and then asked, "Are you sure about these things, Tom?"

Now it was Foncannon's turn to be confused. When Grambling called shortly after noon to ask when he could draw the loan proceeds, Foncannon told him what Hopkyns had said. Grambling was nonplussed. Nothing that Hopkyns had said was a mystery, Grambling explained.

"The telex from the Bank of Montreal was a mix-up, Tom. I had drafted a telex for Mullin to send, and asked my secretary to send it to the Bank of Montreal for approval. She made a mistake and sent it straight to Colorado National."

Foncannon examined the telex he had received. It clearly identified Grambling Energy as the sender. The telex had been a legitimate mix-up, he realized.

But what about Mullin's denial of ever having spoken to Foncannon, and Hopkyns' position, contrary to Mullin's, against participation?

"I can't claim to understand the operation of their minds. But remember, Tom, both Blair and Ivor have been under enormous strain on the $100 million financing. You know what happens when you're at the end of a big deal. Blair has probably spoken to so many bankers these past few days that he could just have been thinking of someone else when he was speaking to you."

To Grambling, the discrepancy on the participation sounded like an unresolved internal bank dispute. Perhaps the Bank of Montreal had not yet decided whether or how to syndicate participations.

"Maybe Blair spoke out of turn when he agreed to your participation in the funding," Grambling suggested.

In his banking career, Foncannon had seen enough similar disputes to appreciate that Grambling's explanation had the ring of truth.

A later call from someone identifying himself as Blair Mullin supported Grambling's suggestion that the confusion was nothing more than internal politicking at the Bank of Montreal. The present Mullin, and Foncannon really could not remember the voice of the earlier one, gave the same general description of the Bank of Montreal financing as had the earlier Mullin. Mullin read Foncannon a copy of the telex which the Bank of Montreal would send regarding the funding. It stated the terms of the credit, the January 31 closing date and concluded "subject to the conditions being met to the satisfaction of the Bank and its solicitors, we are prepared to direct up to U.S. $6 million to your bank in satisfaction of the obligation which you have recently undertaken."

As far as Foncannon could see, it was the same telex as the draft Grambling had inadvertently sent to Colorado National the prior day. As to Colorado National participating in the credit, Mullin was distant and noncommittal.

Just as John had suggested, Foncannon thought. Mullin had gotten himself into trouble with his supervisors by being too loose in promising participation in our first phone call.

Foncannon reported these developments to Hansen. They decided that turf problems within the Bank of Montreal would not affect Grambling's repayment of Colorado National's debt. The Term Sheet in front of the Colorado bankers was explicit: The document permitted repayment. Colorado National disbursed $2,210,573.00 to Grambling on January 11. Pursuant to Grambling's instructions, Colorado National wire-transferred the funds to the account of R.M.T. Properties at Crocker National Bank, Los Angeles, the account from which $2.2 million had been removed by Grambling the prior Tuesday to pay U.S. Shelter. William Miller's threat to Grambling had been satisfied. Never had Grambling repaid a debt so quickly.

Grambling's efforts fell short of total success. Between Monday and Friday, January 7 through 11, Grambling had distressed, and then comforted, Husky's principal officers. Price and Miller just wanted the Bank of Montreal financing to close: They wanted to be done with Grambling.

At Colorado National, the mood was one of comfort. After the nonsensical confusion over the telex mix-up and other things, Colorado National had begun a solid lending relationship.

At the Bank of Montreal in Calgary, the focus was on the pending $100 million funding. Mullin and Hopkyns, and their superior, Scott Hean, were members of the bank's Corporate and Government Banking Group. That the unit had made a personal loan to Grambling was an accommodation to Grambling in his capacity as a corporate client: A personal loan by this unit was an exception to the bank's usual policy, and the Corporate and Government Group had obtained special permission from its credit committee to make the $7.5 million loan. With the personal loan completed, the bankers could now devote their undivided attention to the $100 million corporate loan, their primary concern.

In the course of working on that funding, Hean inadvertently recalled a detail of the personal loan. He mentioned it to Hopkyns the next time they spoke.

"Ivor, isn't it about time that we should be getting the Dr Pepper stock proceeds on that personal loan? When you get a chance, why don't you make a call to see how it's going."

On January 15, Hopkyns had the opportunity to make the call. He dialed the number of Lazard Freres in Manhattan and asked the receptionist to connect him to Robert Wilkis.

Hopkyns asked Wilkis when the Bank of Montreal would be receiving its cash payment pursuant to the Consent and Agreement. Wilkis cut him off.

"I don't know what you're talking about," Wilkis said.

Hopkyns became annoyed.

"I'm talking about the agreement you signed, the Consent, I have a copy of, here right in front of me. It bears your signature, Robert W. Wilkis, and . . ."

"You have a problem," Wilkis interjected before hanging up. "My middle name is Mark."

Redialing the Lazard operator, Hopkyns asked for Peter E.

Corcoran. After an interminable two or three rings, a voice answered.

"Corcoran here."

It took only a second for Hopkyns to know. This was not the voice with whom he had spoken on December 28.

It is not in the nature of a banker to panic or show emotion in public. Hopkyns told Hean and Mullin what had happened. They told their superiors. Counsel at Shearman & Sterling were informed. For caution's sake, the law firm assigned a litigator to the Grambling team. It was all a misunderstanding, everyone was sure, and the morning would bring a good explanation.

CHAPTER 3

SPURIOUS

But what does it mean?

Arthur Norman Field and Jonathan Greenblatt, a senior partner and a senior associate at Shearman & Sterling, sat in Field's office in the Citicorp building, and passed the letter between themselves. The January 17 letter from Lazard Freres & Co. was addressed to James Busuttil. After being received by Busuttil on the 17th, the letter had been given to Field and Greenblatt: "Dear Mr. Busuttil: I have your letter dated January 16 enclosing a copy of a Consent and Agreement purportedly signed by Lazard Freres & Co. Before you sent the letter to me with its enclosure, I informed you that the Consent and Agreement was spurious. Manifestly, we have no intention of complying with its terms. Thomas F. X. Mullarkey."

Mullarkey was in-house counsel at Lazard Freres. Only a member of their own guild, Field and Greenblatt thought, could have written a letter so apparently concrete yet tantalizingly unclear. Lazard was not going to honor the consent—that was apparent. And it would not do so because the consent was "spurious." To the Shearman & Sterling attorneys, Mullarkey's choice of the word *spurious* appeared to confirm Grambling's explanation that Lazard had botched the transfer of his shares. Their attorneys reviewed what they had learned from their client in the two days since Hopkyn's January 15 calls to Lazard.

After the Lazard calls, Hopkyns had phoned Busuttil immediately, and then, Grambling.

"What the hell is going on?" Hopkyns demanded of Grambling.

Grambling was stunned.

"I don't know what's happening at Lazard. But it sounds like a technical error regarding whose signatures can legally bind the firm. Wilkis and Corcoran must have fouled up. Remember, Ivor, I worked there, so I know how they make these mistakes."

As he listened to Grambling, Hopkyns recalled that, when he and Wilkis had spoken in December, Wilkis was confused about who at Lazard could sign the consent.

"Someone's trying to cover his ass," Grambling concluded. "I'll make some calls and get to the bottom of this." Grambling was angry. "Damn them, they screwed up the transfer of my Dr Pepper shares."

That same evening, January 15, Grambling called Hopkyns at his home in Calgary.

"I'm sorry for disturbing you, Ivor, but I thought you'd want an immediate follow-up on the Lazard mistake. It wasn't totally their fault.

"I'm calling from Denver, R.M.T. headquarters, and I just got off the phone with my wife. She read me the mail delivered to our home in Connecticut. E. F. Hutton remitted my Dr Pepper proceeds to my account at Coronado Bank in El Paso, Texas. The transmittal voucher was in today's mail. The stock had been cashed on the 15th, just like we expected, but it was sent to the wrong place."

Grambling promised Hopkyns that he would order Coronado Bank to wire-transfer the funds to the Bank of Montreal.

After reassuring Hopkyns, Grambling phoned Mullin at his home in Calgary. In November 1984, when work on the $100 million credit had begun in earnest, Mullin had given his home phone number to Grambling. For financings of this magnitude, there are no "after-hours" for bankers. They are always on call, for Grambling as well as other clients, and Grambling had called Mullin at home frequently.

This intrusion on the privacy of his home was not the only sacrifice Mullin had made for the Grambling loan. He had given up his Christmas vacation with his family in order to be in New York with Grambling to finalize the loan. As partial recompense for this loss, Grambling had offered to fly Mullin's family to his in-laws in Ontario for the holidays. It was an offer which, after consulting with Hean and another superior, Mullin had accepted. Grambling and Mullin had worked intensely for weeks to bring the loan to a successful conclusion. Mullin was not surprised to receive the January 15 call.

Mullin did not know about Hopkyns' calls to Lazard. Grambling's ostensible reason to call on January 15 was to talk about the progress on their baby, the $100 million funding.

As they chatted, Grambling lowered his voice and confided, "Blair, it seems to me that Ivor is beginning to break under the stress of the financing." Grambling added that he expected to repay his $7.5 million personal loan by week's end.

After speaking with Hopkyns on the 15th, Busuttil fingered through the phone book to make his own call. In law school, Busuttil had studied contracts and corporate law, not forgery. This is not to say that he was a stranger to the evils of the world. Prior to joining Shearman & Sterling, Busuttil had worked in the counter-terrorism section of the State Department. While there, Busuttil had responded to Soviet barbarity in Afghanistan by organizing an international conference on state terrorism. His success as an advocate for the victims of Soviet aggression had earned him membership on a KGB death list.

But when Thomas F. X. Mullarkey returned Busuttil's call on January 16, Mullarkey's message was beyond the scope of Busuttil's experience in the world of business and banking.

"No," the Lazard counsel had said emphatically. "Corcoran and Wilkis did not sign the document that you have in front of you."

At Mullarkey's request, Busuttil had a copy of the Consent and Agreement delivered to Lazard by messenger. On January 17, Mullarkey responded in writing, the brief letter that so puzzled Field and Greenblatt as they reflected on the events of the past two days.

"I don't get it, Art," Greenblatt said. "Why did Mullarkey choose a word other than straightforward, unambiguous *forgery?*"

Greenblatt opened the dictionary he had brought from his office.

"Okay, Art. Here's spurious. 'Spurious. 1—of illegitimate birth, bastard; 2a—outwardly similar or corresponding to something without having its genuine qualities, false, e.g., spurious fruit.' "

Greenblatt flipped back to the "f 's".

"This is forgery: 'Forgery: The act of falsely and fraudulently making or altering a document.' "

Greenblatt and Field mulled the possibilities.

"What if an authorized corporate signatory, a person entitled to sign on behalf of a company, had taken a bribe to sign a document," Greenblatt thought out loud. "To the world, the document would appear authentic. Wouldn't that document be spurious, but not forged?"

"And what if Corcoran and Wilkis had not signed the consent, and their signatures were written without their permission," Field added. " 'Forged' is the best . . . it's the only description of the falsity."

The attorneys shook their heads in confusion.

Mullarkey's avoidance of what would have been the exact word created the suspicion that the consent, though somehow unauthentic, was not a forgery. So long as a document could be spurious without being forged, as Mullarkey implied, Grambling's explanation was plausible: There had been an internal error in signatory powers, and Grambling was not responsible for the screw-up.

Counsel's search for the meaning of spurious was not just an exercise in semantics. The bank had a compelling need to understand why Lazard had repudiated the document, and whether Grambling was responsible. The bank had committed itself to close a $100 million loan on January 31, exactly two weeks after the receipt of Mullarkey's letter. No sane institution would lend money to a forger, but failure to fund Grambling if he was not at fault would have an unpleasant consequence: a megamillion dollar lawsuit which, by Greenblatt's and Field's calculation, would be unwinnable.

They could picture the allegations of the complaint. In justifiable reliance on the bank's promise to finance the R.M.T. buyout, Grambling had spent millions on the buyout. Were the bank to now renege on its promise to lend, the bank would be liable for the costs Grambling had incurred. But that was only the beginning. The attorneys understood that recent court cases had extended the liability of a lender such as the Bank of Montreal beyond simple reliance damages. In recent failure-to-fund cases, juries had awarded damages calculated as the profit lost to the borrower by the breach of the commitment to lend. Such an award could easily be the amount of the loan not given—the not inconsiderable sum of $100 million.

But, Greenblatt and Field feared, a $100 million jury award was not the cap on their client's potential liability. Litigation against banks was a cottage industry with expert witnesses on call, ready to calculate with computer runs, and highlight in dazzling graphics, the lost profits attributable to bank wrongdoing. A sympathetic jury could calculate Grambling's lost profit as what Grambling Energy might have earned over the next five or ten years: A jury could even calculate the lost profit as what Grambling Energy might have been sold for in a future leveraged buyout. A suing borrower's only obstacle to instant wealth was lack of imagination.

The hit could be in the billions and, in the push and pull of developing case law, the attorneys agreed, smart money bet on the aggrieved borrower. That Grambling was a Texan did not help. A disproportionate number of the nine-figure damage awards had been won in the courtrooms of Texas, and one of the most notorious verdicts had been returned by a jury in El Paso, Grambling's hometown. The victor had been William J. Farah, owner of Farah's clothing; and one of the references listed on Grambling's resume.

"Maybe Farah will even recommend his own attorney to John," Greenblatt said only half in jest.

Counsel knew that the outlook was not totally bleak. If Grambling had committed a fraud regarding his collateral, the bank's refusal to lend would have a justification which even a Texas jury might not ignore. However, as Field and Greenblatt pondered the Mullarkey letter, proof of Grambling's fault was precisely the issue that Mullarkey had left unresolved.

As their attorneys in New York pondered the Mullarkey letter, the bankers in Calgary had cause to be optimistic. In banking, the truth is in repayment. True, Hopkyns' call to Lazard had created confusion. But one fact had not been put in dispute. The Dr Pepper proceeds had not been lost. They had not disappeared. They had just been, as it were, mislaid. And on January 17, Scott Hean, Hopkyns' supervisor, had been called by "Jennie," a woman who had described herself as secretary to Ron Keenan, the Coronado Bank president. Although Hean had been unavailable to come to the phone, Jennie had left a welcome message: "The funds are here."

It was only after the "Jennie" call that the bankers in Calgary learned from their counsel in Manhattan of the Mullarkey letter. "We've received a very damaging letter from Lazard" was how Greenblatt explained the letter, which he then sent by telecopier to Calgary.

The bankers in Calgary huddled around the transmission from New York. *Spurious*, they wondered.

Hean, Hopkyns, and Gough located a Webster's dictionary and repeated what Greenblatt had done several hours before in New York.

"It looks like 'spurious' means false and not forgery." Hean suggested. "What do you guys think? Sounds like a back office screw-up."

The three bankers agreed that "screw-up" seemed to be the explanation; their hypothesis was consistent with the recent "Jennie" message from Texas. The stocks had simply been sent to the wrong place, they concluded. Not that they were relieved.

A different and more serious problem was threatening the $100 million loan. After several all-night sessions between the bankers and the Husky officers in late December, the Term Sheet had finally closed on December 31, 1984. It was the bank's understanding that Husky would, without limitation, guarantee repayment of the $100 million. On January 17, that understanding had been dealt a kick to the groin. A week earlier, Mullin and Husky's Miller had agreed to have a lunchtime meeting on January 17 to clean up several small outstanding issues regarding the Grambling Energy loan. This meeting turned into an all day wrestling match.

"You have a misunderstanding," Miller told the banker. "In the event of a liquidation, the guarantee is limited, not full."

"But that's not what we agreed to. Besides, that's not going to happen," Mullin insisted. "The bank will be in the driver's seat if the company gets into trouble. And this is a good transaction. This company has a good future."

"No." Miller was firm. "Husky never intended a full guarantee. We told you this in December. The guarantee would be limited."

Mullin was distressed. In the exhaustion of closing on the Term Sheet, could he have misunderstood an issue as important as Husky's qualification of the guarantee? As the January 17 meeting continued, Mullin reconstructed his recollections with Miller, and calculated the deal's numbers, all with the purpose of convincing Miller that the guarantee was intended to be total.

Miller was unmoved. Not only did he believe that the issue of the guarantee had been left open but also he had begun to wonder about the candor of the Bank of Montreal officers. Husky's New York counsel were the same as Lazard Freres'. The prior day, January 16, counsel disclosed to Miller that the Bank of Montreal had a problem with Grambling's personal loan. The attorney told Miller no details other than that there was a "spurious" document which related to the Grambling loan.

Like so many others that January, the communication from an attorney caused Miller to resort to the dictionary: "Spurious—not what it appears to be on its face." Miller could not imagine what the "spurious" document was, but clearly it could not reflect well on the integrity of the $7.5 million loan. It was equally clear that the Bank of Montreal had not disclosed to Husky any problem regarding the man operating Husky's subsidiary and the man whose loan Husky was about to guarantee. Miller did not realize that, as far as the bank was concerned, it had nothing to disclose.

The January 17 meeting ended with Husky's insistence that the guarantee of Grambling's debt was limited. Stunned by what he believed to be Husky's alteration of the loan terms, Mullin rushed to Hean's Calgary home that evening. Working into the next morning, Mullin and Hean spent five hours trying to figure out how to restructure the deal. Without the 100 percent guarantee, the funding was no longer a commercially acceptable risk: That was obvious to the bankers, as was Husky's insistence that the loan must close without delay. The bankers saw no answer short of canceling the deal.

As the Calgary bankers struggled to think of a way to incorporate Miller's bombshell into the final $100 million loan package, they received more good news regarding the misplaced Dr Pepper stock. On Friday the 18th, Keenan himself, or someone identifying himself that way, called Hean in Calgary.

As Mullin listened in, the Coronado Bank president explained why he had not been available when the bankers initially had called: "I've been unreachable because the bank examiners are here for their routine examination, and you know what that means." Hean and Mullin understood. Keenan then confirmed to Hean that the $8,252,000 in Dr Pepper proceeds had arrived. All that was necessary to transfer the proceeds to the Bank of Montreal was the written authorization of Grambling. The following Monday, the 21st, Keenan again called Hean in Calgary. The money had not yet been transferred since Grambling had guaranteed certain loans at Coronado that had to be paid prior to the transfer. The payments were in progress, according to Keenan, and the transfer would occur shortly.

Though the payment delay was troublesome, Hean was, at bottom, relieved. He had been told by a bank president himself that the Dr Pepper proceeds existed and were residing safely within a bank. Besides, the Bank of Montreal could not receive the funds on Monday anyway; January 21 was a New York State banking holiday.

On Tuesday, January 22, Grambling wrote Keenan to authorize the transfer of the funds. He sent a copy of the letter to Calgary: "Mr. Ron Keenan, President, Coronado Bank . . . As per our previous conversations, you are hereby authorized to release the $8,252,139.00 which you presently have in my account in an interest-bearing market fund and which is to be converted and wire-transferred to the Bank of Montreal. I regret that the funds have not been transferred as per our discussion on Monday and trust that this request for transmittal will be sufficient documentation to allow you to transfer said funds. Please give this matter your immediate attention. Very truly yours, John A. Grambling, Jr." Grambling intended the firm tone of the letter to reassure the Bank of Montreal officers.

It did not. That the stock proceeds had been mistransferred was understandable. That the proceeds had been located, and not sent to the Bank of Montreal by Tuesday was inexplicable. For the first time, the bankers feared that the collateral might not be coming, that the bank might be naked on a $7.5 million loan.

Hean, Hopkyns, and Mullin placed the conference room in the Calgary office off-limits to everyone but themselves. From morning to night, they tried to locate the Dr Pepper stock, and Grambling. They called his El Paso home and spoke to his mother.

"Oh, you're looking for John? He left a couple of hours ago. He was just here overnight."

Hour after hour, the bankers tried numbers in New York, Texas, Connecticut, and Colorado, all without success. Several of their colleagues did not know where Hean, Hopkyns and Mullin had disappeared to and were told to look in the "crisis center." Those who went to the conference room found three men whose nerves had been stretched as taut as the skin of an inflated balloon: The $100 million financing was in jeopardy because of Husky's refusal to guarantee 100 percent of the debt, and the collateral for the already lent $7.5 million was missing. What else could go wrong?

The latest legal advice from their attorneys in New York did little to calm the anxieties of the Calgary bankers. Anticipating litigation, and fearful of a charge that the bank had libeled Grambling, counsel instructed the bankers to be restrained in any comments to third parties about Grambling. "Be button-lipped" was how the bankers heard the advice. So advised, and ensconced in their command module, the bankers in Calgary focused on their single task.

"Musketeers," Hean told Hopkyns and Mullin. "We're staying here until we find our money."

CHAPTER 4

IMPORTANT BUSINESS OUT WEST

As Grambling traveled around the nation, rarely staying in one location for more than a few nights, he understood the crisis of his affairs. Two weeks short of receiving the $100 million that would have papered over his prior crimes, he had almost been discovered. Thanks to Lazard's wooden explanation of the consent, a flat-out forgery, Grambling's explanation had been made to appear sufficiently credible and his borrowing relationship with the Bank of Montreal was troubled, but not dead. He had been handed time, the most precious commodity; time to rebuild his credibility with the Bank of Montreal and to obtain the $100 million.

But he knew that he had painted himself into a corner. His explanation to Hean and Hopkyns had been as explicit as it was false. Since the Dr Pepper proceeds had been mislaid and not lost, Grambling had to transmit $8 million to the bank, and he had to disguise the transfer to make it appear to be the Dr Pepper proceeds misdirected to Coronado Bank. Necessity dictated his battle plan. He would sacrifice $8 million to buy the credibility necessary to get his hands on the $100 million.

Grambling was confident that Colorado National would be a partial source of the necessary $8 million. After drawing the $2.2 million to repay R.M.T. two weeks earlier, Grambling had taken another $1.1 million of the Denver bank loan. The remaining $2.7 million would buy a large chunk of credibility at the Bank of Montreal.

But his search for a new banking victim to fund the other $5.3 million jeopardized the anticipated $2.7 million Colorado National take-down. The day after his January 15 conversations with Hopkyns and Mullin, Grambling, still in Denver, applied for a $6 million line of credit from First Interstate of Denver, a regional commercial bank like Colorado National.

Alert to the rumor-mongering of the Denver banking community, Foncannon heard of Grambling's application to First Interstate. He felt like a jilted lover. Colorado National had advanced $6 million to Grambling to secure Grambling Energy's loyalty and business. Yet, after less than two weeks, Grambling was consorting with one of Colorado National's rivals.

The next rumor whispered into Foncannon's ear was even worse: Grambling's Bank of Montreal loan was in trouble. Fearing the integrity of Colorado National's primary source of repayment, Foncannon called Hopkyns in Calgary on Monday, January 21. The Calgary receptionist transferred Foncannon's call to the crisis center.

"Ivor, we've heard that you've had some problems with your loan to Grambling. What's going on?" Foncannon asked. And tell me it ain't so, he hoped.

Mindful of the advice he had received from counsel, Hopkyns limited his reply to an emotionless account of what the bare facts were thought to be. He said that the bank had been expecting cash collateral from Grambling from the sale of securities.

"But, through what we have been told is a mix-up between E. F. Hutton and Lazard Freres, the cash was transferred to Coronado Bank in El Paso."

Not wanting to in any way interfere with Colorado National's relations with Grambling—that could be tortious interference with contract, counsel had warned—Hopkyns added that "everything is now satisfactory." If there was a qualification in the statement, Foncannon did not hear it.

Hopkyns did not end the conversation with the Grambling explanation of the mix-up. Hopkyns asked Foncannon to explain again how Grambling was spending the $6 million of Colorado National funds. To pay general operating expenses, Foncannon said.

"You should be aware that some of the expenses may not be covered by the Bank of Montreal's interim loan," Hopkyns replied. "However, I am not certain since I did not work on the Husky/Grambling Energy transaction myself."

Hopkyns realized that he could not share with Foncannon all that the Calgary bankers knew and suspected. But the Canadian thought that, with his last comment, he was giving the Denver banker a hint to be wary.

As had the call on January 11, the January 21 conversation with Hopkyns distressed Foncannon. True, Hopkyns had concluded the conversation with the bland assurance, in response to Foncannon's direct question, that the $100 million funding was "progressing" to closing. But if Colorado National could not be repaid from the $100 million, as Hopkyns had hinted, Foncannon did not give a damn about the funding.

Foncannon went to work with his phone. First, he called Ron Keenan of Coronado Bank who confirmed that Grambling's misdirected $8,250,000 was sitting in Grambling's Coronado account. Next, Foncannon called Grambling.

"John, some questions have come up about the Bank of Montreal loan. Could you come to the bank this Wednesday the 23rd?"

That Wednesday, Rockwell and Foncannon met with Grambling at the Colorado National Bank Tower. They told him that the Senior Loan Committee was confused. Why had Hopkyns again suggested that Colorado National's loan could not be repaid out of the $100 million Bank of Montreal funding?

"Colorado National cannot continue to advance funds if its source of repayment is uncertain," Rockwell said.

Grambling saw his desperately needed $2.7 million sink from view. Why couldn't Hopkyns just keep his mouth shut, he thought.

The Denver bankers, however, were not kicking Grambling off the ranch; just fencing him in. They laid out the conditions under which Grambling would be permitted to draw the last $2.7 million.

"You have to give Tom a detailed list of the R.M.T. expenditures that have been and will be paid with the Colorado National funds," Rockwell explained. "Then, John, you're going to have to ask a Bank of Montreal officer to examine the list and verify with Tom that each expenditure is reimbursable under the terms of their $100 million funding."

Grambling readily accepted the suggested procedure.

"But I don't want the Loan Committee to be left with the wrong impression," he said. "Hopkyns is all wrong. He's been working only on matters peripheral to the buyout, and he doesn't understand the terms of the commitment.

"The problem is that you haven't spoken to Scott Hean," Grambling explained. "He's Hopkyns' supervisor, and the senior officer on the R.M.T. deal. I'll arrange for a conference call between Tom and Scott. Then this entire misunderstanding will be cleared up."

The following day, January 24, Grambling telecopied to Foncannon a list of the expenditures to be discussed with Hean. Grambling's secretary called Foncannon's secretary and read each line on the list to confirm that the list had been telecopied accurately. After the confirmation, Grambling and Foncannon scheduled the conference call with Hean for the next day, Friday the 25th.

As the 24th ended, Grambling realized that January 25 would be the make-or-break day for his schemes. If his strategies were successful, he would obtain the last $2.7 million from Colorado National. In addition, he would bring to fruition a plan set in motion shortly before Hopkyns' call to Wilkis on the 15th. He would have a pot of dollars from which the last of the missing "Dr Pepper proceeds" could be transferred to the suspicious but willing-to-be convinced Hopkyns, Hean, and Mullin in Calgary. On January 25, Grambling would be in Salt Lake City to defraud the First Security Bank of Utah of $8 million.

Although Grambling had applied to the Salt Lake City bank prior to the problem created by Hopkyns' January 15 call to Lazard, the timing of the expected loan approval was providential. As he had at Colorado National, George Dibble provided the introduction to First Security. Husky Oil was a longtime First Security customer, whose American operations were well known to the bankers. Husky's former chairman had sat on the bank's board of directors, and a principal owner of the bank had sat on Husky's board. As a former Husky officer, Dibble was a known and welcome presence at the bank, and

sufficiently acquainted with its officers to arrange for Grambling to meet Spencer F. Eccles, a bank director and Chairman
of First Security's Executive Committee.

The meeting occurred on January 16. That afternoon,
Grambling and Dibble met Eccles in First Security's ornately
decorated Heritage Room; also in attendance was Jim Conover,
a senior commercial loan officer. Eccles was the nephew of Mar-
iner Eccles, the prominent financier who, after founding First
Security as the first multistate bank holding company in the
West, had then served as chairman of the Federal Reserve
Board. The room to which Grambling was brought contained
mementoes of the elder Eccles' career: Framed newspaper clippings regarding the bank hung on the walls, as did framed
newspaper cartoons and articles referring to the senior Eccles'
role in President Franklin D. Roosevelt's "brain trust."

As Grambling had anticipated, the First Security bankers
viewed Grambling Energy as the bank had viewed Husky, its
predecessor: With its Salt Lake City refinery and Utah retail
outlets, Grambling Energy was a natural client. It had inherited a prior relationship that was worth preserving. Eccles discussed the parallels between Grambling's expansion plans and
the bank's.

"We're thinking of building a new corporate tower," Eccles
told the young entrepreneur. "You should consider moving
your headquarters to Salt Lake. If you take five or eight stories
in the new building, we could give you a preferential rate on
the lease. We'll make it worth your while."

Grambling nodded in assent.

"That's an attractive proposition," he said. "We should
spend time on it after my more immediate needs are worked
out."

The bank was willing to hear what Grambling proposed.
After outlining his loan request in the Heritage Room, Grambling accompanied Conover to his office. An avid sportsman,
Conover displayed on his walls pictures of big horn sheep and
other game. He began to review Grambling's application.

"Jim, my company needs an $8 million bridge loan to cover
operating expenses, and also to pay legal fees resulting from
my purchase of R.M.T," Grambling began. "I'll fully collateral-

ize the loan. I suggest that the bank take a pledge of my of Southern Union Company stock, 358,000 shares worth over $9.9 million. But the bank will never have to resort to that collateral. My basic source of repayment is the $100 million loan I'm getting from the Bank of Montreal."

Grambling handed Conover a copy of the Term Sheet. As he had done with Foncannon, Grambling and the banker read the document together. And, as with the Term Sheet given to Foncannon, Grambling had doctored the Term Sheet provided to First Security Bank, conveniently excluding the negative covenants precluding repayment of the type of loan Grambling was seeking. Little did Conover realize that, in this transaction, he was the prey.

After Grambling left Conover's office on the 16th, Conover went to work. The financial statement listed a half-dozen bank references, and Conover replicated the process gone through by Foncannon. The results were the same: The references were general or, in the several instances of bankers who had recently been repaid, enthusiastic.

Next, Conover investigated the proposed collateral. Southern Union traded on the New York Stock Exchange, and Conover checked that day's quote in *The Wall Street Journal*: 358,600 shares were worth $9,951,150. Having concluded that the value of the collateral exceeded the amount to be loaned, Conover next considered the physical possession of the collateral.

"The stock is held in my name at the Coronado Bank in El Paso, Texas," Grambling had told Conover during their first meeting. "Jim, you might want to verify the authenticity of the stock with Coronado Bank president Ron Keenan. He's our family banker, and the trustee for my stock account. He'll make the arrangements to transfer possession within Coronado Bank to an account in the name of First Security."

As Conover reviewed the loan request, he saw no reason to disagree with Grambling's suggestion that the physical stock shares stay at Coronado.

Sitting at this desk, Conover drafted his memorandum to the bank's lending committee. He would recommend approval of the loan. What banker would have done otherwise? According to the credit references, Grambling repaid his debt on time if not earlier. The collateral was ample: $9 million in publicly traded stock and, should the Stock Market plunge, guaranteed repayment from the pending Bank of Montreal loan. For a risk-averse creature such as a bank, this was an opportunity to grab.

The opportunities extended beyond the generous rate of interest the bank would charge. Grambling had pointed out that he had permanent financing needs that would require several bank participations. Conover concluded, as Grambling had wanted him to conclude, that this $8 million loan was just the appetizer prior to future big dollar and lucrative financing.

On Tuesday, January 22, Conover called Grambling with welcome news.

"John, the Senior Loan Committee is meeting this Friday, the 25th. I'll be presenting your application for approval that morning. We'll be able to disburse the funds for you that afternoon."

$8 million, Grambling thought. That will buy a lot of credibility, and leave a couple of bucks for pocket change.

"First Security will need two things on Friday," Conover continued. "First, Keenan from Coronado should be available by phone to speak with me and legal counsel. We're going to want to nail down the details of how he can transfer the Southern Union stock to an account for our bank. Also, the committee wants to speak with a Bank of Montreal officer. The committee wants to verify that we're correctly reading the Term Sheet to allow repayment of our $8 million, and that the Bank of Montreal loan is closing on January 31."

Having crafted the forgeries and the falsehoods which were the faulty premises of the pending loan approval, Grambling fully understood the desire of Conover and the committee to verify those two points.

Conover had a last comment.

"The committee will want to be certain about what we've discussed, that First Security will be able to participate in filling your long-term credit needs."

"Of course, you will," Grambling said in his silky Texan voice.

Grambling promised that Keenan would be available by phone, as would, Grambling told Conover, "Blair Mullin, the Bank of Montreal's lead officer on the $100 million debt."

"I think I should come to speak to the committee," Grambling offered. Conover explained that such an appearance was not necessary, but Grambling insisted.

As he ended the phone call, Grambling realized the extent of the tasks he had laid out for himself that Friday. He had committed himself to produce a "Hean" for Foncannon, and now a "Keenan" and a "Mullin" for Conover as well.

As Grambling scheduled the necessary appearances, the Shearman & Sterling attorneys pursued their interpretation of "spurious." After the Hopkyns and Busuttil calls of January 15 and 16, Mullarkey, Corcoran, and others at Lazard immediately realized that the Bank of Montreal had been given forged collateral. Obviously, a civil dispute was brewing, perhaps even a criminal investigation. Confronted by their involvement in a dispute not of their own making, Lazard behaved as would any business entity: a letter was written to disclaim responsibility, and then the organization clammed up. Mullarkey was not amplifying his letter. If anything, he had perhaps been too blunt with Busuttil when, over the phone on January 16, he had stated that the signatures were false.

Lazard, however, did not oppose assisting the bank to stumble along to its own realization of what had occurred. George Wade, a senior litigation partner at Shearman & Sterling, knew Mullarkey. On Tuesday, January 23, eight days short of closing the $100 million loan, Wade called Mullarkey to ask for a favor: Were there publicly available documents that Shearman & Sterling might view to reach an independent conclusion as to the authenticity of the signatures on the consent?

On Wednesday the 23th, Mullarkey delivered to Greenblatt the Lazard Freres "signature books." Financial institutions worldwide grant signatory power to certain of their officers. Within established financial limits, officers are entrusted to bind the firm—to transfer assets, or incur debt—by the signature of their own name or their signature of the firm's name. For a partnership such as Lazard Freres, any of two dozen general partners could bind the firm by his signature of the firm name.

In his office in the Citicorp building in Manhattan, Greenblatt examined the most recent signature book sent by Mullarkey; a copy of the "Specimen Signatures of the firm of Lazard Freres & Co., New York," dated January 1, 1984. Printed in the left column were the full names of each general partner of Lazard: To the right was that partner's signature of the firm name. E. Peter Corcoran was not among the partners authorized to sign for the firm in January 1984 or thereafter.

"Not a good beginning," Greenblatt thought.

Corcoran had once held signatory power, as Greenblatt observed. The prior Specimen Signature Book was dated January 1, 1982. Third in the left-hand printed column was the phrase "Mr. E. Peter Corcoran will sign:" To the right was Corcoran's signature of the firm name "Lazard Freres & Co." Since time immemorial, the law of New York State has allowed laypeople to testify as to the comparison of signatures. The law respects the layman's ability to recognize forgeries.

With a knot in his belly, Greenblatt realized the wisdom of this ancient rule. The Corcoran "Lazard Frere & Co." signature on the Specimen Sheet was plainly dissimilar from the "Lazard Freres & Co." signature on the consent. Equally obvious were the results of comparing the authentic Corcoran and Wilkis signatures sent by Mullarkey with the signatures on the consent: Corcoran and Wilkis had not signed the collateral document.

Greenblatt was in a quandary. That Corcoran and Wilkis had not signed the consent was indisputable. But that did not mean that the signatures were forgeries. The authorized signature of another, as when one spouse signs a check for the other, is not a forgery. What if, Greenblatt thought, someone signed Corcoran's and Wilkis's signatures with their permission? The Lazard materials did not answer that question.

Time for a confrontation, Greenblatt concluded. He drafted a letter which the Bank of Montreal sent to an increasingly hostile Husky Oil Ltd. Addressed to "A. R. Price, President of Husky," and dated that day, January 23, the letter acknowledged receiving Price's letter of the 23rd, which had demanded a prompt resolution of the buyout funding. In its letter, the bank stated:

Another issue has arisen, however, that must take precedence, In connection with a loan made by us to John Grambling personally on December 31, 1984, certain circumstances have come to our attention which raise questions concerning the acceptability to us of the financing for Grambling Energy Inc. Pending clarification of these circumstances, we are not in a position to conclude any financing arrangements for Grambling Energy Inc. A closing on January 31 is therefore unrealistic. We are agreeable to discussions which may clarify the situation and could lead to a later closing. We recommend a meeting among yourselves, Mr. Grambling, and ourselves be held at the offices of Shearman & Sterling in New York at 2:00 P.M. on Friday, January 25, 1985 in an attempt to discuss and resolve our questions and concerns.

A copy of the letter was telecopied to Grambling, who, the next day, finally returned one of the dozen phone messages left for him by Hean and Mullin. Hean listened over the speakerphone as, with anger giving a sharp edge to each word, Mullin read Grambling the January 23 letter that had been sent to Price. Mullin told Grambling to attend the meeting.

"Of course, I'll be there, Blair," Grambling replied in his ever smooth voice, which only further infuriated the bankers. "Boy," Hean said afterward, "Is that guy ever cool."

Hean, Hopkyns, and Mullin flew to New York that day, Thursday the 24th, to prepare for the next day's meeting. Their rush to New York was unnecessary. While the Calgary bankers were in transit, Grambling called the Bank of Montreal in New York.

"I can't make Friday's meeting," Grambling told the bank officer in charge of the Manhattan office. "I have important business out West that can't be rescheduled."

Since Grambling could not be confronted unless present, the Shearman & Sterling meeting was adjourned to Saturday, the 26th.

CHAPTER 5

VICTIMLESS CRIME

On Friday morning the 25th, the members of First Security Bank's Senior Loan Committee took their seats in the conference room. It was a work area with a plain wooden table and drab plastic chairs. The walls were gray, and the bookshelves empty. Hung on the walls were the room's only decorations, maps of the bank's branches. The five members convened to consider various loans, including Grambling's $8 million interim loan request.

Each member had read the review prepared by Conover, who was invited into the room. Grambling waited in Conover's office. Despite Conover's discouragement, Grambling had arrived at the bank to attempt to speak to the committee. As Grambling waited, Conover's secretary brought Grambling coffee.

Why does he carry his entire business in his attaché case, the secretary thought with disapproval.

Behind the closed doors of the conference room, the committee adopted Conover's recommendation of approval, and his observation that the loan could be the start of a significant relationship. But their discussion indicated that there were concerns.

"I've never heard of Coronado," one member said.

The others shook their heads in agreement.

"Jim, could you bring a copy of Polk's?"

Conover returned with the bank directory, which lists banks by state and summarizes the bank's current balance sheet. One of the members flipped to the Texas section and read the entry.

"It's a small El Paso bank. Only $50 million in assets."

He looked around the table at his colleagues.

"Do you think Coronado is large enough to hold $9 million of stock as our agent?"

The shaking heads indicated unanimous disapproval. The chairman instructed Conover, as was the bank's standard practice, to have the stocks pledged to First Security, and to have that pledge documented and perfected.

The chairman moved to the next matter of concern: The Bank of Montreal funding.

Hesitantly, Conover explained that the borrower wanted to address the committee on that issue. The committee members were surprised. Though not unheard of, it was extremely rare to invite a borrower into the inner sanctum of the committee room. The members were in a quandary: This was a new borrower, who had made a special trip to Salt Lake City and did hope to begin a significant new relationship with the bank. Grambling had understood the psychology of these western bankers: They would not offend him by saying "no" to the request to address the committee.

Conover invited Grambling into the room. He launched into the issue that concerned the bankers.

"Blair Mullin is the lead officer you want to speak with. Blair's in Florida on bank business, but he's reachable at this number."

Grambling read from a slip of paper as Conover scribbled on a yellow pad; "305-940-7536". Conover activated the conference call system and dialed the number. The line was answered by a male voice.

"Mr. Mullin?" Conover asked.

"Yes."

"This is James Conover from Salt Lake City. I'm in a room with the Senior Loan Committee."

"Of course, the committee from First Security," Mullin said. "John asked me to expect your call. My papers are in another room in a briefcase. If you could give me a few minutes to get my things in order, I'll call you gentlemen right back."

A minute later, Mullin called the committee room. He was ready to be questioned.

The committee members began. Yes, Mullin responded, the expenditures paid by the First Security funds were reimbursable from the $100 million funding. He referred to specific sections of the Term Sheet which he and the committee members read back and forth over the phone. And the funding would definitely close on January 31, Mullin assured the committee members.

"The Bank of Montreal is very positive about present and future relations with John." Mullin added. As well as being precise in his knowledge of the R.M.T. buyout and funding, Mullin spoke knowingly of Grambling the man, and his business acumen.

Conover was not present during the entire long-distance conversation between the committee in Utah and Mullin in Florida. Five minutes into the discussion, Conover slipped out of the conference room to call the Bank of Montreal in Calgary. He and another banker had noted that, in answering the phone, Mullin had not said "Bank of Montreal." Conover was instructed to call the Bank of Montreal's Calgary office to confirm that, as far as the $100 million funding was concerned, Mullin was truly the lead banker whose statements could be relied on.

Conover called the oil and gas division in Calgary. He located an officer who confirmed that Mullin was the lead officer on the Husky deal. That's all I need to know, Conover thought as he prepared to hang up.

"However, Mr. Mullin is not available to come to the phone," the voice in Calgary continued.

"I knew that," Conover said. "He's in Florida today."

There was silence from the Calgary end of the line.

"I had thought that Mr. Mullin was on the East Coast today," the voice from Calgary said. "Manhattan, to be precise."

"Was he planning to go to a meeting in Florida, too?" Conover asked.

"I don't know. Let me give you our New York number. You can call and ask for Mr. Mullin there."

Dialing the number provided by the Calgary office, Conover reached the Park Avenue office of the Bank. Conover was again informed that Mullin was unavailable, at a business meeting somewhere.

"No, I don't think he's in Florida," one of Mullin's colleagues on Park Avenue told Conover. "No one seems to know quite where he is."

The banker in the Bank of Montreal's New York office was telling Conover the truth. Faithful to the instructions from counsel, the Three Musketeers had been secretive about their whereabouts. Even the few who knew that the three had gone to New York did not know their purpose, which the Musketeers guarded as closely as a military secret: Loose lips sink ships or, at least, result in defamation actions. The Musketeers' discretion had been flawless, so much so that Mullin could not be located to respond to the Conover call.

Conover returned to the committee members, whose lengthy interrogation of Mullin had just ended. Grambling was asked to leave, and Conover related what he had learned about Mullin's responsibility for the $100 million funding, and his travel plans. The latter made no impression on the Utah bankers. The Mullin with whom the committee had just spoken had impressed each member with his detailed knowledge of the funding and the buyout: his knowledge was proof of his identification. It was obvious to the Salt Lake City bankers that Mullin had taken the short plane trip from Manhattan to Miami for a day of business.

The committee returned to the business at hand. Banks in New York lend to Brazil. Banks in Salt Lake lend to the local refinery. Whatever questions the members had about the loan were resolved by the collateral: The Southern Union stock made the loan risk-free. The loan application was passed to the appropriate signatories, and unanimously approved. Conover was reminded to document the pledge of the Southern Union collateral, and the committee asked the loan officer on the next application to enter the room.

Returning to his office, Conover interrupted the successful borrower as he was engaged in a phone call.

"Excuse me, John. Congratulations. The loan's been approved."

Grambling ended his phone conversation, and he and Conover shook hands. Conover then explained the committee decision regarding the Southern Union stock.

"Jim, the bank should make Ron Keenan its agent to hold the stock," Grambling protested. "You can't find a more trustworthy banker."

Not possible, Conover explained, as he telephoned Scott Clark, bank counsel.

While Conover was on the phone, Grambling reflected on his own diligent morning. When not in the committee room, he had been busy on the phone with Foncannon in Denver.

"Tom, have you heard yet from Hean?" Grambling had asked from Conover's office in Salt Lake City.

Foncannon said that he had not. Grambling promised to arrange the conference call.

"I'm about to fly to New York," Grambling said. "We'll have to do the call during one of my stopovers, probably when I'm in Chicago."

At about 1:00 P.M. on the 25th, Grambling, still in Conover's office, called Foncannon again.

"I'm on that layover in Chicago, Tom. Are you ready for the call with Hean?"

Foncannon said that he was, and after about 15 minutes, Foncannon's phone rang again. A raspy female voice spoke.

"Please hold for a conference call with Mr. Grambling in Chicago and Mr. Hean in New York." Grambling came on the line and introduced Scott Hean, who Foncannon knew to be a senior energy lender at the Bank of Montreal.

Foncannon reviewed with Hean the history of the Colorado National loan, specifically the expenditures which had been paid and would be paid with Colorado National's $6 million.

"Scott, Ivor Hopkyns seems to think that not all of the expenditures are covered by the Bank of Montreal funds," Foncannon said.

Item by item, Foncannon read Hean the list of expenditures provided by Grambling.

"Could you repeat that one again, Tom? Yeah, that's covered, and what's next. I got it."

After a pause, Hean said with an air of finality to his voice, "Tom, each of the expenditures you've listed is contemplated by the Term Sheet, and every one can be repaid with the working capital portion of the Bank of Montreal funding."

Foncannon next inquired if the Bank of Montreal expected to close the $100 million loan on time.

"Things are moving along fine," Hean said. "But the closing will probably be a few days late since the lawyers still have details to iron out. You know lawyers, Tom. They always have details to work out."

Everyone laughed.

"By the way John, when are you going to be in New York so we can finalize this thing?" Hean asked.

"I'm in Chicago now. I should be in New York in a few more hours."

The conversation ended, and Hean hung up. Grambling and Foncannon stayed on the line.

"Tom, I need the rest of my money. Was Hean's approval what you needed to forward the balance of my loan?"

Foncannon discussed the Hean conversation with Kropf. They could think of no reason not to disburse the final $2.7 million. When Grambling, still at First Security Bank in Utah, called Foncannon later that afternoon, Foncannon said that the money was ready to be disbursed.

Grambling was in a dilemma. He had to transmit money to the Bank of Montreal immediately. But how would it look if the money was wired directly from Colorado National to the Bank of Montreal? Not possible, Grambling thought. His explanation to Hean, the real one, required that the money originate at Coronado as if it were the misplaced Dr Pepper proceeds.

"Tom, please wire the money to my Connecticut bank," Grambling instructed Foncannon.

The money was sent that afternoon. Grambling would make separate arrangements to have the funds transferred from Connecticut to Coronado, and then to the Bank of Montreal.

After completing the calls with Foncannon on the afternoon of Friday, January 25, Grambling redirected his energies to stalking First Security's $8 million. He now sat in Conover's office as an approved loan applicant. He and Conover discussed the collateral transfer.

"Jim, the stock at Coronado is held in my name. Four certificates, C-164895, C-164712, C-197658, and C-204634, a total of 358,600 shares."

Bankers are comforted by details, and Grambling's details, written by Conover on the same yellow scrap of paper that bore Mullin's telephone number in Florida, were precise.

Scott Clark, counsel to the bank, joined them. To arrange the pledge of the collateral, Conover and Clark called Ron Keenan at Coronado.

"Bank of Coronado," a voice on the phone answered.

Clark was relieved. He knew of the earlier phone call to Blair Mullin at a number which did not answer "Bank of Montreal." There could be no doubt, however, that he and Conover were on the line with Coronado Bank.

Clark and Conover asked that the call be transferred to Ron Keenan.

"Mr. Keenan is not available," Jennie, Keenan's secretary, told them. "I will locate him and have him return your call."

Within 15 minutes of Conover's conversation with Jennie, Keenan called the Utah bank. He verified the ownership details provided by Grambling; number of certificates, serial numbers; number of shares. He also told Clark that the stock had been in the name of a family trust but had been transferred to Grambling.

"Is it pledged for a loan?" the inquisitive attorney asked from Salt Lake City.

"No, we hold the certificates because they had been pledged for a loan," Keenan replied from El Paso. "But the loan's been repaid. The stock is wholly unencumbered."

Clark explained his job to Keenan; to figure out a way to have someone hold the stock in pledge for First Security.

"Where is the stock physically?" Clark asked. "Your office, the bank, a vault?"

Keenan was unsure, and the call ended with Scott's request that Coronado telecopy copies of the certificates to First Security. Shortly thereafter, Grambling told Clark that Keenan was on the line again. Clark took the phone. Keenan explained that the stock had been transferred to Merrill Lynch so Coronado could not telecopy copies of the certificates. But Keenan offered to have the stock returned to Coronado where it could be held for First Security's account.

"Why not have me send you a document hypothecating the stock to your benefit?" Keenan suggested. "I'll do the forms. I'll swear to them, and file them here in El Paso. When they're done, I'll send copies to you in Salt Lake City."

"That won't be necessary," Clark said. Keenan's mention of Merrill Lynch had given Clark an idea. "Ron, we have a Merrill Lynch office in the same mall complex as the bank building. Let me call our broker. We'll arrange to have an account set up here in the bank's name. Merrill Lynch can transfer the stock internally, El Paso to Salt Lake City."

The conversation ended, and Clark proceeded to call his law firm's account officer at Merrill Lynch, Salt Lake City. He and the officer were discussing the arrangements for the stock transfer, when Grambling knocked on the door.

"Excuse me, Scott. Mr. Keenan's on the line. He'd like to talk with you."

Clark ended the Merrill Lynch call and again spoke to Keenan in El Paso.

"Sorry, Scott. I was mixed-up earlier. John's stock is at E. F. Hutton here in El Paso. Now I can pledge . . ."

Clark interrupted.

"That's great, Ron. E. F. Hutton has a brokerage account relationship with First Security. We'll do the same arrangement we were going to do with Merrill Lynch."

Clark hung up, and went back to Conover's office, where he dialed the E. F. Hutton broker he knew.

As Clark was on the line making the arrangements, Grambling again knocked on the door to interrupt.

"Mr. Keenan on the line, Scott."

Again, Clark hung up and went to the room where Keenan and Grambling were speaking on the phone.

"Could you hold on a second, Ron," Grambling said into the phone as he turned to Clark. "I'm sorry, Scott, Ron was confused. The stock is not at Hutton. It's at the El Paso branch of Eppler, Guerin & Turner. Ron can make the arrangements for a transfer to an account pledged to First Security at Eppler, Guerin." Grambling held the phone out to Clark.

Clark did not have to check the local phone directory to determine whether Eppler, Guerin & Turner, a large Texas brokerage firm, had a branch in the same mall complex or city as the Salt Lake bank.

"Ron tells me that Eppler, Guerin has no branches in Salt Lake City, or Utah," Grambling said. "But Ron can transfer the stock to the Texas brokerage house for First Security's account."

Clark didn't take the phone, and Grambling hung up. It was after 5:00 P.M.

Clark and Conover were tired and frustrated. After working all afternoon on the transfer, they were no closer to obtaining the collateral. Since the loan could not be closed that day, they decided that they might just as well send a messenger to El Paso to pick up the physical shares of stock on Monday morning. They prepared a letter for Grambling's signature authorizing Eppler, Guerin & Turner to give Grambling's Southern Union stock to a messenger from First Security.

Clark handed the letter to Grambling.

"Here, John, just sign it. No one seems to be sure where this stock is, so we better just pick it up ourselves. You can get your money on Monday."

What Grambling did astonished Clark and Conover. Without signing, Grambling turned and walked out the door. Clark and Conover were never to see Grambling again.

Conover was not the only banker, and Clark the only bank counsel, to be amazed that Friday. Hopkyns, Mullin and Hean had arrived in New York on Thursday night for their critical 10:00 A.M. Friday meeting with the Husky officers and Grambling. With the meeting adjourned to Saturday, the Canadian bankers spent Friday at the Lexington Avenue office of Shearman & Sterling, three blocks from the bank's Park Avenue office. They met with their counsel that morning.

Greenblatt handed the bankers copies of the notorious Lazard consent. He also gave them copies of the Lazard specimen signature books. The bankers' faces turned ashen. They looked at each other dumbfounded: The truth struck home. These were forgeries, each thought. Plain and simple.

"Stay together," Greenblatt advised. "We don't know what's going to happen today. And don't be on the phone, either making or receiving calls, unless you have a witness on the line. And don't talk to anyone about the situation."

The bankers were led to an empty, windowless conference room. They spent several hours, waiting. As people do when caught in a common dilemma, they compared mental notes to try to comprehend what was happening to them, and the loan to Grambling.

"Look at the phone number for Libman," Hopkyns said, as he passed around several of the letters received from Cumberland Village Mining. "It's 305-940-7525. That's very close to 305-940-7536, the number Grambling gave me to call Corcoran, or whoever, in Florida."

The bankers looked around the room in which they had been entombed. Each observed that there were three phone consoles.

"Let's do it," Hean said.

Each picked up a receiver. Mullin looked at the known Libman number, the number shown on the stationery of Cumberland Village mining. No, Mullin thought, not that one.

He dialed the other number, 305-940-7536, the number at which Hopkyns had reached the phony Corcoran on December 28.

After a few rings, a female voice answered.

Mullin spoke.

"Is Mr. Libman in?"

The female replied, "May I tell him who is calling?"

The bankers hung up.

For several moments, they remained silent. Filing out of the room, heads bowed, they found and told Greenblatt what had occurred. In their collective shock, they did not hear the consoling thought of one of their counsel.

"Look on the bright side," he said. "Maybe you did lose $7.5 million dollars. But think of it as the cost of saving the $100 million."

January 25 had been an exhausting and battering day. The next day, the bankers flew home to their families, and one arrived in time for dinner. Mid-meal, his wife ushered their son out of the room. She did not know what had happened. She would find out later. But she did not want their child to see any more than he had already seen: his father, at the head of the table, holding his head in his hands, sobbing.

"It will be the biggest fraud loss in the bank's history," he told his wife. "How could I have judged him so wrong?" The career they had worked and sacrificed for was over.

CHAPTER 6

LETTER TO HOGAN PLACE

Almost a month since he had handed Busuttil the Consent and Agreement, Grambling returned to the 33rd floor of the Lexington Avenue office of Shearman & Sterling. Accompanied by two attorneys and Robert Zobel, the friend slated to become Chief Operating Officer of Grambling Energy, Grambling and his entourage did not go to the precise scene of the December crime. The December 28 closing, involving a relatively small loan for Shearman & Sterling, had occurred in a small, windowless conference room. The January 26 meeting would determine the fate of the $100 million credit (as well as, the Bank of Montreal officers worried, the future of their relationship with Husky). A more imposing setting was in order.

The receptionist escorted Grambling and his group to the main 33rd floor conference room. It was a distinguished location: 40 feet long and wood-paneled, the room's south side consisted entirely of glass facing a panorama of midtown and southern Manhattan. The room's chairs and table were dark, tastefully carved wood. Several original Audubon prints graced the walls. The silver tea service seemed appropriate to the setting. But the two overhead projectors and movie screen did not. Their presence was the brainchild of Field and Greenblatt, the attorneys intent on demonstrating why their client could not make the $100 million loan. In addition to Grambling and his group, Arthur Price and William Miller of Husky Oil, and their counsel, were present, as were the Three Musketeers, Hean, Mullin, and Hopkyns.

Grambling's counsel looked around the room with a blank expression on his face.

"I don't know why we're here," he began. "We haven't been told what's going to be discussed. So, of course, we haven't investigated anything, other than the stock mix-up."

Grambling nodded in approval. He was as nonchalant as Hean and his colleagues were tense.

To Field and Greenblatt, counsel's alleged befuddlement was exactly what they wanted, an invitation to explain. The Shearman & Sterling attorneys distributed copies of the Lazard Consent and Agreement, and copies of the specimen signatures provided by Mullarkey.

"This is why we're here," Field announced.

The blinds were closed, and the lights turned off. Field projected two images on the wall: one was the "Peter Corcoran" signature from the consent that Grambling had given to Busuttil; the other image was the Corcoran signature on the specimen list. With the dramatic sense of a handwriting expert testifying in court, Field slowly converged the two images. The signatures sprawled atop one another, like a round peg being fitted over a square hole.

Field raised his voice above the increasingly irritating hum of the projectors. "John, how can you explain this?"

The room was silent, but for the relentless humming of the machines. Like little jackhammers, the noise chiseled into everyone's mind the forgery on the screen. Field's words hung unanswered in the air. Finally, in response, Grambling rose from his chair and approached the machines. He turned them off. The painful images disappeared. After a whispered consultation with his counsel, Grambling addressed Field.

"I haven't committed any crime, Art. I didn't sign that consent, and I don't know what happened at Lazard. Though I will tell you that there are people there who want to hurt me." Grambling glanced around the room. His head jerked backwards, startled, as if he noticed something for the first time. "Art, Jim Busuttil already had the consent when I arrived at the closing. Why isn't he here to explain?"

Unbeknownst to Grambling, Busuttil was several doors away at a closing on an unrelated loan. His conduct had been examined by Shearman & Sterling attorneys to determine what had happened at the closing; particularly, how the consent had arrived. As far as the Shearman & Sterling attorneys were concerned, the party solely responsible for what counsel were increasingly referring to as "the fraud" was Grambling. As the Shearman & Sterling attorneys heard Grambling's not so subtle attempt to pin the blame on their young colleague, their feelings for Grambling began to alter, from mere dislike to loathing.

Grambling continued with his soliloquy. He was hurt and offended by Field's accusatory questioning.

"I admit there's been a foul-up. My Dr Pepper stock was held at Coronado. When the stock was cashed out it was sent through E. F. Hutton, not Lazard. But the proceeds are now at Coronado. You know that Keenan's holding the money, since I'm liable for a small debt of Libman's. But that's all being taken care of. You'll be repaid on Monday." Grambling gestured toward the screen and handouts. "As for this signature stuff, I'll do my best to find out what happened at Lazard. But I really don't know."

His explanation completed, Grambling, his counsel, and Zobel left.

Whatever the impression the presentation had made on Grambling, the presentation did not alter the concerns of the Husky officers. Price, the Husky President, brushed the consent and Lazard handout to the side as if they were no more than used coffee cups.

"Now that the show's over," Price began. "Let's get down to the real meeting. The bank has less than a week to close on the $100 million loan."

Field was stunned. He snapped at Price. "Wrong meeting, Art."

"Pardon?" Price said.

"You're at the wrong meeting," Field repeated. "This meeting is about what we just showed you on the screen."

The bankers were ecstatic. For a week, they had suffered Price's criticism that they had altered the terms of the loan and were delaying the closing. Now their counsel had taken their defense.

Lawyering is often the skill of controlling one's outrage. As patiently as their tempers permitted, Field and his colleagues explained, slowly and meticulously, why they could not advise their client to risk a $100 million loan to someone implicated in a patent forgery. And how could you think otherwise, the bank counsel thought.

With equal firmness, the Husky officers could not believe that the bank would renege on a commitment for what was, in its fundamentals, still a good deal. Disagreement became dislike. Within months, Husky had withdrawn its business from the Bank of Montreal.

Grambling knew that the clock was ticking. The tone of the 26th meeting was unmistakable. He would have to repay the entire $7.5 million or the bankers would dismiss the Dr Pepper mistaken transfer story, whose believability faded with each day of nonpayment.

The week of January 28, Grambling tried his home court advantage. His father approached a banking acquaintance at the Interfirst Bank of El Paso. Would Interfirst consider an expedited $6 million loan to his son? The bank agreed. Within the day, Grambling appeared in person in El Paso to request a three-month $6 million loan for himself and, as he told the officer, "my partner, Robert Libman." Grambling offered as security well over $6 million of the publicly traded stock listed in Libman's financial statement.

"Bob's stock is held in street name by Signet Securities," Grambling explained to the Interfirst bankers. "You can verify the numbers with Bob's account officer, Tom Carson." Grambling gave Carson's phone number to the bankers—305-940-7536—and twice the bankers called the securities officer. In response to each call, the ever-willing male who answered the phone, "Carson" for these calls, verified that Signet held the specific stock listed in Libman's financial statement. The bankers, however, insisted to Grambling that the stock shares offered as collateral be physically transferred to Interfirst.

"It takes time to transfer the shares, and I need the financing now." Grambling urged the bankers to be reasonable. "A telex that the stock is held by Signet, and Libman's sworn, notarized assignment to you, surely should be enough at this point?"

It would not, the El Paso bankers insisted. They planned to syndicate the loan among several El Paso banks. Syndications required extra caution on behalf of the agent bank, so Interfirst did need the physical shares. After all, the bankers reminded Grambling, a courier could deliver the shares to El Paso in one business day. Grambling withdrew the application and, as an apparent afterthought, asked Interfirst to return the financial documents he had submitted to support the loan request.

With the Bank of Montreal, Grambling maintained the pretense that nothing was seriously wrong. On Monday January 28, $2 million was wire-transferred to the Bank of Montreal for Grambling's account. Unmistakably, the money came from Coronado Bank in Texas. Hean, Mullin and Hopkins responded with wide-eyed astonishment. Could Grambling be telling the truth? Had the Dr Pepper stock been mistakenly transferred to Coronado?

Hean and Mullin called Coronado Bank to question Keenan. The call was not intercepted by Jennie, Keenan's secretary. A voice identified himself as Keenan, and, as Keenan spoke, Hean and Mullin looked at each other. This isn't the same voice as that of the Keenan we spoke to the other week, is it? Whoever he was, the present Keenan extinguished whatever flicker of confidence the Bank of Montreal officers might have experienced as a result of the $2 million transfer.

"Gentlemen, I cannot answer your questions about John's stock," Keenan said. "If you have questions, ask him."

The time had arrived for the Bank to reach a major corporate decision. Art Field arranged the conference call between himself and his colleagues, and the senior bank officers in Toronto. That the $100 million loan could not be authorized was clear. The decision that had to be made concerned a related issue: the unmistakable conclusion that the $7.5 million had been taken by crime.

"We are a foreign bank doing business in America," the voices from Toronto stated. "What is our legal obligation, if any, to report what we have learned to the American authorities?"

Field's response was clear. The fraud discovered by counsel indicated potential breaches of state and federal law, and a report would have to be made to both authorities. It was a matter of good corporate citizenship, as well as a legal obligation of the statutes under which the Bank of Montreal was permitted to operate in New York State. Other than to ignore the facts on which the bank had relied in breaking the commitment to lend, the bank had no choice but to come forward and report that it had been swindled.

Even the unavoidable decision was not an easy one. Coming forward had adverse financial consequences for the bank. In the financial records of the bank, the personal loan to Grambling, now reduced to $5.5 million, could be accounted for in one of several ways. It could be designated a bad debt and carried on the bank's books as an underperforming loan, one to be criticized by bank examiners but, nonetheless, an asset.

Treating the loan as a theft had a different consequence. A theft is a loss to be written off with a deduction taken from the Bank's loan loss reserve. To attempt some recovery, the bank could also file a claim under its insurance policy. However, in cases of sophisticated fraud, banks often discover, as the Bank of Montreal would, that insurance companies often maintain that the policy definition of fraud excludes coverage for the type of fraud loss for which a claim is being submitted. In any case, the moment the "loan" was characterized as fraud, the bank's assets would decrease $5.5 million.

Disclosure, as the decision-makers in Toronto understood, also invited a harm for which there is no form of insurance: embarrassment. To be victimized by bank fraud is a humiliation; a mockery of a person's intelligence; a statement that one has been taken for a fool. Victimization is particularly embarrassing to professional people, holders of advanced degrees, who, in the wisdom of hindsight, are always pinioned on the standard of "you should have known better."

And, the humiliation is public. If the fraud is large enough, the crime will be reported in the press, general and financial. The public enjoys seeing the wealthy humbled, and correct or not, few institutions and their employees are perceived to be as pompous and deserving of a fall from grace as are banks and bankers. Bankers themselves could be expected to feel a full measure of schadenfreude—pleasure in the misfortune of others—when reading about the duping of their colleagues. Behind the laughter would be the realization that only makes the nervous guffaws more intense—there, but for the grace of God, go I. For good reason, a banker's visceral reaction to being defrauded is no different from that of the rape victim; a genuine fear that going public will only compound the pain.

The bank chose to be a good citizen. It instructed counsel to submit a letter reporting the crime to the appropriate authorities. Field and Greenblatt drafted a letter to be dated February 1, 1985. It was directed to three parties. Two were general, the "Superintendent of Banks" at the New York State Banking Department, and the "Agent-in-Charge" at the Manhattan office of the Federal Bureau of Investigation. The third addressee was a specific individual: "Hon. Robert M. Morgenthau, District Attorney, New York County," the New York County prosecutor.

As it was for the Bank of Montreal, for Grambling also, the last days of January was a time of decision. Although he had defrauded many banks, he had never inched as close to discovery as he now had with the Bank of Montreal. He came from a family of attorneys, and, after the meeting of the 26th, he fully understood where the Bank of Montreal was headed. With no new loan forthcoming, no new victim to swindle out of a kitty to pay the old victim, Grambling resorted to his last defense, sympathy. Late in the evening of Thursday, January 31, midnight Calgary time, Grambling called Mullin at his home in Calgary.

Mullin's wife answered. She woke her husband. It had been a tense month for Mullin. He thought that he, Hopkyns, and Hean may have been under suspicion as potential accomplices of Grambling. During the last week, Shearman & Sterling counsel had advised the Three Musketeers that they and the bank might have different interests. "Shearman & Sterling represents the Bank of Montreal," bank counsel had told them. "We know of no reason why you should obtain individual counsel, but we want you to know that it is your right to do so, and you may want to get your own attorney to advise you."

Neither Mullin, Hean, nor Hopkyns had obtained separate counsel. In their minds, they were good soldiers, falsely suspected and innocent of any wrongdoing. The facts would prove it, they were confident, and to obtain counsel under these circumstances was like an admission to something they did not do.

For his part, by the time of the midnight call, Mullin was at peace with himself and his role in the Grambling affair. The interminable meetings, the traveling, the conferences were over, and for the first time in weeks he had his own life again: He had gone to bed early that evening. After five minutes of reluctance, Mullin awoke and located a pad and pen. Of course, he would speak to Grambling. But he would take meticulous notes so that the truth could emerge through the ongoing investigation.

"Blair, my first priority is to give the bank back its money. I don't want to go to jail. There's been a number of fuck-ups by me and my banker, but I never intended to cheat anyone. There's an explanation. A guy like Field won't like it, but there's an explanation."

Mullin said "Hmm" and "Yes" to indicate that he was listening, as he scribbled notes.

"We can still pull off this deal. If we have a meeting, you, me and the other bankers, I'm sure I can satisfy you. The 31st was not a realistic closing date even if all had gone well. And maybe Husky won't want to come back and deal, but I can explain what happened. If we can talk off the record, I can satisfy you and Scott and the others. Can we talk, Blair?"

Grambling was silent. The lack of words was oppressive. Mullin was overcome by the compulsion, common to people who think they may be under suspicion, to answer the question.

"We've heard your answers, John. I can't answer your question about a meeting. However, we're always willing to listen."

"Let's arrange it for next week, Blair. We'll all sit down, but not the lawyers. I don't want to face a barrage of questions from the likes of Art Field." Finally, Mullin ended the call.

Mullin went back to bed. First thing the next morning, he called the other two of the Three Musketeers, and then counsel.

"Preserve your notes," Greenblatt advised. "We'll talk more next week."

That there would be any further meetings with Grambling, everyone understood, was out of the question. The issue of the "loan" had been taken out of the bank's hands. The letter reporting the crime had been signed by Art Field late that Friday afternoon, and, Monday morning February 4, it was hand-delivered to the District Attorney's Office. When the letter left the Shearman & Sterling office, the Grambling loan ceased being a matter of dollars and cents to be resolved by businessmen and their lawyers. The messenger brought the letter to lower Manhattan, and an Office whose concerns transcend the marketplace.

CHAPTER 7

WE BEAT HIM ON THE FORGERY

The modern office of the District Attorney is in the Criminal
Court Building at 100 Centre Street. To the south are the mu-
nicipal buildings, City Hall, and Wall Street. To the west is a
neighborhood of dilapidated factories; five- and six-story struc-
tures that were modern architecture in the mid-19th century
and which, increasingly, have been renovated to house the
newly wealthy. Surrounding the east side of the office is China-
town, and north, Little Italy.

Centre Street was an appropriate location for the prosecutors. Any member of the Rackets Bureau desirous of a short
lunchtime stroll could walk up Mulberry Street, east of the
Criminal Court Building, and pass the storefront lawyers, bail
bondsmen, and a number of Italian restaurants, including Lu-
na's, where Crazy Joe Gallo was tape-recorded extorting
money, or Umberto's Clam Bar, where crazy Joe was murdered, or SPQR, owned by Matty "the Horse" and forfeited to
the government after his racketeering conviction. The historical stroll would end at the Ravenite Social Club, a dilapidated
tenement. The Ravenite is the headquarters of the Gambino
crime family, one of the five families comprising the New York
Mafia.

Although there had been a prosecutor in New York County
since the 17th century, the courthouse had been located on
Centre Street only since 1838. At the time, the 100 Centre
Street area was in the heart of the notorious Five Points district, a slum of closely packed tenements connected by under-
ground passageways. It was the most impoverished area in the
English-speaking world. "Let us go on again, and plunge into

the Five Points," wrote Dickens in his *American Notes.* "Where dogs would howl to lie," Dickens observed, "men and women and boys slink off to sleep, forcing the dislodged rats to move away in quest of better housing. . . . All that is loathsome, drooping and decayed is here." According to street wisdom, children born in the hovels of Five Points could live into their teens without seeing the sun or breathing fresh air: Crime so infested the area that the unarmed could not venture into the filth-covered streets. When one infamous tenement house was torn down, workmen were seen to cart away bags of human bones. The bones, recovered from the tenement walls, were the remains of generations of the building's inhabitants, and their victims.

Centre Street itself predated the courthouse by only 25 years. The area had originally been a freshwater pond; in its center, had been the island on which the city's executions were conducted. In 1808, sailors unemployed by the Embargo Act led a starving mob which marched on City Hall to demand bread and food. Threatened with being torn limb from limb, the City Council members responded by funding the public works project of filling the pond. The landfill was bisected by a street, Centre Street, which quickly became the home to Manhattan's boisterous brothel district. The city authorities decided that the area's populace needed a combined prison and courthouse which, named the Hall of Justice, was built in 1838. Squat, with columns resembling reeds from the Nile, the building had been patterned after an Egyptian mausoleum. Both because of the funereal appearance, and the fate of those housed there, the building quickly became known as *The Tombs.* Connecting the prison portion of the Tombs to the building's courtrooms was a graceful, stone bridge over which manacled prisoners were led after being sentenced. The bridge also had a name; the Bridge of Sighs. If condemned, the prisoner who walked that bridge soon appeared in the Tombs' central courtyard, the place of execution. Hangings occurred here until the late 19th century when the electric chair, the more modern form of execution, was introduced at Sing Sing.

Franklin D. Roosevelt and the WPA rebuilt the Centre Street area in the Depression. The old Tombs, and courthouse, and Bridge of Sighs, were destroyed, replaced by an Art Deco skyscraper with two 17-story towers: America's most modern prison and courthouse. The Manhattan House of Detention, its legal name proudly chiselled in a granite headstone, was the new prison, as well as the building's north end; no matter what letters were chiseled, however, the prison was still called *The Tombs*. The courtrooms were in the building's center, connected to the Tombs by an exterior 12th floor bridge which, in the less romantic 20th century, was called simply *The Bridge*. The entrance to the District Attorney's Office was at the south end of the building. The street on which the entrance was located was formerly a section of Leonard Street, specifically 155 Leonard Street. In 1981, this portion of the street was renamed *Hogan Place* in honor of the legendary District Attorney. The entrances to the courthouse were wrapped in inscriptions meant to be instructive to those who entered to work or be judged: "Where law ends, there tyranny begins."

On February 4, 1985, the Shearman & Sterling messenger trotted up the steps into One Hogan Place. Between him and the elevators was a barrier, made of metal poles connected by lengths of cloth, as in a bank. At the end of the barrier was a desk manned by a uniformed and armed police officer.

Security at the District Attorney's Office vacillates between periods of intensity and laxity. In the early 1970s, the Black Liberation Army, a gang of street thugs and killers mouthing Marxism, terrorized the city with a series of ambushes of policemen, and police murders. District Attorney Hogan's own two police bodyguards had been attacked while sitting in their patrol car in front of Mr. Hogan's Morningside Heights home, a block from Columbia University. Machinegunned from a passing vehicle, the officers were crippled for life.

During those days of terror, a bomb had been walked through the court building and placed in a bathroom adjacent to the Complaint Room of the District Attorney's Office: The Complaint Room is where arresting officers and civilian victims of street crime, often accompanied by children, first meet the assistants who evaluate cases. Luckily for people in the room, the wall proved to be a testament to the solidity of pre-World War II government-financed construction: The thick concrete wall retained the explosion. In a similar assault on the Justice System, a radical defense attorney had smuggled a gun, handcuffs, and can of mace to his clients, three Black Liberation Army killers about to be sentenced for the ambush murders of two uniformed policemen: The contraband was discovered with no injuries.

It was a dangerous time. The reception desk of the District Attorney's Office was then manned by thoroughly competent but older police officers, close to retirement. It was thought to be a wise step to replace these veterans with younger cops with even quicker gun fingers.

By 1985, the danger had retreated, though the younger cops remained. Barely glancing up from the TV hidden beneath the counter, the reception cop stopped the messenger from Shearman & Sterling.

"Letter for Morgenthau? Drop it in Room 749."

The cop returned to his soap opera, and the messenger turned to the elevators, flanked by the war memorial with fading pictures of young men long dead: "To the Assistants Who Gave Their Lives in the Great War." The messenger brought the letter to Room 749, the receiving area for all correspondence and legal documents, and departed lower Manhattan as he had come, by subway.

A clerk collected the day's correspondence for the District Attorney, threw it in a wire cart, and wheeled the cart to the Executive Suite on the 8th Floor. An officer, nonuniformed but armed, buzzed open the door and, after going through a hallway and a waiting room, the clerk left the mail with Ida VanLindt, the District Attorney's long-time secretary.

The clerk had passed through the hallway a thousand times, and had long ceased to look up at the several dozen photographs that lined the walls. The first photographs were of prints or statutes, and the last were photographs of the men themselves: The District Attorneys who had served New York County from the Revolution to the present. They were all men—grave, middle-aged—and all, except to historians, forgotten. Forgotten that is, but for the last three, the District Attorneys who spanned the past 50 years in the history of New York County—Thomas Dewey, Frank S. Hogan, and Robert M. Morgenthau.

Dewey and Hogan had created the modern prosecutor. In the 1930s the Office of the District Attorney, whether in Manhattan or elsewhere, was not necessarily an office of distinction. Frequently, the county prosecutor and his assistants were political appointees, beholden to the party organization. The result was often a lackadaisical attitude to the prosecution of corruption.

The District Attorney himself was elected, and in 1933, the Mob elected the Manhattan prosecutor. In a 1948 book, *New York Times* reporter Warren Moscow described the 1933 election:

> Squads of mobster "storm troopers," trade-marked for their own purposes by identical pearl-gray fedoras, marched in on polling place after polling place south of Fourteenth Street in Manhattan and took over the voting machinery. They told the policeman assigned to the place to "beat it," and he, knowing where the interest of his superiors lay, took a walk around the block instead of sounding a riot call. The citizenry, waiting in line to vote, was shoved out of the way. One gorilla—one who was able to write—would take over the registry book and sign for those who had not yet voted, while another rang up the votes on the voting machine, as if it were a cash register.

It was not that the District Attorney so elected was himself on the take; he was just uninterested in prosecuting those who had put him in office.

This lack of concern readily became apparent to the New York County Grand Jury, the entity which accuses individuals of serious crimes and compels them to stand trial. The institution consists of 23 county citizens. They sit in secret session with evidence presented to them by the District Attorney or his assistants. The institution of the Grand Jury predated independence and, as every school child was once taught, the New York Grand Jury jealously guarded individual liberties. In 1735, the Royal Governor of New York ordered the Grand Jury to indict the Manhattan publisher, John Peter Zenger, for holding the government up to scorn, and, as proof of its own independence and its respect for liberty of speech, the Grand Jury refused.

In the 1930s, grand jurors in New York County were drawn from the Grand Jury Association of New York County, a self-perpetuating private organization whose membership largely consisted of businessmen and professionals, people who perceived of themselves as good citizens interested in honest government. After the 1933 election, these citizens, sitting as the Grand Jury, were shocked by the evidence they heard. It was estimated that organized crime and related law enforcement corruption was costing city taxpayers $164 million a year, a phenomenal sum in depression America. Yet, the District Attorney and his assistants were unable to present evidence warranting indictments for any of the racketeering activity which menaced the public. Even after the Grand Jury took over the investigation, dismissing the District Attorney, and summoning and examining witnesses on its own responsibility, the evidence was not forthcoming.

The Grand Jury acted on its outrage. In March 1935, in an act consistent with their lineage of courage and independence, the New York County Grand Jury directed a six-paragraph report to Herbert Lehman, the Governor of New York. The report stated the Grand Jury's belief, founded upon months of investigation, that gangsters had come to dominate multiple aspects of life and governance in New York City. The report concluded with the recommendation that "a prosecuting attorney of outstanding capacity and public prestige should be appointed by the Governor to investigate, with the aid of a special Grand Jury drawn for that purpose, all forms of organized crime in the county, and their connection with agencies of law enforcement." In responding to such requests, the historic practice of New York's governors was to appoint as Special Prosecutor an attorney who was not a member of the political party to be investigated. Since New York County was Democratic, the Democrat Herbert Lehman appointed as Special Prosecutor a young Republican attorney, Thomas E. Dewey.

It was a revolution. Dewey and his young assistants, known as "Twenty Against the Mob," successfully prosecuted corrupt politicians and mobsters: Then, as five decades later, the two would be connected. Riding this wave of success, Dewey was elected New York County District Attorney in 1937. He took office in 1938. His pre-election promise, as would be that of his two elected successors, was honest law enforcement with favoritism to no one. Loyal to that commitment, Dewey remade the Office: Assistants were appointed on merit, not party favoritism. The New York County Office became the model for prosecutors throughout the nation.

Dewey earned a national reputation and entered politics. In 1940, the one-term New York County District Attorney arrived at the Republican National Convention in Philadelphia with the greatest number of pledged votes. In the end, he lost the nomination to Wendell L. Willkie. In 1941, Dewey declined to run for re-election as New York County District Attorney so that he could run for governor of New York, an office to which he was elected in 1942. Upon declining to run again for District Attorney, he designated as his successor Frank S. Hogan, a member of the original Twenty.

Elected and re-elected Manhattan District Attorney for the 32 years from 1941 to 1973, Hogan trained generations of prosecutors. The graduates of his and Dewey's Office, filled prominent positions throughout the legal profession. Dozens were appointed to the bench, state and federal. Two of the "Twenty Against the Mob," Stanley Fuld and Charles Breitel, were to become Chief Judge of the New York State Court of Appeals. Several graduates became district attorneys themselves, in New York State and elsewhere, where they replicated the Dewey-Hogan tradition of training young attorneys to be selfless public servants.

As had Dewey, Hogan became a national figure. When a murder occurs in Boston or Chicago, it's another statistic in the national index of 20,000 homicides. But when a boy is killed in a gang fight in Manhattan's Hell's Kitchen, a musical is written; "West Side Story." Attorney Generals come and go with each president, and local federal prosecutors change even more frequently, but decade after decade, Frank Hogan remained— "Mr. District Attorney," the acknowledged dean of the nation's prosecutors. Gravely ill, Hogan left office in 1974.

Robert Morgenthau, the present District Attorney, was among the few attorneys in New York with the experience and reputation to succeed Hogan. Morgenthau grew up in a tradition of public service; his grandfather had served as Ambassador to Turkey under President Wilson; his father had been Secretary of the Treasury under President Roosevelt. In the 1950s, Morgenthau held office as an appointee of New York's Governor Harriman. In 1961, the newly elected President Kennedy appointed Morgenthau United States Attorney for the Southern District of New York, often considered the country's most prominent local federal prosecutor. Morgenthau remained close to the Kennedy family. He was with the Attorney General in November 1963 when the news came from Dallas that the president had been shot.

Morgenthau continued to serve as U.S. Attorney under Presidents Johnson and Nixon. He remained in office until 1970, when he came too close to uncovering illegal Republican campaign contributions. Morgenthau was fired. It was a firing for which Morgenthau remains intensely proud. Prominent in his office is a three-by-four-foot blow-up of a Pat Oliphant cartoon showing Morgenthau, in a Sherlock Holmes hat, following footprints to a Swiss bank. He's stopped at the door by President Nixon, who says, "Ridiculous, Morgenthau. You're fired."

After a brief period in private practice, Morgenthau returned to public service. In a special election in 1974, he was elected New York County District Attorney to replace the recently deceased Hogan. Since then, Morgenthau has been reelected four times. A quiet, intensely private man, Morgenthau had a reputation for an ability, in the words of a Supreme Court decision describing the model prosecutor, to strike "hard blows but fair ones."

Within the profession, he was one of the most respected prosecutors in America. And he was widely known to the public. Like Dewey and Hogan before him, Morgenthau was the District Attorney at the media center of America: A subway gunman, a little girl beaten to death by her adoptive father, a young woman raped in Central Park by a pack of teenagers—the crimes prosecuted by Morgenthau's Office were often known to the nation.

In 1985, reports of major crimes were evaluated as they had been for the past 50 years. Whether originating in phone calls or letters, each report was reviewed by a trusted executive assistant, and, if appropriate, assigned to a trial attorney. The executive assistant who read Morgenthau's mail in 1985 was

James Kindler. A graduate of Harvard College and the University of Pennsylvania Law School, Kindler had been hired by Mr. Hogan. As with the two dozen remaining Hogan appointees, Kindler displayed on his wall a framed copy of the poster from Hogan's last election campaign. In bold print under the benign face of the aging Hogan was the campaign motto: "You can't play politics with people's lives."

Kindler was a career prosecutor. He had been a member of the Narcotics and the Homicide Bureaus, as well as the Bureau Chief of what was known as a Trial Division, the unit whose members prosecuted robberies, rapes and murders, the usual street crimes. He had most recently been Chief of the Frauds Bureau, and to a large degree was responsible for shifting that unit's focus from standard bank embezzlements to the more complex business swindles that had mushroomed towards the end of the 1970s and the beginning of the 1980s. As Executive Assistant, he filled many roles. The primary one was to exercise judgment. Assistants relied on Kindler for guidance in the Office's most difficult cases. Their questions would go to both trial strategy, what the evidence could prove and how to prove it, and core ethical issues, such as the wisdom and fairness of proceeding with certain investigations. Kindler's judgment was among the most sought after and respected in the Office.

Among the dozens of letters crossing Kindler's desk on February 4 was the one on the letterhead of Shearman & Sterling. Like a diamond atop a sea of mud, the letter stood out from the general correspondence, often the inarticulate and angry statements of people who had obviously been hurt, though it was not clear whether the hurt had been caused by a criminal or civil wrong. In four crisp pages, the Shearman & Sterling letter outlined the law firm's discovery of a potential forgery. The conclusion was supported by several attached exhibits, including the Consent and Agreement, and the Lazard Freres signature documents. Kindler's evaluation was a quick one: Wall Street law firm, major institution as victim, $7.5 million obtained, an apparent forgery. This is a real crime, he thought. Which bureau should investigate?

Kindler ran down his options. Obviously not a street crime; Trial Division was out. No suggestion of organized crime, so the Rackets Bureau would not receive this case. The remaining trial divisions were the Special Prosecutions Bureau and the Frauds Bureau, the two units that prosecuted fraud. Special Prosecutions' cases tended to originate in civilian complaints. In several recent and innovative prosecutions, the bureau had obtained prison terms for landlords who had brutally harassed tenants, forcing them to vacate their homes so that the landlords could sell the buildings at an enormous profit. The focus of the Frauds Bureau was business crime. The bureau was a senior unit with several of the Office's most experienced trial and appellate attorneys. Frauds was the bureau with which Kindler was most familiar.

It was a strange calculus, Kindler knew. Assistants would gain their experience prosecuting murders and rapes, savage crimes, and then be transferred to the Frauds Bureau to prosecute bloodless business fraud. There was a method to this madness.

Trying violent crime cases developed a prosecutor's judgment in ways other than courtroom skills. One could talk to any trial attorney in Morgenthau's office and be told variations of the same story. The assistant had suffered an acquittal in a vicious case. The undeniably guilty defendant had beaten the charges due to some mistake; whether attorney or jury, or judicial error, was unimportant. Victims were entitled to know what the jury had done, and part of the assistant's job was to call the complainant and explain what had occurred. "Mrs. Smith, I'm sorry. The man who raped you was acquitted." Or, "Mr. and Mrs. Jones, I am sorry. The person who killed your child is a free man." It was a gutwrenching experience: It gave assistants a sober perspective on responsibility, and the important things in life.

Morgenthau wanted that perspective in the Frauds Bureau. Assistants who had prosecuted the cases of true horror understood that there were gradations to crime; that there were offenses which, though serious, and warranting punishment, were not the worst crimes in the world. It was a perspective particularly needed in the prosecution of white-collar offenses.

What is a business fraud is often not clear. There can be a fine line between crime and aggressive or thoughtless business dealings; and whether the act is a crime is frequently a question of interpretation and analysis. Even when it can be determined that technically a crime had been committed, whether the crime warrants prosecution is a matter of judgment.

The power to prosecute—to designate a given set of facts as warranting treatment as a crime—is the power to destroy, and nowhere is this more so than in the area of white-collar crimes. The perpetrators of business fraud are middle class, largely white. They are soft people insulated from the hard world of the law. Causing such people to be indicted results in consequences—loss of wealth, loss of dignity—that are devastating. For those actually sentenced to the living death of New York State prison, there is the incalculable loss of their very self-image as a human being. The power to prosecute and its consequences are huge, and an assistant with the experience of several homicide prosecutions under his belt is presumed to have the wisdom to use his power with restraint.

Chewing on his cigar, Kindler wrote "Benitez" in the corner of the Shearman & Sterling letter and tossed it into his out box. Peter Benitez was Kindler's successor as Chief of the Frauds Bureau. The Grambling case had been sent to the District Attorney's senior investigative unit for evaluation.

Within the hour, a messenger brought the letter to the suite of offices on the 7th floor designated as the Frauds Bureau. Benitez's office was in the southwest corner. Austerely furnished with government issue desks and chairs, it was a large office, befitting a Bureau Chief. Benitez had been hired by Hogan, and framed on Benitez's wall was the poster: "You can't play politics with people's lives."

Benitez set aside an hour each day to examine new reports of crime. Each report called for one of three decisions. If the incident reported was, on its face, not a crime, or if it was a crime too minor to be treated in the harsh world of the criminal justice system, Benitez sent the complainant a polite letter explaining the Office's decision to decline prosecution.

Sometimes the complaint stated a real crime which deserved to be prosecuted, but the crime was not significant enough to be investigated and tried by any of the 12 senior attorneys in the Frauds Bureau. As with life itself, business fraud was a victim of inflation. In 1975, a $100,000 case was considered significant, and the million dollar fraud was a rarity, the prosecution of which would be the highlight of a career.

By 1985, the numbers had changed. Frauds with million dollar losses seemed as boringly common as cases of fare beating on the subway. The Frauds Bureau attorneys worked on cases—such as the Drysdale securities collapse, a $250 million fraud loss for Chase Manhattan Bank—in which the losses were calculated as portions of a billion dollars. Unless the victim was particularly vulnerable, such as a charity or religious institution, or the fraud involved public corruption or crime by an attorney, Benitez tried to steer to a trial division all cases in which the fraud loss was less than $250,000. The cases deserved serious investigation and prosecution, and were given that attention in the trial divisions: The Frauds Bureau reserved its limited resources for the larger matters.

Benitez's third choice was to keep the case. After a quick perusal, that was his decision regarding the Bank of Montreal letter. Leaving his corner office, Benitez walked down the corridor. He flattened his back to the wall to squeeze by the file cabinets, filled with the bank documents and financial papers—the grist of the multimillion dollar investigations—that lined the corridors.

Benitez knew who he would give the case to. The door was open. Without knocking, Benitez walked into the office of Brian Rosner and dropped the Shearman & Sterling letter on the assistant's desk. Benitez looked at the boxes of documents piled on top of and underneath the tables, and on the file cabinets.

"You got a little time? I want you to look at something."

Benitez and Rosner were both in their mid-30s, with Benitez being older by three years. Each had graduated from Columbia College and Columbia Law School, where each, in his respective years, had been an honor student and an editor of the *Columbia Journal of Law and Social Problems.* Close to six feet tall, Benitez was as handsome as a matinee idol and strongly muscled from a regular regime of weight lifting.

Both were experienced. Benitez began his career in a trial division. He graduated to the Rackets Bureau, where, ultimately, he supervised several of the wiretaps that were to result in the convictions of the city's mob bosses. His principal interest was the prosecution of official corruption: He had convicted several New York County court officials who were selling decisions in civil cases; he also had convicted two assistant state attorneys who had taken bribes in the course of a major state construction project. Rosner had been appointed an assistant in 1975; he was a member of the first class of attorneys hired by Morgenthau. He began his career in the Appeals Bureau, where his job had been to convince appellate courts to uphold the convictions obtained at trial. In his five years in the Appeals Bureau, he had argued a larger number of cases than argued by the entire litigation departments of most law firms. In the Office, he had the reputation of often being able to salvage the most difficult case. Every defendant indicted by a grand jury to which he had presented the evidence had ultimately been convicted of a crime.

"It's a ground ball," Benitez said. "But I think we should do it anyway. Look it over. I'll be back in a few minutes."

Rosner began to read the letter. He understood Benitez's interest in the case: A document, purportedly from one of the city's major investment banks, had been forged; a financier had been impersonated by someone in Florida. That's not surprising, the assistant thought. It was a rare large fraud that did not involve someone in Fort Lauderdale or Miami.

And the letter continued. A second bank in Colorado was referred to as a potential victim, as was a bank in Utah. The letter made more allegations of impersonations: "It has come to the bank's attention that officers of two other banks have informed the bank that within the past month they have communicated with one of the bank's officers about the proposed loan to a corporation controlled by Mr. Grambling. The bank's officers deny having had such conversations."

Rosner leaned back in his chair and thought. The letter alleged a pattern—forgeries, multiple impersonations, conduct spanning several states—that warranted an investigation. That was a matter of duty, job performance. But, whether intentional or not, the letter was more than a complaint warranting investigation.

Beneath their legal veneers, many assistants were detectives, or more to the point, detective novel readers. There was nothing such an assistant liked better than to unravel a real life mystery, to discover and lay out the strands of evidence, and convince a jury what really had occurred. Grambling had blundered. He had caught the attention of the prosecutor: He had made his swindle "interesting."

Benitez came back.

"Nice little investigation, don't you think?"

"Well, it looks like it could be larceny. This Grambling guy makes a representation to the bank that he has real collateral, the Lazard stock assignment. The bank relies on the representation and gives the loan. Grambling knows that the Lazard document is false. It's a straightforward case, but for the usual problem." The assistant waved toward the boxes stacked in his room. "It's like Halloran. Grambling's going to have the same defense of lack of criminal intent."

Rosner was speaking in professional code: "the Halloran defense." Business swindles come in two forms. In one, the criminal intent is clear. Someone submits counterfeit or forged checks (or money orders, or credit card receipts, or loan documents, whatever) to the bank. In the belief that the documents are real, the bank disburses its shareholders' cash. The person receiving the money disappears. At some point, the bank realizes that it has been duped. A crime has been committed. No one denies it. The problem is finding the person who committed it. Indubitable crime; unfindable perpetrator.

The boxes of documents filling the assistant's office were evidence of the second kind of business fraud. The documents were the proof of guilt in the Halloran case, that of two businessmen who had run a $9.4 billion check-kite. The kite was a fraud in which the businessmen had written over 15,000 checks back and forth between their checking accounts at separate banks. The blizzard of paper tricked the banks into allowing the check-kiters to withdraw over $23 million which, the banks thought, were the depositors' funds: In truth, it was the banks' money. In this type of crime, there is no problem finding the perpetrators—they are prominent businessmen, with substantial homes and country club memberships. It is their very availability that creates the often impenetrable defense of no criminal intent.

The defense originates in a basic principal of the larceny law; that, when someone else's property is taken, the thief intends to keep the property permanently. Proving permanence is an easy task when the defendant is a street kid who snatches a necklace in the subway, and sprints for the exit. Or when the swindler uses counterfeit documents and phony identification in the hope that no one will ever figure out his real identity. But in the sophisticated fraud, the swindler is often a known businessperson with roots in the community. How often had the assistant listened to such defendants testify: "I always intended to pay the money back. I just took the money temporarily as an act of desperation to get me over some cash flow problems. But I didn't have a one-way ticket to the Bahamas. My house wasn't for sale. My kids' school tuition was paid for the next semester. The bank, and the prosecutor, knew where to find me." It was an attractive and frequently successful defense.

In the Halloran case, the check-kiters had actually repaid the money taken, with interest (the money used to make the repayment was merely half the profit of the successful real estate investments the check-kiters had made with the swindled funds). Rosner had conducted the Halloran investigation in 1984, and he and Benitez had recommended to Kindler in late 1984 that the Halloran case be presented to the Grand Jury for a decision on whether or not to prosecute. Uncertain about the "lack of permanent deprivation" defense, the Eighth Floor had been sitting on the Frauds Bureau recommendation for months.

"Peter, Grambling has the same defense as Halloran," Rosner continued. "Grambling is probably some kind of wealthy guy; otherwise, the bank wouldn't have dealt with him. Whether his money is real, or it's only on paper, it's all going to be the same to the jury, particularly in light of this $2 million repayment which came from somewhere. How are we going to prove intent to deprive permanently when the guy takes out a loan—my God, he even signs a note promising to repay—and then does repay $2 million. In fact, I don't even have to call the bank to know he had some kind of business problem. He is going to say that he did something stupid (and that's going to explain away the larceny in the jury's mind), but that he never intended to keep the money or hurt anyone. It's a tough case," Rosner concluded. "Although, I admit, it looks interesting."

"Lookit," said Benitez. "If the law of this state is that every rich guy can take money by fraud and then claim lack of intent since he hopes to pay the money back, and actually does pay some back, fine. Then he beats us on the larceny." Benitez turned to the Lazard Frere consent, and tapped it several times with his forefinger. "But the Lazard Frere letter is a forgery, independent of any larceny. Let's look at this case as a simple forgery. There's a public interest in not having business people forge collateral, particularly when they're forging the name of a major Manhattan investment house."

Benitez had a point. As was larceny, forgery was a Class D felony, a crime for which a defendant could be imprisoned for up to seven years. Whether Grambling stole $7.5 million by deception (a larceny), or passed a forged document (a forgery), conviction on either charge would expose him to a maximum prison sentence of seven years which, with parole factored in, would be a real sentence of two and a third to three years. It was a reasonable maximum exposure for what Grambing was alleged to have done. But Rosner was skeptical.

"You know, Peter, the letter isn't even clear whether Grambling passed the forged document to the bank. What does it say?" He flipped through the pages.

" 'It is the recollection of the attorney who handled this matter that Grambling handed over the forgery.' What's that bullshit supposed to mean? The attorney can't even say whether Grambling produced the forgery, and the 'crime' occurred only a month ago. What the hell is the attorney going to remember a year from now when we're on trial?"

"That's okay." Benitez continued. "We don't know who this guy Grambling is. Maybe he doesn't even deserve being prosecuted. We don't know the facts. Make some calls. It looks like it could be a nice simple case."

Benitez looked around Rosner's office. "And no wheelbarrows of evidence."

The assistant nodded his head in agreement. He had tried too many business fraud cases where the evidence filled boxes. The more paper there was, the easier it was for a jury to be confused.

"We'll look at the complaint as a simple forgery," Rosner agreed.

"And if Grambling deserves prison," Benitez said, "he'll have an exposure of seven."

"So he beats us on the larceny," Rosner said.

"And," Benitez finished, "we beat him on the forgery."

"And, listen," Benitez added, "work fast." Pointing to the list of addressees on the first page of the letter, Benitez tapped the line listing the F.B.I. as a recipient.

"If there's a case here, we don't want to lose it to the feds."

PART 2

INVESTIGATION

CHAPTER 8

CONVENING THE GRAND JURY

Alone in his One Hogan Place office, Brian Rosner reread the letter. In his mind, he outlined a plan for the investigation.

Criminal complaints typically elicit an emotional or an intuitive response. The conduct reported is clearly wrong, or unfair, or immoral; therefore, complainants and their attorneys often conclude, the wrongdoing complained of must be a crime. This conclusion is dead wrong. A crime is defined by the precise phrases of the Penal Law. Every jury that has ever decided the fate of a defendant has been firmly instructed that their verdict must be guided by legal definitions, not their inner moral sense, or personal conception of right and wrong. This instruction is the fundamental meaning of "the rule of law," and the basic analytic tool of prosecutors as well.

Leaving innuendo and emotion aside, Rosner reread the Shearman & Sterling letter. It suggested two crimes; larceny and forgery, each as old as Leviticus, and each codified in the New York statutes. Although he had read the statutes a thousand times, the prosecutor turned in his chair and reached for the second volume of his seven-volume New York State Penal and Criminal Procedure Law. His "library"—the Penal and Criminal Procedure Law, several commentaries on writing and trial practice, and a dictionary—marched along the bottom of the window. He could not reach for the law without seeing the building 50 feet across the alley. "They're quiet today," the assistant thought.

His window faced the alley separating the central portion of 100 Centre Street from the building's north end, the Tombs. The prison's lengthy rectangular windows revealed its interior hallways and the common areas of several floors. He could see the prisoners dressed in their brightly colored jumpsuits. With his window open on a warm day, he could hear the prisoners shout. Sometimes, they waved.

The lawyers in a criminal case played roles. At sentencing, he, the judge and defense counsel would argue about the possibility that a given defendant could be rehabilitated, that the defendant deserved, not 20 years in prison, as the assistant might argue, but only five, or maybe even probation, according to defense counsel. The judge would decide. Out of the courtroom, outside their roles, the court and counsel acknowledged the dismal reality. Rehabilitation was like a miracle—always to be hoped for, but not to be depended on. The end purpose of the criminal justice system was to take men off the streets, justifiably so (that, Rosner never doubted), and put them in the cages he saw through his window everyday. In a world in which attorneys often complained about a lack of purpose to their jobs, the assistant was never at a loss to appreciate the results of his work. And the results began with the Penal Law.

Rosner placed the volume on his desk and spread the black covers. By their own weight, the pages opened to the much-read Section 155.35: "Grand Larceny in the Second Degree. A person commits Grand Larceny in the Second Degree when he steals property and when the value of the property exceeds $1,500." He flipped over the annotations to a prior page, Section 155.05: "Larceny; defined. Larceny includes a wrongful taking committed in any of the following ways—by trespassory taking, common law larceny by trick, embezzlement, or obtaining property by false pretenses." The statutory definitions ended. The methods of theft named in the Penal Law—trespassory taking and the rest—were Common Law crimes, derived from centuries of New York and English case law. The assistant knew the definitions by heart: False pretense—a person takes property by false pretense when he makes a representation that he knows is untrue and induces a second party, in reliance on that representation, to part with property. Representation, reliance, and conversion (the taking of the property). The Shearman & Sterling letter appeared to state the pieces—the "elements," in legal jargon—of the offense. But, Rosner thought, is New York County the proper location to bring the complaint?

Rooted like a tree, the power to prosecute is defined by geography. States are divided into dozens of governing units, the counties. Each elects a county prosecutor, the law enforcement officer responsible for enforcing that state's laws in the county. The state is empowered to prosecute a crime only in the county in which the crime occurs.

This limitation is a fundamental part of an American's rights. A person is entitled to be tried by a jury of his peers selected from the local neighborhood that was the scene of the offense. Centuries ago, it was thought that the local people would know the actors in the offense and better understand the crime. That logic made good sense in medieval England, or young America when, without planes, cars, or telephones, criminal acts usually began and ended in a confined location. The logic was certainly more persuasive in the days when jurors were presumed to be knowledgeable about the crime, unlike today, when jurors are required to be ignorant of the acts they are to judge.

Whatever the collateral logic, the basic premise of geographical jurisdiction has remained: The judgment of a person's guilt or innocence is a fundamental act of community, akin to the election of one's leaders. In a sense, the community holds itself responsible for policing the conduct that occurs in its own neighborhood. It is a fine premise, basic to the civil society without which there could be no democracy. That being said, Rosner wondered, how does the premise apply to a bank headquartered in Toronto that closes a loan in Manhattan for properties in Colorado and Utah to be purchased by a Texan living in Connecticut?

The law had adjusted with the times, as the assistant's own cases had proved. He thought of his first murder trial. Weighted and nibbled by fish, the victim's body had floated to the surface of the East River near a Brooklyn pier, after having been dropped, alive, into the river from its Manhattan side. Which county prosecutes: Manhattan or Brooklyn? Or his first Frauds Bureau case—a German securities broker, in Germany, stole money from a client's account in one German city and transferred it to the broker's personal account in another German city by sending telexed transfer instructions to the ledger maintained at the firm's Manhattan headquarters. Fearing arrest by the German authorities, the broker sought a safe haven in London, where he was arrested on a New York County warrant. Both he and the killer in the floating-body case were prosecuted, and convicted, in Manhattan because of the basic rule of geographic jurisdiction: A county may prosecute a crime when an element of the offense occurs within the county's borders. It does not matter which element it is, whether the murder in the floating-body case, or the conversion in the international embezzlement.

As he examined the letter and the memo in his office, Rosner knew that his first job was to determine whether Manhattan had geographic jurisdiction. Did Grambling commit any act in New York County that was an element of larceny or forgery?

Assuming that there was jurisdiction, the next step would be to determine whether a complete crime, as defined by the strict legal elements, had been committed. Aside from the "permanent deprivation" problem, the ephemeral element in the prosecution of a business fraud was "reliance." Sophisticated business transactions are comprised of multiple representations and reliances. Without knowing the details of the negotiations that resulted in the Grambling loan, Rosner already knew one of the defenses: The Bank of Montreal had really relied on something other than the Lazard Freres document in deciding to make the loan.

Perhaps the claim would be that the bankers had relied on other collateral, or on third party statements that the borrower was creditworthy. The assistant had seen cases where indicted borrowers had convinced juries that the bank had made the loan independent of any reliance. As if it was yesterday, he could hear the testimony. "The bank was filled with funds," the indicted borrower had said. "And it made the loan to me just to get more money on the street earning interest. The bankers had a loan quota to meet. They did not care what documents I submitted. It didn't matter that the papers were phony. The bankers didn't even read them." The defense was more aptly made by Texans investing savings and loan money in oil and gas gambles or the black hole of Houston real estate, the assistant thought. It would be a tough but not impossible argument to make against the Bank of Montreal, which the assistant perceived as a staid and risk-averse institution.

He did not know how the defense would play out, but he was certain that it would be made. On a scratch pad on his desk, Rosner reminded himself to take a hard look at what was really going through the bank's institutional mind when whoever approved this loan approved it. If the loan would have been made without the Lazard Freres document, if it was made in reliance on anything that could not be proved to be illegitimate, the assistant would recommend that there be no prosecution.

The forgery alleged in the complaint raised the same double problem of jurisdiction and proof. The February 1 letter did not state clearly whether the allegedly forged document had been passed to the Bank in Manhattan. The context of the letter suggested that it had to have been—the closing was here—and the letter's hesitation on the point, the prosecutor suspected, was a lingering fear by Shearman & Sterling that, by accusing Grambling, their client bordered on the commission of libel. Institutional law firms were only a slight degree less risk-averse than their institutional clients; their natural inclination was to hedge. I'll get an answer to this at the first witness interview, the assistant thought. But the prosecution had already been harmed. If a witness testified at a future trial that Grambling had handed over the forgery at the closing, the witness would have to explain why the letter written a month after the closing was ambivalent on the point. Not a helpful letter, Rosner thought. But, if the facts proving a crime are strong, the case will survive.

In Rosner's view, the proof of the alleged forgery suffered from a bigger problem. The assistant compared the "Peter Corcoran" and "Robert Wilkis" specimen signatures with the signatures on the consent. He would not need an expert witness. Any juror, whether a chairman of the board or a cleaning lady, would be able to see that these signatures were different. But, as Greenblatt has realized two weeks earlier, the assistant knew that a signature is not a forgery just because it is not penned by the person whose name is written. The issue was whether Corcoran or Wilkis had authorized someone to sign their names.

The prosecutor was confused. Attached as an exhibit to the Shearman & Sterling letter was the January 17 letter to Busuttil from Mullarkey at Lazard Freres: "I have your letter . . . enclosing a copy of a Consent and Agreement purportedly signed by Lazard Freres & Co. . . . the Consent and Agreement are spurious. Manifestly, we have no intention of complying with its terms."

What a bizarre letter, Rosner thought. After examining "spurious" in the dictionary, his confusion was confirmed.

Spurious is not forgery, at least, not necessarily. The use of the word suggested an internal problem at Lazard. Perhaps, the banking firm was trying to distance itself from an employee who had helped Grambling by tricking authorized signatories into signing the consent. The prosecutor made a mental note that Grambling may have had one or more accomplices at Lazard.

"Jurisdiction," "reliance," "forgery"—these were the legal concepts that would define the scope of the investigation. But behind the legal analysis was a concern that would ultimately be the decisive factor in the decision whether or not to prosecute. The assistant searched the Shearman & Sterling submission for an answer to the ultimate prosecutorial question: Is this a case about which the District Attorney's Office, or a jury, should care?

Jurors were not machines that processed facts in accordance with strict definitions of law. In his life as a citizen, a juror would probably render no more difficult decision than the verdict of guilt or innocence, and, although not governed by emotion, jurors could not avoid being affected by it.

True, the jury decision, and verdict, were unanimous. But none of the 12 jurors could hide his responsibility in the unanimity. After the foreperson announces the community decision, the jury is polled. Each juror stands individually in the jury box and, the defendant also standing, his spouse and children sobbing in the front row, the juror is asked by the court clerk, "You have heard the verdict of guilty read by the Foreperson. Is that your verdict?" One by one, every juror answers, and is made responsible for the group decision. It takes internal fortitude to stand in the jury box and say "guilty." Rosner often wondered how jurors gathered the strength to come back with a verdict of "guilty."

He had been through the debate a thousand times in his own mind. The answer is that jurors do not convict unless the crime for which they are sending a man to prison is an offense of seriousness to which they can relate emotionally. This reality presented a special problem in the business fraud case.

Burglaries, robberies, and murders were, whatever the legal problems of proof, morally straightforward to a jury. Once the community members were convinced that there was a murder, the emotional and moral issue was narrowly focused. "Did the defendant do it?"

To prove that a crime had been committed, and that the defendant had done it, was rarely enough to obtain a conviction in the business fraud prosecution. In a business fraud, the "victim" is perceived by jurors to be an institution. No juror has ever felt sympathy for the bricks and stone of a bank building, nor has any prosecutor. Jurors required an evil result— whether in the ruination of the careers of the bankers involved, or an adverse economic impact on the life of a community— before they say the word *guilty*. To a lesser extent, prosecutors also looked for the harmful consequence of the crime before being willing to crush a defendant with the enormous weight of the criminal justice machine.

A hard-working business person who commits a foolish act due to genuine financial distress is not going to be indicted or, if so, not convicted. That the Grambling complaint looked interesting, the assistant did not doubt. That the public or the District Attorney's Office should care about the Bank of Montreal loss was the open question.

The prosecutor began the investigation by resorting to the lawyer's basic tool for gathering information—the telephone. He called Art Field.

"Sorry," his secretary responded. "He's at a meeting. May I take a message?"

"Have him give me a call back. Assistant District Attorney Rosner, Frauds Bureau, New York County District Attorney's Office. The number . . . ."

"Oh, wait a moment, Mr. Rosner. We were expecting a call. Let me transfer you to another attorney working on the Grambling matter. You'll be speaking with Mr. Greenblatt, Mr. Jonathan Greenblatt."

Four years earlier, Greenblatt had represented Citibank in a case Rosner had prosecuted. It was a simple embezzlement. The only twist to the case—the assistant remembered the name now "Hagen, Ronald Hagen"—had nothing to do with the facts. The Hagen crime had been reported simultaneously to the Manhattan District Attorney and the New York State Attorney General. The two prosecutors had argued over which office should proceed. The result was that each office had fought over the evidence, had each obtained half of it, and had then separately indicted Hagen for the same crimes.

Ultimately, the offices had, in a prosecutorial sense, kissed and made up. Hagen, who had fled to the Caribbean, was jointly extradited, and jointly convicted. The assistants in both offices had become friends, and the two offices had cooperated on several subsequent investigations. Rosner expected that any initial competition with the feds would end in the same type of reconciliation. It was like army boot camp: Units might compete against each other during basic training, but you knew who your teammates were when you were sent into battle overseas.

"Brian, how have you been? I should have figured you might be getting this case. Listen, this is a good one, better than Hagen."

"We read your letter, Jon. Interesting situation. Let me just see if you're even talking to the right prosecutor. Where was this loan negotiated?"

"New York and Calgary, according to my witnesses. They are available for you to talk to."

The representations probably occurred in Manhattan, the assistant thought. If the representations were false, and relied on by the bank, we have jurisdiction of the larceny.

"Where did Grambling get the money, Jon? Calgary or New York?"

"New York. The money was credited to an account in Grambling's name at 430 Park Avenue, and wired out from there at Grambling's direction to various banks across the country. We have a second letter we're preparing. It has more details about what we've discovered. I think we attached the disbursement material to it. I'll make sure that the letter is sent straight to you."

If Greenblatt was correct, the bank's money had been converted to Grambling in New York County. If there was a larceny, representation and conversion had occurred in New York County. Clearly, this was a case for New York to look into. Rosner moved to the forgery charge.

"I read this attachment here." The prosecutor flipped through the exhibits to the letter. "Jon, I'm looking at the Lazard Freres letter from Mullarkey to Busuttil. Mullarkey says the Consent and Agreement is 'spurious'. Spurious? I even looked it up in the dictionary, but I can't figure out what it means. Do you have information that there's some kind of forgery here?"

"We don't know," Greenblatt replied. "You're going to have to figure that out. But I'll tell you, Brian, there's something going on at Lazard. There's an investment banker named Wilkis who discussed the consent and Grambling's stock with one of our attorneys and with a banker. I think Wilkis was Grambling's accomplice, but you can hear it from our witnesses."

"When can you start bringing the witnesses in?"

"Our attorney who was at the closing is in New York. He's available anytime. The bankers who did this deal are in Calgary, but we'll fly them in whenever you want to see them."

Arrangements were made to see Busuttil that week, and Hopkyns, Hean, and Mullin the next. The prosecutor turned to the matter of the "friendly" federal-state competition: Obtaining possession of the physical evidence was how to win the race.

"Jon, if there's going to be a Grand Jury investigation, the jury will need the original documents: all the loan documents, including the Lazard consent. I'll want to pick them up this afternoon."

"Brian, give me a subpoena and they're yours." After a pause, he continued, "And don't worry about the feds. They've already called, but you know it will take them days to get authorization for a subpoena."

"Have the feds come down to see your witnesses?"

"No. You'll be seeing them first."

"Okay, Jon. You'll have our subpoena today. Bring the documents down on Friday with Busuttil."

Rosner reached into a desk drawer and withdrew a pad of white legal-sized forms bearing the title "Grand Jury— Subpoena Duces Tecum." He was about to activate the Grand Jury, one of the most ancient and powerful institutions in our lives. Comprised of 23 county residents, the jury sits in secret session to determine whether felony charges should be voted against an individual. It is the only body in New York State that can vote a "true bill," the indictment charging a person with a felony.

The assistant's role before the Grand Jury is special: He presents the evidence they consider. No defense counsel is present in the room (except under narrow circumstances) and no judge, although a transcript is kept of the proceedings for subsequent judicial review.

The jury is intended to be a shield between the individual and the state. Where there is reasonable cause to believe a crime has been committed, it may indict. Even where there is evidence to charge, the jury, rendering mercy as the conscience of the community, may choose not to charge. Every jury to which the assistant had presented evidence had been told in no uncertain terms of its mercy-dispensing function, and many had applied that power.

Nonetheless, the conventional wisdom is that the Grand Jury is a tool of the prosecutor. Sol Wachtler, the Chief Judge of the New York State Court of Appeals, has said, "If the prosecutor asked, the Grand Jury would indict a ham sandwich."

Though perhaps true elsewhere, the criticism is not accurate when applied to Manhattan. Every Grand Jury to which Rosner had presented evidence had at least one member who had heard Judge Wachtler's criticism, or read one of the many books and articles faulting the jury for its allegedly passive role. As a result, the assistant and his colleagues had found, New York County grand jurors participate actively in the cases presented to them.

The real problem, assistants had discovered, was not that jurors "rubber-stamped" prosecutors' requests to indict, but the reverse. The juries frequently threatened to become an assistant's worst fear—a "runaway" grand jury. As legal advisor to the Grand Jury, the assistant instructs the jurors whether or not the evidence they have heard is legally sufficient to charge a crime. Often, the assistant must charge that, however despicable a person's conduct might have been, the evidence is not legally sufficient to charge a crime, or so barely sufficient that guilt could never be proved at trial. In either case, the assistant requests the jury to vote "no true bill."

The jurors' most frequent assertion of independence is when they dispute that legal advice and insist on their power to voice the harsh sentiment of the community. Many assistants have had the experience of asking a jury to withhold its vote until the prosecutor could find a supervisor to persuade the jurors not to vote an illegal indictment, or one in which a conviction could never be obtained. It was ironic. Despite the criticism of their role, Assistant District Attorneys more often than not put a restraining hand on the grand jurors.

Each assistant was the surrogate of the District Attorney, whose statutory and constitutional power to choose which cases to present to the Grand Jury was absolute and unreviewable. In instances of violent crime, the decision was clear-cut. A robbery was committed, and a perpetrator was arrested: The case was presented to the jury usually within a day of the crime. For allegations of white-collar crime, there was truly an investigation with extensive preliminary analysis of documents and witnesses. During the initial stage of an investigation, the Grand Jury itself did nothing. The prosecutor issued subpoenas, legal process demanding the production of documents to be analyzed by himself and, if necessary, the Office's forensic accountants and detectives. When and if the assistant decided that there was a real crime for the Grand Jury to consider, not a business mistake or lapse in judgment, the evidence already gathered was presented to the Grand Jury panel.

More often than not, probably by a ratio of two to one, the subpoenaed documents produced no evidence worthy of further pursuit, and the investigation ended where it had begun, in the assistant's mind.

Rosner looked over the blank subpoena form. It called for documents to be produced in the "case of _____." He crossed out "case of " and wrote "In the Matter of the Investigation into John Doe Borrower." He filled in the address of "The Bank of Montreal, c/o Shearman & Sterling," and turned to the body of the document. "You are hereby commanded to produce the following:" He wrote a description of all of the documentation conceivably relating to the Grambling loan. The subpoena was dated, and the "due date" called for production that day. He called a messenger to deliver the legal process to Greenblatt. On receipt, Greenblatt would become temporary custodian of the evidence on behalf of the New York County Grand Jury.

The Grand Jury's investigation had begun.

CHAPTER 9

REELING OUT THE ROPE

The prosecutor turned his attention to the forgery.

The simplest way to resolve the Lazard Freres confusion was to ask. He called Mullarkey. Lazard's in-house counsel was not in, and Rosner left a message with Mullarkey's secretary. Within the hour, Rosner was called by Martin Flumenbaum, a litigation partner at Paul, Weiss, Rifkind, Wharton & Garrison, a respected Manhattan law firm. Flumenbaum was outside counsel to Lazard Freres.

The assistant knew Flumenbaum. Rosner's senior by one year at Columbia College, Flumenbaum had attended Harvard Law School. After a federal court clerkship, he did a tour of duty with the United States Attorney's Office for the Southern District of New York, where he ended his career with the tax fraud conviction of the Unification Church's Reverend Sun Myung Moon. People do not change from what they were in college, or high school for that matter. If the assistant remembered Flumenbaum correctly, he would be intelligent and aggressive, traits that, in a lawyer, translate into a meticulous concern for the protection of one's client. Rosner and Flumenbaum had not spoken for over a decade.

After college-related chit-chat, Flumenbaum mentioned his years as a prosecutor. This was a standard introduction when a former prosecutor spoke to a present prosecutor. It was a statement—"I was once on the firing line where you are"—that the private counsel understood the assistant's concerns. That's the way the old-shop talk began and, often, the way the conversations were maintained.

But as Rosner knew from experience, once he did something with which the former prosecutor disagreed, the tone would invariably change: "That's not how we used to do it when I was an assistant." Or, from those who had preceded the assistant at One Hogan Place, a very specific "that's not how Mr. Hogan would have done it." Former prosecutors lived a fallacy of the "lost golden age": when the attorney in private practice was young and an assistant, prosecutors exercised better judgment. At the beginning of the relationship, however, defense counsel's reference to his origins as a prosecutor was the simple statement, "Trust me."

"Brian, I'm surprised it was you who called. Lazard reported a forgery to the Bureau two weeks ago. We've even gotten a call back on the matter."

The Bureau was insider argot for the F.B.I. In a sentence, Flumenbaum had resolved two ambiguities. "Spurious" had been a lousy choice of a word: Lazard, the putative signatory to the consent that Grambling had handed to Busuttil, had reported the consent as a forgery. And the feds were on the case.

"Lazard should have called us, Marty. The D.A.'s Office does forgeries. I'm calling because we received a letter from Shearman & Sterling, counsel for the Bank of Montreal. I can't quite tell what's going on, but it seems that there's a Lazard employee, Wilkis, who should be talked to. Do you represent Wilkis?"

"I represent Lazard, and that includes Wilkis, although I'll double-check. Let me get back to you."

Flumenbaum called back that day to confirm that he did represent Wilkis. "He's a witness you want to talk to, Brian. Wilkis was duped by Grambling. He can fill in a lot of what you need to know to make your case."

Although Rosner knew what the response would be, he asked the question anyway.

"Well, Marty, why don't you bring Wilkis in so I can meet him?"

It was the invitation to the immunity dance.

"You'll be giving Wilkis immunity, won't you?"

"Sure, Marty. If I decide to use Wilkis as a witness, he gets immunity when he's sworn in before the Grand Jury."

"Not good enough. He wants a promise of immunity before he talks to you."

Flumenbaum's voice was firm. Rosner feigned surprise.

"Marty, you're telling me the guy's a witness. Why does he need immunity in advance?"

Flumenbaum did not respond. Good response, Rosner thought. He's just going to let me sputter.

"I don't even know what the guy's going to say, Marty. How can I offer immunity in the dark? Tell you what. Bring him in to make me an offer, off-the-record. Let me get a sense of who I might be giving immunity to. When you were an assistant, no one expected you to act in the dark."

"Let me come in later this week, alone," Flumenbaum replied. "I'll make an offer of proof on what Bob can say. Then you can decide whether you want his testimony—and, believe me, you will—and he'll come in and talk to you on your promise that you'll confer immunity."

"Let me get back to you," Rosner said.

He thought through the possibilities. The decision to confer immunity was a basic exercise of a prosecutor's judgment, and one that usually occurred early in the investigation. Immunity is a mutual exchange of rights between the state and the individual. The individual relinquishes his constitutional right to refuse to incriminate himself—to refuse to make statements, oral or written, that might be used to prove his guilt in a court proceeding. In exchange, the state relinquishes its fundamental power to prosecute the witness for crimes he may have committed. Immunity, the promise to not prosecute, is the price the state is willing to pay to obtain a witness's testimony.

"Transactional" defines the scope of the immunity in which New York State cloaks the witness: The witness will not be prosecuted for any crime deriving from any transaction about which he is questioned by the assistant. "Transactional" is defined broadly. Were an investment banker to testify, he would be immunized for every crime—securities fraud, insider trading, drug sales to colleagues—in which the witness' statement "I am an investment banker" could arguably be used as evidence of his guilt. Nowhere in America is immunity defined as broadly as it is by the courts of New York State.

So expansive are the court decisions interpreting the breadth of the immunity conferred that an assistant is trained to act on the simple assumption that he would lose any court dispute over the scope of the immunity granted. The court decisions made for a "bright line" rule of practice; never confer transactional immunity on a witness the Grand Jury might for any reason later want to indict for his pre-testimony conduct. Clairvoyance is part of an assistant's job description.

Despite the uncertainties, the assistant acknowledged that he and his colleagues were often compelled to give an immunity bath to an accomplice. The best witness to a crime is often an accomplice, particularly in fraud cases, where the critical element of the crime is the culprit's elusive state of mind. Accomplices are partners and, whether in business or crime, partners tend to be open with one another. As a consequence, the partner-accomplice is often present when the partner-defendant says "No one will ever catch us for this crime," or shreds documents, or forges a signature. This is the incriminatory evidence an assistant needs to prove the defendant's guilt. For the purposes of a trial, an accomplice willing to tell all can be a useful life form.

The problem with a rat, Rosner thought—and at bottom, that's what a turncoat accomplice is—is his utter lack of credibility. An accomplice is a criminal that hopes to buy a little freedom by sinking his former confidante. Though always professing remorse on the witness stand, the turncoat accomplice is motivated by the purest self-interest, to save his own neck. It's a motivation that invites testimony tailored to be whatever the prosecutor wants to hear. Using turncoats and granting them immunity, or doing a "deal" in which the accomplice pleads to a lesser crime with a promise of "consideration" at his sentencing, is a dirty business, offensive to all assistants. Rosner preferred not to use such witnesses: better to suffer an acquittal than tarnish the government's integrity by using a witness with such a compelling motivation to lie.

What was interesting about Flumenbaum's "request," Rosner thought, was its modesty. When selling his client as a witness, a defense counsel trys to seduce the prosecutor into believing that the client, the accomplice, merits immunity because of his critical testimony. The time-proven sales pitch is to paint the client, now remorseful and rehabilitated of course, as having once been the devil incarnate: The worse the witness once was, the more likely that he was privy to the detailed information needed by the assistant. In the perverse world of "deals," a prosecutor would often spurn the minor accomplice, the peripheral player not culpable enough to have been intimate with the critical criminal acts; that accomplice could be forgotten and serve his prison time. The best deals were reserved for the worst people. Only the major rat, the target defendant's most trusted lieutenant, had the critical inside knowledge that warranted a deal.

But Flumenbaum had characterized Wilkis as a dupe, someone more victim than victimizer. Presumably, Wilkis would not be able to testify to a direct statement from Grambling that Grambling was committing a crime.

Rosner informed Benitez of Flumenbaum's offer. They decided that, unless the preliminary interviews with the bankers created a suspicion that Wilkis was a knowing accomplice, or there was proof of fraudulently obtained money going to Wilkis, he would get his immunity up front, prior to his testimony.

The prosecutor advised Flumenbaum to come in and make his offer of proof. Meanwhile, Greenblatt sent Rosner the second Shearman & Sterling letter. It spoke of impersonations by which frauds had apparently been committed against the Colorado National Bank of Denver and First Security Bank in Salt Lake City. On February 1, 1985, the letter explained, Mullin had finally returned Jim Conover's phone message of January 25: "Thank you for speaking from Florida to the Committee," Conover had told Mullin, who was stunned. Then Conover gave Mullin the phone number at which the Salt Lake City bankers had called "Mullin" in Florida, and Mullin understood.

The letter tempted Rosner to expand the case. Jurors have the humane tendency to forgive a swindler for one mistake. What often convinces lay people to convict the business person is proof of an ongoing pattern of deceit. It is a jury's rough justice: The first bite of the apple is gratis, the second is not. Rosner knew that proof of a second or third crime could win the conviction on the Bank of Montreal case.

Rosner suppressed the temptation to expand the case. The prosecutor too eager to make too many cases doesn't put any case together correctly. Rosner decided to widen the investigation within modest limits. He would keep track of what happened at Colorado National since a loss was involved, and investigate the Salt Lake City bank case later.

The Shearman & Sterling letter identified Colorado National Bank's counsel, Michael Stanton, a litigation partner at Weil, Gotshal & Manges, another highly regarded midtown firm. As Rosner reread the Bank of Montreal letters to prepare for his call to Colorado National's counsel, his phone rang. It was Stanton. Word was traveling fast that Morgenthau's Office was involved in the case.

Though pleased that the Manhattan District Attorney had an interest in Grambling, Stanton was dubious that the Office could prosecute what appeared to be a Denver case. After all, he explained, Grambling negotiated the loan in Denver, and received the money there. Rosner told Stanton his theory of jurisdiction: "It appears that a crime occurred in Denver as part of a New York-based conspiracy. If that's what happened, New York County has jurisdiction." And in any case, Rosner thought, whether or not Grambling's charged in New York with the Denver crime, evidence of the additional crime is the proof I need to decide that he's worth prosecuting on the Bank of Montreal case, and to convince a jury to convict him.

Stanton eagerly related Colorado National's story. The prosecutor took copious notes. It was a jumble; telexes that were later repudiated; bankers who subsequently denied their conversations; but, unalterable in the confusion, a document, a firm piece of evidence, on which the bankers had relied in making the loan, only to learn later that the document was a forgery. "It's not easy to follow," Stanton said. "The bank will fly the officers involved to New York immediately to speak with you."

Stanton's offer startled Rosner. Crime imposes many burdens on a victim. One is the cost of pursuing a prosecution. Rosner habitually used his initial talk with victim's counsel to explain these costs. Producing documents is costly. Drawing people from work to be interviewed is costly. Flying witnesses across the nation and housing them in a Manhattan hotel is costly.

Rosner's purpose in emphasizing the costs was to flush the complainant out. Better that the bank has its doubts about proceeding at the beginning of a case, rather than months later, after the District Attorney's Office had invested hundreds of hours in an investigation and committed itself to the prosecution. That the Colorado Bank attorney had unhesitatingly offered to fly the witnesses to New York, in a case in which even the bank questioned the jurisdiction of the District Attorney's Office, suggested that Colorado National had been badly hurt and wanted vindication.

After the talk with Stanton, Rosner made several further calls prompted by the second Shearman & Sterling letter. According to documents attached to the letter, Grambling had disbursed the Bank of Montreal funds to banks in Arizona, Texas, Kansas, Connecticut, and Tennessee. A fertile area of inquiry, Rosner thought.

For years, he had prosecuted swindlers, men and women who, until the moment of their arrest, had been perceived to be leading an exemplary life in their communities. That perception was rarely correct. Business people do not suddenly commit a fraudulent act when, as in Grambling's case, they are 36 years old. Honesty and dishonesty are lifelong habits, usually ingrained by grade school. More often than not, a business person's first arrest, as Rosner had seen, is just the first time he had been caught, not the first time that he had taken money by fraud.

Rosner acted on his experience. If Grambling had committed a forgery to trick the Bank of Montreal into extending a loan, Rosner assumed that Grambling had done similar acts on earlier occasions at other banks. With a series of calls, the assistant reached across the nation to bring to the New York County Grand Jury the physical evidence of Grambling's other crimes.

As does every county prosecutor in America, the New York County District Attorney's Office is invested with nationwide subpoena power. Most people do not know that this extraordinary power exists. Most local prosecutors never use it. Nonetheless, every state is a party to an interstate compact on subpoenas. The agreement commits the local courts of each state to honor the grand jury or trial subpoena issued by the local prosecutor in another state. By an established process, a local court, whether in El Paso or Topeka, summons the local resident into court, converts the New York County subpoena it has received into a local subpoena, and orders the local resident, whose testimony or documents are needed, to appear and testify forthwith in New York County. Should a witness be foolish enough to refuse to comply, he will be fined or imprisoned, or both. The interstate compact is a powerful evidence-obtaining device.

There was hardly a bank in the country that seemed aware of the local prosecutor's power. The practice of the Frauds Bureau was to call the out-of-state bankers to advise them that a subpoena was coming. It was a polite way to direct the bankers to the interstate pact and their obligation to honor the out-of-state subpoena. Personal service of the subpoena was required, and, to actually serve the subpoena on the banks in Iowa or Texas, Rosner relied on the national network of local prosecutors. Over the next two weeks, Rosner's word processor cranked out a dozen interstate subpoenas for documents. Each one resulted in a call to a bank—"A subpoena is coming. No, you don't have to testify at present. You need only produce the documents by mail."—and a call to the local District Attorney for assistance.

The local prosecutors eagerly helped. Every year, from jurisdictions across America, hundreds of felons flee to New York County, where, with luck, some are arrested by the local cops and extradited by the local prosecutors, just as felons fleeing from New York are arrested out-of-state and returned to New York. County prosecutors across America are bound by a web of mutual indebtedness.

Rosner called a Texas colleague.

"John, how're you doing? I have a subpoena for a bank in Dallas. Can you serve it for me? We need the documents, not the witness."

"Sure, Brian," the Travis county prosecutor replied in his western drawl. "Just send me the documents. By the way, how are Joey and his partner? We appreciate their picking up that mutt for us a few months back."

"They're doing fine, John. I'm trying to get Joey assigned to the case with me. Listen, can you do me a favor on this one? Move quickly on the subpoena? We're in a little foot race with the feds."

"Always willing to help someone beat those damn feds. Up north, do the feds cooperate the way they do down here: You do the work; they take the credit." The Texan chuckled. "You know you got arrest power under the Interstate Act. You want me to arrest these banker witnesses, hold them until you get your documents?"

"No, we don't need arrests yet. If you could just serve the subpoenas, we'd be happy." Although out-of-state witnesses often had to be reminded of their obligations to respond to New York County subpoenas, the New York assistant never yet had to order an arrest to obtain compliance.

With his calls to the out-of-state assistants, Rosner completed the opening structure of the investigation. He would interview witnesses on the Bank of Montreal and Colorado National frauds, and collect documents on the rest.

As the week ended, the possibiity of an arrest was already on the mind of the prime actor in the case. Stanton told Rosner that Colorado National had called the loan—that is, demanded its immediate repayment. In response, Stanton explained, Grambling and his counsel were trying to convince the Colorado bank not to sue Grambling or throw him into bankruptcy.

Rosner's ears perked up at Stanton's mention of counsel.

"Who's Grambling's counsel?" the prosecutor asked.

"He has two. Barry Kingham and Joe Kelly from Curtis, Mallet-Prevost, Colt & Mosle in Manhattan."

Rosner knew the firm. The head of its litigation department was Peter Fleming. If trial work were baseball, Fleming would be a starter on the All-Star team. Fleming had made his reputation as defense counsel for John Mitchell, President Nixon's Attorney General. Mitchell had been indicted for perjury during the Watergate investigation, and, with Fleming as lead counsel, acquitted. As with many great trial attorneys, Fleming was a former prosecutor, having served under Morgenthau as an Assistant United States Attorney in the 1960s. Rosner also had heard of Kingham, a former Assistant United States

Attorney who had served after Morgenthau's resignation. Kingham was a member of the trial team that in the late 1970s had put away Nicky Barnes, the head of what was then the biggest narcotics ring in New York City.

A lot of talent for a loan dispute, Rosner thought. Grambling understands his predicament.

"It's all a waste of time," Stanton explained to Rosner. "Grambling's been in Denver this week trying to convince the bank to forebear from litigation. He even brought his partner with him—Libman, a multimillionaire who says he's willing to guarantee Grambling's loan. The bank is willing to hear Grambling out."

To Rosner's ear, Stanton's comments were in the nature of a question. When banks are victimized, the defrauder invariably tries to prevent prosecution by contacting the victim and promising repayment. The promise puts the bank in a quandary. If it cooperates with the authorities, it risks not being repaid. After all, a swindler will never be able to restore the money if he's put in jail. But just as the swindler does not want the victim to speak to the authorities, many prosecutors don't want the victim to discuss settlement with the swindler. When a victim pursues civil and criminal remedies simultaneously, a District Attorney's office is made to look like nothing more than a collection agency, with the complainant's threat of prosecution being the club to beat the borrower into paying his civil debt. Stanton's casual remarks about Grambling's meetings in Denver were pregnant with the unasked question: Does the Manhattan District Attorney's Office object if Colorado National both prosecutes and tries to collect civilly?

Rosner did not care. No matter what the bank did, defense counsel would argue at trial that the bank was misusing the criminal justice system to collect a debt. The way to beat that argument was with convincing facts that the borrower had committed a crime. Moreover, the District Attorney's Office understood that a bank's primary obligation was a fiduciary one to its shareholders. No responsible prosecutor would expect a bank to disdain a civil settlement in order to enhance the prosecutor's case at trial.

Besides, a basic practicality was at work even if Grambling had defrauded the bank. If Grambling could repay, the victim would be satisfied and have no desire to invest hundreds of unremitted hours in a prosecution. Nor would the District Attorney's Office. Rosner understood this reality, as no doubt did Fleming and Kingham.

Of course, in Rosner's mind, there was a caveat to the argument for allowing Colorado National to seek repayment. No proof is more damning than the commission of a new crime to silence the victims' complaints from an earlier crime. Rosner did not know what Grambling could do to repay Colorado National and the Bank of Montreal. But if the allegations made thus far were true, Grambling's method of repayment would be fraudulent, and more evidence of guilt. Rosner had no qualms about the advice he gave Stanton.

"Mike, the bank has obligations to its shareholders. It should do what it would normally do to resolve this matter civilly, as if there was no criminal investigation. Just keep me informed. Once I understand what Grambling did in December and January, I'll try to figure out what he's doing now."

Rosner encouraged Stanton to pursue the repayment promised by Grambling, as he would encourage Greenblatt when he raised the topic a few days later. Rosner would give Grambling a chance to make his victims whole and end the investigation, or take more rope to hang himself.

CHAPTER 10

TRUST THE DOCUMENTS

Rosner's head hurt.

Greenblatt had brought Busuttil to One Hogan Place and with him, the loan documents—memoranda, consents, letter agreements, stock transfer forms, stock certificates—all originals, except for the physical shares of Biosystems and Cumberland Village Mining stock. Greenblatt and Busuttil sat in the two rickety wooden chairs in front of the assistant's decades-old oak desk.

As he put the documents on Rosner's desk, Greenblatt commented, "The bank has the original stock certificates in its safe, just in case they have value and we can sell them."

For wallpaper, the assistant thought.

The three attorneys had been studying the loan documentation for hours. Rosner's eyes glazed over as the documents melded into a single stack of paper. If I can't keep the papers straight, he thought, how will the jury? He drank some more coffee and focused his eyes on Busuttil, neatly attired in a dark, vested, pin-striped suit.

The very image of a bank counsel, the assistant thought, but for the beard. Busuttil? He rolled the name over in his mind. Eastern European?

"Did anyone check to see if the stocks had value?" Rosner asked Busuttil.

"No, my instructions were to pay particular attention to the Lazard Freres consent," Busuttil answered precisely. "The rest of the collateral was there as part of the loan, and we prepared all the necessary documents to secure the property as collateral. But we did not look beneath the surface of Grambling's representations as to the stocks' value."

"Except as to the Dr Pepper stock?" Rosner inserted.

"Yes," Busuttil said. He emphasized his answer with a movement of his hands. Good, the assistant thought. Jurors like hand gestures.

"My instructions from Ivor in Calgary were very specific," Busuttil continued. "The loan was not to close unless and until I received that Lazard Freres consent. I can't tell you what the bank would have done if other collateral documentation was missing on the 28th—I'm not the banker, so that was not my decision—but my instructions as to the Lazard consent was clear. No consent, no loan."

Busuttil's answers had resolved several ambiguities in the case, not least of which was the importance of the consent. But the content of Busuttil's answers was the cause of only half of Rosner's satisfaction. He could never interview a witness without visualizing that person in the witness box in front of the jury. He liked what he was seeing. I'm going to use him to teach the jury, the assistant thought.

Rosner knew in law school that he was bound for a career in criminal law. He attended classes in Contracts and Corporations—he had to in order to graduate—but he had steered clear of the advanced courses on the Uniform Commercial Code and Secured Transactions. The great criminal cases of the 1960s and early 70s, the cases that had shaped his view of criminal law and what it was to be a trial attorney, were cases of murder, political corruption, basic social principles, and articles of impeachment. Business fraud was there, he supposed, but little did he foresee how the weight of legal talent would so shift in the direction of white-collar crime that, by the mid-1980s, an attorney could be considered a great trial attorney without ever having tried a homicide case to a jury. What would Mr. Hogan have thought? Rosner had learned his business law on the job, from witnesses such as Busuttil.

As he and Busuttil began to weed out the surplus documents to identify the core of the transaction, the assistant's thoughts returned to the trial problems of a fraud prosecution based on documents. The problem isn't me. I've been to law school. I'll have the opportunity to read the documents a dozen times, and commit the critical portions to memory. If I misunderstand a detail, I can ask for an explanation, or two, or as many as I needed.

The problem is the jury. For most of them, business transactions with multiple documents are a mystery. They'll get to hear the case once and, if defense counsel is any good, he'll see to it that the jurors hear the case only in a disjointed, heavily interrupted manner. I have to teach the lay people what the papers mean, and what's important. I'll have an uninterrupted opening, and a closing, but the primary instruction time will be the direct examination of my witnesses. Busuttil's going to be a teaching assistant and my first witness.

"You know guys, I was trained that if you can't put it into a single sentence your case is too complex." Greenblatt and Busuttil smiled. "Let's see if I understand where we're headed on this."

Rosner and Busuttil had narrowed the case to two documents—the loan agreement and the Lazard Freres consent. Busuttil repeated the requisite sentence: "If Grambling had not produced the Lazard consent, there would have been no loan."

Representation and reliance, and conversion, the assistant thought. The sentence said it all. But what of the forgery?

"James, you've said that you received this consent at the closing," the prosecutor stated.

"Absolutely. I can see in my mind right now. The Lazard Freres consent was the last document as Grambling and I moved around the table. When we got to the last folder, I asked for the consent, and he pulled it out of his attaché case."

Busuttil reached for a phantom attaché case by the side of his chair.

"He did it just like that. It was the document that was utmost in my mind during the last days prior to the closing."

"Are you sure that Grambling gave you the consent at the closing?"

Busuttil looked surprised, as if it was the dumbest question he had ever heard.

"I've never been surer of anything in my life," he said.

Rosner looked to Greenblatt, who grimaced.

"Brian, James didn't look at the February letter before it was sent. Whatever ambivalence is in there is the fault of the letter writers, not the witness."

The assistant was satisfied. The production of the consent was so important that receiving it from Grambling in Manhattan was something that Busuttil would remember. His recollection of the consent's importance was supported by documents—the paper, as the Frauds Bureau assistants called it. You could always rely on the paper, the assistant thought. He often joked with his street crimes colleagues that the important witnesses in business cases never came to court drunk or with heroin needles stuck in their arms. The key "witnesses" were paper, and all Rosner had to do was keep the jury sufficiently awake to pay attention and understand.

Rosner realized that the importance of the consent created a theory of defense counsel cross-examination of Busuttil. Although the assistant knew the answer, he wanted to see how Busuttil would respond to the inquiry.

"James, this Lazard consent was critical, wasn't it?"

"Yes," Busuttil replied with an emphatic nod.

"So much so that it was the only collateral for which you did a background check, unlike the Datavision and Cumberland Village Mining stock, for which you didn't do any reality check, right?"

"Yes."

"You and Hopkyns even went so far as to call Corcoran to question him about the transfer of the Dr Pepper stock?"

Busuttil nodded his head in agreement.

"You know that investment firms, like banks, have specimen signature lists, don't you?"

Busuttil nodded again, and began to look concerned.

"If this Lazard consent was really so important to the bank, James, why didn't you obtain the Lazard specimen signatures and compare them with those in the consent?"

"Brian . . . ," Greenblatt began to talk. The assistant silenced him with a stare.

Busuttil hesitated. "Well, we didn't know until the closing who would be signing for Lazard."

"But you could have obtained the list for all the partners in advance," the assistant said quickly, pointing a finger at Busuttil. "And then you could have compared the list with whatever actual signature was on the consent."

Busuttil shook his head side to side, and held his hands in the air, palms towards the assistant, as if he was a soldier surrendering. He was perturbed for the first time that morning. Then he spoke with stacatto precision, and abrupt hand motions. Mediterranean, Rosner thought. Definitely.

"But we don't do that, Brian. This was a loan closing. The bank was dealing with somebody it trusted. We wouldn't have been at the closing if we had the slightest suspicion that a document would be forged. Calling Corcoran for a chat was one thing. It was a normal precaution, to make sure that he understood what the bank needed by way of his signature on the consent. But what you're asking is why 'didn't we do a criminal investigation in advance?' If we thought we had to do that, that we couldn't trust a borrower to give us authentic documents, we wouldn't have been in the room to close the loan."

Jurors have 20/20 hindsight, and the question the assistant had asked was one they would want asked at trial. The bank was dealing with somebody it trusted. Lay people would understand that, Rosner thought. So much of their lives proceed on trust: Trust in their colleagues at work, their teachers, their doctors, their spouse and children and friends. Trust was a concept that the jury could appreciate, and, with Busuttil's answer, take a giant leap towards comprehending how the crime had been committed against the bankers and their counsel. This was not a case of banker-cowboys, running high-risk ventures with their depositors' money, as the assistant had seen in other of his cases. The Bank of Montreal loan was a matter of business people dealing in a prudent manner in the ultimate belief that each person at the bargaining table shared the same, basic moral values.

Rosner was warming even more towards Busuttil. He would be a credible witness. The jurors will like him.

The tension in the room had eased palpably.

"Let's go back to something we went over earlier, James. Your conversations with Wilkis."

"They were pretty cut and dried. I called to confirm the stock ownership numbers that Wilkis had given to Ivor. Wilkis confirmed them. He told me, though, that he did not have the authority to sign the consent. After I sent a copy of the consent to him a day or two prior to the closing, I called him, and he told me again that Grambling would have to find someone else at Lazard Freres to sign."

"Did he tell you that Grambling owned the $8 million of Dr Pepper stock?," the assistant asked.

"I never asked him directly, 'Does Grambling own the stock identified by X, Y, and Z stock numbers?' But it was implicit in what he did tell me. I asked him about the stock information that he had given Ivor—the numbers of shares owned, and actual certificate number for each batch of shares—and Wilkis said, 'yes, that's the right information.' He never told me that he was Grambling's personal investment advisor."

Busuttil paused for a second.

"In fact, Wilkis said quite directly that he was not. But he did give me the exact stock numbers, or what I thought were exact numbers, for Grambling's shares, and Wilkis knew that I wanted the numbers to put into the consent."

"Is that what Lazard told you, Brian?" Greenblatt asked. The assistant looked at Greenblatt. There was silence.

"Okay," Greenblatt retreated. "I know you can't tell me what you're finding out in the investigation. But it sure looks like Grambling had Wilkis working for him."

The attorneys analyzed the documents a last time. Rosner withdrew several documents and gave them back to the Shearman & Sterling counsel. The assistant's operating premise was spartan: The more documents admitted at trial, the more confusion among the jurors. This was not a derogatory attitude. Rosner recalled a complex business fraud trial in which, during jury selection, he heard the defendant's college-educated wife ask her wealthy and college-educated husband, "Why are you challenging all the jurors who are like us?" He replied, "I don't want anyone who's going to understand the case." The jurors—doormen, cleaning ladies, office workers—understood and convicted. Still, there was no reason to make the juror's job more difficult by drowning him in paper. The assistant weeded out the noncritical.

Rosner stopped at the December 14 Datavision letter promising to buy Grambling's Biosystem stock. It was the original letter. Its black type had made palpable impressions in the stationery and the signature of "Crawford," the Datavision Chairman, was written in original, non-photocopied, blue ink. Across the top of the page was an inch thick black band with "Datavision" superimposed in white letters. An occasional speck marked the uniformity of the black band. The prosecutor held the letter above his head to the ceiling light. He slowly ran his fingers over the paper. There was no water mark, or grainy feel. A letter committing a company to spend $3.5 million is serious enough to merit being typed on original top quality stationery, not a piece of Xerox paper, the assistant thought.

"Jon, you know that this Datavision letter is typed on a photocopy of Datavision stationery?" Rosner queried Greenblatt.

"We see that all the time in private practice, Brian. People save their stationery by typing their letters on Xeroxed stationery."

"I see it all the time, too," the assistant said.

It's a forgery by white-out, he thought. Grambling—and the prosecutor thought of Grambling in a generic sense, meaning that it was he, or an accomplice, who had forged the letter—had access to a letter from Datavision on original Datavision letterhead. He had whited out the body of the letter and typed a new letter on what appeared to be stationery from Datavision. Someone then signed the name "Richard Crawford," the Datavision Chairman. Two counts of forgery, Rosner concluded; one for dummying up the Xerox to make it look like a letter being sent by Datavision, and another for falsifying the "Crawford" signature. He made a mental note: "Call Crawford, and find out how Grambling had access to Datavision stationery."

As Busuttil and Greenblatt rose to depart, the assistant asked a last question of Busuttil. The assistant knew that simultaneously with bringing the case to the District Attorney's Office, Shearman & Sterling would be commencing civil process, whether negotiating repayment with Grambling, or suing him, or filing an insurance claim, or all three. When Busuttil testified in the Grand Jury, the jurors would be entitled to know about his involvement in the effort to recover the money civilly. The jurors could decide, in their role as fact-finders assessing credibility, that Busuttil was an interested witness, lying or shading his Grand Jury testimony to further his client's civil recovery. The prosecutor wanted a preview of what the grand jurors would hear.

"James, regarding the insurance claim the bank has filed, are you . . ."

"I don't know anything about any insurance claim," Busuttil responded blankly.

The assistant was confused.

"The bank hasn't notified its carrier of a potential fraud loss?"

He looked towards Greenblatt.

"Brian," Greenblatt explained, "when we, that is, when Art Field and I and others at S&S realized that this might be something other than a straightforward bad loan, we removed James from all dealings with the matter. We figured that he's going to be a witness, so we'd just keep him out of any process other than the report to the authorities."

"I know very little," Busuttil added. "I mean, I'm here, and I can guess what's been happening. But, since getting the Mullarkey letter, I've had no first-hand knowledge of what's going on."

It was not often that Rosner met bank counsel who were sensitive to the realities of trial work. By isolating Busuttil from the civil proceedings, Greenblatt and his colleagues had smothered an entire line of cross-examination.

"James, could you leave so that Jon and I can talk about some other case matters?"

After Busuttil had gone, the assistant commented to Greenblatt, "Good witness, competent guy," and then got to the point. "Is his job in jeopardy?"

"Absolutely not," Greenblatt said. "A hundred different attorneys could have handled that closing, and no one would have done it more competently, or with different results. That's the frightening thing, Brian. It could have been you or me, if we did closings. Grambling was bound to succeed.

"You hit it with your questioning. Unless you're going to act like an F.B.I. agent suspicious of a crime, you've got to trust the documents. You make sure they're all signed, of course. But no one is supposed to hand you a forgery at this level of business. This guy was about to get a $100 million loan."

Rosner nodded his head in agreement as he held the forged Lazard Freres consent in his hands. You've got to trust the documents.

CHAPTER 11

A SERIOUS MATTER

Busuttil was interviewed on February 8, 1985, the Friday of the week in which the February 1 letter had been received. Greenblatt brought in the "Three Musketeers" the following Thursday, February 14. Busuttil knew that he had been understood and exonerated by his Shearman & Sterling colleagues. Hopkyns, Hean, and Mullin were still uncertain of what was being thought of them. They felt as if they had been blown off the face of the earth, and the strange environment that greeted them at One Hogan Place gave them no comfort that they had landed in cognizable or friendly territory.

As Greenblatt collected the four red visitors' passes at the front desk, the bankers were startled by the first major difference between this Office and those with which they were familiar: the weaponry. Like gunslingers in the movies, the uniformed officers carried sidearms, holstered in leather belts. Other officers carried their weapons every which place. Detectives, identified by the shields pinned to their suit's chest pocket, wore their guns in shoulder holsters, causing a noticeable bulge under their jackets, or, if one looked towards their feet, in ankle holsters. The undercover officers, dressed like street bums or drug pushers, favored the holster stuck in the rear of their pants waistback. An occasional officer carried a rifle. And everyone, including the women officers, loudly and frequently cursed. The bankers shared glances. This was not like the Bank of Montreal, they thought.

"Excuse us," a big man in a tie and jacket, a detective obviously, said in a gravelly voice. He shoved a hefty, well-muscled black man to the rear of the elevator in which Greenblatt and the bankers had piled. The black man smiled, his arms hand-cuffed behind his back. Defendants, witnesses, detectives, and grand jurors used the same One Hogan Place entrance and its three elevators.

Greenblatt motioned his clients to squeeze out on the seventh floor. The long hall with its linoleumed floor and green walls extended the full length of the building. The Frauds Bureau was at the far end. With the joy of condemned men walking their last mile, the bankers headed for the Frauds Bureau through the dimly lit halls, every second light fixture broken or housing a burned-out bulb. Holes lined the corridor walls. Hean thought of the handcuffed thugs. He had seen many since the elevator ride, and wondered, "Are the holes the work of fist punches, or slammed heads?"

"This way." Greenblatt led the bankers around a corner into the Frauds Bureau.

After being announced, Greenblatt brought the bankers into Rosner's office. There were enough chairs, in various degrees of sturdiness. To the bankers' minds, the office was long and narrow, confining. They felt compressed.

"You've all spoken together about what has happened," the assistant began. Hopkyns, Hean, and Mullin nodded in agreement. It would have been unnatural had the three not discussed what had been done to them, and what had caused them to be produced like packages at the District Attorney's Office.

"I'm going to talk to you separately, then together," Rosner said. "Please, in answering my questions, be very careful to separate what you know based on your own, first-hand knowledge from what you've heard from others. And if you can't separate on any given point, let me know that, too."

Hopkyns and Hean were excused, as the assistant began with Mullin. Rosner had written several topics on a sheet of paper. Though there was a thick yellow pad and pen on his desk, he planned to take infrequent, if any, notes.

"If there's a trial, and you're called as a witness," the assistant explained, "I have to turn over to the defense, in advance, every scrap of paper you prepared relating to the loan, and every paper I prepare regarding what you've said. In state law, it's called Rosario material, and, in essence, it's your pretrial written recollections. All the notes I take will be Rosario material, as will Jon Greenblatt's notes."

Rosner looked sharply at Greenblatt. He put down his pad.

As did his colleagues, the assistant abhorred creating Rosario material. It was not that he disagreed with a defendant's entitlement to such papers. Rosner would readily produce them—notes, correspondence, Grand Jury testimony—in neatly ordered, indexed files. And, as a trial attorney, he recognized Rosario material's value in impeaching a witness. If a witness' trial testimony conflicted in an important detail with what that witness had said on an earlier occasion, the jury should take the difference into account and, unless a good explanation was forthcoming, discount the witness' present testimony.

The assistant's problem with Rosario material was that his mistakes in note-taking would invariably be misunderstood as the witness' inability to testify accurately. "But, Mr. Witness," the defense counsel would ask at trial, with the requisite tone of sarcasm. "You've testified today, two years after the alleged crime, that you made the loan only after speaking with the borrower on several lengthy phone calls. But isn't it a fact that, one month after the incident, when your recollection was much clearer, you were interviewed by the prosecutor, and you told the prosecutor that there was only one call?" And, when the witness says "no, I told him about several calls," the defense attorney would triumphantly offer into evidence the prosecutor's notes, which, of course, has the written word *call* with a period after it, which the prosecutor knows, and the jurors will never find out, is a poorly written "s" and not a period.

Rosner's solution was to take no or few notes. The assistant would let his witnesses commit themselves to details—and put their recollections in a documentable form—when they testified under oath in the Grand Jury. Sworn testimony given under solemn circumstances was a more reliable format for the witness to memorialize his recollection than an assistant's attempt to ask questions, understand the answers, direct further inquiries, and, at the same time, write the answers completely and accurately.

With his pen idle in his desk, Rosner scrutinized the first banker witness. As did Hopkyns and Hean, Mullin appeared to be in his mid-30s, the same age as the assistant. But Mullin seemed less nervous than the other two bankers.

"Let's begin at the beginning," Rosner said. "When did Grambling request the personal loan?"

"The second week of December," the banker answered. "But that's not the beginning, far from it. Let me explain how John came to the bank."

Like a fork being scratched across a plate, the use of the first name grated on the assistant's ear. First names were terms of familiarity. A defense counsel used the first name when referring to his client in front of the jury. It was so, well, human. A juror could more readily convict the "defendant" than a person named "John." Rosner made a mental note that, for the Grand Jury, he would instruct Mullin and his colleagues to call Grambling "the defendant," or at least "Grambling."

Mullin continued with his explanation of the Husky transaction. "So, you see, John did not just walk into the bank to ask for a loan. He was introduced to the bank by a highly regarded and respected customer. It was the finest character reference our bank could receive. By the time John made his request for a personal loan, we had worked with him and his accountants and counsel, all highly regarded professionals, for weeks."

As the assistant listened, he reflected on Mullin's use of Grambling's first name and Mullin's reliance on Grambling's aura of credibility. Mullin was a person of competence and integrity who had spent a career dealing with people similar to himself. After working with Grambling, Mullin had concluded that Grambling was hard-working and trustworthy, as were almost all of Mullin's clients. I don't know, Rosner thought, would my conclusions have been any different?

Mullin moved into his January recollections and, inexorably, he tugged the assistant towards a broader investigation.

"So we spent Friday, January 25, at Shearman & Sterling on Lexington Avenue. When I went back to the bank's Park Avenue office that afternoon, I saw that I had been called by a James Conover from a bank in Salt Lake City. In the rush of events, I never called him back. The next Friday, February 1 it was, I finally call Conover back. He insists that I had spoken to him on January 25. To a whole committee, he says, while I was on a business trip in Florida. And he asks me, 'How could you have told me last week that you were so confident about doing the financing, and then I read in the paper that the Husky deal had fallen through?' I didn't know what he was talking about."

Mullin continued with his recollections. Aside from the January 31 midnight call from Grambling, they were group recollections. Rosner decided to talk to the bankers together on those issues. The next individual interviewee was Hopkyns. He was a thin man of medium height. A small scar ran down one cheek. He was fidgety, clearly uncomfortable.

"Let's begin with the Husky loan, and your involvement in that," Rosner said.

"There's not much I can tell you," Hopkyns said in his precise, clipped voice. "I knew about the loan from Blair and Scott, but that was really their loan. I became involved in this affair when Scott, he's my superior you can say, asked me to consider a personal loan which was an outgrowth of the Husky deal. Our unit of the bank, Corporate and Government, usually does not extend personal loans. This was a special circumstance since Grambling was a new and highly regarded corporate client of the bank."

Step by step, the assistant focused Hopkyns on the part of his job, and his memories, that related to the specific elements of the crime, and the Office's decision whether or not to go forward.

"Ivor, what's the process by which loans are reviewed?"

"It's a committee affair. I would investigate the loan and report my findings with a recommendation."

"Was there any question that a person with Grambling's credibility—the guy was about to receive a $100 million loan—was going to be approved?"

"I don't think I can answer that 'yes' or 'no.' The bank was not going to just stamp yes on the application and give him $7.5 million. When we initially reviewed Grambling's request, our first decision was, yes, we'd make the loan, but only if it was fully collateralized by liquid assets."

He uses the name "Grambling," the assistant thought. There's an edge to his voice.

"Was that decision about the liquid assets communicated to Grambling?" the assistant asked.

"Absolutely. From the first. Initially, he offered as collateral the Cumberland put agreement. The offer was wholly inadequate to the bank. Not even to be considered, and Grambling was told that. Almost all of my discussions with Grambling focused on the type of liquid assets he would have to pledge to obtain the loan."

"By liquid assets, you mean cash or publicly held stock?" the assistant asked.

"Or treasury securities," Hopkyns added. "Grambling gave us his financial statement which showed that he owned $4 million worth of Dr Pepper shares free and clear. From the bank's point of view, it was an adequate type of asset, but the amount was insufficient. I told Grambling that the bank wanted more than the amount of the loan in liquid assets. At that point, Grambling mentioned a trust agreement through which he had recently inherited an additional $4 million in Dr Pepper shares. He said that his grandmother had left him the stock, but since she had died after June 1984, when he had last prepared his financial statement, the inherited shares were not reflected in the statement he had given us. But now he had over $8 million in shares, he said. The $8 million total was communicated to my superiors, and we decided that this was adequate liquid collateral to proceed with the loan."

"You guys were giving him a big break," Rosner laughed. "A $7 million loan secured by $8 million of liquid assets. I thought you said that the bank relied on his credibility and wealth when making the loan?"

Hopkyns smiled, albeit wanly. "We're a conservative bank. But for the fact that he was introduced to us by a prominent client and appeared fully capable of repaying the loan, we would never have spoken to him. But loans are loans, and whoever the borrower is, we have the responsibility to our stockholders to secure all credits with collateral."

So much for the argument that the bank really made the loan in general reliance on Grambling's appearance of wealth, Rosner thought.

The prosecutor began to narrow the focus.

"So, the bank told Grambling that there would be no loan without the Dr Pepper stock?"

"Yes."

"It was the only liquid asset?"

"Yes."

The assistant readied the key question for the purpose of representation and reliance in a larceny case. He leaned forward slightly in his chair.

"Ivor, would the loan have been made without the Dr Pepper stock?"

Hopkyns looked to Greenblatt, who raised his left hand and began to speak.

"Brian, we're involved in civil proceedings and, as you know, the bank also received Biosystems and, what's it called . . ."

"Cumberland Village Mining," Hopkyns said.

"Yes, the mining stock," Greenblatt said. "I'm not sure the bank can really say that some of the collateral was not important."

"Okay, Jon. I see your point. Let me go on." The assistant leaned back and thought for a moment.

"Ivor, you made some calls regarding the Dr Pepper stock, and you made the calls because that stock was an important piece of collateral?"

"Yes."

"Did you call Crawford at Datavision regarding the option to buy the Biosystems stock?"

"No, I did not."

"Any calls regarding the mining company?"

"No."

"If Grambling showed up at the closing without the Biosystems and mining stock, would you have authorized the bank to disburse the money?"

Hopkyns glanced at Greenblatt, who remained silent. The banker looked at Rosner.

"But with the Lazard consent?" Hopkyns asked.

The assistant nodded.

"Yes. I would have authorized the disbursement," Hopkyns said. He again glanced at Greenblatt and, seeing no sign of disapproval, continued.

"The consent was the necessary collateral for the loan."

Representation, reliance, disbursement—if Hopkyns was believed, Grambling had committed a provable offense. And, Rosner thought, there was no reason to disbelieve Hopkyns. The documents supported his account.

"Let's talk about your conversations with Lazard," the assistant said.

Hopkyns' face turned red with anger.

"I had several discussions about Grambling's stock with someone calling himself Wilkis. I was led to Wilkis by Grambling. Wilkis told me about the Dr Pepper buyout in general, and the specifics of Grambling's own stock ownership. I remember that conversation as if it were today. I had called Grambling to tell him that, as we were getting close to the end of December, I needed the location and share numbers for his holdings. You must remember, the bank received this loan request the first week of December on a very urgent basis from Grambling. We were giving his request top priority, but not receiving the requisite information."

"Okay." The assistant nodded.

"So, it was December twenty-something, already late in the month. I called Grambling and told him that we had to have the numbers. He told me to call Wilkis again, because he would be getting the numbers that day. After a short while, I called Wilkis and, just as Grambling had said, Wilkis told me that he had just gotten off the phone with the transfer agent for the Dr Pepper stock, and Wilkis rattled the numbers off to me."

"Did Wilkis ever say directly that Grambling owned Dr Pepper stock?" Rosner asked in a soft voice.

Hopkyns looked puzzled. "He and I had several conversations about the stock. We both discussed it as if it was real, which is what I thought, and certainly what he caused me to believe."

"Did Wilkis claim to be Grambling's account manager?" the assistant asked.

"No, that he did not. He said he was a former colleague and friend, but that the stock was managed from, what did he say, the 'back office.' I do not know what more he could have said to lead me to believe that it was real. He was very specific. He told me that he had the numbers in front of him."

Next, Rosner moved to the call to Florida to Peter Corcoran.

"It was just normal chit-chat," Hopkyns said. "We didn't know until the day of the closing who the signatory would be, and Wilkis had told us on several occasions that he did not have signing power."

Time to play devil's advocate, Rosner thought.

"You mean, Ivor, that you didn't believe the signature was authentic?"

"No, not at all," Hopkyns replied without hesitation. "One of the problems at the closing was that we could not read the signature on the consent. Grambling said that it was 'Peter Corcoran,' but our New York attorney said the signature was all scrunched up."

"But you had planned to call in advance, hadn't you?"

"Well, yes. James was to call to tell me that the consent was in. I had planned to talk to the signatory."

This was a point that almost confused the prosecutor and, he feared, might confuse a jury. If Hopkyns really trusted Grambling and the consent, why call Corcoran? And, if he suspected that there was a fraud occurring, and the suspicion of fraud was the reason he had called Corcoran, why didn't he go all the way and demand to see the Lazard signature books. Once a jury began thinking along those lines, they might go the next step and think that Hopkyns either was not being careful—and jurors tend to acquit defendants whose success is, in part, due to banker's negligence—or that Hopkyns did not truly care about the authenticity of the consent. And if Hopkyns did not care, that would be an argument that he and the bank truly did not rely on the consent in disbursing the funds. The train of thought had become extenuated, but, as one of Rosner's law school professors had instructed, and the assistant had seen numerous times in court, winning arguments often begin with such loosely connected thoughts of counsel.

"Ivor, did you think that the signature might not be authentic?"

"No, but I did want to be certain that there was no mistake. I did not for a moment think that a Lazard Freres partner—and that's who I thought I was talking to—would lie to me about his power to sign."

And if he thought that, Rosner thought, he would not have bothered to call, or to loan Grambling the money. It was like when people leave their apartment for a night out and, after walking a few steps down the hallway, go back to make sure the lights are off. Of course, they remember turning the lights off, and the lights are never on when the people open the door to check. But they just wanted to be sure. He liked the analogy and scribbled it down on his note paper. He would use that argument in summation to the jury.

After Hopkyns, the assistant spoke to Hean, and then the three together. The bankers' statements, together with Busuttil's, proved that crimes had occurred in Manhattan. The sophistication of the actor, and the manner in which he had convinced the bankers to accept the authenticity of the forgeries, argued that the case warranted prosecution. Now was as good a time as any for the assistant to give his "Grand Jury" speech to the three potential witnesses.

"We're just at the beginning of the investigation. The case may end up going to the Grand Jury for a possible indictment. Let me tell you a little about that process.

"The Grand Jury is a serious matter. If Grambling is charged with a crime, his life is over. The whole process of the presentation is secret, of course. Though, what with the civil proceedings and nature of the crimes, it won't be secret to anyone familiar with the situation. And, if indicted, Grambling will be presumed innocent until convicted. But, in the real world, indictment means guilt, and this Office won't begin the process unless we're aware of the consequences.

"That's what I want you to think about. Grambling hurt you. You probably want to kill him. It would not be human to feel otherwise. But, if convicted of a crime, he's going to be taken from his family and thrown in jail."

Rosner motioned over his shoulder towards the Tombs.

"I want you to remember one thing. Control your anger, and always tell the truth. Don't exaggerate. Don't remember things you're not sure of. Don't think of the process as revenge. I'm not saying I detected any of that in your comments. But if Grambling deserves to be hurt for what he did, trust to the system to see that justice is done."

Hean was the leader of the three. He looked to his colleagues and said, "We hear you. Grambling hurt us all, but we understand what this," motioning around the room, "is about. I hate the guy for what he did to me and my family, but I'm not out for revenge."

After the three had left, the assistant spoke alone with Greenblatt.

"They got snookered but good, Jon. Does the bank understand?"

"I think so, but I can't tell for sure. This is a Canadian bank, and these things don't happen up there."

Rosner thought about the comment. Though under stress, the Canadians still appeared to be more conservative and thoughtful bankers than many New York bankers the assistant had met.

"The bank's certainly not going to go under because of this," Greenblatt said. "I think the immediate reaction was that the decision-making officers must have done something outrageously wrong, or that one of them must have been an insider. The bank's over that. But there's still a high degree of institutional shock over the fact that this occurred, that a customer could have violated them in this way."

"Interesting," the prosecutor noted, leaning back in his chair, fingers intertwined behind his head. "By the way, Jon. Have the federales been around?"

"Yeah, an agent was up to my office last night to meet Hopkyns, Hean, and Mullin. He didn't go through anything near the detail that you did."

In federal prosecutors' offices, F.B.I. agents did investigations and presented the results to a prosecutor for a decision on whether to proceed. In Morgenthau's Office, and most state offices, the attorneys and detectives worked together from the investigation's inception.

"Don't worry," Greenblatt added. "You're light years ahead."

CHAPTER 12

THE OLD-FASHIONED WAY

Late in the week of February 12, Flumenbaum visited Rosner to make the offer of proof on Wilkis' behalf. Having heard the Bank of Montreal witnesses, the assistant had a basis to review, and accept, Flumenbaum's offer.

The following Wednesday, February 20, Wilkis traveled to Hogan Place to be bathed in immunity. He and his attorney were a contrast: Both in their mid-30s, Flumenbaum was short and stocky with wire-frame glasses; Wilkis tall and thin, no glasses.

Prior to the interview, Flumenbaum and Rosner had spoken. Flumenbaum wanted the prosecutor to tell Wilkis, face-to-face, that he was immunized. No letter on District Attorney's stationery would be necessary, Flumenbaum had said. One less piece of paper to impeach this guy with, the assistant thought with relief.

Wilkis entered Rosner's office and sat in the witness chair in front of the assistant's desk. Flumenbaum took a seat at Wilkis' side. Jurors like tall people, the assistant noted as he began his silent evaluation of Wilkis as a witness.

"Thank you for coming in today, Mr. Wilkis," Rosner said in his most formal manner. Wilkis sat ramrod straight, a sour look on his face.

"As your counsel has no doubt told you, you'll be receiving full transactional immunity today, just as if you were in the Grand Jury testifying. That means that you can't be prosecuted for any crimes derived from what you tell me. Of course, should I put you into the Grand Jury, and you don't tell the truth, or refuse to answer questions, you can be prosecuted for perjury or contempt. But you're talking to me today will be just as if you were in the Grand Jury; you get immunity. If you have any questions, or would like to confer with counsel . . ."

"No, I understand what's going on. Let's get on with it."

"Okay. Let's begin at the beginning. How did you become involved with Grambling?"

"I knew John from Lazard Freres. We began there together. We even shared the same secretary, Sheila."

"Were you friends?"

"No, not at all. Just business acquaintances."

"Did you keep in touch with him after he left Lazard?"

"No. I saw him once or twice on deals. I was representing Lazard, and he was dealing for himself. But no sustained contact."

"Okay," the assistant nodded. He would just let Wilkis talk.

"In early December, I gave him a call," Wilkis said. "Lazard had just finished a big deal that I was involved in, and I wanted to let people know what I had done. I sat down at my desk with my Rolodex, and started calling everyone on my cards—classmates, associates, acquaintances—just to let them know. Grambling was one of the dozens of people I called."

The prosecutor raised his eyebrows in disbelief. What a different profession, he thought. We win our trials, our appeals, and those who want to know about them will find out. In the District Attorney's Office, self-promotion was a cardinal sin.

Wilkis saw the assistant's look of surprise. He said quietly, "I was just tooting my own horn. That's the way the Street works. Wall Street, I mean. You have to let people know what you've done, and that you're around, so that they think of you for their next deal."

"Deal," "Street"—Rosner pictured Wilkis in front of the 12 jurors. For many of them, it would be like going to the movies, or the moon.

"So it was Wednesday, December 19," Wilkis continued. "Grambling calls. I'm not in, so he leaves a message with Sheila. It's in my message book."

"You still have your message book?" the assistant asked.

"Yes."

Rosner looked to Flumenbaum.

"Just put it in the subpoena," Flumenbaum said.

Rosner made his first entry in the list of the documents to be subpoenaed from Lazard.

Wilkis continued, "So I talk to Grambling and we're gladhanding each other. 'How you doing?' 'What you been up to?' That stuff. And then he goes, 'Listen, Bob, could you do me a small favor?' "

Wilkis' face grimaced with the words. "Jesus, if I only knew what I was getting into." Wilkis' voice broke as if he was about to cry.

"I understand, Bob, just . . . . "

"It's okay. It's just . . . well, so he asks, 'Can you do me a small favor?' and he starts to tell me about this great Husky deal. Multimillion dollars, oil, gas. And I'm thinking, 'Hey, this ain't a bad guy to do a favor for.' You know what I mean. I scratch his back today, tomorrow he scratches mine? Well, that's how the Street works.

"And he tells me how he has this problem with bankers. They're Canadians, real slow, dim-witted, he says. And he has to explain to them how, because of a leveraged buyout, his Dr Pepper shares are worth so much in cash. Now, Lazard had done the Dr Pepper deal, so I knew about it. And, we're talking, and I ask, 'How many shares,' and he goes '360,000 or so.' And I think, 'Jesus, when he was here everybody knew he was filthy rich, a Texas oil brat, but here's this guy, he has 360,000 shares of Dr Pepper hanging around'—I do some quick calculations in my head, that's $8 million we're talking about—'and he hasn't even converted the stock yet.' You see, the stock had been convertible for months, with mid-January 1985 being the cut-off date. And this guy, I'm thinking, he has so much fucking money he doesn't even notice that his stock can be converted to $8 million of cold cash immediately.

"So, he asks me if I can talk to these dim-witted Canadians. 'You know,' he says, 'they don't understand LBOs and high-finance, and if you could just explain to them how the deal worked, and how the money comes out at the end.'

"And I agree. Why not? If I can help the guy out in such a little manner on such a big deal, why not? So I say 'yes,' and

Hopkyns, the Canadian banker, calls that day. I explain the LBO to him, and the cash conversion process."

"Did you tell Hopkyns that Grambling owned 360,000 shares of Dr Pepper?" the assistant asked.

"I told him I wasn't Grambling's account officer, and couldn't give him the details about Grambling's stock," Wilkis said sharply.

"Did you disagree with Hopkyns when he referred to Grambling owning 360,000 shares?" Rosner asked.

"No. I thought Grambling was a multimillionaire. The rumors, from when he was at Lazard, were that he was worth $50 million. So $8 million of Dr Pepper stock was just, yeah, it seemed right."

"So, the next day . . .," Wilkis continued.

Flumenbaum tapped Wilkis' forearm. "Tell him about the stationery."

"Oh, yeah. I didn't think about this until late January, after the Hopkyns call. But when Grambling called me on December 19, and I wasn't in, he spoke to Sheila, his old secretary and my present secretary. He asked Sheila if she could send some blank Lazard stationery to his lawyer in New York."

"Did she tell you that on the 19th?" Rosner asked. He tried to suppress his look of incredulity.

Wilkis looked to Flumenbaum, who had a placid look on his face.

"Yes," Wilkis said. "She told me on the 19th shortly after work."

"Did you tell anyone?"

"You're going to think I'm a jerk or a liar, but no. I just thought, 'What a weird request. Is he crazy?' And I just stored the thing in my mind."

"When did you first tell one of your superiors at Lazard?"

"After the Hopkyns' call in January."

This is how a jury trial becomes a horse race, Rosner thought. Is Wilkis telling the truth, and if true, will the jury believe it? A request for the firm's stationery is a shrieking siren calling for a response. If Wilkis did not tell anyone about the request until January, maybe he is an accomplice. But if he is an accomplice, why is he telling me the stationery story now? Is he 'fessing up now because Sheila the secretary is a witness? But presumably, she didn't tell anyone in December either, except Wilkis.

"Marty, is Sheila available?" the assistant asked.

"Yes, she tells it the way Bob does. She'll need a subpoena."

"Okay, bring her in the day Corcoran comes in."

Flumenbaum wrote a note.

"So what happened the next day, Bob?" Rosner continued.

"Grambling calls me the next day. 'Bob,' he says, 'can you do me another small favor?'" Wilkis chuckled. "I can't believe what a schmuck I was. 'Do me a small favor.'"

Wilkis's demeanor had softened. He was becoming more animated in his speech.

"What Grambling wanted was that I should take a call from Continental Illinois Bank, the transfer agent for the Dr Pepper stock. The Canadian bankers needed the precise stock information, but he was busy closing the $100 million loan. So could I just take the call on the Dr Pepper numbers and have them available when the Canadian banker called. Grambling was all apologetic about how he knew it was an inconvenience, 'but Bob, you know how short time is at the end of a deal.' So, okay, I agreed. He played me just right.

"Literally five or ten minutes after I hang up with John, I get a call from a guy who says he's from Continental Illinois. He just rattles off these numbers—number of shares, certificate numbers, that there's bifurcated share holdings, 170,000 at Lazard, 180,000 at Hutton. The guy was really good. He had a gruff voice, that of an older man. You could just picture him sitting in the back office of Continental Illinois surrounded by dust-coated ledger books. And I'm scribbling down these numbers on a scrap of paper laying on my desk.

"A few minutes later, Hopkyns calls. And I tell him that I was expecting his call, and I have the numbers. And I rattle off what the 'Continental Illinois' guy had just told me. I think it was then that Hopkyns asked me if I would be signing the consent, and I tell him 'absolutely not. I'm an associate, not a partner. John is going to have to get someone else to sign.'

"The next day, I went on vacation, and I was back in the office on December 27. That day Grambling calls me and asks, again in his oh-so-sweet voice, if I could just sign the document for him. I told Grambling 'you got to be out of your mind.' By this time, I was pissed. I mean, a favor is one thing, but this had gone on for too long. It's vacation time. Things are slow. So I have my daughter in my office. You know, seeing what daddy does."

Wilkis smiled broadly. It was the first time he had smiled during the interview.

"She's sitting there, eating french fries and playing with the typewriter. We're going to go out and walk around Rockefeller Center. You know how pretty it is at holiday time."

Rosner grinned and nodded.

"And I just didn't want to be bothered anymore with Grambling's favors," Wilkis said. "Then this attorney calls, Bususomething."

"Busuttil?" the assistant said.

"Yeah, Busuttil. And he's running these numbers by me, and asking about signing a document, and I just exploded. I said 'I've already told you that I couldn't sign.' So he says that he'll send the document to me by messenger, something about leaving the signature place blank, and I hang up."

"Did a document come by messenger?"

"Yeah, a messenger comes with this package from Shearman & Sterling. It's a cover letter and a document—the consent I saw later in January—and while I'm sitting at my desk looking at it, who do you think calls? Grambling. He wants to know if I got the package, and am I sure I can't sign. I just tell him 'enough is enough.' And Grambling says 'that's okay.' He backs off. He'll get someone else at Lazard to take care of it, he says, and I should just rip up the documents and throw them away. Which is what I did.

"I went to Baltimore the next day, the 28th, for vacation to visit my folks. I was out most of the day, and when I got back, my mother gives me a message. I had been called by someone from the Bank of Montreal—Hopkyns. I just crumpled up the message and threw it away.

"On January 2 or 3, I'm back in my office at Rockefeller Center, reading the papers, and I see a clip in *The Wall Street Journal*—'Husky Sells U.S. Refineries to Grambling Energy, Inc.' My God, I thought, the son-of-a-bitch pulled it off. He actually did it, and I was a little bit responsible for helping.

"All of a sudden, I began to feel bad for being a little abrupt with him on those last phone calls. So I called to congratulate him. I was a little apologetic. I said, 'You know, John, I couldn't sign that document.' Grambling told me not to worry about it. He got Peter Corcoran to take care of it.

"Then basically nothing happens," Wilkis continued, "until January 15 when I get that call from Hopkyns wanting to know when the money will be available. 'What money?' I say, and he goes on about how he has this consent with my signature on it, 'Robert W. Wilkis' 'You got a problem, pal,' I said, 'the name is Robert M. Wilkis.'

"By that afternoon, the 15th, we had figured out what happened."

Wilkis was at a loss for words. He looked around a few times, and screwed up his lips.

"Christ, I could have killed that shit. All of a sudden my job is on the line. The first reaction of everyone is that I helped him do this."

He threw his hands in the air.

"Of course, I did help him. But I didn't know what he was doing. But even saying that makes me feel like a jerk. Credibility is important on the Street. All of a sudden, after so many good deals, my credibility's down the drain. Now Wilkis is the sap who got done in by Grambling."

With his fingers extended, Wilkis ran a hand through his hair, and looked at the floor. He sighed and spoke.

"I was mad. I called Grambling that night and cursed him out. 'How could you do this to me, you son-of-a-bitch. You forged my signature.' And all of a sudden, Grambling changes from that sickly sweet voice of his, to like he's affronted, like I've done something wrong. How dare I accuse him of forgery, he says. He didn't write the signatures, he says. He had another friend at Lazard help him out."

Rosner glanced to Flumenbaum. "We've checked it out. It's bullshit. Grambling's just talking."

"Okay, Marty. We'll talk about it."

Wilkis looked around, and spread his arms as if embracing the room.

"And now I'm here."

He shook his head side to side.

"How could I have been so dumb? But you got to appreciate Grambling. The way he set up the calls between Hopkyns and me, and that 'Continental Illinois' guy."

"Any other calls or transactions with Grambling in December or January?" the assistant asked.

Wilkis thought for a moment.

"Yes. Just one, or just almost one. Nothing ever happened, and I didn't know what it was about. But sometime in December, I got a message that someone from a company called U.S. Shelter had called. It had something to do with Grambling. Grambling called me shortly afterwards and told me not to return the call or talk to the U.S. Shelter guy. He said that whatever the reason for the call, it had been taken care of. Okay, I thought, and didn't think anything else of it. And in January, very soon after the beginning of the year, someone called and left a message about a cable venture and Grambling. But the guy never called back. And that's it."

The assistant made a note that, at some point, he would figure out what the U.S. Shelter calls were about.

"Is there anything else, Bob?" he asked.

"No, but," and a hard expression returned to his face. "That son-of-a-bitch hurt me. Here's a guy born with a silver spoon in his mouth, and I'm just a poor schmuck just trying to make my money the old-fashioned way, and this is what the guy does to me."

He was about to say something else, but stopped, and clenched his hands. After Wilkis and counsel had left, Rosner strolled to Benitez's office.

Benitez looked up from his desk. "What's up?"

"It's a real crime," Rosner explained, as he sat down and began his assessment of the facts and the witnesses. "The bankers are likable guys, prudent, conservative, not out there throwing money away on wild ventures."

Benitez nodded in understanding. The bureau had seen many cases of banker irresponsibility. He understood the impact that had on a jury.

"The bankers are also all non-New Yorkers," the assistant went on. "There's less of a frenetic pace about them and I think the jury will like that.

"The crime is there, representation and reliance. Wilkis turned out as we expected. It's amazing. He and Hopkyns, the Calgary bank officer, were simply talking past each other. Grambling had created such an aura of wealth and financial credibility, that Hopkyns and Wilkis each assumed the truth of what Grambling was saying about his own wealth. Of course, Grambling helped it along a bit." Rosner explained how Grambling had set up the Continental Illinois call.

"What's the story with Libman," Benitez asked. "Is he the Corcoran from Miami?"

"Don't know. All we know is that a phone call was made to a line which somehow feeds into his business number. But we don't know who actually picked up the phone and did the talking. The suspicion is that it's Libman, but the evidence isn't even close to proof beyond a reasonable doubt. By the way, I did a little background on Libman."

As soon as the first Bank of Montreal documents had been received, Rosner had noticed an incongruity. Libman had told the bankers that he was President of Cumberland Village Mining and the manager of the company's mines. Yet his address, as was the address of the mining company, was in North Miami Beach, Florida, a strange place for digging coal.

But a typical address for the fraud records of the District Attorney's Office. For a decade, the Frauds Bureau had investigated fraud in the coal industry. In the mid-1970s, the energy crisis had fueled a boom in the coal industry. Like vultures flocking to a corpse, lawyers and accountants in New York, aided by operators in Appalachia, responded by creating a sub-industry of tax-sheltered coal investments, most notable for their steep tax write-offs and high up-front fees to attorneys and promoters. Once the fees were paid, scarcely any working capital remained for mining: Consequently, little or no coal was taken from the ground. There were hundreds of such shelters, and the prosecutor had never seen an honest one. Assistants joked among themselves that more coal was being mined in the law offices of Park Avenue than the coal fields of Appalachia. In response to the sale of the fraudulent tax write-offs, and the havoc the tax shelters had created for legitimate coal producers, the prosecutors' offices of several Eastern coal-mining states and the Manhattan District Attorney's Office joined forces in a multi-state, federally funded coalition—the Leviticus Project—to investigate and prosecute fraud in the coal industry.

"I ran Libman through the Leviticus computer," Rosner told Benitez. "I got a hit regarding civil fraud litigation in the Atlanta federal court. It's the usual complaint; false representations to investors to get them to ante up for a coal investment. I can't recall if it was Kentucky or Tennessee property at issue, but it was a different company than Cumberland Village Mining. Libman is the guarantor on the $7.5 million Bank of Montreal loan. And I've been told by counsel to Colorado National that Libman's trying to negotiate a civil resolution to that loss."

The assistant explained how Grambling had defrauded a second bank, Colorado National.

"People like Grambling never do frauds as a one shot deal," Benitez commented.

"I figured that. Look at what I've started to get back on my interstate subpoenas."

The assistant spread several photocopied documents on Benitez's desk.

"Spring of 1984, this Topeka Bank made a $2 million loan to Grambling, secured by the Cumberland Village Mining stock. Here's the memo when they made the loan. The bankers are falling all over each other praising Grambling and his business. They also evaluated the stock at $4,680,000."

"Is that the value the Bank of Montreal put on it?" Benitez asked.

"No, the Bank of Montreal's buy-back agreement, signed by Libman, or at least made to appear to be signed by Libman, attributes a purchase value of $8.5 million to the stock."

"Sounds like a rising investment to me." Benitez smiled.

Leaning over the desk, the assistant pointed to the relevant pieces of paper.

"Peter, look what happens in Iowa. The loan comes due. No payment. Then there's these letters between the bank and Libman. The bank tells Libman, 'you're the president of Cumberland Village Mining, this stock is for sale. Do you want to buy it?' Libman writes that the company is interested. He strings the bank along for weeks. Finally, by the fall of 1984, the bankers realize that they're going to have to foreclose on the stock so they send inquiries to a half dozen brokers. The brokers all come back with the same response. 'The stock has no market, and no value. It's worth nothing.'

"You see what's happening, Peter? Grambling swindled the Topeka Bank. He got the loan with the false pretense that the stock had value." Rosner rose from the papers.

"Why did the bank believe him?" the Bureau Chief asked.

"I haven't spoken with them but you can see it from the internal memoranda. They thought Grambling walked on water. Somewhere in this guy's life, some banker got the idea that he had a lot of bucks. It's like high school. You do real well in your sophomore year and reputation alone carries you to graduation.

"You can also see where the guy got his reputation, at least his reputation that he pays banks back. When the Topeka bankers are at their wits' end—Grambling isn't paying, Cumberland Village Mining's not buying back the stock, there's no real market to sell the stock—Grambling comes through and pays the loan, with interest, by defrauding the Bank of Montreal."

"Robbing Peter to pay Paul." Benitez drummed his desk with his fingers.

"Your basic Ponzi scheme," the assistant said. "And look how neat Grambling keeps it going. He knows that the Topeka Bank tried to sell the stock, only to discover that there was no market. So when he offers the stock to the Bank of Montreal, he also gives the bank this purchase option which gives the stock a guaranteed value of $8.5 million. Who said you couldn't teach an old dog new tricks?"

Benitez thought for a while.

"Nice work, Brian."

Benitez sorted through the papers on his desk and found a two-page letter, which he handed to the assistant. "Here look at this." The letter had just been received by the Office.

Honorable Robert M. Morgenthau
District Attorney
New York County
One Hogan Place
New York, New York 10013

Re: Bank of Montreal and John A. Grambling, Jr.

Dear Bob:

As you may know, the Bank of Montreal and its attorneys recently brought to your attention and the attention of the United States Attorney's Office alleged criminal conduct by John A. Grambling, Jr. In sum, it appears that Grambling obtained a $7.5 million personal loan based on fraudulent documents he prepared.

It appears that Grambling's scheme includes similar criminal conduct in Colorado and Utah. Thus, this investigation will require the use of nationwide process which is available to the federal grand jury. Similarly, access to Federal Bureau of Investigation offices in other parts of the country will enable us to pursue this inquiry expeditiously and thoroughly. In fact, the New York office of the Federal Bureau of Investigation has already commenced an investigation into these allegations and is asking its offices in their other relevant cities to assist.

This case is a case where concurrent jurisdiction exists. It can be pursued federally as well as locally. Given the high volume of your case load in other very serious areas and the need for subpoenas being served in areas beyond your jurisdiction as well as some of the other advantages by using a federal grand jury and the nationwide resources of the Federal Bureau of Investigation, this case is an excellent candidate for federal investigation.

I am advised that papers from the Bank of Montreal were submitted to an Assistant District Attorney and that he has certain original bank records under subpoena. We would like to proceed promptly and therefore I suggest that your assistant contact the Chief of our Criminal Division so they can discuss the best method for utilizing federal jurisdiction and resources to investigate and possibly prosecute this matter.

Very truly yours,
RUDOLPH W. GIULIANI
United States Attorney

"How soon can you put the case in the Grand Jury?" Benitez asked.

"It's not ready for the Grand Jury," Rosner protested. "I have to talk to the Colorado bankers, and Corcoran and Crawford, the people whose signatures were forged. Also, I haven't quite figured Libman's role. For all we know, someone is impersonating him. And I have some other cases."

Yeah, get done with the excuses, Benitez's face said.

"But I can see finishing the investigation in two to four weeks. And the letter's bullshit, Peter. They haven't even spoken to the important witnesses."

Rosner looked at the letter again. "You know, Peter. Bankers aren't the only ones who never heard of interstate subpoenas."

CHAPTER 13

IN THE NEIGHBORHOOD

On Tuesday, March 5, Colorado National's Tom Foncannon and Ken Hansen flew to New York. Accompanied by Philip Byler, a senior litigation associate at Weil, Gotshal & Manges, they went to One Hogan Place the morning of March 6, and marched down the dreary lime green seventh floor corridor.

At the end of the hall, they arrived at the doors of the investigative divisions. "Rackets Bureau" read the sign straight ahead. "Frauds Bureau" beckoned the sign to the left.

"That's us." Foncannon sighed. They turned left.

They weaved through the interior hallway of the Frauds Bureau and came to Brian Rosner's office. It was all familiar: The hallways never painted; the antique metallic doorknobs boldly inscribed "City of New York"; the armed detectives. The set for Kojak, Foncannon thought.

As they entered the Assistant District Attorney's office, Foncannon noticed the boxes, piled on the file cabinets and tables and on the chairs, where Rosner pointed for the bankers and their attorney to sit. Lifting a heavy box labeled "Transit Mix," Foncannon cleared a chair. This isn't happening to me, he reflected.

They look beat, Rosner thought. Though the Bank of Montreal had suffered the larger loss, at the end of the day, that bank would survive. The $7.5 million would be charged against loan loss reserves and, but for the shattered confidence and careers of several bankers, and a small individual loss for each of the bank's stockholders, the bank's business would continue.

Colorado National was a different story. Agriculture and mining, staples of the Colorado economy, had entered a downturn: 1985 would be a disastrous year. The $6 million Grambling loss would be more than Colorado National's 1985 net profits, and Colorado National's shareholders would see no dividends in 1985. Although the full extent of the economic depression and bank loss would not be known for months, the intimations had begun, and Colorado National's employees were deeply concerned. Foncannon and Hansen carried the burden on their faces. Better loosen them up with some small talk, the assistant decided.

He thanked them for coming to New York and explained that, if there was a Grand Jury presentation, they would be back in April.

"Nice time to be in New York," he said. "Springtime, start of the baseball season. You follow baseball?"

"Looks like a good year for the Mets," Foncannon commented.

They talked about baseball and children. Foncannon noticed the framed pictures of mountains on Rosner's wall.

"That from out our way?" Foncannon asked.

"Wind River Range," the assistant said.

"Yo man," a voice shouted.

Foncannon and Hansen were startled. They looked around the room. Rosner turned in his chair towards the window.

"Yo man, yo."

Reaching out, he pulled the window shut, closing out the noise from the alleyway.

"The Tombs," he explained.

Foncannon nodded in complete understanding. Of course, he thought, the Tombs.

They began the interview.

"We thought the loan was absolutely risk-free," Foncannon explained. "If the deal didn't close, we could be repaid out of the escrow fund, and, if it did close, we'd be repaid from the Bank of Montreal financing. I can't tell you how many times—well, it's all in the affidavit we prepared for the civil case. You have that, don't you?"

Rosner nodded. The bank has recently sued Grambling to prevent him from moving his unencumbered assets. In support of the lawsuit, Foncannon has submitted a meticulously detailed 30-page affidavit recounting the events of January.

"I checked and double-checked that the Bank of Montreal financing was a reliable source of repayment. I had Grambling give me a list of expenses and I ran each single expense by 'Hean.' Now the Bank of Montreal tells me that it wasn't Hean I was talking to. But I did talk to real people at times, a real Mullin and a real Hopkyns. In the beginning, they said pretty much what, I'll call him the fake Mullin, what the fake Mullin had told me. When Hopkyns finally told me something different, that's when Hean got on the phone with me . . . well, it's in the affidavit."

"Tom," the assistant began. "When Grambling gave you the Term Sheet in Denver, did you think to check, or did you have any procedure to check, whether it was a forgery?"

Foncannon sat on the question. As always in the unnatural setting of being interviewed by an assistant, the seconds dragged as if minutes.

"I guess I just look like a dope, but Mr. Rosner . . ."

"Brian," the assistant said gently.

"Brian, I've been in banking one way or another for 14 years," Foncannon replied. "No one ever gave me a forged document. Exaggerated balance sheets, sure, and we discount for that." He glanced to Hansen, who nodded. "But a forgery?" Foncannon stopped speaking, and held his hands in the air in futility.

"Let me say something," Hansen vigorously interjected. "Maybe we're just simple, slow-moving folk from Colorado. But business people out there don't forge documents. I've never seen one either. It's just not our way of doing things. And it's not that we just dumbly trusted this guy." Hansen turned to Foncannon. "Tell him what you did, Tom."

"When the loan application came in—and remember how the introduction came in, through Mr. Dibble, a highly respected oil and gas man, and right through the chairman's office—still, I did exactly the due diligence that you'd do on a loan of this size. I called every bank reference. They were among the best I'd ever heard. Keenan at Coronado, and I know

Keenan, could say only good things. The fellow from Bank of Scottsdale, he called Grambling 'super.' He was sorry that Grambling had repaid his account in full, and early, and left the bank."

As they unburdened themselves, Foncannon and Hansen appeared to be more comfortable. Time to see how they respond to a hostile question, the prosecutor thought. With a wave of his hand, he stopped Foncannon's narrative.

"Get off it, Tom. Bank references are nonsense. Everyone's scared of a defamation suit, so whenever a banker is asked questions, he gives some vague, useless response."

"That's not so," Hansen and Foncannon objected in unison. Hansen looked at Foncannon. For the first time that morning, they cracked smiles.

"You have to be able to read between the lines," Hansen said. "Like the time I called a banker down in, well, Texas of all places. A fellow was applying for a loan. Let's call him Johnny Smith.

"So I call the banker," Hansen continued, "and ask him about Johnny Smith. What reputation does he have in the community? Does he pay his debts? Is he an able business person?

"The banker thinks a bit and says, 'Johnny Smith, Johnny Jr., that's what we call him in town. His daddy's one of the most respected folks around here. Owns a business. Has had it for generations. His uncles, too, highly respected people. Their word is their honor.' And the banker goes on and on about Johnny Jr.'s dad, and uncles, and cousins. After several minutes of this, I cut him off. 'Thanks for all that information,' I say. 'But it's not Johnny Sr., it's Johnny Jr. I'm asking about.'

" 'Oh, Johnny Jr.,' the banker says, and after a pause, 'Now Johnny Jr.—he must take after the mamma's side of the family.' "

They all laughed.

"Brian," Foncannon said as he calmed his chuckling. "I read between the lines of the references. They were superb and unqualified. The man repaid his debts, with interest and, at times, early. You can't ask for better."

The "Johnny, Jr." story had lightened the interview. Rosner stored it in his mind. It was the best real life explanation he had heard of bank references. Still smiling as he said goodbye to his witnesses, Rosner thought, I'll have Hansen tell that one to the jury.

It was not to be. Hansen would be gone from the bank in six months. He would relocate to a different state and take a job at a salary half of what he had been making. Rockwell, the bank chairman, would accelerate his already planned early retirement. Foncannon would remain—Boards of Directors fired captains, not crewmen—one of the many Colorado National officers trying to dig their company out of the pit Grambling had put it in.

As the interviews occurred, and the bank records flowed in from across the nation, the prosecutor wrote memoranda to Benitez and the Eighth Floor detailing the progress of the investigation. Facts are inevitable. Slowly they accumulated, and, by early March, the facts indicated what the ultimate decision would be. Grambling was a sophisticated swindler engaged in a long-term, cross-country pattern of fraud: The case would be presented to the Grand Jury. The memoranda thickened, and the recent ones ended with a request: A detective should be assigned to the case.

Second week in March, Rosner walked to the ninth floor of the District Attorney's Office. For decades, the Police Department had assigned a special cadre of detectives to work directly with the prosecutor's office: The District Attorney's Office Squad, commonly known as DAOS. It was a prestigious assignment. Each detective was at least a 10-year veteran who, after his beginning years as a patrolman, had spent several years in a special assignment, doing undercover narcotics work for example, or homicides. A position in the squad was an opportunity to work directly with a prosecutor on some of the most significant cases in New York City.

The assistant walked by the candy machines and wall displaying wanted posters into the squad room. It was like detective offices everywhere—rows of desks facing each other, each with a phone, several with a typewriter. The room was filled with the noise of 50 people, talking to each other, talking on the phone, talking to unhappy defendents seated in chairs. It was rare that a defendant would be handcuffed in the squad. "Listen, pal," the detective would say. "Sit here. I'll take the cuffs off. Make you comfortable. You move for the door, I shoot you. My aim is lousy. I'll try for your legs, but will probably hit you in the head. If I miss, there's 50 guns between me and the elevators. Got it?" No uncuffed defendant has ever fled from the squad.

"Hey, big guy, where you been?"

A giant of a man rose from a desk and, taking the cigar from his mouth with one hand, held out his other huge, meaty hand for a shake. Half the time, he shakes, and half the time he crushes my hand as a joke, the assistant thought, as he waved a greeting.

"Where's Merv?," Rosner asked as he looked around.

"Am I the Polack's keeper?" The detective chewed on his cigar and sat down. "Try the wireroom."

Polish, blacks, Irish, Italians, women, Hispanics—the unit was a composite of the city. If pressed for interpreters during investigations, the squad could produce an officer who spoke Spanish, Hebrew, or Sicilian. The prosecutor crossed the hallway and went into the room with two cells, each with inch thick steel bars, two inches apart, extending from the ceiling to the floor. This was where prisoners were kept when in transit between the Tombs and an assistant's office. The wireroom was at the rear.

Quietly, he entered. Shelves holding tape recorders lined the walls. Tapes spun in several machines, as a half dozen men sat and stood with intent faces and earphones on their heads. A surveillance was under way. He saw Sergeant Woike.

"Hey, Merv," he spoke softly and waved. Woike and the assistant stepped out of the room. The detectives in the squad were divided into teams commanded by sergeants. Each sergeant sought different skills for his unit. For his team, Sgt. Woike had gathered several detectives who relished the paper cases, bank fraud.

"Sorry, Bri." The sergeant held his hand over his head. "We've been up to here on the wires. High priority stuff. Almost the entire squad is working on them overtime and weekends."

The assistant understood. The greatest disincentive to running a wiretap was the manpower involved: three detectives by the recording machine for each tapped line, eight-hour shifts, 24 hours a day, seven days a week.

"How many plants you got up?"

"Three now. And we just got a great overheard. They're talking about a hit this weekend."

"Yeah, who they going to hit?"

"One of our witnesses."

"Is he a good witness?" the assistant asked. They smiled.

"Bri, I know what you want, but I'm all jammed up."

"It's not an in-depth investigation, Merv. No fancy interviews, or any of that. It's a document case, and I can read the documents. But there's a little bit of detective work—some calls, some background checks."

Sgt. Woike took his cigarette from his mouth, and blew a cloud of smoke. "I have a new guy. He's good, I think. First grade detective."

The assistant looked perplexed. Of the city's 30,000 member police force, only 2,000 had been promoted to detective. Once promoted, the detective earned one of three badges. He began with the basic shield, designated third grade. After 15 or 20 years on the job, a few, maybe a dozen each year, were promoted, "made second grade" as cops put it. Most members of the DAOS, among the best detectives in the Department, were two-decade veterans fighting to make second grade. It was a promotion and an honor, and, a hefty raise, as much as $5,000 a year on a detective's $36,000 base pay; $8,000 a year if they went from second grade to first. It meant a couple of hundred dollars a paycheck, and more for the long term. Since an officer's pension was based on his salary for his last year on the force, a promotion prior to retirement translated to more money in each pension check. Sergeant Woike was offering the assistant a first grade detective, an officer who had achieved the highest level of accomplishment in the detective force.

"Merv, I thought with the budget cuts and all the Department stopped promoting to first grade."

"No, we're still making one or so every few years."

The Sergeant paused and puffed on his cigarette. The cellroom, dank and airless, began to stink of smoke.

"You'll like Eddie. He's never done an investigation," Woike added. "At least, not what you're used to."

Let's hear this one, the assistant thought.

"He was on bodyguard detail the last couple of years. The bigwigs. The Commissioner. The usual visitors to New York; Reagan, Carter. Like the Secret Service. And prior to that," Woike grinned. "He was in the Red Squad."

"The Red Squad?" the assistant said in disbelief. He remembered the Red Squad from his college days at Columbia. The Police Department, as did the F.B.I., and, Rosner guessed, every major police force in the country, had special units to infiltrate subversive political organizations. The units had existed for decades, in peacetime and in war.

In the 1960s, political dissent became confused with subversion, and the Red Squad kept track of "politicals," including left-wing students at Columbia University. When first appointed to the office, the assistant had studied one of the squad's most pronounced failures; the infiltration of a radical black group allegedly plotting to dynamite Bloomingdale's and other Manhattan establishments. The result of the infiltration was the 1971 Panther 21 trial, one of the most embarrassing prosecutions in District Attorney Hogan's tenure. After a much publicized multiweek trial, the jurors took 90 minutes to acquit each defendant of all the charges. In the jurors' minds, it was unclear how much, if any, of the discussed violence had been planned by the Panthers, and how much by the group's police infiltrator from the Red Squad.

The juror's confusion over the inclinations of the Panther 21 defendants was resolved by events. Two weeks after the acquittal, Richard Moore, the Panther 21 leader, machine-gunned and crippled for life the two policemen assigned to bodyguard District Attorney Hogan. In one of Rosner's first homicide cases, the killer was another acquitted Panther 21 defendant. It was not a political crime. The killer, a hero of the Left only months before, was a street punk who robbed and killed a university student for drug money. Another of the acquitted defendants murdered a New Jersey state trooper who had stopped her car for a registration check: The killer fled to Cuba, where she still is.

Murder is such a permanent crime, Rosner thought; children who will never see their fathers, and families that will never be. If a defendant deserves to be put in jail, the assistant had learned from the Panther 21 fiasco, make sure you bring a case that will stick.

"I thought the Red Squad had been disbanded years ago," the assistant said to Woike.

"No," Sergeant Woike smiled. "Renamed, and moved. I'll send the detective down to your office. His name is Collins, Eddie Collins."

Collins came to the prosecutor's office that afternoon. He was of moderate height and thin, with short, reddish blond hair. He had a positively boyish appearance. Pinned to the lapel of his jacket was the Big Apple pin worn by City detectives: A red, lacquer button in the shape of an apple with a tiny replica of a detective's shield and the letters "D.E.A." for the Detectives Endowment Association, the detectives' fraternal organization. He smiled as he entered the assistant's office, as he would smile for the period Rosner knew him. Collins carried a pad and pen.

"Interesting case," Collins said. "I've read your memos."

"Have you ever worked a case before?" Rosner asked.

"Not like this."

"Ever testified?"

"Once. When I was walking down the street, I saw some people chasing a robber, and I helped in the chase. I testified in the Grand Jury."

"How'd you make first grade?" the assistant asked.

"You don't know the story? I worked deep undercover for 11 years. I led another life: different name, background, social security number, the works. While I was undercover, the Department gave three sergeant's exams. I couldn't take them, since someone might see me. I couldn't risk blowing my cover. But I knew that I wouldn't be able to take the exams when I went undercover. I had been promised that I could get to take a make-up exam. But no one ever figured that I'd be undercover for 11 years, and it would have been very expensive for the Department to create three make-up exams just for me and the three other guys in my position. So I appealed to the Department, and they agreed to figure out what I would have been promoted to had I been a normal officer allowed to advance in a public manner. It was all polite. No hostility. They concluded that by my fifth year on the force, I would have made second grade detective and, by my tenth year, first grade. So that's what the Department appointed me to, first grade."

Rosner nodded.

"This is my first investigation," Collins said. He chuckled. "Am I going to get a collar?"

"Probably," the assistant said, responding to the officer's question whether an arrest would be made. "It looks like Grambling committed a crime, and Libman's involved, or, at least, someone using his phone number is involved. I can't figure exactly what his role is."

"Maybe we should visit him in Florida." Collins smiled broadly at the thought. "Wish I could bring the kids. The kids love Florida." Noticing Rosner's picture of his family, Collins asked, "How old is your son?"

"One and a half. And yours?"

"Eddie is almost six, and Corey's three and a half."

Collins took out his wallet and showed pictures of his son and daughter to Rosner.

"They're why I'm here. You know I did bodyguard work, don't you? It's an interesting assignment. You work with Secret Service to protect dignitaries when they're in town."

"Who'd you bodyguard?"

"The Presidents, Reagan and Carter. I protected Margaret Thacher when she came in for a United Nations meeting, and also Sadat and Begin. It's amazing, but these people were all real gentlemen and ladies. You'd not necessarily expect it, what with their status and all, but they always were very polite to me and the others on the guard detail. Got quite a good autograph collection, too."

Great so far, Rosner was thinking, as he sized up Collins as a witness. Family man, and he's been entrusted with the lives of the world's leaders."

"Did you ask to be reassigned?"

"Yeah. Bodyguarding is a detail for young guys. But once you get married and start having kids." He tapped the wallet with the photos of his children. "Well, all of a sudden you got something more to live for. You start to hesitate about whether you're willing to take a bullet meant for the President. Once you start thinking like that, you're no good anymore for the people you're guarding. I realized this when Eddie was growing up."

"Didn't you stay and bodyguard the Police Commissioner?" the assistant asked.

"Oh, that," Collins laughed. "Well, that was more being a jogging companion than anything else. Commissioner McGuire liked to run in the evening along the East Side Drive. Not the safest neighborhood late at night. So the Commissioner needed a bodyguard who could jog with him. I keep in pretty good shape—at the local school, I teach kids, five- and six-year olds, how to swim—so the Commissioner asked for me.

"He didn't carry his own gun. He was a real stickler about that. He's a tough kid from the South Bronx, and he figured he could just duke it out if there was a problem. So I carried the gun. You know what it's like jogging with a 36 on your waist? But McGuire was fanatical about running, and I was his bodyguard."

"So, detective, what do you think we do next?"

"Talk to Libman in Florida," Collins replied without hesitation.

It was the logical step, which the prosecutor had been avoiding. "Okay, we drive down in your car."

Collins left. A few minutes later, John Moscow entered. In his mid-30s and broad chested, Moscow was the most experienced trial attorney in the Frauds Bureau. He had obtained convictions in some of the most difficult homicide and business fraud cases ever prosecuted by the Office.

"Collins working the Grambling case?" Moscow sat down. "Best witness you can find. Looks like an altar boy. He could break into a bank, steal everything in sight, and a jury would look at his smile and acquit him."

"He also teaches swimming to children," Rosner added.

Although the smile was still on Moscow's face, his voice became serious. "Make sure he does something that makes you use him as a witness. The jury will love him, and the goodwill will rub off on your case."

It was time to update Kindler on the case, and make a request which the assistant dreaded. In the 1960s, the salaries of young assistant district attorneys were not much less than those of their classmates who had gone to Wall Street law firms. With the stock market boom that decade, however, the pay scale at Wall Street firms broke loose, and the District Attorney's Office never came close to catching up. Then came the fiscal crisis of 1975 and the Office entered a permanent war of attrition between necessary costs and tight money.

Though unwritten, the rules of permissible office expenses were known. If a killer fled the jurisdiction, the Office would pay to extradite him from anywhere in the world: Two-and-a-half tickets, two for the detectives picking up the prisoner, and a one-way return for the killer. Rapists and armed robbers justified a more limited expenditure: If arrested after fleeing from New York, they would be brought back from locations east of the Mississippi. As to burglars and white-collar criminals, an assistant could forget it. The cost of extradition was too prohibitive. Though, in several instances of major fraud, including the embezzler extradited from London, the Office had allowed the victim to pay the expense of returning the culprit to New York to be tried. Kindler's job was to evaluate proposed expenses. His receptivity to such requests was reflected in his nickname, which also was that of his predecessor—"Dr. No." It was a thankless task.

Rosner entered the Executive Assistant's office. "How's the case going?" Kindler asked. The assistant explained, and Kindler focused immediately on the open question.

"Who's this guy Libman?"

"Don't know, Jim. His name is on documents, and his signature, maybe. His phone number is used in Florida. He's either an accomplice, or someone who's being set up, like Wilkis."

"You should talk to him." Kindler drew on his cigar. "Anyone given him a call?"

"Not yet. He's not the kind of guy I'd want to talk to over the phone. Whether he's a dupe or an accomplice is going to be a judgment call. You're going to want to look at the guy while he's talking. If I heard Wilkis' story over the phone, instead of seeing him, it would have been unbelievable, but in person . . ."

Rosner's voice trailed off, as Kindler nodded in agreement.

"Libman ever visit New York?" Kindler asked.

"Don't know. I could find that out. But if we're going to make a decision on whether to charge him, we got to see him. What we do with him is the only issue holding up the indictment."

"Jesus, Brian," Kindler smiled. "How come you always get the cases that take you to nice places like Florida. Okay, you and Collins, one night, coach. You going to need a car? Yeah, probably. Don't rent a Cadillac. But before you make these plans, call Libman. Make sure he'll be willing to talk to you, and that he's not coming up to New York soon. If you can, see him here."

"Thanks, Jim." Rosner left the room before Kindler could change his mind. Two round-trip coach tickets, a hotel, meal money: it could probably all come to about $1,000, enough to bring a killer back from Florida, or pay two weeks salary to a first-year assistant.

The prosecutor raced to the squad to catch Collins before he left for the day. He found the detective by the candy machine. He had put a bag of M&M's in his jacket pocket and was pushing the button to buy another.

"Hi, Brian. For the kids. I've spoiled them. They expect their Dad to bring a treat home everyday."

"Listen, Eddie, I think the Office is willing to send us to Miami to talk to Libman. Give him a call, see if he's willing to speak with us. Don't say we're coming down. Let's see if he's going to be up here any time soon. Real low-key."

"Should I tape the call?"

Rosner thought for a moment.

"Yeah. Why not."

The prosecutor returned to his office, and in a half hour was joined by Collins, who was carrying a tape recorder. The assistant listened to the tape. Collins sounded like a lost boy asking for directions.

"I'm doing an investigation into John's problems with the Bank of Montreal," he told Libman, who knew of the problems and, of course, volunteered to help. "Would you have a chance to look over some letters with me when you're next in New York?"

"Sure," Libman replied. "I come up every couple of weeks."

"Any chance that you'll be in New York in the next few days?"

"No," Libman replied. "I have no traveling plans until next week, but that's not to New York."

"Well, we might be in Florida on another investigation in the near future. Would you be willing to see us?"

"Yes. Just give me a call," Libman answered.

Collins turned the machine off.

"Nice job, Eddie. Do you think he's really willing to talk to us?"

"I don't think he's about to come in to the office next time he's in New York, but he wasn't adverse to me on the phone. You can hear it. He sounded a little stiff, but not surprised that he was getting this call. He certainly didn't sound like a guy who thinks he's involved in a crime."

"Maybe he's not. That's why we have to talk to him." The assistant looked at his watch. It was after 7:00 P.M. What if we fly down and Libman doesn't let us in the door, Rosner thought. I'll never get another expenditure approved in the case.

"No use letting him forget who we are, Eddie," the assistant said. "Book us on tomorrow morning's first plane to Miami."

Rosner and Collins met early the next morning at LaGuardia, and worked out their strategy on the plane to Miami.

"Low-key," the prosecutor was talking out loud. "Let's start with the innocuous documents signed by Libman—the Cumberland Village promise to buy Grambling's stock, the consent assigning the promise, the guarantee. We'll work our way to the December 28 call to 'Corcoran.' "

As the assistant spoke, Collins opened a package of clear plastic envelopes he had purchased the previous day at Woolworth's.

"These papers must have been handled by a hundred people," Collins said as he slipped an envelope over each of the documents thought to be signed by Libman. "All the fingerprints are probably smeared off, but let's let Libman think we're going to do a fingerprint check. It might get him to tell the truth."

Continuing to plan their strategy, the assistant and detective agreed that before meeting Libman, they would try to count the number of people in the office, and walk by as many desks as possible to see whose phones could take a call on line 7536.

"Should one of us take notes?" Collins asked.

"I'm not sure, Eddie. I don't know about you, but if I take notes, either the notes are bad and my questions are good, or vice versa. I'd just as soon not."

"Think it might spook Libman?"

"It wouldn't be in keeping with the casual front we'll be putting on. Let's just skip notes. How's your memory?"

"Pretty good. On my old assignment, the one before body-guarding, I had strict orders not to take any notes at the location where I was planted, or even on the subway ride home. All my notes were written in my apartment probably two hours after leaving the location. I'm used to taking my notes afterwards."

It was the most detail that Collins would ever mention about his undercover work.

They arrived in Miami at 11:00 A.M. and drove their rented car to Libman's North Miami address. It was a modern multi-story apartment building on the beach. A tawny color, the building looked as if it was made of sand and rocks.

"Let's pull into that place," Rosner said, pointing to a motel. "We'll call from there."

"What a racket," Collins said as they walked to the motel lobby. The morning quiet was broken by the jackhammers and bulldozers of a work crew. Collins tried to make the call. The phone rang and rang. There was no answer. Did he skip, Collins wondered.

"Don't bother," a woman wearing an apron said as, pushing a tray, she hurried by. Motioning with her head to the street, "They just cut the phone cable. All the lines are out."

"Thank you, ma'am," Eddie smiled beautifically, as the woman, mouthing a "You're most welcome," disappeared through revolving doors.

"Well, at least we're not going to be interrupted by any phone calls," Rosner shrugged. The two drove to Libman's building and entered the lobby. "Condos," Collins said. The directory indicated that several units were being used for offices. They took the elevator to Libman's sixth floor apartment and buzzed the door labeled "Southern Management."

An attractive, slender woman in her 30s opened the door. She saw two men wearing suits. One wore a button in the shape of a red apple pinned to his lapel.

"Can I help you?"

"Yes, we're here to see Bob Libman."

"Is he expecting you?"

"Yes, I'm Assistant District Attorney Rosner, and this is Detective Collins. We're from New York."

"Wait a moment. I'll tell him you're here."

She walked across a reception area and went through an open door into an office. Uninvited, the assistant and detective followed. They craned their necks to glance at the phone numbers on the reception desk and to count the offices. Going to the room the woman had entered, they walked in as she was finishing her sentence, ". . . and a detective from New York."

A man in his 50s rose from behind a desk. Medium height with a tough, hardened face, he wore a short-sleeved shirt, open to his hair-covered midchest. A chain hung around his neck. He had a phone receiver in his left hand. On the wall behind him were wood-framed photographs of grown children and an older woman, his wife.

He looked flabbergasted.

Rosner spoke as he extended his hand for a handshake.

"We were in the neighborhood, Mr. Libman," the assistant said. "So we thought we'd drop in."

CHAPTER 14

LIBMAN CAN'T REMEMBER

"I was just trying to make a call," Libman said. He pushed several buttons on his phone console. "But the phone's dead. Just went out. No more than . . . 10 minutes ago."

Rosner smiled.

Libman smiled.

Good beginning, the assistant thought as he glanced at Collins. Libman thinks we cut the phone wires.

"You gentlemen are in luck," Libman said as he hung up the phone. "When I'm not in West Virginia running the coal mine, I'm here spending most of my time on the phone. Cecilia—gentlemen, this is Cecilia Rudd, my secretary and assistant—get our friends some drinks."

Cecilia, the woman who had answered the door, asked the assistant and the detective what they wanted.

"Not while I'm on duty," Collins said with a chuckle.

"It's seltzer or coke," she replied smoothly.

"Get one for the boy," Collins said, as he motioned to a 10-year old peering around the doorway. It was Cecilia's son, out sick from school and spending the day with his mom.

As Cecilia left, Libman asked, "What can I do for you gentlemen?"

"We're here about John Grambling, and the loan he obtained from the Bank of Montreal," the assistant began.

"Awful situation. I told John to be careful with the Canadian bankers. John's problem is that he was borrowing long and short from the Canadians. They're much less forgiving than American bankers when short-term debt is unpaid when due." Libman shook his head from side to side with a sorrowful look on his face. "I warned John not to deal with the Canadians."

"That's the loan that brought us here," Rosner said. "Some documents were submitted to the bank that look like they have your signature."

"I've heard about these."

"Eddie, do you have the December 3 letter agreement and the consent?"

The assistant and the detective sat in chairs in front of Libman's desk. Libman's phone console was to his right, next to a recording machine. Collins approached the desk and neatly placed the letter and consent in front of Libman. Collins lingered to glance at the numbers on the phone lines—7523, 7524, 7525, 7536. He sat down. Rosner had read the numbers when he had leaned across the desk to shake Libman's hand.

"The December 3 letter, that's the one on Cumberland stationery," Rosner continued. "It's a promise by Cumberland Village Mining to buy Grambling's Cumberland stock for $8.5 million, and the consent assigns that promise to the bank. Both appear to be signed Robert Libman. Are they your signatures?"

Libman scrutinized the letter and consent, each encased in a clear plastic envelope.

"I've never seen either of these before," he said. "It sure looks like my signature though."

"Have you ever signed blank stationery for John?" Collins asked.

"No, I wouldn't do that ever, certainly not on the stationery of Cumberland. The mine is owned by several prominent Nashville businessmen, proper, religious gentlemen, public figures. I would never do anything to hurt the company."

Libman paused. He seemed to be deep in thought. Then he banged his hand on his desk and spoke with animation.

"Wait a minute. About six months ago, John asked me to sign some Cumberland Village stationery for him. I didn't do it. I wouldn't even give him the stationery."

"Any way he could have gotten the stationery?" Collins asked.

"It's only available here and the mine in West Virginia. John's here frequently, but never at the mine." He called out, "Cecilia, could you come in?"

Libman whispered to his visitors, "She knows my signature better than anyone in the world.

Cecilia went to Libman's desk.

"Cecilia, look at these. Are they my signature?"

She looked down at the documents.

"They appear to be your signature," she said. Rosner and Collins looked at each other and smirked. Cecilia sensed that she had said something wrong.

"But it's not my typing," she continued. "The typeface is different from the machine I use, or any of our machines. I did not type these," she said emphatically. "And I do all of Mr. Libman's typing."

Libman sighed with relief.

"Cecilia, remember the time John asked me to sign some Cumberland Village stationery for him in blank, and I said I wouldn't do it."

Cecilia stared blankly at Libman. She did not want to mess up her cue as she had with the signatures. What answer does he want, she thought.

Reddening, and slowly nodding his head up and down, Libman repeated the words slowly, as if speaking to a child.

"Remember, Cecilia, John asked for stationery. You were here in the room. I said I would not do it."

"Yes," Cecilia said flatly. "I remember. It was awhile ago."

Her last sentence ended with the raised inflection of a question.

"Six months," Libman said. He stared at her and raised his eyebrows.

"Yes, summertime," Cecilia replied with false conviction.

Rosner and Collins peeked at each other. They were covering their mouths to hide their smiles. Get a good look, Eddie, the assistant thought. I'm going to have you describe this scene for the jurors: A secretary's loyalty to the boss.

"You can go Cecilia. Thank you," Libman said.

Libman became agitated.

"I can't understand why you two were so interested in these documents. They're meaningless. No company could commit itself to such a purchase without a resolution from the Board of Directors, and any banker stupid enough to accept this," he passed his hand over the December 3 Cumberland Village letter, "is guilty of gross negligence, and should be fired. You have a case of incompetent bankers using your Office to collect a debt, and cover up their stupidity."

Libman's face was flushed, and his comments had been spoken with sincerity.

"You're being used," he continued. "John has a loan dispute, and you're a lever that some dumb bankers are using to gain an advantage in the civil settlement."

This guy's in the wrong moral universe, Rosner thought. I'd better set him straight, firmly but softly enough to keep the dialogue going. Does he really think it's not a crime to rip off a bank?

"Bob, we were going to get to that point ourselves," Rosner said. "Many people misperceive our Office as a collection agency when it does a bank case. You could not be more wrong. Civil resolutions are not our concern. We won't obstruct the Bank of Montreal or any other victim if it tries to get its money back. But if the Bank of Montreal thinks we're a collection agency, they're in for a shock. Detective Collins and I are investigating a crime, a swindle by forgeries and false documents. We take those crimes seriously in New York, and we prosecute them in the name of the People of the State of New York. Not the bank, but the People. This investigation will probably be presented to a grand jury, and, if people are indicted and convicted, they're going to jail. This has nothing to do with civil resolutions."

The assistant's monologue sobered Libman.

"Let's leave these documents," Rosner said. "Could you tell us a little background about how you came to know Grambling?"

"I got to know John about two years ago when he bought his shares in Cumberland. I'm the manager for the mine."

"Is it a real mine?" Collins asked.

Libman laughed.

"Sure. I spend half the week in Mingo County, West Virginia, running the mine. You ever been to Mingo County? It's a union area, and we're a nonunion mine. Sometimes it's too dangerous to drive to the mine, so we take a helicopter in—flak jackets, automatic rifles for protection—and we still get shot at from half a dozen little hollows in the mountains.

"When John wanted to buy the Husky unit, I warned him not to do it. The price was too high. But he's a Texan and he wanted to be like the big boys back home. Anyway, John asked for my help. I have a background in marketing. I made some trips out West with him, and he asked me to operate the service station part of the business. It's a solid part of the assets. With good management, it could be a winner."

"Any talk of compensation?" Rosner asked.

"John said that he'd 'take care of me,' and we left it at that. I think I was going to be an officer of the company, but we never talked a title or compensation."

"Did you have anything to do with the Bank of Montreal loan?" the assistant asked.

"John wanted me to talk to the Canadians, and I did."

The prosecutor glanced at Collins. "Eddie do you . . . ?" Collins looked through the files and took out the guarantee. He handed it to Libman.

"Oh that. Yes, the bank wanted a guarantee from a reputable third party, so I gave them one. It's not worth much," Libman said nonchalantly. "I don't have any assets. I was sued a couple of years ago."

Rosner knew of the lawsuit. Its details were stored in the Leviticus computer.

"So I put all I owned in my wife's name. I'm judgment proof. But the bank wanted a guarantee, so I gave one."

"So this is your signature on the guarantee?" the assistant asked.

"Yes. It was witnessed by Cecilia and notarized by one of the notaries on the second floor of this building."

"But the December 3 Cumberland letter . . .?"

"Sorry, can't help you. It sure looks like my signature, but it's not. I would never have signed a letter committing Cumberland without approval from the Board of Directors."

A tactic that sometimes worked with witnesses was to jumble the order of the questions, to go back and forth between topics to see if the answers were consistent.

"Have you ever been fingerprinted?" the prosecutor asked.

Libman was surprised.

"Years ago, when I worked in the Miami hotel business. I was fingerprinted by the state. All employees were." Libman picked up the December 3 letter and began to remove it from the plastic envelope. "What does fingerprinting have to do with this?"

"Don't touch that," the assistant and Collins shouted in unison as they rose from their seats. "Let's not put your fingerprints on it now," Rosner explained. "Mr. Libman, if we went to the state to get your fingerprints, and compared them to the prints lifted from that letter, are we going to find your prints?"

Libman fingered the plastic envelope and thought for a moment.

"What if you did. My stationery's lying around the office. Grambling could have taken it."

"After you touched it?" the assistant asked.

"If it was on a desk, I could have touched it." Libman thought for a few moments. "Maybe for some business reason I did sign a sheet in blank."

"We went through that," Rosner reminded Libman.

"Now I can't recall if I did or didn't sign something in blank for John. But I can see where you're heading."

"Well, let's get to something else," the assistant continued. "The guarantee. Did you submit a balance sheet to the Bank of Montreal?"

"Did I? Absolutely not. I never submitted a balance sheet. I never did."

Libman's emphasis of the word "I" spoke the proverbial volumes.

"Did John?" Rosner asked.

"I don't know. But I wouldn't be surprised if you found that there was a balance sheet of mine floating around."

"There is," the assistant said. "Didn't you discuss your balance sheet with bankers from the Bank of Montreal?"

◄ John A. Grambling, Jr.,
leaving the courtroom after
his arraignment on the first
indictment for conspiracy
and larceny.
(N.Y. Daily News Photo)

▲ The R.M.T. refinery in Cody, Wyoming — part of the $100 million
purchase which brought Grambling to the Bank of Montreal.

▲ Robert H. Libman, Grambling's "multimillionaire" partner, later indicted and convicted

▲ Libman's balance sheet, presented to and accepted by various banks (marked as a People's Exhibit for Grambling's sentencing). (©Alan S. Orling)

▲ The Cumberland Village Mining stock (purportedly worth $8.5 million), the additional collateral for the Bank of Montreal $7.5 million personal loan. (©Alan S. Orling)

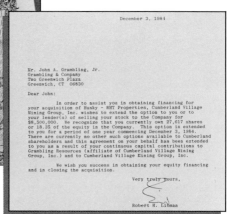

▲ The stock purchase agreement, later assigned to the Bank of Montreal, by which the Cumberland Village Mining Group agreed to purchase Grambling's mining stock for $8.5 million. (©Alan S. Orling)

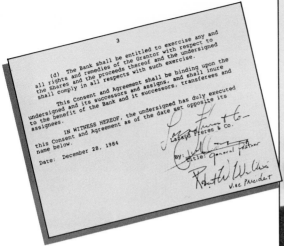

▲ The Lazard Freres Consent assigning the $8.2 million of Dr Pepper stock to the Bank of Montreal. Without the Consent, the $7.5 million personal loan would not have been made. (©Alan S. Orling)

▲ James Busuttil, counsel to the Bank of Montreal. The consent was "spurious," Lazard Freres counsel wrote to Busuttil. "Manifestly, we have no intention of complying with its terms." (©Alan S. Orling)

▲ Scott Hean, Bank of Montreal. Hean gathered his subordinates into a conference room and said, "Musketeers, we're staying here until we find our money."

▲ Blair Mullin, Bank of Montreal. As Hopkyns and Hean listened, Mullin dialed the number Hopkyns had used to reach Corcoran. Hean asked, "Is Mr. Libman in?" (©Adonis Photo Studio Ltd.)

◄ Bruce Rockwell, Chairman, Colorado National Bank of Denver. An energy company headquartered in Denver seemed a natural recipient for a $6 million loan from the bank. *(Berkeley Lainson)*

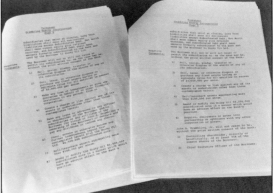

▲ The Bank of Montreal/Husky Oil Term Sheet. The provisions of the Term Sheet presented to Colorado National Bank of Denver (the forgery on the right) permitted repayment of the Colorado National $6 million loan. The provisions of the real Term Sheet (on the left) did not. *(©Alan S. Orling)*

▲ Jonathan Greenblatt, counsel to the Bank of Montreal. He presented the case to the Manhattan District Attorney's Office. *(©Alan S. Orling)*

▲ The Lazard Freres & Co. Specimen Signature Book. Greenblatt did not have to be a handwriting expert to recognize that Peter Corcoran had not signed the Consent. *(©Alan S. Orling)*

◄ Robert M. Morgenthau, District Attorney of New York County. His Office acted quickly to investigate the Bank of Montreal's complaint of a fraud.

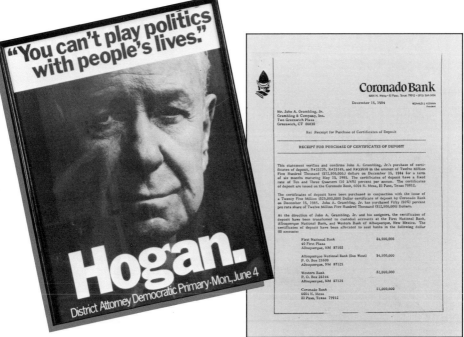

▲ Frank S. Hogan, the District Attorney of New York County, 1941-1973. The last campaign poster and the credo for the Office. (©Alan S. Orling)

▲ The forged Coronado Bank receipt for $12.5 million of CDs. Even as his attorneys negotiated with the District Attorney's Office, Grambling continued with his crimes. (©Alan S. Orling)

▲ James Kindler, Executive
Assistant District Attorney.
His judgment was among the
most respected in the Office;
he authorized the nationwide
Grambling investigation.
(Jim Sousa, N.Y.C. D.A.O.)

▲ Peter Benitez, Chief of the Frauds
Bureau, later a judge of the criminal
court. A sentence of less than state
prison, he insisted, would send a
message that society did not strongly
disapprove of white-collar crime.
(©Alan S. Orling)

▲ Detective Edward Collins. He had
worked deep undercover and was
a bodyguard for the presidents.
This was his first white-collar
investigation.

▲ John Moscow, Assistant District
Attorney, later Frauds Bureau Chief.
He said of Grambling, "Bankers
thought he was sort of slow. But he
showed them. He took their money,
and he took their jobs."
(Jim Sousa, N.Y.C. D.A.O.)

◄ Hillel Bodek, the psychiatric social worker retained by the People. He submitted to Judge Cahn a 353-page psychiatric review, the most comprehensive analysis of the white-collar criminal mind ever presented to a judge at Hogan Place. (©Alan S. Orling)

▲ A Corrections Department bus, used to transport prisoners from the courthouse to Rikers' Island, the New York City penitentiary. (©Alan S. Orling)

▲ The 12th Floor Bridge (from the outside), the passageway by which prisoners are brought from The Tombs to the Courthouse. (©Alan S. Orling)

▲ The interior of the 12th Floor Bridge. "Go man, go!" the prisoners shouted as the corrections officer pulled Grambling away from the cells and toward the elevators. (©Alan S. Orling)

▲ Brian Rosner, Assistant District Attorney, appearing in court in one of his trials. His explanation of Grambling: "Grabbing at money and power over other people's lives was his definition of self."

▲ Trish Grambling, the defendant's wife. As much a victim as any of the bankers, she urged the court to protect her sons from the harmful influence of their natural father.

▲ Herman Cahn, Acting Justice, New York State Supreme Court. "I hope the message is clear to other people in this city, in this state, indeed in this country," he said in imposing a twenty-year sentence. "People who commit white-collar crimes are subject to incarceration in the same way and in the same places as other people are." (©Alan S. Orling)

"No, they took the guarantee without speaking to me," Libman insisted. "That shows you how competent they are."

Having spoken to Miller earlier that week, the assistant knew that Miller and Price had met Libman in Miami. Didn't they talk about the balance sheet, Rosner thought.

"Do you remember meeting Miller and Price from Husky?" he asked Libman.

"Yes, they flew down. We met in this office, and lunched in the Jockey Club."

"Did you talk finances with them?"

"Not my own. We talked about how I thought I could help John and what I could do for Husky."

"Did you give them or talk with them about your balance sheet?"

"No, absolutely not," Libman said firmly.

That's not what Miller said, the prosecutor thought. They talked at length about the balance sheet. It was the reason Husky accepted Libman's guarantee on the loan to Grambling.

Rosner had heard enough about the balance sheet. He moved to the critical subject.

"Mr. Libman, we're concerned about a call that came to your phone on December 28. The call came in on (305) 940-7536."

"That's not one of my numbers," Libman replied. With a quizzical look on his face, Libman looked at his phone console. The assistant and Collins rose, and leaned over Libman's desk.

Collins pointed to the button labeled "7536."

"It's the one on the end."

"Oh, that one," Libman replied. "I never use it."

Reseated, Rosner said, "Let's see who was here on December 28 who might have used that line."

"December 28? That's a Friday, wasn't it?" Libman looked at a desk calendar. He called Cecilia into the room. "We were on our holiday schedule in late December. That means we were closing the office at noon."

"Or that we were at least leaving by 2:00 P.M., that's what Mr. Libman means by a noon closing," Cecilia added with a soft laugh.

"Who could have been here with access to the phone?" Rosner asked. "Anyone rent office space?"

"We rented office space to Signet Securities. That was John's brokerage company, and a person named Padykula sat at the Signet desk. He was here off and on in December. He was spending time at the Mayo Clinic." Libman paused and a somber look came over his face. "Getting chemotherapy."

"Is he here now?"

"No, Signet moved out in January."

"Is Padykula around?" Rosner asked.

Libman shook his head slowly.

"Cancer?" the assistant asked.

"Yes," said Libman. "Sad."

The best defense in the world, Rosner thought. The dead man did it.

"Was anyone else here?" Collins asked.

"There was a person named Steve, a real estate wholesaler that we rented space to. But he's gone, too," Libman said.

The assistant excused himself, as Collins and Libman continued the conversation about who had access to the office. Rosner had forgotten the exact time of the "Corcoran" phone call, and, when the prosecutor looked through his notes, he realized that he had not brought the Bank of Montreal telephone records. In light of Cecilia's remark that she and Libman had been in the office until 2:00 P.M., it was important to know whether the call came in before or after that time. Cecilia showed him to a phone, and he called Greenblatt at Shearman & Sterling in Manhattan.

"Hello, is Jon in? This is A.D.A. Rosner."

"No, he's at a deposition right now," Greenblatt's secretary said. "Can I help you?"

"Maybe." The prosecutor asked Greenblatt's secretary to locate the Bank of Montreal phone information.

"Well, with what's happening in this case . . . the phone calls . . . let me ask Mr. Greenblatt."

After several minutes, she came back to the phone. "Hello? Mr. Greenblatt said that we don't know who you really are, so we can't give you the information."

"Get that son-of-a-bitch to the phone."

"But," the secretary continued in her even tone of voice, "Mr. Greenblatt said that, if you are the assistant, you would know the name of a case he and you worked on several years ago, and that, if you knew the name, I could give you the information."

"Give me a minute," the assistant said. "He used the money to buy gold coins. Shipped them to a post office box. Fat guy. Yeah, Hagen, it was. Ronald Hagen."

"Oh, thank goodness, Mr. Rosner. I thought it was your voice, but you can't trust callers anymore. I have the information here. The call was made at 11:06 A.M., Calgary time. It lasted for six-and-a-half minutes."

The prosecutor returned to Libman's room, where Libman and Collins were still talking about who rented office space.

"We're interested in a call that came in at 1:06 P.M., Miami time," Rosner said. "It was Calgary to Miami. Six minutes. The voice at this end—the 7536 extension—said that he was an investment banker with Lazard Freres, a New York brokerage house. Would you have been here at 1:06 P.M.?"

Libman became animated, and he began to talk with his finger raised in the air.

"I didn't take that call, and I don't know who could have. But I'll tell you, I'm going to find out. I'll get to the bottom of this."

Libman stopped. He looked as if he had just recalled something. "Wait a minute. We had problems with a lock in December. And some things were missing, from the office. Paper cups, I think. Maybe someone broke in."

"To use your phone?" Collins asked in a deadpan. "Did you report the break-in to the police?"

"No, I don't think so," Libman said in a quieter voice. "I didn't think much of it. Maybe Cecilia did."

Libman motioned as if to call for her.

"Don't call her," Rosner said. He leaned forward in his chair. "Listen, Bob, people do things for friends, things to help them out in a jam. In hindsight, it might look kind of stupid, what's done that is, but it's human nature to help a pal. I understand. Eddie understands. And there's no point denying it."

Rosner took a deep breath.

"I wonder, to help John, did you ever impersonate anyone, make believe you were someone else?"

Libman pursed his lips.

"Yes, a couple of times."

"Who did you say you were?" the assistant asked gently.

"Bankers, brokers. Mostly bankers."

"How many times?"

"Six, maybe. I haven't done it for awhile."

"Over the phone?"

Libman nodded.

"How would the call be set up?" Rosner asked.

"John would call me. He would tell me who would be calling, and who I was supposed to be. I'd give him the fourth extension as the number that he should have me called at—that was the 7536 number we looked at. I would ask John to have the calls come in around lunch time when Cecilia was out. She wasn't involved in any of this. She hates John. She won't even speak to him on the phone. He said something to her once."

"Do you remember any of the impersonations you did?" Rosner asked.

"Yes, I talked to some banker in Salt Lake City, some lawyers in Detroit. In a call to a bank, I said that I was a Mr. Keenan. But I can't recall the details of the calls."

Libman raised his hands as if in self-defense.

"Don't get me wrong. I never helped John close a deal. I did the calls out of friendship, but I always turned the conversations to matters that caused the deals to fall through. I made sure I said something to alert the banker or business person not to go ahead. I remember talking to a Conover from Salt Lake. What I said killed the deal. You check on the calls, and you'll find that, because of a problem I raised, the deal died."

Libman shook his head sadly.

"They might say I pushed the deals if you talk to the bankers now. But they're just covering their mistakes."

"Did anyone else make these calls for John?" Collins asked.

"Yes. He mentioned other people. But I don't know who they are, or how many times others made calls."

"About this December 28 call," Rosner said. "Someone from this number got on the phone and said he was Peter Corcoran, a partner at Lazard Freres in New York. You've heard of Lazard?"

Libman nodded.

"He spoke for a little over six minutes according to the phone records," the assistant continued. "Bob, was that you?"

Libman held his hands palms up in a sign of futility.

"Brian, I don't remember."

"Bob, I can see you saying 'no' or 'yes,' but how can you not remember?"

Libman shrugged.

"I just can't."

"Bob, that's ridiculous."

"Brian, if I say I can't remember, how are you ever going to pin anything on me?"

Libman smiled triumphantly.

"Okay, Bob, let's play a game. Let's play that it's a trial and I'm cross-examining you.

"Mr. Libman," the assistant began in a bass voice, "impersonating a partner from Lazard Freres is not something you do every day, is it?"

Libman nodded.

"To impersonate such a partner would be a rare event, would it not?"

Libman nodded again.

"Rare and memorable, correct?"

Libman shook his head.

"And are you telling this jury that you cannot remember such a rare and memorable event, which occurred less than, what the heck was it," the assistant said in a normal tone. "Oh yeah," returning to the deep octave, "which occurred less than three months ago?"

Libman smiled.

"You're pretty good. I see the point, Brian."

"You say you can't remember, Bob," the assistant said. "If that's your position at trial, I'm going to crucify you. And I'm not even a good cross-examiner."

"You probably won't believe this, Brian, but I'm an honest person. I really can't remember. But if you give me immunity, I'll testify truthfully."

"That you can't remember?" Rosner asked incredulously.

"Give me immunity and I'll testify truthfully," Libman said calmly.

The assistant pointed at Libman. "There's a problem giving you immunity. I give you immunity, and then Grambling's defense becomes that you're the main man. I ain't much good at cross-examination, but Grambling has this lawyer, Barry Kingham, former federal prosecutor. He's going to eat you alive at trial. These are bad circumstances for me, Bob. I got to get something substantial in return for giving you immunity."

Libman nodded, and spoke slowly.

"I've met Kingham and Kelly, John's other lawyer. You know that Colorado National attached one of John's bank accounts in New York? John wanted me to sign a document that the money was really mine so the attachment could be vacated. Kingham and Kelly gave me the document. I wouldn't sign it. I told them, 'You tell me that the money attached is mine, then I'll sign it.' I know John's attorneys. In fact, I've been helping them get the loan to solve this whole problem."

Libman motioned to his phone.

"We've had long talks about what we're going to do."

Libman saw the look of surprise on the faces of Rosner and Collins.

"Oh, Barry thinks it's all legitimate, so does Joe. But I can tell what John's trying to do."

Libman leaned back in his chair, and thought for several seconds.

"No, I don't think that John or his attorneys would be able to touch me at trial."

"Do you use a special attachment?" Collins asked. "Or do you just tape right from the phone?"

"Right from the phone," Libman said. Turning in his chair, he opened a drawer in the wall unit behind him. "See for yourself."

The drawer contained what appeared to be at least 20 cassette tapes.

"Immunity," Libman began.

"And the tapes are ours," Collins finished.

"I'm from Missouri," Rosner said. "How do I know there's anything good on those tapes. You lay people misunderstand what it takes to convict at trial. You can have a conversation you think is devastating, but when you listen closely, there's holes that a guy can drive a defense through. Not that I'm doubting you think the tapes are good, Bob. But you don't understand the quality I need."

Libman took the bait. He picked up several tapes and read their labels.

"This is a good one. It's about what John's trying to do now."

"Would he always give you your instructions by phone?" Collins asked.

"No," Libman said as he put the cassette in the machine. "He usually gave his instructions by letter. Here, listen to this."

The tape began with Libman's voice answering the phone. "Hello," he said, "what's up, John?" Then there was silence. Then Libman's voice asked that something be repeated. Then silence. Then Libman's voice was speaking again, asking a question about a loan. The tape had recorded only one side of the conversation.

Libman reddened. He fumbled with the machine.

"Maybe I have something turned on wrong."

"No, you just weren't picking up the other side." Collins commented. "I could give you a lesson on how to do this right."

"This was a good call," Libman said. "It was from two days ago. John wanted me to do something with a bank. Had to do with CD's. If you listen to what I'm saying, you can tell what he must be saying, and . . ."

Rosner cut him off.

"No good, Bob. Even crystal clear tapes can be turned on their heads by good defense counsel. And this, well, this tape is just meaningless. Sorry, I can't make a . . . ."

"I understand," Libman interrupted. He was embarrassed. "Okay, you don't believe me. I'm going to convince you. I said John wrote letters."

Libman opened a desk draw and took out a folder three inches thick with papers.

"How would you like to get your hands on this?"

"No disrespect, Bob," Collins said. "But are the letters as good as the tape?"

"See for yourself." Libman took the top pages off the file and held them out. Rosner seized the document.

Why the heck didn't I ever take a speedreading course, he thought. Mississippi bank. CDs. Other banks. Texas and New Mexico. Four pages. Bunch of zeros. In the millions.

It's a commitment letter for a loan to close in a few days, Rosner realized.

"Only a glance." Libman snatched the letter out of the assistant's hands.

"It would be easier for us to make a decision on immunity if you let us copy that," the prosecutor said calmly, his fingers smarting.

Libman shook his head from side to side.

"Immunity," Libman insisted.

He restored the letter to the folder, and the folder to the drawer.

It was past 5:00 P.M. "Lucky the phones were out," Libman said as he escorted the assistant and Collins to the door. "Otherwise, we wouldn't have had a chance to speak."

Rosner and Collins talked as soon as they were out of the building.

"We got an answer to our basic question, Eddie. Is Libman a bystander or an accomplice."

"That's for sure," Collins laughed. "By the way, is he commiting a Florida state crime by taping interstate calls?"

"I hadn't thought of it, but he probably is."

"Can we get a search warrant for the tapes and letters?"

"Yeah, but it would be a mess," Rosner explained. They got into their car. "We'd have to get a warrant through the locals, the Dade County prosecutors. They're probably gone for the day now, and we're leaving tomorrow. We could try to get one tomorrow, but we might not make it before the weekend. And I'm not sure if we want one. Assuming there's anything on the tapes, Libman made it sound as if there's plenty of conversa-

tions with Kingham and Kelly, and who knows what other attorneys. The tapes are probably saturated with attorney-client
privileged materials that we're not entitled to hear. The letters
too. Once they're seized, there's a royal legal battle to decide
what we can hear and read, and what we can't. I've been down
that road before. We'll be tied up in court proceedings for two
years. And I'm not sure it's worth it. We got enough paper to
convict these guys. Besides, Libman's probably already hid the
folder and tapes, so we wouldn't seize anything with a warrant.
Let's just get our notes together."

"You going to give him immunity, Brian?" The detective
pulled the car into the traffic on Collins Avenue.

"Who needs him? If he wants to rat out Grambling, he can
plead guilty to something and do a deal."

That evening, Rosner and Collins made plans to stay in
Florida for personal reasons. Collins called his wife to arrange
for her and the children to fly to Florida for a short vacation.
As he always did on his business trips to South Florida,
Rosner visited his elderly Aunt Toby, a former New Yorker
now resident in Miami Beach. When it rained the next day,
Collins changed his family's plans, and Rosner and his aunt
drove the detective to the airport for his return to New York.
During the drive, Collins regaled Aunt Toby with stories of
crime and his experiences from his bodyguarding days. She
was fascinated: Her uncle had been one of New York City's
most prominent and respected defense attorneys, and she had
never lost her interest in the criminal law. As he left the car,
Collins removed his Big Apple police pin and put it in her lapel. Aunt Toby beamed.

Back in New York the next day, Rosner and Collins each
followed a lead provided by Libman.

The assistant called Miller, the Husky financial vice president, in Calgary.

"Are you sure you spoke to Libman and not someone saying
he was Libman?" the prosecutor asked.

"I went to the address in North Miami," Miller said. He described the tawny building and office—including the family
pictures on the wall—that the prosecutor had just been in. And
he described Libman.

"Of course, we discussed the $23 million balance sheet," Miller added. "That's why Art Price and I went to Florida."

Collins and Rosner discussed the second call.

"Eddie, what if it's true what Libman said about how he always botched the deals when he impersonated people in phone calls?"

"That's not what the witnesses have been saying, Brian."

"But we haven't spoken to the guy from Salt Lake. It's time for a call."

Collins thought for a moment. "Tape it?"

"I don't like taping people who may end up being my own witness." Rosner paused to think. "But, if we don't, the defense may claim that we prepped the witness into saying something. Tape it."

Collins called Conover that Monday, March 26. It was a classic interview. Step-by-step, Collins let Conover lead him through the loan process. Five minutes into the call, they reached Conover's account of the January 25 call with "Mullin."

"We called Mullin at a number supplied by Mr. Grambling, (305) 940-7536," Conover said. "We called Mullin at that number and then he returned our call and communicated to our senior loan committee vis-a-vis a conference call. He had said 'I do not have my briefcase here with me, I'll call you back.' And Mullin said that he was very knowledgeable about the transaction, and very high on the management team of Grambling Energy, and very high on Grambling."

"Are you aware of anything Mr. Mullin might have said to sour the deal?" Collins asked.

"No, I am not," Conover replied.

The evidence buttressed Rosner's and Collins' initial conclusion that Libman was an accomplice. When Libman called the assistant on March 29, the prosecutor refused to speak with him other than to say, "You should obtain counsel and have him call me."

That same day, Greenblatt called the prosecutor about a subpoena matter and, in passing, noted, "You know Grambling's been negotiating to pay the bank back with some new funding. He sent us the commitment letter, but with the new lender's name whited out so that we wouldn't know who it was. We learned today who it is. Some bank in Mississippi, Jackson Savings and Loan, I think."

Rosner called the Jackson, Mississippi District Attorney that afternoon, and, the following day, the Mississippi prosecutor served a New York County Grand Jury subpoena on the Jackson bank.

CHAPTER 15

ASSISTANCE OF COUNSEL

February and March were hectic months for Grambling. Repayment, in any form or amount, would be his salvation. He frantically tried to pacify the banks as he searched for a new victim.

To his surprise, the Bank of Montreal closed the door on further meetings. "Call us when you have the money," was their attitude. "Until then, bug off." Grambling had mistaken the Canadians' civility for lack of resolve. But Colorado National was eager to discuss repayment with Grambling, anywhere and anytime. 1985 was turning into a bad year for the bank. Agriculture had remained in a depression and mineral extraction, another staple of the regional economy, was not rebounding as expected. The bank had just increased its loan loss reserve by $5 million, a whopping 50 percent. It was desperate to retrieve the $6 million from Grambling.

On Friday, February 8, as the assistant met Busuttil, and took his first bleary-eyed look at the bank documents, Bruce Rockwell, Colorado National's Chairman, met Grambling in Stamford, Connecticut to discuss repayment of the Colorado National debt.

"It's terrible what the Bank of Montreal did to me," Grambling whined. "Pulling my commitment with no cause."

Rockwell could sympathize with whatever bad words Grambling had for the Canadian bank. It was shocking, Rockwell thought, how the Bank of Montreal officers had led on he and Foncannon. Even if the Canadian bankers had not made all of the phone calls, as they and their counsel were now claiming, the Canadians must have suspected that Grambling was not the legitimate businessman he claimed to be. How else could they have abandoned a $100 million commitment? And why did they let Colorado National be fleeced without even a hint of a warning?

The release of the last $2 million of Colorado National's money particularly angered Rockwell. The money had been released solely on the basis of the January 25 Scott Hean call, and the reassurance about the $100 million funding that the call had provided. That the $2 million was transferred immediately to repay a large chunk of Grambling's Bank of Montreal debt did nothing to placate Rockwell's hostility towards the Canadians.

As they sat in the Stamford office of Grambling's attorney on February 8, Rockwell and Grambling parsed Grambling's financial statement line-by-line for assets to repay or collateralize the Colorado National debt.

"What about this Southern Union stock?" Rockwell pointed to Grambling's list of stock holdings. "150,000 shares, $4 million."

"I might be able to make the Southern Union available. But I don't think that much is necessary. I'd rather sign over my $500,000 note from Datavision."

The meeting ended inconclusively. But Rockwell persisted. He returned to Stamford on Monday, February 11. In addition to local counsel, Rockwell had at his side Randall Weeks, a senior partner at Davis, Graham & Stubbs, the Mile-High City's equivalent to a Wall Street law firm.

Accompanying Grambling were his retained counsel, Barry Kingham and Joe Kelly of Manhattan's Curtis Mallet-Prevost, Colt & Mosle. As Grambling knew well, attorneys put the imprimatur of credibility on one's business affairs.

"John is working toward a refinancing," the attorneys assured Rockwell and Weeks at the Stamford meeting on February 11. "He has two prospects in the works. One facility under negotiation is for $10 million. The other potential loan is a five bank participation for a $12 million credit."

Painfully cognizant of Colorado National's stinging lack of collateral, Rockwell asked, "What are these loans going to be collateralized by?"

"Certificates of deposit from Grambling family members," the Curtis Mallet attorneys replied. "Family members hold CDs of several million dollars on John's behalf, which will be pledged to support the loans."

"What family members?" Rockwell wanted to know. "And why not assign the CDs to Colorado National to collateralize our debt?"

"John expects that the financing will resurrect the R.M.T. purchase," counsel said. But they would not identify the potential lenders or the collateral. As they told Rockwell and Weeks, "John's scared that Colorado National might seize his assets and kill the new funding."

"Barry, you can't expect Colorado National to do nothing," Rockwell protested. "The bank is facing a $6 million loss. And the stories surfacing in Denver—the press is reporting that false documents were submitted to the Bank of Montreal—don't give us any comfort that John can repay. What can John do for us now?"

The attorneys had expected the question, and prepared an answer.

"John has a substantial business associate willing to guarantee the obligation to Colorado National. His name is Bob Libman. Here, you can look at his balance sheet."

Kingham and Kelly handed copies of Libman's $23 million balance sheet to Rockwell and his counsel.

"Look at the numbers yourself, and the quality of Bob's portfolio—mostly blue-chip, public-traded securities," Grambling's counsel continued. "We've met Bob, and we're impressed with him."

"Is there anything John can give us now?" Rockwell wanted to know.

In response, Kelly and Kingham handed Rockwell copies of the put agreements; Cumberland Village's promise to buy Grambling's Cumberland shares and Datavision's promise to buy Grambling's Biosystems shares. "John has binding commitments to buy his stock for $8.5 million and $3 million. That should be some comfort until new financing is in place to take out Colorado National."

Rockwell turned to Grambling and asked, "John, will you

pledge the Cumberland Village Mining and Datavision stock to Colorado National?"

"If that's part of the process, we can talk about it," Grambling replied noncommittally. He did not volunteer that the stock of both companies had already been pledged to the Bank of Montreal, as had the put agreements, or that the stock and agreements were worthless anyway.

Rockwell asked again about the $4 million of Southern Union Mining stock, and Grambling did not object to its assignment. He did object, however, to Rockwell's suggestion that Colorado National be assigned the $4 million of Dr Pepper stock shown on the Grambling financial statement.

"No, Bruce," Grambling said. "That stock secures my loan from the Bank of Montreal."

Four days later, Kelly called Weeks, Colorado National's attorney, in Denver.

"I'm sorry, Randall. But, well, . . . Barry and I misspoke on Monday." The discomfort was evident in Kelly's voice. "The Cumberland Village Mining and Biosystems stock is already pledged to the Bank of Montreal. But we're working on the new financing and expect some good news soon."

An attorney's basic source of information is his client, and the Curtis Mallet attorneys had just experienced their first taste of who their client was. But counsel attributed Grambling's "mistake" about the availability of the put agreements to the turmoil—the collapse of the Husky deal, the threat of indictment—of the last few days. The important point, in their minds, was to look forward to the new funding, which would end both Grambling's financial problems and the bubbling criminal investigation.

Libman was helping. He met with Rockwell at the Colorado National Bank office in Denver, and he called Rockwell frequently.

"The family is organizing a payback," Libman said in his February 19 call to Rockwell.

That's well and good, Rockwell thought. But I'm more concerned about obtaining the guarantee of the man with the $23 million balance sheet.

"Bob, Joe and Barry gave me your balance sheet. They said that you're willing to guarantee John's debt to Colorado National."

"Oh, I know of that balance sheet," Libman told Rockwell on the 19th. "I stand behind John, but a guarantor is no longer necessary, Bruce. Husky has decided to go ahead with the R.M.T. sale. The only point in the air now is who the purchasers will be."

In a confident tone, Libman continued his explanation to Rockwell.

"The principals of Cumberland Village Mining want to expand their coal business to oil and gas. Husky and Cumberland are talking about finishing the R.M.T. buyout."

"But there's a delicate personal issue involved," Libman confided. "The other Cumberland investors and I are John's friends, and we don't want to cut him from the deal after he's done all the work. We want to give John that little extra time to get his finances in order so he can participate in the buyout."

"Are you saying, Bob, that the Cumberland people would be willing to finish the Husky purchase without John?"

"Well, they want the property badly. Cumberland and the Bass Brothers from Texas are talking about a joint venture. But we want to keep John in it. I'm talking to my friends at Citibank to arrange the financing for a Cumberland purchase of R.M.T. We'll know in a week. But even if that doesn't work out, Colorado National will be taken out. The Grambling family has agreed to refinance John's debt. And you'll be hearing about that soon."

A few hours after Libman's call, Kelly and Kingham called Rockwell to confirm what Libman had said about the Grambling family. And two days later, Libman called Rockwell to confirm that the Bass Brothers had agreed to join Grambling in financing the R.M.T. purchase. Over the next three weeks, Libman, Kingham and Kelly made similar encouraging calls, and more promises, with no results.

Towards the end of February, Colorado National attached Grambling's few unencumbered assets, including the balance of a checking account in New York. If Grambling was to forestall further collection efforts, it was time to produce.

To produce, he needed a new bank, and for a new bank, he needed an introduction. Relying on the reputation he retained in some circles—that of a borrower who paid his debts, with interest, though sometimes a little late—Grambling called his business friend Barton Tuck, the President of U.S. Shelter.

"Sorry that the cable deal did not work out," he said, "and the repayment was a little late. But I was in the middle of a major deal, and U.S. Shelter was repaid."

Tuck, of course, did not know the history of the repayment—that Grambling had defrauded Colorado National to repay R.M.T., which he had defrauded to repay U.S. Shelter, which he had defrauded. Nor did Tuck know that the loan now desired by Grambling was needed to silence Colorado National and the Bank of Montreal, the most recent victims on Grambling's merry-go-round.

Grambling got to the point.

"I need an introduction. It would be a loan in the amount of $6 to $10 million, fully secured, of course. I've exhausted my usual banks with the Husky deal. Bart, could you suggest a place?"

Tuck knew the president of the Security Savings and Loan Association in Jackson, Mississippi. He made the introductory call on Grambling's behalf.

With the follow-up call, Grambling continued the process of robbing Peter to pay Paul.

CHAPTER 16

SHELL GAME

On February 27, 1985, Grambling began to discuss loan terms with Ken Warren, Executive Vice President and a senior lending officer of the Jackson Savings and Loan Association. They never met. The loan negotiations occurred by letter and phone between the Mississippi offices of the bank and its counsel, and the Manhattan offices of Grambling and his Curtis Mallet lawyers.

"Ken, I need an interim facility to pay down some of the debt I've incurred in a LBO," Grambling told Warren in his first call. "As Bart might have said, I'm looking in the area of $10 million. It's a short-term loan. I'm currently working with Citicorp Industrial Credit and Bass Brothers Enterprises to refinance the Husky purchase. But that financing won't be ready for six to eight weeks."

Though the Jackson bank was not a player in the LBO arena, Warren realized that Grambling was a personality to be cultivated. "From one of the most prominent and respected families in Texas, Tuck had said. And he had repaid a $2 million unsecured loan," were Warren's thoughts. Besides, whatever the ultimate business purpose of this transaction, the terms of the $10 million loan contemplated by Jackson Savings were as conservative as a loan could be.

"John, $10 million is an amount we're prepared to do. Now, you all mentioned collateral to the bank. The bank, of course, would want full liquid collateral. Was it CDs you were suggesting?"

"Yes," Grambling replied. "I'll secure the loan with $12 million in CDs, held for my benefit by an El Paso cousin of mine, Eldon P. Harvey. He's an oil and gas millionaire. The CDs are part of a $25 million jumbo certificate the family buys as a group. We roll it over every six months. I'll pledge the CDs by way of a pledge agreement until they mature, oh, six weeks from now, on May 15. When the CDs mature, the proceeds will be made available to the bank until the loan is paid."

"John, send me proof as to the amount and location of the CDs, and we'll issue you a commitment," Warren said, and the phone call ended.

That same day, Grambling mailed Warren a cover letter on the stationery of Grambling & Company and the proof; copies of two one-page documents, each on stationery picturing in its upper left hand corner the profile of a bearded and helmeted conquistador, the logo of the Coronado Bank.

Warren received the Coronado Bank documents the next day. One was a February 25, 1985 letter to Grambling verifying that he owned "50 percent of the jumbo CD of $25 million" bought by the Grambling family and transferred "to safekeeping accounts at selected banks in New Mexico." The second document, a December 1984 "Receipt for Purchase of Certificates of Deposit," confirmed that Grambling's three six-month CD's matured on May 15, 1985 and, "at the direction of John A. Grambling, Jr. and his assignees, have been transferred to custodial accounts at the First National Bank, Albuquerque, New Mexico ($4.5 million), Albuquerque National Bank (Sun West) ($4.5 million), and Western Bank, Albuquerque ($2 million), with a $1 million certificate retained at Coronado."

As Warren could see, both the December receipt and the February letter had been typed on the personal stationery of "Ronald J. Keenan, President"; the letter bore Keenan's signature. Warren referred to his foot-thick Polk's Directory and located the brief entry for "Coronado Bank, El Paso, Texas." Texas was a one-branch banking state, and the directory plainly indicated that Coronado was a small bank.

$500 million in assets. Surely, Grambling is one of their larger clients, Warren thought. That Coronado had transferred the CDs to other banks made sense in light of Coronado's size. But what Warren was looking for was not assets, but the section on personnel. The bank had 70 employees, chief among them was "Ronald J. Keenan, President." Keenan certainly was the appropriate officer to sign the letter, Warren concluded.

The Polk's Directory does not contain signatures, but it would not have mattered had Warren compared Keenan's real signature with the signature on the February 25 Coronado Bank letter. Over a month later, when the assistant obtained the Jackson bank documents, the Keenan signature would be the first detail he would examine: it was a true Keenan signature. The second detail would be the documents' typeface. It was readily apparent that the Coronado documents had been typed on the same machine that had produced Grambling's February 27 cover letter to the Mississippi bank. The Coronado "documents" were photocopies of real Coronado stationery with the body of the true letter blocked out, and then filled in with the message Grambling wanted Warren to see. First-class job of cutting and pasting, the assistant was to conclude.

Warren, however, did not compare typefaces in February 1985; no banker would have had cause to, certainly not when the borrower is of the stature of a Grambling. Based on the Coronado material received from Grambling, Warren issued a commitment letter on February 28. "Security Savings & Loan Association will loan to Grambling & Company, Inc. $10 million which will be secured by $12 million of Certificates of Deposit in FDIC insured banks." The loan was required to close in 30 days.

The commitment letter written by Warren accepted Grambling's proposal regarding the mechanism to assign the CDs. Each bank holding a CD would provide Security Savings with an assignment and pledge, and an estoppel letter verifying that the CD it had issued was not assigned or liened. The banks would not be required to transfer the CDs themselves to Security Savings. Nor would the banks be required to transfer the CD proceeds prior to the May 15 maturity date. As Grambling had planned, he would be able to collateralize the $10 million Jackson loan by having signatures placed on documents prepared by attorneys. Whatever his other shortcomings, compliance with such a requirement was an area in which he excelled.

In March, Warren received the signed commitment letter from Curtis Mallet and Grambling's $50,000 commitment fee. He began making the calls necessary to close the loan. The first person Warren called was Keenan. He was not in.

"I believe that he's around, sir," Keenan's secretary said. "I'll make sure that he gets back to you."

Keenan would not be immediately available on the half dozen occasions that Warren would call over the next several days. On each occasion, the same events would transpire: within 10 or 15 minutes of the secretary's promise that Keenan would "get back to you," a Keenan would call Warren.

"Hello, Ken, what can I do for you?" Keenan said on his first return call to Warren on March 8, 1985.

"I'm calling about the Coronado CDs to be assigned to the bank for John's loan."

"New Mexico banks hold the proceeds of three of the CDs, which are made out to Coronado as the account holder," Keenan explained. "What you need, Ken, is an assignment of the CDs from Coronado and the New Mexico banks. I'll have the banks sign the documents for you, and I'll sign for Coronado."

"Ron, we also need to make certain that we in Jackson have a perfected security interest in the collateral."

"John tells me that the loan transaction will be governed by Texas law," Keenan said.

"That's correct," Warren replied. "That's the governing law clause that counsel has drafted for the loan documents."

"Your bank is protected then," Keenan assured Warren. "Under the Texas Uniform Commercial Code, you, the lender, have a perfected security interest in the CDs if you have the receipt for the CD purchase. Coronado has the original CD receipt. I think you've seen a copy of it—the December 1984 receipt John has sent you. We have the original, and I'll send it to Jackson for the closing. That receipt will be absolute security for your bank under Texas law."

"Very good, Ron. The first draft of the loan documents, including the assignments for the CDs, is prepared. There's an assignment and estoppel agreement for Coronado to sign. I'd like to send the drafts to you to have them approved by your legal counsel."

"Of course, Ken. I'll give them my personal attention."
Keenan paused for a moment. "I'll be leaving El Paso this
afternoon for Dallas; I have a few days of meetings there. Could
you send the documents to me in Dallas? That way, I can make
certain that I review them quickly. Here's the address where
I'll be."

Keenan read off the location and Warren wrote it down:
"Ron Keenan, President, Coronado Bank c/o Signet Securities,
14180 Dallas Parkway, Suite 710, Dallas, Texas."

"You send it there, Ron, and I'll be sure to get it."

After Keenan hung up, Warren called John Shows, the
bank's outside attorney. Shows was not uncomfortable with at
least part of the bank's relationship with this new client. Shows
knew Kingham. They had served together in the army, and Curtis Mallet used Shows' firm for legal work it needed done in Mississippi. Shows liked Kingham and his colleagues. It was an affection that Shows did not extend to Curtis Mallet's client.

A Texan living in Connecticut who wants to borrow from a
bank in Mississippi to fund some project in Colorado: Sounds
like bullshit, but I'm not the banker, Shows thought.

Warren addressed his attorney.

"John, could you mail the draft documents to Keenan at
this address. He's traveling," Warren explained.

It was the banker's job to be enthusiastic, and Shows' job to
protect the bank. Shows asked Warren, "How are we perfect-
ing the bank's security interest in the collateral, Ken?"

"I've spoken to Keenan," Warren replied. "The bank will
be getting the original receipt for the CDs. Keenan, the Coronado president, will deliver it to us himself. He says that possession of the receipt is perfection under Texas law."

"I'm not sure that that's a perfected security interest under
Texas law, Ken. But I'll check. Meanwhile, I'll send the documents to Keenan."

As Warren had requested, Shows mailed the draft loan documents to Keenan "c/o Signet Securities" in Dallas. Never before had Shows mailed documents to a bank officer at an address other than the bank address. A creature of firm habit, he
refused to change his practices totally. Shows called in his secretary.

"I want you to Federal Express a second package to Keenan. Yes, I know you just sent him one. Send a second one— exact duplicate of the first—but send this package to the Coronado Bank in El Paso, Texas. You got the address?"

The package of loan documents arrived at the Coronado Bank the next day, March 9. Jennie wondered what to do with it. Grambling had given her instructions about phone calls. "Jennie, I'm expecting someone from a Mississippi bank, a Mr. Warren, to call Mr. Keenan. They're unimportant calls, and Ron shouldn't be bothered with them. When the banker from Mississippi calls, just call me, and I'll handle it." It was a small bank. Jennie knew the customers, and Mr. Grambling was one of the best. She had told him about each call from Mississippi, just as he had asked. But Mr. Grambling never asked me to do anything about packages from Mississippi, she thought.

She delivered the package to the bank president.

What's this, Keenan wondered. He began to read the documents.

"Estoppel Agreement. Whereas, John A. Grambling has pledged certain certificates of deposit in the amount of $12 million to Security Savings & Loan Association. Whereas, Coronado Bank has issued certain certificates of deposit numbered R33239, R33149, and R33650 in the full face amount of $12.5 million in the name of Grambling. . . ."

"What the hell is going on?" Keenan shouted.

He read more and realized that the papers were the loan documents for a $10 million loan to Grambling to be collateralized by $12 million of Coronado Bank CDs.

This is not what Keenan had expected when John Grambling, Jr. had become a customer of the bank. It had been only the prior October. Grambling, Jr. had been introduced to Coronado by the father, and there was no genuinely more distinguished man in town. In Keenan's mind, the Gramblings were to El Paso what the Rockefellers were to New York, and Keenan had been overjoyed to lend $1.6 million to the son and his partner, that Libman fellow from Florida. The money had been repaid as promised. So pleased was Keenan with the relationship that only a month earlier Coronado had offered to buy a $700,000 participation in a $6 million loan that First Financial of El Paso was putting together for Grambling. It would have been a good loan, Keenan thought, secured by millions of dollars of blue-chip securities held by Libman in his Signet Securities account. Although that loan never came about—I never did ask John why, Keenan remembered—Coronado did loan $500,000 on its own to Grambling in early February.

But what are these papers about, Keenan thought. He read the Estoppel Agreement's description of the CDs allegedly placed at Coronado. "$12.5 million of CDs. Someone's crazy." Keenan shook his head. "That's almost a third of our assets and half our loan portfolio. The largest CD Coronado ever issued was only a few hundred thousand dollars." Keenan went back and reread the numbers identifying the so-called CDs.

"That's not even our enumeration system for CDs." Keenan read the numbers again. "But they do look like our numbers for loans."

He asked his secretary to bring him the Grambling file. It was a match. The identifying numbers attributed by the Estoppel Agreement to the three so-called Coronado Bank CDs were the numbers from three of the promissory notes that Grambling and Libman had signed to evidence their recently repaid $1.6 million Coronado Bank loan.

"Jennie," Keenan called to his secretary. "Next time John Grambling calls, make sure you find me wherever I am. I want to talk to him."

Grambling called that afternoon.

"John, I got this package from an attorney in Mississippi. Something about a loan in Mississippi and collateral from here. CDs in some crazy amount. What the hell is going on, John?"

"Don't worry, Ken," Grambling replied. "It's just a shell game. I'm getting a loan from the United Bank in Arizona. It's a shell game to protect the loan."

"But what is this talk about CDs here at Coronado?"

"It's just a way to keep the Canadians and the Colorado bank from interfering with my loan."

Canadians, Colorado bank, Keenan thought. He had spoken to bankers from all over the country on Grambling's behalf in the past months. He remembered speaking to Foncannon. In

January, he had spoken to some Canadians: That was when John had wire-transferred his Dr Pepper proceeds to Coronado though, now that he thought of it, Coronado never had received the full amount that had been expected. But Keenan could not recall ever having spoken to anyone from Mississippi.

The thought gave Keenan comfort. Whatever the game Grambling was playing with the Mississippi bank, no bank could be hurt in the end. So long as I didn't sign anything, or speak to anyone, this Mississippi loan can be no more than talk, Keenan figured. No banker would take an assignment without a call to me and my signature on a document.

Keenan was relieved.

"John, I want this nonsense to end," Keenan said.

He looked again at the documents he had received. There was a cover letter from counsel for the Mississippi bank. There is the man's name, Shows, and phone number with a 'cc' to an 'Hon. T. Barry Kingham.' Should I call and tell the Mississippi attorney what's being done by one of Coronado's largest customers, a son of one of the most respected families in town?

"Ron, just throw those papers away," Grambling said firmly. "Next time I'm in town, I'll tell you what was happening."

Keenan tossed the papers into the bottom of a drawer. He would be making no calls to Mississippi. But neither would he be destroying the documents, which would later be produced for the New York County Grand Jury.

Despite the silence of the true Ron Keenan, a Keenan did call Warren about the draft documents delivered to Texas on March 9. The package mailed to "Keenan c/o Signet Securities" was held by the receptionist for Grambling, who delivered the documents to his Keenan. The next day, Grambling's Keenan replied to the documents sent by Shows. By this time, however, Shows had lectured Warren on the security perfection requirements of Texas law.

"Ken, I have the package Shows mailed to me," Grambling's Keenan began in his call to Warren on March 10. "The papers look fine. I'll get the necessary signatures, and I'm ready to come to Jackson to present the original CD receipt at the closing."

"Thank you, Ron. That won't be necessary now. My attorney tells me that he's checked the Texas case law, and the receipt might not be enough. We're going to want the original CDs at the closing. Coronado is holding onto them, isn't it?"

"Ken, the CDs are not necessary," Keenan protested. "Believe me, I know Texas law, and it's not necessary. All you need is our receipt for the sale."

"Sorry, Ron. Our counsel is insistent. Also, we're ready to send the latest drafts of the loan documents to you."

"Okay. Listen, Ken, I'll be leaving for Dallas again today. So if you could mail the package to that address I gave you last time, c/o Signet Securities. Thanks."

Damn, Grambling's Keenan thought. Forging receipts or assignments is easy; just a matter of putting a signature on a typed piece of paper. But certificates of deposit are printed forms. How is John going to forge an original one of those?

As requested by Keenan, Warren asked Shows to mail the new drafts to Keenan. Shows complied, in the same way as he had with Warren's first request: one package to Keenan in Dallas "c/o Signet Securities," and one to "Keenan, Coronado Bank, El Paso." Shows liked this loan less and less as time passed.

On March 13, Shows called his client with a question.

"Ken, we can't finalize these papers until we have the details on the CDs, like the exact name of the account holder. Did Grambling send photocopies of the CDs to you like he was supposed to?"

He had not, so Shows and Warren called Kingham that afternoon, March 13. They reached Kingham in his Manhattan office.

"The attorneys working on the financing and John are down the hall in a conference room," Kingham said. "Let me go there and call you back."

Within a few minutes, Kingham was on the line again. He had set up a conference call between Shows and Warren in Mississippi, and the Curtis Mallet attorneys and Grambling in Manhattan.

Shows listed the information needed about the CDs for the final documentation.

"We're working on it," Kingham and Kelly replied. "John will send you copies of the certificates, and you can take the necessary information from the copies." Grambling agreed with his counsel's remarks, and repeated the location of the CDs.

But Shows had another complaint.

"The commitment requires John to provide the bank with a signed financial statement. What's the hold-up on that?"

Grambling's counsel were perturbed. Although they did not know exactly what evidence was filtering into the District Attorney's Office, they knew that allegedly incorrect financial statements were a part of it. Their experience with offering the Cumberland and Datavision put agreements to Colorado National, only to be compelled later to withdraw the offer, was like a burn on the finger. It sensitized them to the disarray in Grambling's financial affairs. In this turmoil, it was dangerous to allow Grambling to commit numbers to paper. If John made a mistake in his numbers, they thought, the mistake would be misunderstood as a crime.

"You and Ken don't need a financial," the Manhattan attorneys argued. "The bank is getting FDIC insured CDs in an amount exceeding the loan by $2 million. The loan's risk-free. Having a financial statement is not going to make a difference."

"A financial statement from a borrower is a regulatory requirement," Show replied flatly. "If there is no financial statement, I cannot recommend to my client that it proceed with this loan." Period. Shows had ended that discussion.

"And the commitment expires in two weeks," Shows added. "So let's get moving. When are you going to get possession of the CDs?"

"We're talking to counsel for Grambling's family in Dallas. Kathy, one of our associates, is scheduled to go to Dallas at the end of the month, Sunday, March 30. There's going to be a family meeting to arrange the transfer of the CDs."

On Thursday, March 27, 1985, Grambling complied with one of the demands made by the bank in the March 13 call to Manhattan. He sent Warren copies of the three CDs, one from each of the three Albuquerque banks, Sun West, First National, and Western Bank. The account holder on each certificate was the same: "Coronado Bank has deposited the above amount for the account of Eldon P. Harvey, Jr." Each certificate had a similar format; typed information inserted onto a printed CD form bearing each bank's distinctive printed emblem.

That Sunday, the Curtis Mallet associate flew to Dallas for the much anticipated family meeting. No original CDs were presented for submission to the Jackson bank. For all his skills at forgery, Grambling had been unable to manufacture original printed CDs to be turned over at the meeting.

Curtis Mallet's efforts for the past 30 days had been a waste. On Tuesday, April 2, the Curtis Mallet attorneys informed the Jackson bank that the CDs would not be forthcoming. Similar calls were made to Colorado National and Bank of Montreal.

The most depressing event for the attorneys on April 2 was not the calls to the banks, but the meeting. Aware of the increasing activity in the criminal investigation, Kelly had called the assistant the prior Tuesday, March 25.

"Brian, we hear that you're working actively on the case. Barry and I would like to talk with you about the investigation. He's out of town until next week. Are you planning to arrest John prior to that? If not, could we see you next Tuesday, the 2nd?"

"We're not planning an arrest prior to Tuesday," Rosner replied.

Tentatively, since he did not know Rosner or his practices, Kelly reached out for a commitment in an area of critical concern to defense counsel. Should there be an indictment, would his client be permitted to surrender—allowed to come to the District Attorney's Office to be arrested—rather than being arrested and handcuffed by the police at his home, in front of his wife and children, or at work in front of his colleagues. In the heat of an investigation, assistants and detectives sometimes forgot the sole reason for an at-home arrest or the handcuffing of a defendant: To prevent flight. Government power should not be used to humiliate the defendant, or just to let him know who the boss is. The criminal justice system, even when it worked, humiliated all defendants adequately. There was no need to shame a man without cause.

"Brian," Kelly said. "John's not going anywhere. He's known of your investigation for weeks, and he plans to fight it. When the time . . ."

Rosner cut Kelly off.

"Joe, when the time comes for your guy to be arrested, we'll tell you. And you can bring him in to surrender."

"Also, Brian, John doesn't have any money. Are you going to ask for a cash bail or . . . ."

"Joe, we'll talk about that on Tuesday. See you and Barry on the 2nd."

It all could have been so much simpler, Kelly thought, had John obtained the $10 million Mississippi loan.

PART 3

JUDGMENT

CHAPTER 17

OPEN FILES, OPEN CELLS

On Tuesday, April 2, Kelly and Kingham trudged to One Hogan Place to meet the prosecutor. The officer on duty distributed the red visitors' passes, and Kelly and Kingham took the elevator to the seventh floor. With no greater enthusiasm than that of the victims who had preceded them, they walked the dismal corridor to the Frauds Bureau, and to the hardly more cheerful assistant's office.

They look like business attorneys, Rosner thought, as he shook their hands and took their cards. When's the Office going to print cards for us to hand out?

The format of the pre-indictment meeting is chiseled in stone. Defense counsel express their bewilderment that a civil dispute is being mistaken as a crime. Calmly, the prosecutor assures counsel of the impartiality of the investigation. The only factor that changes over time is that, as the assistant matures, he alters careers and may assume a different role.

"It's just a loan dispute," Kingham, the former assistant, began. "John got jammed up by Husky on a bad deal, and he may have done some dumb things, but he's not a bad person. He's a businessman who got in over his head."

"That's a fair point," the present assistant said. "The Grand Jury will decide. If your client wants to testify to explain what happened, let me know. And let me know if there's any exculpatory evidence. If there is, the Office will put it before the Grand Jury."

Having fulfilled their ritualistic role, Kelly and Kingham turned to the real purpose of the meeting.

"John's short on money," the attorneys said. "There's no reason to make him put up bail."

Rosner did not immediately respond. At this junction in Grambling's life, no person knew Grambling's finances better than the attorneys who had taken a retainer. Since their client might have to scramble to put together the money to make bail, they were entitled to know if the People would be making a bail request.

Rosner thought through the implications of the decision he was about to make. The purpose of bail is to guarantee that the defendant appears at future court proceedings: That he had learned in law school. For a business criminal with firm roots in the community and every intention to appear in court to fight the charges, bail was redundant, however much a high bail made for a good headline in a newspaper story.

"He's not going anywhere," counsel stressed as they sat in the assistant's office. "His wife is here. His kids are here. He's not a flight risk."

"I won't be asking for bail," Rosner agreed. "And, as I told Joe last week, if there's an arrest, Grambling can surrender."

After Kelly and Kingham left, the assistant sprinted up the two flights to the ninth floor. His destination was the middle of the corridor, and the two swinging wooden doors—"Grand Jury, Room 906."

The juries should have been impaneled yesterday, Rosner thought as he pushed his way through.

Grand Juries were convened the first Monday of each month. "You are summoned to appear at 100 Centre Street," read the court order mailed to hundreds of Manhattan residents selected from the voter registration rolls. Presiding over a courtroom crammed with hundreds of responding citizens, the impaneling judge picked as the Grand Jury the first 23 whose names were selected at random from the list of the summoned. The selection was unlike that of a trial jury, for which attorneys were allowed to remove potential jurors without explanation. The impaneling judge excused no one except for narrowly circumscribed hardships—young children at home with no available child care, or severe medical problems bordering on death. Invariably, panels included workers of all types: retirees, artists, students, the rich, the poor, and, due to the unusual demographics of Manhattan, a concentration of business and professional talent. No panel more representative of the community sat in New York County.

The juries had not always been so representative. Prior to the 1970s, the members of the Grand Jury were drawn exclusively from the Grand Jury Association, the organization whose members had comprised the Jury which, in 1935, had urged Governor Lehman to appoint a Special Prosecutor. The Association believed in exclusivity: The power and responsibility of Grand Jury membership, it was assumed, was too great to invest in more than a small portion of Manhattan's populace.

For convincing statistical reasons, grand juries drawn from the Association came to be called blue-ribbon grand juries. Although New York County's roll of registered voters exceeded 600,000 persons by 1964, the Association's membership, the pool from which grand jurors were drawn, was limited to 2,000 persons. Though it had served an honorable purpose, the Association was gradually passed by history. Under evolving constitutional theories of fairness, power and responsibility of governance were to be available to all. By the time of Rosner's appointment as an assistant, grand jurors were chosen from the same roll of registered voters which served as the juror pool for trial juries. Though he had presented cases only to the newer, non-blue ribbon panels, the assistant had never encountered a juror, whatever his or her educational background or class, who had been unable to understand the transactions at issue, however complex, or articulate his or her judgment. The assistant had no doubts that democracy worked.

The impaneling judge chose six Grand Jury panels, three to sit in the morning, three to sit in the afternoon. Although the panels could hear any case—and, when there was a backlog of cases, an assistant would make his presentation to any available panel—the juries had specialized functions: a morning and an afternoon jury for street crimes; two similar panels for narcotic cases; one for homicides; and one, traditionally an afternoon grand jury, for the long-term investigations of the Frauds and Rackets Bureaus.

As he pushed through the doors, Rosner was greeted by the pandemonium that typefied the first full working day of the newly-impaneled juries. Witnesses—the arresting officers and civilians, several with bloodied bandages or fresh bruises on their faces—sat tightly packed on the shiny, light-colored wooden benches. Noticeable in the crowd were young men and women in conservative business attire: The young assistant district attorneys. The hands of some were filled with files. Others hugged the files to their chests. Leaning in the direction of the witness' face, constantly talking, the young assistants were prepping their witnesses one last time before the testimony.

Crossing the invisible barrier that separated the waiting area from the entrance to the juries, Rosner entered a corridor with two doors, one to each of the Grand Jury rooms. Across from each jury room sat the jury's warden, the court officer who acted as the Grand Jury clerk. A dozen assistants crowded around the warden's desk opposite from the first Grand Jury room, the street crime Grand Jury.

The assistant saw that his colleagues were hurriedly filling out the grand jury forms—defendant's name, proposed charges, names of witnesses—for their presentations. The Grand Jury's responsibility—to decide whether there was cause to believe that a person had committed a crime—could be discharged in 10 minutes. The victim testified: "A man came up to me. He pointed a gun and demanded my wallet. I gave it over." And then the cop: "While turning the corner, I noticed a young male with what appeared to be a weapon pointed at the individual who just testified. Upon observing the radio patrol car, the young male ran down a side street. My partner and I gave chase, and apprehended the young male, from whose possession we retrieved a wallet and a loaded weapon, exhibits A and B".

Of the panel of 23, 16 members were required to hear the critical evidence on any given case, and twelve had to agree on the action to be taken. Subsequent to the presentation of evidence, the assistant would read the proposed charges and legal instructions to the jurors. After a few days, the jurors became familiar with the law, and would tell the assistant not to bother reading the legal instructions again. The jury's deliberation and vote occurred in secret, so, after the assistant read the proposed charges, he would leave. Seconds later, the assistants milling around the warden's desk would hear the buzz. "They voted," the buzz meant. The warden would enter the jury room and retrieve the charge slip from the foreperson. One check next to a proposed charge meant that the Grand Jury had voted to indict; two checks was a "no bill," a vote to not charge.

The assistant recognized several of the dozen assistants crowding around the warden to the street crime Grand Jury. Having completed their charge slips, the assistants eagerly waited for the sound of the three buzzes, the signal that the jury was ready for the next case. "First come, first served" was the rule of entrance into the street crime Grand Jury. The warden was the gatekeeper.

Excusing his way through his colleagues, the assistant approached the warden seated at the desk outside the second Grand Jury room, the sanctuary of the investigative jury. It was quiet. He was the only assistant there.

"How you doing, Mario?"

"Well, Mr. Rosner." Mario extended his hand for a shake. He was an oldtimer who had been with the court system for years.

"Haven't seen you for a while. Got something big this month? You got time reserved tomorrow and a couple of more days."

The investigative Grand Jury sat for three hours each afternoon. It's availability to an assistant was on a reserved basis only, with time being exhausted usually two weeks prior to its impaneling.

"Just the usual case, Mario. I'd like to go in and introduce myself to the new panel."

Rosner nodded his head toward the jury door.

"Anyone in there now?"

The warden rolled his eyes towards the ceiling.

"Yeah, one of your colleagues. She's been in there for a half hour trying to get them to understand a two-minute grand larceny."

The door to the jury opened. The noise of 23 arguing people rolled over Rosner and Mario. One of the assistant's colleagues, flushed and angry, emerged and slammed the door.

"I should have known better. It's a new jury. It's their first larceny. Simple. Bookkeeper takes the business' money by checks. Puts the checks in his personal account. And they're acting like this is Sherlock Holmes' greatest mystery. 'Why didn't you do a fingerprint analysis on the checks?' one of them wanted to know. What the fuck do they think? Some martian put the checks into the defendant's account?"

She chopped at the air with the side of her hand.

"The hell with it. I'm going to come back and finish this case later this month. Let them get some experience about what they're supposed to be doing with someone else's case."

She seemed to notice the assistant for the first time.

"Brian, do you have a case for these people? Hope it's black and white."

She stomped out of the Grand Jury area.

Mario shrugged.

"These jurors nowadays. They think they're holding a trial in there or something."

He shook his head.

"Never had this problem in the old days, never with the blue-ribbon juries. Let me get you a stenographer, Mr. Rosner, and you can go in."

Accompanied by a stenographer, the assistant entered the Grand Jury room. The room was a semi-amphitheatre. At the lowest level was a table and a chair for the witness, and a chair for the stenographer. The seats rose in two rows of 10 seats apiece, bisected by an aisle. At the top of the aisle was a raised platform the length of the row of seats. To the rear center of the platform were the seats of the foreperson, vice foreperson, and secretary. The foreperson swore witnesses to tell the truth; the secretary retained the jury's attendance records. The impaneling judge selected the officers, and usually chose educated or business people for these duties.

Rosner scrutinized the jurors as the stenographer prepared her machine. He did not speak. Although he had heard of instances in other counties of assistants speaking off-the-record to the jury, even telling them how to vote, the practice of New York County assistants was unvarying and strict: Every word spoken by the assistant would be recorded. The transcript would be then reviewed by the judge who had impaneled the juries; the impaneling judge supervised the juries' work during their one-month term. Part of this supervision was to ensure that the assistant's conduct before the jury was fair.

The assistant saw that each of 23 members were present, as was common on the panel's first day. The stenographer nodded that she was ready. The assistant cleared his throat and introduced himself. He explained that a presentation covering several days would commence the following afternoon.

"I urge you all to attend. As the presiding judge instructed you when you were impaneled, you may only vote on a case if you have heard the essential and critical evidence."

Several jurors nodded their heads in agreement.

"Although, as your legal advisor, I have not yet concluded which witnesses will be essential and critical, it may turn out that you will have to have been present on each day of testimony in order to vote on the case. At the beginning of each week, I will tell you the afternoons that you'll be hearing witnesses on this case. We have 23 grand jurors so that we can have a cross-selection of our community deliberate and vote whether to indict or not indict. I urge each of you to make every effort to attend so that you can be a part of that vote."

The foreperson spoke.

"An assistant from the Rackets Bureau told us that we should have a code name for each case, so that we can keep all the cases we hear distinct. Do you have a code name for the case you'll be presenting?"

Rosner laughed. "You won't need a code name to remember the case. See you tomorrow."

Trial work is historical reconstruction. The next morning, the assistant began to assemble in his office, for one last review, the witnesses to the Bank of Montreal and Colorado National events. That afternoon, with 23 jurors again in attendance, the witnesses began their appearances in the Grand Jury. The assistant's practice was simple. He would question the witness and then open the floor to questions from the grand jurors. After the witness had left the room, the assistant would answer jurors' inquiries on how the investigation should proceed.

"Shouldn't we speak to the real Corcoran?" one juror asked.

"He's scheduled for later this week."

"Does the bank have phone records to prove that the call to Miami was made," another wanted to know.

"I can't testify to what the evidence is or will be. But, as your legal advisor, I will tell you that, were there phone records, this last witness could not as a matter of evidence authenticate the records in a manner that you could rely on for your vote. A later witness today will be able to authenticate phone records, so why don't you folks wait to hear what he has to say."

After the first hour or two of testimony, the jury and the assistant worked out a relationship for the presentation of evidence. The jury would allow Rosner to present the witnesses in the order he thought best, with a suggestion every so often. During recesses, and at the end of the afternoon's session, the assistant left that day's evidence, and evidence from prior days when requested, on the witness table for the jurors to examine. Whenever he left the room, he saw several jurors head for the table, and, when Rosner gathered the evidence at the end of the day, he could tell from its disarray that the jurors had been reviewing the documents.

The presentation proceeded through the first two weeks of April. Towards the end of the first week, Rosner met several witnesses for the first time on the same day as their testimony.

Crawford, the Chairman of Datavision and putative signatory on the Biosystems purchase agreement, flew to New York from Michigan to testify. Prior to his pre-testimony interview, he and Collins sat in the assistant's office. One by one, Collins handed Crawford three-by-five index cards. On the side without lines, Crawford wrote his signature. As the assistant watched, Crawford signed his name on 20 index cards.

Let him think we're going to do a handwriting analysis, the assistant thought. In his 40s, just a little older than Grambling. Looks depressed.

Crawford handed the last card to Collins, and turned to face the assistant. It was the signal for the interview to begin.

Rosner handed Crawford the December 1984 letter committing Datavision to purchase Grambling's Biosystems' stock for $3.5 million. The letter bore a signature, "Richard Crawford."

"Did you sign this letter agreement?" Rosner asked.

Crawford breathed heavily and shook his head.

"No," Crawford replied.

After a pause, he continued.

"But it's close to something that did occur. I met John in 1981, when the company he was with, Dean Witter, arranged financing for Datavision. The board was so pleased that it elected John a member of the board. He still is. Of course, I've written him letters on occasion."

That explains how he got Datavision stationery, the assistant thought.

Crawford continued.

"About two years ago, I introduced John to the owner of Biosystems. The reason was that John wanted to buy the company, and he did buy it. Back then, around the time that John bought the company, Datavision considered a merger with Biosystems. But the thought was abandoned. Biosystems didn't have the cash to justify a merger. But this December letter. It's . . . well."

Shaking his head, Crawford reread the December 1984 letter for what must have been the 12th time. He still can't believe it, the assistant thought.

"Datavision doesn't have $3.5 million in cash even if the Board voted to buy the stock. You can look at our filings with the SEC. We don't have that money."

The assistant knew that Datavision didn't have the money to buy Biosystems. He had already examined the SEC filings. Copies were in his files.

And the Crawford signature on the Datavision annual report is close to but not quite like that on the December letter, the assistant thought. He writes in an unambiguous, easy-to-copy pattern.

Crawford handed the December letter back to Rosner, and began to speak again, with hesitation.

"This isn't the only instance of John . . . of John doing something. John is holding a $500,000 note from Datavision. We've heard that he's pledged the note as collateral for a loan."

Crawford shifted uncomfortably in his chair.

"We've heard from the lenders who have it pledged."

With a nod, Rosner acknowledged that he was following.

"The note's been pledged to a couple of lenders at the same time," Crawford concluded.

"Thank you for that information, Richard."

Rosner rose from his chair as he looked at his watch. It was 1:50 P.M. The Grand Jury convened at 2:00 P.M.

"I'll be storing that piece about the note. We won't use it today in the Grand Jury. All I'll be asking you about are the forgeries."

It was the first time that Rosner had used the Penal Law description for the crimes that Crawford had described, the falsification of his signatures.

Crawford also rose. He was a big man. Quietly, he wiped tears from his face.

"John's a friend," Crawford said. "I'll do what I have to. Since he involved the company. But . . . ."

"I understand," Rosner said.

He patted Crawford on the shoulder and gently guided him through the door.

Friends, the assistant thought. The last ones to turn against Grambling, until he left them no choice.

The following Tuesday, April 9, Rosner completed the presentation regarding the Bank of Montreal and Colorado National, and he charged the jury. With 23 jury members in attendance, the jury voted conspiracy, larceny and forgery charges against Grambling and Libman. Where they had acted jointly to commit a crime, Grambling and Libman were each responsible for the other's conduct. As a result, even though he had never set foot in New York, Libman was charged as an accomplice to the larceny and forgery that Grambling had committed against the Bank of Montreal in New York County. In addition, the jury charged Grambling individually with a larceny and a forgery regarding the Colorado National Bank fraud. All in all, Libman was named in four counts, and Grambling in 13.

The same day of the Grand Jury vote, the U.S. Attorney for the Southern District sent a second letter to District Attorney

Morgenthau. When the assistant went to Benitez's office that afternoon to report the vote, the Bureau Chief handed him the Southern District letter.

Dear Bob,

I would like to take this opportunity to reiterate our view that this is an investigation more suitably conducted by federal authorities. Although the Bank of Montreal brought this matter to your attention, they also brought it to our attention at about the same time . . . I know that careful and efficient use of resources is a matter of importance to you. I understand that at least one Assistant District Attorney from your office and perhaps other city law enforcement personnel have been traveling to Florida and other distant jurisdictions in order to obtain evidence in your investigation. As you know, the Federal Bureau of Investigation has offices throughout the country and we have nationwide subpoena power. Both of these facts make it easier, less expensive, and more expeditious for us to collect evidence in other jurisdictions. In any event, we are moving forward with our federal investigation. If you believe that in doing so we can relieve your office and the overburdened state courts of the necessity of going forward with this matter, you know that I would consider any arrangement that would be in the best interests of getting this case done effectively.

Very truly yours,
RUDOLPH W. GIULIANI
United States Attorney

The assistant dropped the letter on Benitez's desk.

"Is there a federal investigation?" Benitez asked.

"Not that I can tell. I've been speaking to witnesses from Mississippi to Texas to Utah to Michigan and back again. There was a flurry of F.B.I. interest when the Bank of Montreal reported the case, but nothing since."

"Finish the case," Benitez said. "Don't rush so that you miss anything. But let's do it quick."

Returning to his office, Rosner informed Kingham and Fred Hafetz, counsel for Libman, that an indictment had been voted. Hafetz, one of Manhattan's best and most experienced trial attorneys, was a graduate of the offices of both the Manhattan District Attorney and the United States Attorney. He had been retained shortly after Rosner's last phone conversation with Libman. Although arrest warrants had been issued with the filing of the indictment, the assistant, as he had promised, told counsel that their clients could surrender.

That Thursday morning, April 11, Libman and Grambling received their introduction to the criminal justice system. Accompanied by counsel, they went to One Hogan Place, took the elevator to the ninth floor and, after walking by the candy and soda machines, and wanted posters, surrendered to Collins in the Squad Room. Collins thanked them for coming in early and introduced Ronnie Moss, a second grade black detective. A broad-shouldered police veteran, Moss had taken Collins under his wing when Collins had joined the squad. The two liked to work together and tried to be assigned to each other's cases. Collins had asked Moss to assist him in processing the arrests.

Processing is the paperwork that accompanies an arrest. The most time-consuming part is the fingerprinting. Not the actual taking of the prints: By 9:00 A.M., Moss had inked the fingers of Grambling and Libman, and, one by one, pressed the tips of their fingers on their separate fingerprint cards. The fingerprint check caused the delay. When arrested, the arrested person's prints are sent electronically to Albany for comparison with the prints in the master computer in Albany, the state capital.

Matching fingerprints, not names, the Albany computer produces a "rap" sheet, a chronological list of all the arrests of the person whose fingerprints are under examination, as well as a listing of the various "aliases" used by the person with those prints. The rap sheet is the only way to determine if the recently arrested defendant committed his current crime while free on bail in another case, or if he is a fugitive from justice. For the white-collar criminals, the computer check is unnecessary. As with Grambling and Libman, their backgrounds are thoroughly investigated prior to indictment. But by statute, all arrestees must wait for the return of the rap sheets before they can be arraigned.

By 9:00 A.M., Moss had submitted the prints to Albany and received the usual reply: "Computer down, no rap sheets this morning." Sometimes, Albany took 24 hours to produce rap sheets.

For a defendant such as Grambling or Libman, processing was humiliating: He was fingerprinted and confined. The computer breakdown made processing dangerous. After being fingerprinted in the relative tranquility of the Squad Room, Police Department regulations required that all arrestees be taken to Central Booking to wait for the rap sheets. Central Booking was the primary police detention facility where, in a spirit of true democracy, the arrestees—rapists, killers, drug pushers and swindlers—were herded without distinction into a huge holding pen.

Business criminals in Central Booking were objects of hatred. Aside from the usual race hatred to be expected from the other detainees—poor, illiterate young blacks and Hispanics—there was the class hatred. As had Grambling and Libman, the white collar criminal comes to his surrender and arraignment wearing what he would wear for business—a suit, a tie, a watch, and fine shoes. The white-collar criminal wants the arraigning judge to see him as what he believes he is—a business person. But the reaction to this dress by the thugs in Central Booking is visceral: "This is the dress of the people I rob."

During their stay in Central Booking, white-collar criminals are often relieved, by their cellmates, of their cigarettes, wallets, rings, watches and, depending on tastes, belts, ties, and shoes.

The humiliations to be suffered in Central Booking raised a dilemma for Rosner. Equal treatment is the foundation of justice. But, as was plain from experience, the normal pre-arraignment process was cruel to the nonhardened criminals prosecuted by the Frauds Bureau.

After the surrender, Rosner went to the Squad Room to speak with Collins. Moss was with Grambling and Libman in a separate room.

"Eddie, I promised counsel that we wouldn't be using cuffs if we didn't have to."

Collins responded with annoyance. "Brian, the regulations say I'm to keep them in cuffs when they're not in a cell. One of these guys takes a run when I'm walking him across the street to Central Booking, it's my ass in a sling, not some assistant's."

"You mean me?" Rosner smiled. "Listen, Eddie, do what you think is right. But remember, these guys aren't running anywhere." The assistant looked around. Other detectives were coming in for their day tour. "Also, Eddie, let's keep them out of Central Booking."

Collins dropped his pen and looked up from his desk.

"I can't keep them out. I have to bring them over with the papers."

"Eddie . . . ," Rosner began to protest.

"I understand," Collins said. "Ronnie and I will keep them there as briefly as possible. When we're waiting for Albany to send the rap sheets, we'll bring them back and put them in the cells by the wireroom."

Later that morning, Rosner returned to the squad to check on the prisoners. He walked by the soda machine, and peeked around the door leading to the cells. He saw Grambling and Libman, each in one of the two cells in the fingerprint room. Someone tapped him on the shoulder. It was Collins. Moss was with him.

"How are we doing on the rap sheets?" Rosner asked.

"The computer's still down," Moss replied.

"Well, let's wait through lunch. If the sheets aren't back by then, I'll waive prints." As the statute permitted, the assistant could consent to arraignment without prints. It was never done in street crime cases. "I'll waive prints," Rosner said, "and we'll get these two arraigned after lunch."

Collins pointed to Libman's cell—the door was unlocked and slightly open.

"He said that closed doors give him claustrophobia," Collins explained. "And we didn't use cuffs."

Rosner nodded.

"Brian," Moss motioned with his head to the assistant. Moss was very much like Collins. The mild and good natured exterior made him exceedingly effective when interviewing witnesses and prisoners.

"What is this, Brian?" Moss asked. "Special treatment for white men?"

The mildness of the style hid the bitterness. Moss had made hundreds of collars. He treated all the people he arrested, however despicable, with respect. But no cuffs, open cells, and avoiding the Central Booking pens was special, and a treatment he had never seen accorded to a black man like himself.

"Ronnie, it's class, not race. These middle-class guys are pushovers. They'd be eaten alive if we threw them in with the skells." The assistant used the police slang for street criminals. He motioned with this head towards the wireroom cells.

"If it was you arrested, or your kid, I'd treat you the same way I'm asking you to treat these guys."

"Okay, Brian. But people who are arrested should be treated the same; polite if they deserve it, but equal. I don't like this."

And neither do I, Rosner thought.

The Albany computer did not provide prints that day, so the assistant told counsel that he would agree to an arraignment without prints. After lunch, the detectives brought Grambling and Libman to Part 40 on the 11th floor. The courtroom was one of the most majestic in the building: A 20-foot ceiling and a huge spectators' area that could seat hundreds. The detectives and their collars sat in the first row.

At the front of the room was the bench—the judge's seat and working area—raised five feet above the floor. The jury box, with 16 comfortable wooden chairs, was to the left of the attorney's tables. Attorneys waiting for their cases to be called lounged in the jurors' seats. Once a trial courtroom, the room was now an arraignment part. The judge handled pretrial matters for a 100 cases a day. The assistant and defense counsel stood at the bench and spoke to the judge. After a hushed off-the-record conference, Rosner returned to his table. The parties were now speaking for the transcript.

When the judge, Herbert Altman, asked the People for its position on bail, the assistant recommended "ROR," that the defendants be released on their own recognizance. At the arraignment's conclusion, Grambling and Libman, unaccompanied by detectives, left the courtroom through the front door. They were free men.

But their lives had been profoundly altered. With the arraignment, Grambling and Libman were no longer suspects. They were defendants awaiting trial. As part of the pretrial process, they were now entitled to obtain from the prosecution the evidence to be used against them. Rosner made the offer he always did in frauds cases—open file discovery. Defense counsel were invited to come to the assistant's office and examine the evidence that the prosecutor would use to prove their clients' guilt, and send them to prison.

CHAPTER 18

MESSAGE FROM THE COURT

Rosner's mind focused on a superseding indictment. As soon as the April 11 arraignment ended, he arranged a Grand Jury presentation for the crimes committed against the Salt Lake City and Jackson, Mississippi banks, as well as First Interstate in Denver. The evidence-gathering process was identical to that employed earlier—an interstate subpoena to the bank followed by a call and, if the witnesses were cooperative, a preliminary interview on the phone. The assistant listed his necessary witnesses—Conover and Scott from Salt Lake City, Shows and Warren from Mississippi and, from El Paso, Keenan.

The banks involved in the second part had not lost money, and the difference raised the cost of the presentation. The institutions agreed to let their witnesses testify, but refused to incur any out-of-pocket expenses.

Rosner prepared another disbursement request for Kindler. Between the flights and the hotels, the request exceeded $3,000, a month and a half's salary for a young assistant. The largest expense was the $900 round trip airfare for Keenan. Rosner brought the list to Kindler for approval and sat across from the Executive Assistant as he chewed on his cigar. The assistant sensed what Kindler would say.

"Do we need the guy from Texas?" Kindler asked. He held his pen, hovering over the papers, ready to sign the form.

Rosner explained the prospective indictment, and the risks involved. The Bank of Montreal crimes had been committed in New York County, and there would be no serious legal challenge regarding the Office's jursidiction to prosecute. But the Grand Jury had indicted on the Colorado National crimes, and would be asked to indict on the new crimes, on a jurisdictional theory never tested in court: That if a crime is committed as part of a conspiracy based in New York County, then New York County is empowered to prosecute that crime, even if committed in another state, and even if committed by a defendant, like Libman, who had never set foot in New York State. It was not the first case in which the assistant had proposed an expansion of New York County jurisdiction.

"Is this another one of your theories of universal New York County jurisdiction?" Kindler laughed.

"Our argument makes sense, Jim. Manhattan is the financial capital of the world. If all money crimes come back to New York, that's only a reflection of what this county is. That's why you and I work here. Besides, if we're ever going to test this jurisdictional theory, we might as well do it on this case, where the facts are so strong."

Kindler smiled and shook his head. He had authorized the first Grand Jury presentation, and the indictment for the Colorado National Bank crimes, because the facts argued powerfully for a jurisdictional leap.

"Benitez behind you on this?"

Rosner nodded.

"Moscow too?"

Another nod.

"The entire bureau is crazy."

"Just like when you were there," Rosner replied with a grin.

Kindler signed the vouchers and handed them to Rosner.

The assistant presented the expanded case to the Grand Jury during the end of April and the beginning of May, 1985. Normally impaneled for one calendar month, the Grand Jury, all 23 in attendance, voted to extend their existence for the sole purpose of completing the Grambling investigation.

The witnesses came to New York. Few had a sense of how close they had come to the precipice. Conover, the loan officer from the Salt Lake City bank, was an example. That Grambling had left his bank without the loan was unusual, Conover explained as he sat in Rosner's office. The assistant then showed the banker the real Husky Term Sheet.

Conover's mouth dropped. Gripping the true Term Sheet in his hands, his eyes were transfixed by the clause prohibiting repayment of the $8 million loan which had been approved by the Salt Lake City bank.

"Brian, it's like it was in 'Nam. When you heard the bullet whistling by your head."

Additional strands of the investigation came together. Theodore Etter, the founder of Signet Securities, came to New York to testify. He had sold the brokerage firm to Grambling, and, in March 1985, repurchased it. Etter had been in Signet's Dallas office in March when the two Federal Express packages came from Mississippi for "Keenan c/o Signet."

"I checked the Federal Express every morning," Etter said as he sat in the witness chair in the assistant's office. "I remember seeing the packages. I didn't think much of it. John had called earlier, saying that the packages would be coming and that he'd stop by to pick them up. I knew of Keenan, and about John having a banking relation with Coronado. I just thought that these packages were part of John's continuing business with the bank."

"Did Signet carry an account for Robert Libman?" the assistant asked.

"No, Signet only has accounts for businesses, not individuals."

And Grambling probably has a stack of your stationery, the assistant thought.

Shows and Warren, the Mississippians, came to New York. Their testimony raised a red flag in Rosner's mind. He asked Moscow to accompany him to a meeting in Benitez's office.

"Grambling made Kingham and Kelly into accomplices to the crime," the assistant began. "They negotiated a loan based on phony documents."

Moscow raised his hand as if he was a traffic cop stopping the flow of cars.

"Don't even think it," Moscow said to Rosner. "Kingham's what you're going to be when you leave the Office, a straight-shooter. He couldn't have known what was going on."

"Libman said the same thing to Eddie and me," Rosner added. "I'm sure Kelly and Kingham were suckered, just like everyone else I'm putting in front of the Grand Jury."

"Okay, what do you want to do?" Benitez asked in a crisp businesslike voice.

"I need them as witnesses," the assistant said firmly.

The room was silent. The legal profession was a guild. Calling people as witnesses was what attorneys did to everyone else in the world, but not to one of their own.

"Fleming's a friend of the boss," Moscow said. "You make his partners into witnesses, you disqualify him as trial counsel."

Moscow shook his head from side to side to indicate his disapproval. Benitez sat impassively.

"You don't want to do that, Brian," Moscow continued. "You want to try the case against Fleming. It will be the best learning experience you ever had." Moscow, one of the Office's most skilled trial attorneys, had recently been beaten by Fleming at trial.

"No, John. I need these two as witnesses."

"What for?" Benitez asked brusquely.

Benitez is playing devil's advocate, Rosner thought. He's always supported me on the tough calls.

"We've been beating our head against the wall on the jurisdictional issue," the assistant said. "Okay, we got a theory on jurisdiction by the back door of conspiracy law. But Kelly and Kingham give us direct evidence of a fraudulent act in New York for the Mississippi crimes. They were on the phone, in their New York office, when false representations were made over the phone to the banker and his attorney in Mississippi. That's a straightforvard jurisdictional act occurring in New York County. No fancy legal principles. A false statement made in New York, period."

"You have other witnesses to the phone call?" Moscow asked in a low voice.

"Sure, I got the Mississippi people, the lawyer and the banker. But Fleming's going to impeach them at trial."

"You don't know that," Benitez said. "The defense might stipulate that the statements were made and take the whole issue out of the case. Why else do you want Kingham and Kelly as witnesses?"

"I need them to win this trial, Peter." Agitated, Rosner rose and paced the room.

"It's the usual banking case. I got the paper on my side, but Fleming's going to make my witnesses look like asses on cross-examination. He'll make them look like they were greedy and careless; that they never relied on anything Grambling did. It was their greed that made them jump ahead and make the loans."

"Get off it. I've seen your paper, and I've read your memos. That's not your case," Benitez insisted.

"Yeah, but you know what happens to a case on cross-examination when someone like Fleming's doing the questioning. Kingham and Kelly are living proof that my witnesses are credible. They're identical to the bankers—professionals who trusted in Grambling, and got screwed. If there's a suggestion at trial that my witnesses were foolish or greedy, I sum up on Kingham and Kelly. Grambling swindled his own attorneys just like he swindled the bankers. And those attorneys weren't careless or blinded by greed any more than the bankers were."

"You're talking about disqualifying Curtis Mallet as counsel and making them into witnesses against their own client," Moscow said. "That's the worst thing you can do to a defense attorney."

"What do you want me to say, John?"

The three were silent. They were seasoned trial attorneys. Rosner's argument made powerful sense.

The assistant tapped the arms of his chair, as Moscow rocked back and forth in his. They looked to the Bureau Chief.

"Does Kingham know the problem?" Benitez asked.

"I haven't spoken to him about it," Rosner replied.

"Ask him in for a talk," Benitez said slowly. "Lay out the problem, and let's see what he thinks."

Rosner called Kingham and explained what the Office had learned about the forged Coronado documents and New Mexico CDs.

Kingham's tone of voice changed.

"I didn't know any of that," he said quickly, in a higher pitch. "I want to talk to you. I have an appointment now that I can't cancel. Can I come in right after that, at 4:00? Is that okay?"

Within two hours of the call, Kingham and Kelly were back at One Hogan Place. Had Rosner harbored any doubts that the two had been victimized, the doubts evaporated as Kingham walked into the assistant's office. In his career, the assistant had seen many things. He had seen skillful cross-examination make honest men appear to be liars: He had seen a killer walk out of a courtroom as a free man. But until Kingham walked through the door, never had Rosner seen a defense counsel blush.

Kingham and Kelly insisted that they knew nothing of the deceptions. However, they could not disclose what they did know because it had been learned in the course of their confidential attorney-client relationship. And they strenuously opposed being disqualified as Grambling's counsel.

That Friday, April 19, Fleming, Kingham, and Kelly met with the three assistants in Benitez's office to negotiate the disqualification. The attorneys agreed to disagree. The Curtis Mallet attorneys refused to step down as counsel. The assistants put Curtis Mallet on notice that the Office would seek both to disqualify the firm as counsel and to call Kingham and Kelly as trial witnesses, necessary to prove their client's guilt.

The Grand Jury investigation concluded. The first week in May, the Jury voted 19 new counts charging Grambling with crimes against the Salt Lake City bank, Jackson Savings and Loan, and First Interstate in Denver. For his role as the "Mullin" imposter in the call to the loan committee of the Salt Lake City bank, Libman was charged as an accomplice to that attempted grand larceny. In total, there were now 32 counts charging Grambling, and five counts charging Libman. A sufficient number of counts, Rosner thought, to give the court adequate scope at sentencing. Before leaving the Grand Jury room for the last time, Rosner thanked the 23, each of whom had attended every session, for their service.

On May 9, Grambling and Libman were again allowed to surrender to Collins, and again arraigned with the generosity that had been shown a month earlier.

Now began the long interregnum of legal papers, and waiting. Within two months of the second arraignment, Grambling and Libman brought a motion to dismiss the indictment. The arguments had been anticipated by the assistant: There was no larceny since Grambling always intended to repay the money taken; New York County had no jurisdiction over any of the crimes since no element of any crime had occurred in Manhattan; the Grand Jury's decision to prosecute Utah, Colorado and Mississippi crimes in a forum as distant from the events as New York was gross prosecutorial overreaching.

In August, Rosner responded with a memorandum of law and cross-motion to remove Curtis Mallet as the trial counsel. His argument for disqualification was simple: at least two Curtis Mallet attorneys would be necessary witnesses to contested factual issues at trial, and it was a given legal principle that an attorney could not both be a witness and a counsel in the same proceeding.

Although the focus of the Grambling case had shifted to legal argument, Rosner never stopped the investigation. Through the issuance of trial subpoenas, as powerful a tool as grand jury subpoenas, the assistant continued to track Grambling's "business activity."

In late May, Rosner received a package from the Western Savings and Loan Association in Phoenix, Arizona. The documents disclosed a defendant undeterred by the criminal justice system.

The documents showed that the first week in May, as the Grand Jury prepared to vote the superseding indictment, Grambling had applied for a $150,000 loan from the Western Savings and Loan Association. Called by the Western banker for a reference, Robert Zobel, the Touche Ross partner designated to become Grambling's controller at R.M.T., vouched for the accuracy of the $20 million net worth Grambling had listed on his financial statement. "Zobel did not bring up anything negative about Grambling," the banker's internal memo noted.

The assistant shook his head. Maybe it wasn't Zobel who the banker spoke to, or, if it was, maybe Zobel really believes that Grambling has money.

Rosner read more of the file.

The Western Savings bankers also telephoned Foncannon, who was less kind than Zobel, though discreet. Foncannon read the Arizona banker the first two paragraphs of the April 12 *El*

Paso Times article reporting the first indictment, and then referred the Arizona banker to the Bank of Montreal.

Tom read him the article. Rosner laughed. He pictured Foncannon speaking in his slow, careful voice, ever so cautious of not creating grounds for a libel case. The assistant returned to the documents.

On May 10, the day before his second arraignment, Grambling called Western Savings to ask if the loan had been approved. Informed of the bad references, Grambling complained, "I've gotten some bad press when the Husky deal blew up, but I can get you new references."

And I'm sure he could have, Rosner thought as he examined the financial statement on which Western Savings had relied in approving the loan pending a reference check. The financial falsely stated that Grambling owned over $4 million of Dr Pepper stock: Even Zobel had told the Arizona banker that the Dr Pepper stock should not be on the financials. Western Savings had rescinded its approval of the loan.

Good evidence of continuing criminal intent, Rosner thought. But not worth bringing to the judge's attention: It was only an attempt.

On May 13, after the second arraignment, an accountant from R. R. Donnelly & Sons, a commercial printing company in Chicago, informed Rosner of Grambling's second recent crime.

"Donnelly contracted to do printing for Grambling's venture capital company in March," the accountant said. "Grambling promised to pay with a $450,000 letter of credit from the Coronado Bank in El Paso, Texas. When we called Ron Keenan, the officer Grambling told us to contact, the secretary said that Keenan was not in, but would call us back. Later, someone identifying himself as Keenan did call. He apologized, saying that he was hard to reach because the bank auditors were in, but he verified that the letter of credit existed though he wasn't able to send it right away. Donnelly was just about to begin the printing, so we started based on Keenan's promise that the letter would be coming. We didn't get one. But when we called Grambling, he said that he had received the letter of credit and would forward it.

"Before we got it, we called Keenan again. We reached him at Coronado and started talking about the L/C. He didn't know what we were talking about. He referred us to his attorney, who told us that Grambling had been indicted in New York for forging letters on Coronado stationery.

"We called Grambling to tell him that Keenan had denied that a letter of credit existed. We didn't tell him what Keenan's counsel had said about the indictment. Without missing a beat, Grambling said that Coronado had problems regarding a Bank of Montreal loan related to a Husky deal, and that Keenan was just being overly conservative in talking to us because of Coronado's problems."

"Are you finishing the printing?" the assistant asked.

"Yes. We made Grambling assign us his accounts receivable."

The printers sent a copy of the Coronado letter of credit to Rosner. He could see at a glance that it was another forgery by white-out; the Keenan signature was legitimate, but the body of the letter had been typed in by Grambling.

When Rosner called the printers two months later, they told him that, based on the accounts receivable, the printer had been almost paid in full. They had no interest in pursuing charges.

Without a loss, or a complaint from a victim, there was nothing to report to the court, the assistant concluded: Nothing but the audacity of Grambling continuing to commit crimes while under indictment.

On September 14, two Connecticut detectives called Rosner to report yet another Grambling crime. Grambling had attempted to draw $260,000 out of a Stamford Savings Bank account in what appeared to have been a check-kite. The teller, suspicious because the account had been recently opened, called the police. When Grambling saw the police park their vehicle in front of the bank and head for the bank entrance, the detectives explained, Grambling told the teller that he did not want to withdraw money, and, when the teller appeared surprised, denied that he had ever wanted to withdraw money.

After hearing the detectives' account, Rosner rapidly served several trial subpoenas in Arizona and Connecticut.

The subpoenas produced documents proving that, in one week in September, Grambling had kited checks between four banks, First Interstate and Grand Canyon State Bank in Arizona, and Stamford Savings and Connecticut National in Connecticut. The Arizona banks had reported the crime to the F.B.I. but, by the Friday of the week in which the kite had begun, Grambling's father had deposited $265,000 in the victim banks to cover the loss. The F.B.I. and Connecticut police investigation ended: No loss, no crime.

If I report the kite to the court, the assistant thought, I'll probably be criticized for overzealousness. He could hear defense counsel's argument to Judge Cahn: It was just a misunderstanding over account balances, your Honor, and everyone was made whole in the end. Save it for trial, Rosner concluded.

But what did Grambling do with the money, Rosner wondered. With the aid of law enforcement colleagues in Phoenix, he learned that Grambling had placed a $150,000 down payment on a recently built $2 million mansion in the exclusive Biltmore Estates section of Phoenix. Rosner spoke with the builder, Edmond Mason, toward the end of that September.

"I did ask John about his indictment once I heard about it," Mason said. "But he told me not to worry. The judge was about to dismiss it, and Grambling told me that he'd be paying back all his bank loans by springtime 1986."

Rosner thought back to the courtesies he had extended Grambling at the arraignments, and to the detectives' complaints. Maybe, Ronnie was right, he thought: Treat a bum like a primrose, and he starts to think that he's something special.

Meanwhile, defense counsel and the District Attorney's Office awaited the court's decision on the motion to dismiss the indictment. Typically, the arraignment judge decided the pretrial motions. This was an onerous burden even in the street crime cases where the grand jury transcript and motion papers rarely totaled over 20 pages. The arraignment judges had 100 cases on their calendar each day. The Grambling motion papers and transcripts amounted to 700 pages to be reviewed, an impossible burden for an arraignment judge. In September, Justice Altman assigned the case to his colleague, Herman

Cahn. A trial judge with a smaller caseload, Judge Cahn had the time to study and adjudicate the pretrial issues.

Rosner reported the assignment to Benitez.

"Peter, do you know Judge Cahn?"

Benitez grimaced. "He's a nice man, and a good judge. But he's terribly weak on white-collar crime. You know that six-month long commodities fraud trial the Attorney General's Office just completed? It was before Judge Cahn. He gave the defendants a slap on the wrist at sentencing."

Rosner sighed. Had he put so much work into the case, only to have a judge who was going to give the case away at sentencing?

Benitez smiled.

"Don't let me get you depressed. It could be a lot worse, Brian. I tried a case in front of Judge Cahn. A bribery case, back in the Rackets Bureau. He mischarged the jury on whether the statute should be read in the disjuncture or the conjunctive. You know how, for some reason, our indictments historically read 'and' in defining the methods of committing the crime even though the jury can find guilt if they decide that the crime was committed in any of the listed manners?"

The assistant nodded.

"Judge Cahn charged the jury the way the indictment read. Instead of telling them that they could find guilt if the People proved the crime in any manner, he said that the People had to prove all the ways listed in the indictment. I told him he was wrong. I even got the Court of Appeals case that said he should charge 'or,' not 'and.' You know what he did?"

Rosner was silent.

"Judge Cahn went to chambers and read the cases. Then he recalled the jury and told them, 'I'm sorry, I made an error in charging you that was pointed out by counsel.' Then he charged them correctly."

"What happened?"

"The jury acquitted anyway," Benitez said with a wave of the hand. "It was a weak case. But I had never seen anyone like him before. You know the way a lot of judges are when you tell them they're wrong? They get pig-headed and bend over backwards to deny that they made a mistake, particularly in front of the jury. But Judge Cahn, with no rancor, read the cases and corrected himself."

Benitez looked toward the ceiling for a few moments, and then continued talking.

"He's weak at sentencing, and you're going to have to educate him on white-collar crime. But he's a hard-working man, and he does his homework. And he believes in doing the right thing."

Benitez thought out loud. "A white-collar case with some tough legal issues? You could have done a lot worse, Brian, a lot worse, than getting Judge Cahn."

A judge who could admit that he was wrong, Rosner thought as he walked back to his office. That's as rare in a judge as in a prosecutor. Should be an interesting man to meet.

The meeting occurred in November. Judge Cahn asked counsel to appear in his courtroom, Part 48 at 111 Centre Street. The courthouse at 111 Centre Street was the stepchild of the court system. The courtrooms at the 100 Centre Street courthouse were huge and, though rundown with peeling paint and clocks beating to their own time, the dimensions alone suggested a restorable majesty. The same could never be said of the courtrooms at 111 Centre Street. Small and windowless, with few spectator seats, the courtrooms had originally been designed with a rail in front of the jurors that was so high that the sitting jurors could not see a testifying witness. The rails had been cut down. But little could be done with the remaining inadequacies. The courtooms suggested little of the majesty of the law, and, with the rooms' notoriously poor acoustics, little of the law's practicality either.

Every morning was a constant reminder of the building's shortfalls as a courthouse. When Rosner went to 111 Centre Street for his November court date, he and hundreds of people—lawyers, litigants—jammed themselves into the lobby to wait 30 minutes for an available elevator. The building had not been designed to accommodate the hundreds of people simultaneously arriving at 9:30 A.M. for court.

Part 48 was a little box at the western end of an upper floor. There were only two rows for spectators. Rosner checked the physical structure: Jury to the right; assistant's table to the left of the jury, and the defense table to the left of that. Ahead of the tables was the bench, lower than those at 100 Centre Street, but still raised. In the rear right was the door to the jury room and the holding pen for prisoners.

While at his table, Rosner called to John McCormack, the gangling, Irish clerk seated at a desk to the left of the bench. McCormack raised his head. Acoustics okay, the assistant thought. No hum from the air vents. He read some papers on his table. Acceptable lighting, but not great. He walked behind his table, and in the area between the table and the jury box. Limited pacing room. Then he sat in various seats in the jury box; front seat closest to the courtroom door, the foreperson's seat; rear seat sixth from the courtroom door, that of juror number 12. Good sight lines. It will do for a trial, he concluded.

The assistant noticed that his adversaries and their clients had entered.

A court officer banged three times on the back rear door, then opened it.

McCormack stood and shouted, "all rise," as a small man in a black robe entered from the rear door and assumed the bench.

Early 50s, Rosner thought. Wearing a wedding band, probably has kids. Thick glasses; a scholar.

The judge spoke to the clerk in a polite, low voice.

"Added to the calendar," the clerk shouted. "People of the State of New York against John A. Grambling, Jr., and Robert Libman, Indictment Number 2800/85. Counsel present? Assistant present?"

The attorneys nodded, as the stenographer sat with his fingers poised over his typing machine.

"Could you gentlemen come to the bench?" Judge Cahn asked. The stenographer relaxed. The conference would be off-the-record.

Fleming, Hafetz, and the assistant approached. They stood in a row before the bench. Rosner and Hafetz looked up to meet the judge's eyes. Fleming was at eye-level.

"I want this to be informal since my answers aren't final," the judge said in his soft voice. "You are all busy practitioners and you need to know what your trial schedules will be.

"In essence, I will be denying the defendants' motions. I am troubled by the jurisdictional argument raised on behalf of Mr. Libman. And I want to study that more closely to make sure that the jury understood the limits of its power to indict someone who did not enter New York County or State. But the bulk of the indictment will survive. I suggest that you gentlemen clear your calendars for February as a trial date."

"Your Honor," Rosner asked, "will Curtis Mallet be trial counsel?" Fleming nodded his head, and Judge Cahn directed his answer to him.

"Mr. Fleming, I will be granting the motion to disqualify your firm as trial counsel. In light of the facts on the Mississippi loan, and the possibility that your partners may be People's witnesses, I do not think that it is tenable that you try this case in front of a jury."

"We can, of course, do the pretrial work?" Fleming asked.

"Yes. The disqualification only runs to the trial in front of the jury. You may remain as counsel on pretrial matters and, should you wish, even prepare the case for trial. But you cannot be appearing in court, at the defense table, at the trial."

"I'll inform John, your Honor, and we'll retain trial counsel."

The assistant was impressed with the judge's decision and its scope. Fleming could not cross-examine his own partners at trial, so he could not try the case. But, as Judge Cahn had ruled, there was no reason for a disqualification beyond the actual trial.

Since a trial was in the air, it was time for defense counsel to raise the topic they had avoided previously in the hope that the indictment would be dismissed.

"Your Honor," Libman's attorney began. "Could we get a sense of what kind of sentence you'd consider appropriate. My client is a businessman. Were he to plead to any crime, his career would be ruined. He wouldn't be able to do important work. Right now, he's trying to obtain a franchise, and this indictment is preventing him. Any plea is punishment enough, and jail time in addition would be cruel. Can we get a commitment on probation?"

The judge was affronted. "That Mr. Libman may have trouble getting a franchise is probably the least punishment he should be worried about. A great deal of money was involved, and I will not diminish this crime by promising no jail."

Like a sailor scanning the winds, Fleming evaluated the conversation and approached his sentencing question from a different tack.

"Your Honor, there is a great deal of money involved here, much of it my client's. This is a disaster for everyone. He went to the edge on the Husky deal, and broke down. But now he's trying to pick up his life, and get together repayment for the banks. I won't diminish the dollars involved, certainly my client understands that. He's trying to get the loans back together. But no one was killed. This was an institutional crime. The banks will survive, and the person who'll be most hurt no matter what you do, will be John and his wife, and his four young boys."

Judge Cahn was listening intently and nodding.

"I don't expect you to consider probation at this point, you hardly know John, but perhaps we can at least limit the prison time we're discussing. I think city time of less than a year is enough."

One year sentences were served on Riker's Island, where, the assistant knew, a one-year sentence usually meant parole after eight months or less. State sentences were served in prisons, usually upstate. Twelve months without parole was the minimum state time.

With discomfort, Rosner observed Judge Cahn's receptivity to Fleming's argument. It appeared to appeal to the judge: some prison, but compassion for the defendant and his family.

"What's the People's position?" the judge asked the assistant.

"We won't consent to anything less than state prison time. This is a major crime involving a great deal of money. . ."

"I know," the judge interrupted. "But no one has been hurt other than economic harm to the banks, and restitution will be part of the sentence. Several months in prison should be enough, and I think that you're being cruel by asking for more. I hope that the District Attorney's Office will rethink its position. In any case, this is all preliminary. We'll talk again when I've rendered my decisions in the motions. Please step back, gentlemen."

The attorneys returned to their tables. For the record, Judge Cahn stated his preliminary decision on the disqualification motion and the likelihood of a February trial date. The case was adjourned until January 1986.

Rosner returned to One Hogan Place, and went straightaway to Benitez's office. The assistant related the judge's sentencing thoughts to Benitez. Had they known that the case would result in a one-year sentence, the bureau would not have bothered to do the investigation.

"Don't worry," Benitez consoled Rosner. "Judge Cahn's only read the Grand Jury transcript. You can't get a sense of a case from that. The judge doesn't know what Grambling's like. He'll learn that from seeing your witnesses live at trial. And he hasn't heard about the check-kite and other crimes Grambling's been doing, has he?"

Rosner shook his head. "You should have seen it, Peter. Fleming talked abut Grambling's wife and kids, and the judge looked like he was going to cry."

"He's a sensitive man. It hurts him to put fathers in jail. Look it, you've got a long road to trial and sentencing. A lot can happen. Don't get the wrong message from a three-minute bench conference."

Rosner would try not to. But at the bench, the conversation was loud enough for the defendants, waiting at the defense table, to hear. The assistant had glanced at Grambling while Justice Cahn had spoken about sentencing. Grambling had listened intently to every word.

What, Rosner thought, was the message Grambling was getting?

CHAPTER 19

KEEPING A GOOD MAN DOWN

Once Judge Cahn had ruled that the indictment would not be dismissed, and had given his view of the appropriate sentence, Fleming and Kingham scheduled a meeting with Benitez and the assistant to discuss a plea of guilty by their client. In the usual plea arrangement, a defendant pleads guilty to a count or counts to "cover" the indictment, meaning that the counts not pleaded to are dismissed. A defendant has no legal right to plead guilty to an indictment without the prosecutor's consent, unless he pleads to every count in the indictment, which is a rare occurrence.

The meeting took place on December 19. Rosner entered Benitez's office after Fleming and Kingham had already arrived. He nodded to Benitez and shook Fleming's and Kingham's hand. Defense counsel sat in chairs directly in front of Benitez's desk. Rosner sat to the side. He always felt tense discussing prison time.

"Have you heard the one about the Lone Ranger?" Fleming began. Not for 30 years, Rosner thought. It was an old joke, and they all guffawed. Fleming had eased the tension: He was in control. That's how he must be in front of a jury, the assistant thought. He can size up the mood, dominate the situation.

"John may want to plead," Fleming said. "But he needs to know the kind of time the Office is pressing for. This is a business crime. Despite all the counts, it's really one transaction, the Husky deal and John's crackup over seeing that go down the tubes. He's a first offender, and a family man. Can we have a commitment that a long sentence is not necessary?" Fleming was talking to Benitez.

"You're conceding that prison time is appropriate?" Benitez asked.

"No," Fleming shook his head. "But we can see an argument for it. What we can't see is an insistence that it has to be lengthy time for a first offender on what is really one offense."

Rosner shook his head, but it was Benitez who spoke.

"I think we disagree on that. He is a first offender, but all white-collar criminals are first offenders. Felons can't go into a Bank of Montreal and apply for a $7.5 million loan. So the first-offender argument cuts no ice with us. The problem with figuring out how to treat Grambling is the nature of the crimes. He is manipulative, and the worst thing that you can do to a manipulator is to give him a slap on the wrist. That's a message that society approves, or at least doesn't sanction too severely, what he did. It ends up being an invitation to commit the crime again."

Benitez has been reading the memoranda outlining Grambling's post-indictment skirmishing with the law.

"There's a particular problem here. Being indicted hasn't deterred Grambling." Benitez continued.

He nodded to Rosner, who explained the fraudulent Arizona loan application and the September check-kite.

"Are you charging John with those crimes? If not, they're not crimes that John's answerable for," Fleming said sharply.

"But we know the facts," Benitez replied with equal firmness. "The indictment hasn't deterred Grambling. The only deterrent left is prison."

Kingham joined the discussion.

"We're not arguing that John isn't manipulative." He smiled, as did the others in the room.

You're the one to know, was Rosner's unspoken thought.

"But the question is, how much time is appropriate?" Fleming interjected. He spoke with passion.

"You know what John needs? He has to be taken out of this damn fast-track where he thinks that he has to be an empire builder. The best thing you can do for him is to give him work release, let him pump gas in some small west Texas town. That's what he needs to keep him out of trouble. He is going to be deterred by prison time. Prison time is what is going to break him, make him see the light. It doesn't matter now much prison time. It's the time itself that will deter him from ever doing this again."

"How much time do you think is appropriate?" Benitez asked in a calm voice. Prior to the meeting, Benitez and Rosner had agreed that they would not be the first to mention the possible length of a sentence. Why bargain against ourselves, Benitez had said.

Kingham and Fleming looked at each other.

"What do you think, Barry?" Fleming asked.

"Eight months. That would do as much for John as a couple of years in state prison."

The assistants shook their heads simultaneously.

"Too short," Benitez said. "It has to be state prison time."

Fleming was disappointed.

"How can I recommend state prison?" he asked. "The problem with state prison is that you don't know when the parole board will let him out. If John gets a sentence of a few years, he could be coming out in one, two, three, or who knows? With city time, you have a certainty with the release date."

They were going in circles.

"We just agree to disagree." Benitez rose.

"One other thing, Peter," Fleming said as he stood up. "The disqualification motion. Can we work out a way that I can try the case. It's possible that we can stipulate to whatever facts you would have Barry testify to. There's no argument that a call was made from our office and certain statements made. There won't be any contest on the jurisdiction for the Mississippi crime. We're representing John in all his civil matters. There must be a half dozen of them. The point is that we know this case. We did the pretrial motion." Fleming searched for something else to say.

Benitez looked to Rosner, who addressed Fleming.

"Peter, I'm sure that I'd learn more about how to try a case by getting my ass kicked by you in front of a jury than I'm going to learn by beating someone else at this trial. But I can't see backing off on the disqualification. Barry's living proof of what a manipulator Grambling is, and I need Barry to make my bank witnesses credible."

The meeting ended. As Kingham was walking out of Benitez's office, Rosner called to him.

"Barry, why don't you come to my office for some pretrial discovery?" Kingham accompanied the assistant.

"I can't help but asking," Rosner said as they walked down the hall. "Grambling screwed you over. He made you and Joe a part of crime."

He looked Kingham in the face as they entered his office.

"Why the hell do you want to continue representing this guy?"

"When you get into private practice," Kingham replied. "You'll understand what it means to accept a fee."

Judge Cahn did not render a written decision on the motion to dismiss in December 1985. At the January 1986 proceeding in Part 48, Kingham approached the bench and asked Judge Cahn to delay the decision.

"Mr. Grambling is considering a plea of guilty," Kingham explained. "We'd ask that you not rule on the dismissal action until he decides what to do. If he does choose to plead guilty, he'll withdraw the motion to dismiss. He'll want to plead to as many counts from as many different states as possible so that out-of-state prosecutors won't have any incentive to indict him."

Judge Cahn looked to Kingham and then to Rosner, and back.

"Would you like to discuss sentencing now?" Judge Cahn asked.

"We thank you, your Honor, but not yet," Kingham replied.

At various times in February and March, usually in Part 48 while waiting for the case to be called, Kingham and Rosner again discussed a disposition of the case. They would sit side-by-side in the spectators' seats.

"Brian, John needs a good influence. If he got an honest job in Texas, close to his family, they could give him the support that would keep him out of trouble."

"You talking probation?"

Kingham shook his head up and down. Rosner shook his head side to side.

At the March Part 48 proceeding, Judge Cahn asked Kingham and Rosner to approach the bench. He explained his sentencing position.

"Mr. Grambling would have to plead to a felony," Judge Cahn told counsel. "Prison time is warranted. I'm thinking of real prison time on the order of eight months, that's after parole or work release or whatever. I know that you think it's too light, Mr. Rosner, but this is a financial crime case. I've reviewed the grand jury transcript very carefully. The harm done here was economic harm. I'm not downplaying it."

The Grand Jury presentation was skeletal. It was not appropriate to have elicited testimony on the personal harm Grambling had caused, and Rosner had not done so.

"But when Grambling makes restitution to the victims," Judge Cahn continued, "and whenever we have discussed this issue, the assumption has always been that there would be restitution. As I was saying, when Grambling makes restitution to the banks, he will be undoing the institutional financial harm he caused, and that undoing of the harm is something I can't ignore."

Kingham was flustered. "Judge Cahn, John hasn't made a decision yet. He and Peter have to talk, and Peter's on trial until April. But I don't want to mislead you. John hasn't said whether he'll accept any time, so . . ."

"I understand you," the judge said gently. "It's a very important decision for him to make."

"Also," Kingham reached the point he wanted to make. "We've been working with the bankruptcy counsel." After the failure to obtain the $10 million Mississippi loan, Colorado National had put Grambling in bankruptcy. "I'm not certain how much there is for restitution," Kingham concluded.

The judge looked perplexed. "But I thought . . . well the Grand Jury minutes contain testimony on Mr. Grambling's wealth, and that of his family. I had thought . . . but, no matter. My thinking now is eight months and restitution. Mr. Rosner?"

"Yes, your Honor."

"I know you disagree with what I'm saying."

"Anything less than state prison time, that's a minimum of a year, is just too little. Restitution is nice, but Grambling shouldn't be able to buy his way out of prison."

"But my concern is that Grambling is in many ways different from the type of prisoner we send to state prison. He is not a violent criminal and I don't know whether the prison system has facilities to treat people other than violent criminals. Could you find out whether there are facilities for business criminals such as this defendant? Also, could you get me information on what kind of real time he would serve if I sentenced him to state prison, as you suggest, but on the condition that he be eligible for work release?"

Rosner's lack of enthusiasm for this assignment was evident on his face. The judge continued.

"I'm not certain that there's a difference in real prison time between a state prison sentence, as your Office requires, with parole or work release, and the seven or eight months that I'm talking about. Also, I don't believe that, whatever he has done, Mr. Grambling deserves to be in Attica."

Judge Cahn had referred to an upstate New York maximum security prison that was the scene of a prisoners' takeover in 1971, during Nelson Rockefeller's governorship. The prison was retaken in a bloody shoot-out in which dozens of lives, prisoners' and guards', were lost. Attica is the destination of the state's worst felons, often multiple or particularly malevolent killers. Within the criminal justice system, Attica was a synonym for the hopelessness and brutality of prison life.

Libman's counsel also discussed a plea of guilty with Judge Cahn and Rosner during February and March 1986. Counsel insisted that the plea be to a misdemeanor and not a felony. The distinction was important to Libman. A misdemeanor, such as the conspiracy with which Libman was charged, was a crime punishable by less than a year in prison. Within the public's mind, a misdemeanor was perceived to be not very serious, like a traffic ticket, and no obstacle to a ready reentry into business activity. Felonies, a crime for which a person could be imprisoned for a year or more, were less easily made light of.

At the March and April court appearances, Libman's counsel asked the judge to consider a misdemeanor plea. At a bench conference on April 4, Judge Cahn told counsel that classification as a felon was what Libman deserved, though, the judge said, "I would be willing to consider misdemeanor time." Judge Cahn turned to the prosecutor. The look was an invitation to speak.

Grambling is the main defendant, Rosner thought. But if the judge is fighting me on state time for Grambling, he's going to oppose state time for Libman. It was not worth the fight.

"The People would accept misdemeanor time on a felony plea. We would want something on the order of at least six months on Rikers Island." Rikers Island, located in the Long Island Sound between Queens and Bronx counties, housed the prisoners confined for up to "a bullet," one year.

"I'm not that far off from the assistant," the judge noted. "I was thinking more of 90 days in Rikers. With good time off, that's a real sentence of 60 days."

Defense counsel protested, but recognized the bottom line: a felony plea with misdemeanor time of 90 days, or a trial. Libman had been excused from appearing in court on April 4. "I'll have to discuss the plea offer with my client," Libman's attorney told Judge Cahn.

Outside of the courtroom, defense counsel motioned to the assistant. "My only authorization today was to accept a sentence of 30 days maximum. That's the straight sentence, not after good time or early release. I'll tell Libman the numbers you and the judge put up and get back to you."

Also on April 4, Judge Cahn rendered his long-awaited written decision on the motion to dismiss. In a tightly reasoned 11-page opinion, Judge Cahn dismissed all the charges against Libman but for the misdemeanor conspiracy count. The opinion noted that the Grand Jury evidence regarding Libman was peculiar: He was an accomplice who had never set foot in Manhattan. This peculiarity required the Grand Jury to meticulously understand its authority to decide the factual issue of venue, whether or not New York County was the proper location for the prosecution. Judge Cahn concluded that Rosner had charged the jury incorrectly on venue: The charge had merged the subtle differences in the jurisdictional standards to be applied to an accomplice and a co-conspirator so that the jury may have misunderstood the law governing whether it could indict an accomplice who had not entered the county. The result of this analysis was that Judge Cahn dismissed the counts in which Libman had been charged as an accomplice. Since the error had been made in good faith, Judge Cahn authorized Rosner to re-present the felony counts to a grand jury.

"Thank you, your Honor," Rosner said after Judge Cahn had explained his decision on April 4. "We'll be re-presenting the case immediately, and should there be an indictment, we'll move to consolidate the new Libman indictment with the existing Grambling indictment, and existing Grambling-Libman conspiracy count." Judge Cahn nodded in approval.

The case was re-presented to a new Grand Jury that week. A re-presentation was necessary since the judge had dismissed all the felony counts against Libman. But, Rosner thought, it is not necessary to re-present the entire case. In the indictment voted in May 1985, Libman had been indicted for felonies committed against both the Bank of Montreal and the Salt Lake City bank. Asking the Bank of Montreal to again fly Hopkyns in from Calgary was no problem. The bank agreed to pay the airfare and hotel bill. The Salt Lake City witnesses were a different matter. It would cost almost $1,000 to again fly Conover and Clark to New York for their testimony, and it was a $1,000 that the Office would have to pay.

"Not worth it," Rosner explained to Benitez. "We're talking misdemeanor time for Libman anyway. I'll have felony counts for him to plead to based on the Bank of Montreal crimes. He's not going to get any extra time if there are Salt Lake City bank felonies. And, if Libman doesn't plead and I try the case, I'll be able to get the proof of the Utah crimes into evidence anyway since those crimes are charged as part of the conspiracy."

Libman was reindicted on the Bank of Montreal felonies. Uncertain how to instruct the jury on accomplice liability, the assistant had taken the charge verbatim from Judge Cahn's opinion dismissing the indictments. That charge passed Judge Cahn's legal scrutiny when he reviewed the transcript of the re-presentation, and the new Libman indictment was consolidated with the old. After 10 months of oral and written argument, the final result of the Grand Jury review was an indictment identical in all ways to the original, but for the omission of Libman as a codefendant on the Utah bank felony counts.

The re-presentation had given the assistant an opportunity to prepare his witnesses for trial. Among the witnesses necessary to reindict Libman was Robert Wilkis. He came to One Hogan Place to be reinterviewed that April. As Wilkis left the assistant's office, he met Warren Reiss in the hallway. Reiss, one of the Office's most talented young trial attorneys, had just been transferred from a street crime unit to the Frauds Bureau.

"Hey, hey, hey Bob, how you doing?" Reiss put his cigarette in his mouth and extended his hand for a shake. The assistant heard the greeting and came out of his office.

Wilkis saw the perplexity on Rosner's face.

"Oh, I had brought a complaint to the Office," Wilkis said to Rosner. "Nothing much. I never got around to telling you."

"It's okay," the assistant said without conviction. "Warren will tell me."

Rosner shook Wilkis' hand. "Thanks again for coming in, Bob. I'll let you know when we have a firm trial date." Rosner watched as Wilkis walked through the reception area and, out of sight and hearing, into the central hallway. He turned to Reiss, and motioned him to come into the assistant's office.

"Okay, let's hear this," Rosner asked after they had sat down. The cigarette dangled from Reiss' mouth. Smoke curled around his face. No one in the Frauds Bureau smokes, Rosner thought, except these guys from street crime.

"Nothing much to tell, Brian. Bob came in with a complaint a couple of months ago. His housekeeper, from Brazil or somewhere, allegedly snatched the cash that Bob kept in a shoe box in the closet. Not much of a case. No proof she took it, other than her fingerprint on the shoebox. But she explained that away. Part of her job was to dust in the closet, rearrange the boxes. It was natural that her print was there. But what's the Grand Jury to do, indict on that evidence? They no-billed the case."

"Money in a shoe box?"

"Yeah, $30 thousand bucks." Reiss took a drag on his cigarette.

Rosner rolled his eyes towards the ceiling.

"Bob says he made loans to his brothers, one was running a restaurant in Boston and the other had some cellular phone business," Reiss continued. "The 30 grand was the repayments."

"What the hell do you think Wilkis was really doing?"

"Hey, an investment banker. Big-time, fast track, doing deals." Reiss put the back of his index finger to his nose, sniffed, and raised his head and finger in jerky motions.

"They're all coke heads. Maybe he was doing some sales on the side."

The assistant laughed at Reiss' joke.

"Hey, what do you want me to do? Down in the trial bureaus, we just do our investigations, put the cases in and let the Grand Jury decide. If Wilkis' money was taken, it would be a larceny no matter where the money came from. By the way, what was Bob in for, the Grambling case?"

Rosner nodded.

"Piece of cake," Reiss said.

"No, not really," the assistant replied. "It's the usual lack of intent defense."

Reiss dismissed the problem with a wave of his hand. "Intent? The argument's easy to make. You just have to make the jury understand that they can infer intent from the facts. Did I ever tell you about my last trial, the St. Andrew's Churchyard stabber?"

Yeah, about 40 times, Rosner thought. He smiled. Few assistants told a trial story better than Reiss.

"Victim's having a stroll in the St. Andrew's Churchyard," Reiss began. "You know, down on Broadway?"

Reiss stood up and, pumping his arms, walked back and forth in the assistant's office. Then he appeared to be startled, and looked over his shoulder with a frightened expression on his face.

"So my guy comes up to the victim, starts stabbing him right in the chest, right near the vital organs, the heart, the lungs. And each time, he plunges that knife into my victim's chest, he screams 'Ugh! Ugh! Ugh!' "

Reiss stabbed the air with an imaginary knife and shouted the guttural "Ugh!" sound with each plunge.

Reiss stopped his movements, and was silent.

"Miracle my victim lives. So we charge the defendant with attempted murder and assault with intent to cause serious physical injury. The defense concedes the attack, but fights the intent. Defendant even takes the stand. He didn't intend to kill the guy. He didn't even intend to seriously harm the guy, he says. 'Hey, asshole,' I ask him, 'What'd you think you were doing when you're poking the guy with the knife and screaming, 'Ugh! Ugh! Ugh!'?"

"Nice cross-examination, Warren."

"You know what he says? 'I wasn't poking the guy!' " Reiss shook his head. " 'No,' the defendant says, 'the guy was just falling on my blade.' "

Rosner laughed. Reiss continued.

"So I sum up to the jury. 'Ladies and gentlemen, what more eloquent proof of intent to kill can there be than this defendant making the disgusting noise 'Ugh! Ugh! Ugh!' as he plunged a knife four times into the area of this victim's vital organs? What more eloquent statement of intent to kill could this defendant make? And what could his intent possibly be, but to kill, when he stabbed the victim repeatedly and deeply near the heart?' The jury goes out. They deliberate."

Reiss paused.

"So what happened?" Rosner asked.

Reiss took a drag on his cigarette, and snapped his fingers. "Conviction . . . on the assault."

Rosner winced.

"They acquitted on the attempted murder. Hopefully, Brian, you got more convincing evidence of intent than I had."

"Only in Manhattan," Rosner shook his head. "And I have to prove Grambling intended to deprive the banks of money permanently when he signed notes promising to pay the money back!"

As April progressed, the plea discussions continued, and the court solidified its position. Judge Cahn adopted the assistant's position as to Libman: Six months real time. That would mean a nine-month sentence, reduced by a mandatory one-third off for "good time," a sentence reduction always earned unless the prisoner attacked a corrections officer while incarcerated. As to Grambling, Judge Cahn had moved to a sentence of three years of state prison. With good time off, Grambling would be before the parole board in a year, and probably out. But restitution was mandatory.

Fleming appeared in Part 48 in April. He resisted the one to three offer by Judge Cahn.

"Your Honor," he argued at the April 14 court proceeding, "John could come before the parole board on a one to three, and not get paroled. He'll end up serving two years."

Also, Fleming added, "I don't think that John can make restitution. The father has only a net worth of $3 million."

Fleming spoke slowly, and looked Judge Cahn in the face. "Any restitution in the case is going to have to come out of John's future earnings."

Fundamentally, it is unfair to penalize a defendant for his lack of wealth. Judge Cahn told counsel that restitution would not be a condition of the plea.

Having moved Judge Cahn to a one to three promise with no restitution, Fleming then worked some more on the District Attorney's Office. As they left Part 48 on April 14, Fleming spoke to Rosner.

"Brian, you don't care where he serves his time, do you?"

"There's lots of prisons in New York State. I don't care where he goes."

"That's not what I meant. Being near his family would be a good influence."

"No problem, Peter. The family's in Greenwich, Connecticut. That's right on the New York State border, near a couple of state prisons."

"No, that's not what I was thinking. John's wife and his boys will probably be moving back to El Paso, with John's folks. If John could serve there, he might be able to make some good of his prison time. Think about letting John plead guilty to some federal crime. He's being investigated by the U.S. Attorney's Office in El Paso."

Rosner was aware of the federal investigation. He had spoken frequently with an El Paso federal prosecutor and F.B.I. agent about Grambling's crimes against the Coronado Bank.

"Let John plead here and in El Paso, with sentences to be served at the same time in a federal prison in Texas," Fleming said.

"A place like Allenwood?" the assistant asked. Allenwood was a notorious minimum security prison in Pennsylvania. Built like a campus, the inmates had access to tennis courts, VCRs and a library. It was confinement: they couldn't leave. But the lifestyle was more luxurious than that lived by millions of honest, hard-working poor people.

"Yeah, that would be nice," Fleming laughed. "I sometimes think that it wouldn't be so bad to serve nine or ten months in Allenwood. Catch up on my reading, lose 20 pounds playing tennis, write my memoirs. But," and Fleming grew serious, "the federal prisons in Texas aren't Allenwood. They're not necessarily all maximum security, but they're all pretty bleak—hot and dusty. It won't be vacation time for John."

"I don't like the idea. But I'll talk to Moscow," which is what Rosner said whenever he wanted to avoid saying a flat out "no."

"Do you mind if I make an appointment to see Bob on this?" Fleming asked.

"Not at all," Rosner said. I knew you'd be seeing Morgenthau at some point, the assistant thought.

The meeting with Morgenthau was set for the first week of May. The representatives of the Frauds Bureau were Rosner and Moscow, the new Bureau Chief. When the city corruption scandals had erupted several months earlier, the head of the Department of Investigation, the chief watchdog over the honesty of city employees, had resigned, to be replaced by Kenneth Conboy, a former Chief of the Rackets Bureau. Conboy had asked Benitez to be his Deputy, and Benitez had accepted. He was replaced by Moscow.

On the appointed afternoon, Rosner raced up the stairs, but still arrived at the meeting late. As he entered the District Attorney's Office, Fleming and Moscow were already there.

". . . 'no', the Lone Ranger said . . . ." Fleming finished the joke, and they all laughed. The office was long and wide, the walls covered with mementoes of Morgenthau's years of public service: awards, certificates, the signed photograph from President Kennedy. On one wall were several water colors of Navy vessels including a watercolor of the cruiser that had been sunk beneath him in the Mediterranean during the Second World War. Morgenthau leaned forward slightly to listen. He favored his left ear. The hearing in the right ear was impaired as a result of the wartime sinking 40 years before.

Fleming explained the facts in a moderate, non-argumentative manner. Fleming knew the diplomacy of the argument. He did not contest Grambling's guilt, or the need for prison, or the number of years Grambling needed to serve.

"In the Southern District, Bob, we never cared where a person served his time so long as he got the time he deserved."

Morgenthau chewed on his unlit cigar and nodded.

"This kid . . ."

"He's a man with children, isn't he?" Morgenthau asked.

"Yes, a young man . . ."

"Who's pretty experienced at committing sophisticated crimes," Morgenthau added, rolling the cigar in his mouth, "a well-trained man." Morgenthau wanted Fleming to understand that the District Attorney was informed about the case. He would be fair in resolving all disputes, but he was informed.

"I'm not arguing that jail's not right for him, Bob. But he also did federal crimes."

Morgenthau smiled and lit his cigar.

"If he pleads both federally and in state court," Fleming continued, "he can serve his time in a prison near his family in Texas. I know that John's and Brian's concern is that my client will go to a resort prison like Allenwood. You know the Texas federal prisons. They're not resorts. Why should the Office fight about where Grambling does his time so long as the number of years is right?"

Fleming had put it in such moderate terms that there could be no reasonable objection to the proposal. Morgenthau looked to his assistants. They didn't speak.

"It's easy to forget what our purpose is," the District Attorney said. "It's not the arrest or indictment." He drew in on his cigar.

"It comes down to sentencing. Our purpose is to convince the judge to impose the right time. We don't care where he serves it."

No one spoke. Fleming, Moscow, and Rosner rose, as did the District Attorney. Hands were shaken. As Fleming and the assistants walked out, the District Attorney motioned to Rosner to stay.

"You did a great job on the case. Nice work putting it together," he said and thought for a moment. "Peter spoke to me. He's really pissed that he was disqualified."

"Mr. Morgenthau, we had . . ."

The District Attorney stopped the assistant with a wave of his hand. "I know. And this request about the sentence, we're not giving him anything. Again, nice job." The District Attorney sat down, and the assistant left.

Just as Fleming was successfully obtaining a commitment for a sentence of one to three in a federal prison, Grambling was working to undo all of Fleming's efforts. On May 15, Robert Ward, a partner at the Manhattan law firm Shea & Gould, called Rosner. Ward was counsel to the accounting firm Touche Ross.

"Can you send me a copy of the Grambling indictment," Ward asked. "I want to attach it to court papers I'm filing in Connecticut."

Ward explained that Touche Ross was applying for an injunction to prevent Grambling from presenting forged Touche Ross financials to businesses, as he had been doing since April. Over the next two days, based on Shea & Gould's information, the assistant made calls to Connecticut and Denver to determine the extent of the new crimes. He went to Moscow's office to tell him the results. The furniture was the same as when Benitez was Bureau Chief, but Moscow had added his personal touch to the room. A ragged, oriental rug was on the floor and various mementoes and pictures were on the walls—a framed Rembrandt print, a photograph of the Putnam County country home owned by his parents, a lengthy extract from a Judge Learned Hand speech entitled "The Spirit of Liberty." Also on the wall was a framed, black and white glossy photograph of Mr. Hogan.

"John, this guy's incredible. I spoke to a real estate owner in Stamford, Connecticut, a guy named Phillip Greenblatt. Greenblatt's looking to rent a building he owns in Westport, and a broker brings in Grambling as a potential tenant. Grambling's working to rent space for some company he has named Venture Marketing Group. Now Greenblatt is giving a $70,000 move-in concession to the new tenant, so he doesn't want to rent to a deadbeat. He asks Grambling for some financials to prove that Grambling's company is creditworthy, and Grambling produces some financials, including one for a business of his named Western Education Enterprises, Inc. Grambling also says to Greenblatt, 'Call my reference at Touche Ross, Robert Zobel.'

"Remember Zobel, John? He's the guy who was going to be Grambling's controller at R.M.T. He's also the guy that gave a great reference for Grambling when that Arizona bank, Western Savings, was considering a loan after the first indictment. Obviously, when Grambling talks to Greenblatt, Grambling figures that Zobel is a guy he can count on. And Grambling even called Zobel in advance, to tell him to expect a call from Greenblatt.

"So Greenblatt calls Zobel, and Zobel's doing the usual bit. 'Yeah, I know Grambling, we've done work for him.' Of course skating over the fact that Grambling's under indictment for $36.5 million of bank fraud. And then Greenblatt says to Zobel, 'I wish I was renting to Western Education and not Venture Marketing. The certified statement Touche Ross did for Western Education is pretty impressive.'

"Now this is too much even for Zobel. He knows that Touche Ross had done some work for Grambling, but he's never heard of a certified statement for Western Education. 'Send me a copy of that,' he asked Greenblatt. Zobel gets it, and circulates it among the Touche Ross offices. Sure enough, it's a forgery. He didn't even have to circulate the financials. You look at the statement, and you can see that it's one of Grambling's cut and paste jobs.

"So Zobel tells Greenblatt, and then calls Grambling. Friendship's one thing, but forging documents over the letterhead of your pal's firm is another. But Grambling gave Zobel the usual apologetic bullshit. 'Oh, Bob, I heard that there's this forgery going around I didn't know about it. People on my staff prepared it without my authority. I fired the person.'"

"Grambling's a man who knows how to 'fess up to his responsibilities," Moscow commented dryly.

"There's more. The entire story I just told you about the Westport property and Zobel—let's see," the assistant looked at his notes, "that occurs between April 10 and April 16."

Moscow reflected on the dates.

"While Fleming's successfully convincing Judge Cahn that Grambling's remorseful," Moscow said.

"You got it, John. And it gets worse. In April, Zobel contacts all the Touche Ross offices to ask about Grambling. On May 12, the Denver office calls Zobel. The Western Education Touche Ross financial had surfaced again. It had been given to a Touche Ross client in Denver, a Beaumont Properties.

"I've spoken to Beaumont. It's a construction company. Grambling wanted to build a school for dental assistants in Denver. It was somehow related to Western Education and Biosystems, the school for rehabilitative therapy that Grambling owns in Tempe, Arizona. Anyway, Beaumont is going to build this school on its own for $1.5 million, and then lease it to Grambling for $150,000 a year. But before building, Beaumont wants Grambling to give it some evidence that Grambling's companies are capable of carrying the rent. So Grambling hands over the Touche Ross financial.

"As it turns out, the Beaumont officer that Grambling is dealing with is a former Touche Ross accountant. He looks at the financials, and he notices that something's wrong. The last paragraph in the cover letter to the statement says that the financial opinion is unqualified, but a sentence in the first paragraph is a disclaimer. The Beaumont officer knows that Touche Ross only puts disclaimers in balance sheets or unaudited statements. It just doesn't read right, so he calls Touche Ross in Denver, which ultimately calls Zobel in Philadelphia. The Beaumont officer also does a newspaper check, and finds the *Denver Post* stories about the $6 million Colorado National Bank theft."

Moscow thought for a moment. "We have to tell the judge, and then he'll withdraw the plea offer." He paused. "Good, it was too low."

"You know what it means, John? No plea, and it's a 10-week trial, and we can lose it. I'm not backing off or nothing. I'm as much of a trial dog as the next guy. But you should always think about the risk before withdrawing a plea offer."

"I'm listening," Moscow said.

"This is how I think we should go," Rosner continued. "A letter to Fleming. Moderate. Polite. Give him advance notice of what we found out. That way Fleming can't accuse us of ambushing him at the next court appearance. Who knows? Maybe Grambling has a good explanation for what's happened."

"He does," Moscow smiled. "One of his employees did it."

"You'd think that a 32 count indictment would put a crimp in a guy's activities," Rosner chuckled. "But I guess you just can't keep a good man down."

The Office followed the strategy suggested by Rosner. On May 20, a letter outlining the Touche Ross crimes was mailed to Fleming. The next court date was May 29. Greenblatt from Shearman & Sterling was at civil court that day. After his proceeding, he came to Judge Cahn's courtroom to see how justice was done. Fleming sat at the defense table, and Rosner at his. Greenblatt was in the first row of spectator's seats. The judge had not yet arrived.

Rosner approached the wooden bar in front of the spectator's area and, leaning over, whispered to Greenblatt. "Have you ever met Peter Fleming?" the assistant asked. Greenblatt said "no," and Rosner motioned to Fleming, who came over. The assistant made the introductions.

"Peter, Jon Greenblatt from Shearman & Sterling, counsel to the Bank of Montreal."

Fleming extended his hand for a shake, and spoke.

"Bank of Montreal. They're the fucks persecuting John."

In a sentence, Fleming had captured the moral inversion of criminal defense work: the defrauder as the victim, the swindled as the persecutor. Greenblatt was struck dumb. Judge Cahn entered the courtroom and took the bench.

When the case was called, Rosner and Fleming approached the bench for an off-the-record conference. The assistant handed the judge a copy of the May 20 letter sent to Fleming.

The judge read in silence. He adjusted his glasses, and appeared to read the letter again.

"Mr. Fleming, I am very disturbed by this letter. It calls for an explanation."

"Your Honor, I have spoken to John about these matters," Fleming said in a grave voice. "They are very disturbing to him too. He has searched into them, and this is what happened. An employee, Pam Ficarella, his sister-in-law, became distressed by the problems John's businesses were having, problems created by John's problems here." Fleming nodded toward Rosner.

Like it's my fault, the assistant thought.

Holding the letter, Fleming continued. "She did this in a foolish attempt to help. Having said that, John accepts full responsibility for what was done."

"Your Honor," Rosner began. "That's a . . ."

"Be quiet, Mr. Rosner," Judge Cahn snapped. He turned to Fleming. "That explanation is not satisfactory."

"I'm sorry, your Honor, that is the only explanation I have."

"My inclination is to withdraw the plea offer," Judge Cahn said. He looked over counsel towards the defense table.

"Your client's presence was excused today, wasn't it? I want him here on future court dates."

Fleming motioned to speak.

"Please return to your tables and make your applications," Judge Cahn said as he turned to his stenographer. "We'll be going back on the record now."

Rosner asked that the bail condition be revoked and Grambling remanded.

"The only way to stop him from committing crimes is to put him in prison while he's awaiting trial, your Honor."

"We'll talk about it at the next court date," Judge Cahn responded. "June 3. And I want your client here, Mr. Fleming."

"May we approach, again," Fleming asked.

Judge Cahn waved them to come up.

"Your Honor, it appears we might be getting close to a trial. I've worked with John on this case for a year. I know the case, and he trusts me. You know how important that is for a defendant at trial. Rescind your disqualification decision. No one from my firm has to testify to any fact that can't be stipulated to."

"If there's a stipulation of facts, discuss it with counsel. June 3."

The judge leaned back in his chair and turned to his court clerk.

"Call the next case." The Grambling proceeding was over.

"No, Peter," Rosner whispered as, side by side, Fleming and he walked down the aisle out of the courtroom.

On June 3, Grambling was present in court. On the record, Judge Cahn withdrew the plea offer of one to three years. He declined to remand Grambling, but he did require a $50,000 bail, cash or bond, to be posted at the next court date. And Grambling was told to obtain a trial attorney in compliance with the Court's disqualification decision. Trial was set for September 12.

The assistant had begun his trial preparations when, on July 2, A.D.A. Reiss walked into Rosner's office. Reiss, a cigarette dangling from his mouth, was reading a *New York Times* as he entered.

"Nice picture of Bob. Where do you think they get it? Business school yearbook?"

Rosner was seated at his desk. The *New York Law Journal* was spread out before him. The assistant was reading the related story. He put out his hand, and Reiss passed him the *Times*. It was a front page story:

> *Two Wall Street Executives Settle In Big Insider Trading Case.*
> Two investment bankers were charged yesterday with participation in an insider trading ring with Dennis B. Levine, the Wall Street professional who pleaded guilty last month in what the authorities have described as the largest insider trading case ever uncovered. The two, Robert M. Wilkis, formerly with Lazard Freres & Company . . .

Reiss spoke first.

"Bobby made $3 million, the *Times* says. And he was doing it while talking to us."

He blew a ring of smoke to the ceiling.

"I guess we know where that dough in the shoe box came from," Rosner replied.

Reiss scratched his head, "Damn. And I thought he was just a coke dealer."

Rosner frowned. Immunity is not transferable between jurisdictions, so however immune Wilkis was against state prosecution, the federal government was not prevented from proceeding with its case against Wilkis.

"Puts a little crimp in your case, doesn't it?" Reiss asked. Although Reiss continued to smile, it was the smile assistants used when they talked business. "Can you get around it at trial?"

"I think so," Rosner said. "Let's say Wilkis is telling the truth. He's an inside trader, but, as far as Grambling goes, Wilkis was duped. He wasn't an accomplice."

"That's great if you get the jury to buy it. But what if they don't?"

"Does it matter? Let's say Wilkis is lying. He intentionally helped Grambling."

"Any money goes to Wilkis, any benefit?" Reiss asked.

"Nope. Absolutely none."

"It's clear that Grambling was calling the shots." Reiss was thinking out loud. "I'm beginning to see what you mean."

"Wilkis helped Grambling commit the crime," Rosner explained. "Whether Wilkis was a dupe, or a knowing accomplice, doesn't matter. Grambling was committing the crime no matter what Wilkis' state of mind."

"Perfect," Reiss concluded. "You can prove it coming or going."

Rosner said something that Reiss couldn't hear.

"Come again, Brian?"

"Oh, I was just thinking, Warren," the assistant sighed. "About making money the old fashioned way.' "

CHAPTER 20

LIBMAN KNOWS WHAT TO SAY

Grambling's continuing criminal conduct made Judge Cahn mad, but he was not a man to hoard his anger. That August, in the midst of a trial that would not end for six months, Judge Cahn again met with counsel to discuss a possible disposition. A guilty plea would abort what Rosner had been characterizing as a 10-week trial and what could readily extend to a trial of twice the anticipated length.

Judge Cahn asked counsel to approach the bench.

"Gentlemen, I have reconsidered the matter. The sentence I propose is 45 months of state prison with a minimum of 15. That should satisfy the People's request that the prison authorities have leeway to keep Grambling in prison for more than an insignificant sentence."

"No, your Honor," Brian Rosner said. "Forty-five months is less than four years, and he'll probably be out in the 15 months. It's too little. And, if he does get out early, society has no hold over him to deter him from committing more crimes."

"Your Honor," Fleming interjected. "If the People are concerned about having a 'hold' over John, then you should consider probation on top of the sentence. That way, if John messes up after being released, he can be put back in prison."

"Does that mean, Mr. Fleming, that your client would accept a sentence of 15 to 45 months?" the Court asked.

"No, your Honor. It would be his decision, of course. But I can't recommend a sentence of more than one to three years, with probation afterwards."

"Judge Cahn," the assistant said, "I don't know what the federal sentencing rules are," and Rosner nodded towards

Fleming, the former federal prosecutor, "but you can't impose a split sentence of prison and probation for a felony. The only way you can give the People the 'hold' they want over Grambling is to impose a sentence with a maximum on the order of seven years. If you set a one-year minimum, he can come before the parole board after 12 months or so, and probably be out. Then, if he screws up on the outside, he can be put back in to finish his sentence."

"To serve up to seven?" Fleming asked incredulously.

"Absolutely," Rosner replied.

Fleming reddened. "How can I recommend that? It's easy to stand here and say that he's going to get paroled early, but the Parole Board would pass him over for two or three years."

Rosner nodded. "I'll be perfectly candid. We're going to recommend that he not be paroled."

The judge was taken aback. "That is a little harsh, don't you think?"

"Even if John gets paroled," Fleming continued. "If he screws up, as the assistant puts it, he gets thrown back in for the full seven years. Who's to know what the Parole Board considers a screw-up. No," Fleming shook his head emphatically, "I can't allow John to accept that uncertainty. We'll have to go to trial on this case."

Rosner shrugged. "Fine with me, Judge Cahn, you have no sense of how rotten a person Grambling is from the cold transcript. After a trial, you'll understand why the sentences we've been discussing have been too low."

The judge could see that counsel were moving further apart on sentencing. "I think that the 15 to 45 months is fair. You know, Mr. Rosner, I could impose it over the People's objections."

The assistant became angered.

"Judge Cahn, Grambling has the constitutional right to plead guilty to the indictment. He does that and the People have no leverage in forcing you to impose more than 45 months." Rosner spoke with emphasis.

"But the People aren't going to participate in any plea that results in a top sentence of 45 months. You want to impose that without us—fine, go right ahead. If you don't want to do that, then let's set a real trial schedule and get moving." The assistant had had his fill of plea discussions.

It was summer. Little trial work was done then: witnesses are on vacation, as are attorneys and judges. Judge Cahn adjourned the case to September 30, 1986. Before leaving the bench, the People made their last plea offer: one-and-a-third to seven, state prison. Fleming refused to recommend more than one to three, and Judge Cahn declined to impose a plea bargain without the consent of the People. Judge Cahn set October 27 as a firm trial date. In trial work, there are trial dates, and trial dates. October 27 was a real date. Judge Cahn ordered Grambling to have substitute counsel ready to try the case.

In the hallway outside of the courtroom, Rosner and Fleming had a last plea conversation.

"Peter, I'm assuming that Grambling can't go to trial, and he's going to plead. My last offer is the one-and-a-third to seven. It's open until October 14. If he doesn't plead by then, I'm going to start preparing for trial. It means flying my witnesses in from all over the country. Once I start doing that, all bets are off. If Grambling doesn't tell me by the 14th that he's going to plea, and then he pleads, you'll have to throw yourself on the mercy of the court. The District Attorney's Office will be free to make any recommendation it wants for the sentence."

Fleming listened in silence. He nodded his head and said tersely, "I hear you."

As the plea discussions with Fleming sputtered to an end, discussions continued with Libman's attorney, Larry Goldman. Goldman had replaced his partner as Libman's counsel. Bushy-haired, with a mustache, Goldman was a former Hogan assistant, a graduate of the Office's Rackets Bureau, and as skilled a courtroom attorney as his partner.

Quick with a wisecrack, Goldman used his humor as a prod in the negotiations.

"Brian, why are you coming down so heavy on Libman. He's hardly the biggest ganef in the case, is he?"

Rosner could not disagree. "Ganef " was Yiddish for thief, and in the realm of the greater and the smaller, Libman was unquestionably the lesser ganef.

"No, Larry," the assistant admitted. "Libman's not the main man, and that's why he has an outstanding offer of nine months city time instead of state prison. And that offer was a mistake, and you know it. Judge Cahn began too low."

"You need Bob, Brian," Goldman said consolingly. "Offer Bob something good, like probation, and Bob will be your witness."

"I don't need him. I have the paper."

"Bullshit, you have the paper. Paper can't talk," Goldman said with a raspiness in his voice. "Listen, you try your case any way you want to, but you know that jurors don't understand paper unless you have a witness explain it to them."

Rosner wanted to disagree, but could not. Sitting comfortably in his office, sifting through the documents a hundred times, the paper told a blunt story—one that the jury could maybe understand. But nothing clarified ambiguities as much as an accomplice to say that the defendant intentionally lied and cheated.

"I'm not interested, Larry."

"Are you really going to try Libman separately?"

Goldman had succeeded in separating Libman's court appearances from Grambling's. The attorney hoped the separation would result in a separate trial for Libman.

"If not me, someone else will. But it won't be a separate trial. Grambling's going to trial on October 27. So will Libman."

"Not if I can help it. I have some more pretrial motions that will delay things for a few more weeks, or cause a severance if you try to try Libman with Grambling. Is Libman so important to the Office that it's willing to staff a separate 10-week trial? All that work to get Libman a year in prison?"

Damn, Rosner thought, what Goldman said made sense. Even with Libman convicted after a multiweek trial, how can I justify a sentence of much more than a year after the plea discussions? Even if I convinced the judge that Libman deserved a state prison sentence, was it worth it? A separate 10-week trial with witnesses flown to New York from Calgary, Denver, Salt Lake City, Texas and Mississippi—and Rosner would have to do that all since Libman was named in the conspiracy which charged all the bank frauds as a crime—just for Libman?

"You're right, Larry. If I'm only going to get a year or so for Libman after a separate trial, it's not worth it. But I don't think it's going to be a separate trial, and Libman saves me no time by pleading out if there's a joint trial."

"Are you going to punish him because his codefendant goes to trial? Is that fair?" Goldman spoke with agitation. Then he thought for a moment, and asked, "What time would you give Libman if Grambling pleaded?"

Rosner thought over Goldman's argument.

"Okay, Larry, this is the deal. If Grambling goes to trial and your guy pleads, it's nine months. Libman doesn't save me any time by pleading. If Grambling pleads, I'll give your guy a break, just to save the Office the expense of a 10-week trial. If Grambling pleads, and Libman pleads, six months."

"He won't plead to the Bank of Montreal larceny."

"Okay. He'll have to plead to the conspiracy, and a felony, a forgery having to do with the Lazard Freres consent and the Corcoran impersonation. I'm going to ask the questions at the plea, and I'm going to have him admit to the theft, even though he won't be pleading it. If he has some kind of business reason that he thinks a felony plea to a forgery is better than a felony plea to a larceny. . ."

"He's innocent of the larceny," Goldman interrupted. "He had no intent to deprive the bank of funds permanently."

". . . that's fine," the assistant concluded. "Just one thing, Larry. You know how defendants crap around at pleas. 'Yes, your Honor, I'm guilty, but I didn't do nothing wrong.' Libman has to plead to the crime. No pussyfooting that he didn't think it was a forgery, or that he didn't intend to deceive the bank. If he's going to plead for this light sentence, he has to allocute correctly. Or the plea's off. And Larry," Rosner added. "He has to plead under oath."

Libman next appeared in Part 48 on October 7, 1986. When Rosner entered Part 48, he and Libman exchanged nods, as they had on all the court dates. They had not spoken since the March 1985 call when the assistant had told Libman to obtain an attorney. Rosner motioned to Goldman. He approached and they spoke by the jury railing. The judge had not entered yet.

"Is it a plea or trial?" Rosner asked.

"Nine months for Bob if Grambling goes to trial, and six if Grambling pleads?" Goldman asked.

"Yeah," Rosner replied.

"It's a plea." Goldman began to walk away.

"Remember, Larry." Rosner called after Goldman in a low voice. Goldman stopped and turned. "He has to admit the crime during the plea. No evasions or excuses."

Goldman walked to Libman, sitting at the defense table, and whispered in Libman's ear. Libman rose and the two moved to a corner of the courtroom. Goldman was speaking. The assistant could not hear the words, but he saw Goldman's head and body move with the rhythm of his argument. Goldman spoke forcefully. Libman shook his head side to side. Goldman spoke with even more exaggerated arm and hand motions. With equally abrupt body movement, Libman replied. Then, there was a stillness. Libman shrugged his shoulders, and held his hands in the air, palms up.

Goldman spoke gently. Libman waved in resignation with a hand. Rosner heard Libman say, "If I got to say it, I'll say it."

Goldman strolled to the assistant who, slouching against the jury railing, arms akimbo, had taken in the show.

"He's ready to plead," Goldman said. "He knows what to say."

"Wait a minute, Larry," Rosner shook his head from side to side. "I don't want him to 'know what to say.' I want the truth. If he's guilty, fine. He can plead. If he's not guilty, he can go to trial. I don't take pleas from innocent men."

"He has trouble saying that he impersonated Corcoran," Goldman explained.

"Let's go to trial." The assistant stood up. "I can prove beyond a reasonable doubt that he impersonated Corcoran, and I ain't taking a plea if he's protesting that he's innocent."

Goldman patted Rosner on the shoulder to calm him down.

"He's not protesting that he's innocent, and he wants the plea," Goldman said. "Let's take the plea. Trust me."

"All rise," the clerk shouted. Judge Cahn entered the courtroom.

"Come up counselors," the judge said. Goldman and Rosner approached the bench. They explained that Libman was prepared to plead guilty.

"And the plea will be under oath," the assistant added. In pleading guilty, Libman would say under oath that he had impersonated Corcoran at Grambling's instruction. Were Libman called as a prosecution witness in the Grambling trial, Libman would be asked to repeat, again under oath, how and why he had impersonated Corcoran. Were Libman to deny at trial what he had said at his plea, one of his sworn statements would necessarily be untrue. Inconsistent sworn statements are perjury, another felony. As Goldman knew, Rosner would not hesitate to seek a perjury indictment of an inconsistent Libman. A plea under oath was powerful insurance that Libman would repeat at a trial what he said at a plea.

Counsel returned to their tables.

"Your Honor," Goldman began. "Pursuant to a series of discussions involving the Court and the assistant, and other members of his Office, the defendant at this time offers to plead guilty to count three of indictment 2358 and count one of indictment 2800, to cover both indictments in accordance with a plea agreement reached between the assistant, myself and the court."

The court clerk spoke.

"Robert Libman, with your attorney present and standing next to you, do you now withdraw your previously entered plea of not guilty to indictment 2358 of 86 and do you now plead guilty to criminal possession of a forged instrument in the second degree under the third count of indictment 2358 of 1986, and conspiracy in the fifth degree under the first count of indictment 2800 of 1985, to cover both indictments, is that your plea?"

"Yes," Libman said.

"All right," Judge Cahn said. "Swear him in."

Goldman stood to object.

"Your Honor, as I told you at the bench, I object to any swearing. Mr. Libman will allocute in accordance with the Criminal Procedure Law. I see no provision . . ."

"I understand," Judge Cahn interrupted. He turned to the court clerk. "Swear him in."

Libman was sworn to tell the truth. Judge Cahn proceeded to ask a series of questions, mandated by United States Supreme Court and New York State Court of Appeals case law, to ensure that the defendant understood the constitutional liberties he surrendered by pleading guilty.

"Are you ready to talk to me about a plea this afternoon?" Judge Cahn asked.

"I am, sir," Libman replied.

"Do you understand that by pleading guilty now, it's exactly the same as if you were convicted after trial?"

"I do, sir."

"Knowing that, you still want to plead guilty?"

"Yes, sir."

"You understand you have the absolute right to continue to plead not guilty as to each of these indictments and each of these charges. And, if you do that, Mr. Goldman will represent you and, if you don't have the money to hire or to keep paying an attorney, if necessary Mr. Goldman will represent you without fee. Or some other attorney would be appointed to represent you without a fee. Do you understand that?"

"I do, sir."

"Do you understand that you're giving up some substantial rights by pleading guilty now?"

"I do, sir."

"I'm going to go over some of these rights with you right now. If there's anything that you don't understand, please stop me, ask me about it or ask Mr. Goldman about it. Specifically, one of the rights you have is the right to continue to plead not guilty. If you do that, your guilt or nonguilt will be decided by a jury of 12 people. Do you understand that?"

"I do, sir."

"Also, you have, you and Mr. Goldman have the right to question the prospective jurors before they become members of the jury, and to object to any of them that you feel could not be fair, or that you otherwise would not want on the jury. Do you understand that?"

"Yes, sir, I do."

"Do you also understand that the jury has to be unanimous in finding you guilty or not guilty. If they're not unanimous, you get a new trial. Do you understand that?"

"Yes, sir, I do."

"Do you also understand the fact that the prosecutor has to prove your guilt of each and every one of the charges beyond a reasonable doubt and, if a juror has a reasonable doubt, that juror is instructed, all of the jurors are instructed, if they have a reasonable doubt, they must vote to find you not guilty. Do you understand that?"

"Yes, sir."

"Do you also understand the fact that you and Mr. Goldman have the right to question and cross-examine the prosecution witnesses. You have the right to call witnesses on your own behalf and to testify on your own behalf. Although you don't have to testify, or do any of these other things if you don't want to. Do you understand that?"

"Yes, sir, I do."

"Knowing that you're giving up all of these rights by pleading guilty, do you still want to plead guilty?"

"Yes, sir, I do."

"One of the charges you're pleading guilty to is a felony. As a practical matter, what that means is that if you are convicted of another felony within 10 years, certainly in New York, I'm not sure what the law of Florida is, then you will be punished more severely, much more severely for that next conviction because of your plea this afternoon. Do you understand that?"

"Yes, sir, I do."

"Have there been any threats made to get you to plead guilty?"

"No, sir, there have not."

"Mr. Libman, has anyone told you what you'd be sentenced to?"

"Yes, sir."

"What did they tell you?" Judge Cahn asked.

" 'If Mr. Grambling goes to trial, then my sentence will be nine months, and if Mr. Grambling does not go to trial, then my sentence would be six months.' "

" 'If Mr. Grambling does not go to trial' means, as a practical matter, if Mr. Grambling pleads guilty?"

"Correct, sir."

"Assuming that there's a plea negotiation between the District Attorney's Office and Mr. Grambling, whether or not the District Attorney accepts the plea is completely up to them. You have no right to second-guess them or to say to them in any way 'you, the Assistant District Attorney should have accepted Grambling's offer.' Do you understand that?"

"Yes, sir."

"As far as I'm concerned, if Grambling offers to plead guilty, no matter what the District Attorney and Grambling agree to, if the court doesn't agree, that's completely up to me. Again, you have no right to get involved or complain about that. Do you understand that?"

"I understand."

"Other than what you just told me, have there been any promises made to you at all?"

"No, sir."

"Now, I'm not going to accept your plea of guilt unless you actually are guilty. The Assistant District Attorney is now going to ask you some questions about the third count, the criminal possession of a forged instrument in the second degree."

"Thank you, your Honor." The assistant began. "Mr. Libman, I'm going to read you the count. 'The Grand Jury aforesaid by this indictment further accuses the defendant Libman of the crime of criminal possession of a forged instrument in the second degree, in violation of Penal Law section 170.25 committed as follows: The defendant, in the County of New York, on December 28, 1984, knowing the same to be forged and with intent to defraud, deceive and injure another, possessed and uttered a forged instrument the same being and purporting to be and calculated to become and to represent, if completed, a commercial instrument and an instrument which does evident create and otherwise create a legal right, interest, obligation and status, to wit, a consent and agreement purporting to bear the signatures of the authorized agents of Lazard, Freres & Co.'

"Did you hear me read that count?"

"I did," Libman replied.

"Does the count accurately state what you did on December 28, 1984?"

"It does."

"On December 28, 1984," Rosner continued. "did you receive a phone call from John A. Grambling, Jr.?"

"I did."

"Where were you?"

"In my office on 156-45 Collins Avenue, Miami Beach."

"Did Mr. Grambling make a request of you?"

"He did."

"What was that request, Mr. Libman?"

"He requested that I take a phone call."

"From who, Mr. Libman?"

"From an executive of the Bank of Montreal."

"And did Mr. Grambling ask you to do something during the phone call?"

"Yes. He asked me to confirm that a document that the Bank of Montreal officer had in his possession was a valid document."

"An authentic document?" Rosner asked.

"Yes. An authentic document."

"Is the document you're referring to the Consent and Agreement purporting to be a Lazard, Freres & Co. Consent and Agreement?"

"It is."

"Did Grambling ask you to impersonate a specific person?"

"He did."

"Do you recall who that person was that you were asked to impersonate?"

"Peter Corcoran."

"Do you recall the position of the person at Lazard, Freres who you were asked to impersonate?"

Libman looked puzzled.

"Was it an executive?" the assistant asked.

Libman took the cue.

"It was an executive or a managing director or partner."

"On December 28, 1984, were you aware that John A.

Grambling, Jr. was seeking a loan from the Bank of Montreal?"

"I was."

"What was the amount of the loan?"

"Seven-and-a-half million dollars."

"And you were aware that Grambling had submitted documents to the Bank of Montreal to induce the Bank of Montreal to grant the $7.5 million loan?"

"I was."

"Were you aware that the Consent and Agreement was one of these documents?"

"I was."

The assistant moved to the heart of Libman's guilt.

"On December 28, 1984, did you receive a phone call from a person identifying himself as a Bank of Montreal officer?"

"I did."

"How did you identify yourself?"

"As Mr. Corcoran."

"Did you authenticate the document, the Consent and Agreement which had been given to the Bank of Montreal by John A. Grambling, Jr.?"

"I did."

"How did you authenticate it?"

"There were certain questions asked and answered properly. The Bank of Montreal was satisfied with the answers."

"The answers which you gave purporting to be a Lazard, Freres officer?"

"Correct."

"Pursuant to the instructions from Mr. Grambling?"

"Correct."

"Were you aware that the Consent and Agreement, purportedly the Lazard Consent and Agreement, allegedly evidenced the fact that John A. Grambling, Jr. held shares of Dr Pepper stock at Lazard, Freres?"

"I was."

"On December 28, 1984, were you aware that this Consent and Agreement falsely stated that John Grambling owned the stock at Lazard, Freres?"

"Yes, I was."

Judge Cahn had been following the plea intently. He asked, "In other words, you were aware that Grambling did not hold the stock at Lazard, Freres?"

Libman hesitated.

"I felt that he did not hold it."

He's beginning to stray, Rosner thought.

"Mr. Libman," the assistant drew him back. "You believed that he did not own the stock, did you not?"

"I believed that he did not."

"And at the time you impersonated the Lazard, Freres officer, was it your purpose to induce the bank to rely on that document which Grambling had presented to them?"

"It was. I was told it was the last document for him to obtain this funding."

"And was it your intent by this impersonation to defraud the bank into believing that the Lazard, Freres document was authentic?"

"Yes, it was."

It could not have gone better, the assistant thought. Misrepresentation, inducement, reliance—all the elements of fraud had been proved.

"The plea to count three is acceptable to the People, Your Honor."

"All right," Judge Cahn said. "Before we go further, Mr. Libman, these questions and answers that you've given this afternoon were given under oath. I know Mr. Goldman objected to it, but they were given under oath. My point to you is this. If there's anything that you have said that is incorrect or incomplete, if you want to change anything that you've said or add to it, now's the time to do it. If you said anything that was not true, that in itself would be a crime. That would be the crime of perjury. So, if there's anything you want to change or add, think about it. If you want to talk to Mr. Goldman, feel free to discuss it with him at this point. Do you want to change anything?"

All eyes in the courtroom turned to Libman.

"No, sir," he said firmly. "I appreciate the opportunity, but what I said was true."

The plea to the conspiracy count was an anticlimax. Judge Cahn restated the litany of rights Libman was waiving, and Libman stated that he understood. The assistant conducted the allocution. Sentencing was set for 2:00 P.M., Wednesday, October 29, 1986. In a half-hour proceeding, 23 months after a phone call to which he probably had given no second thought, Libman had become a convicted felon.

Rosner's attention turned to Grambling and the trial. Fleming had not called to accept the plea by October 14 and the District Attorney's Office began to fly in the witnesses for their last trial preparation. The assistant also reinterviewed Wilkis who, despite his federal indictment and pending plea of guilty, offered to testify at the Grambling trial.

"What I told you is the truth," Wilkis said as he sat again in Rosner's office. "And I'll repeat it at trial no matter what the cross-examination is."

The effect of a prosecution can be seen on a defendant's face, the assistant thought. Some defendants, though mouthing remorse and regret, showed clearly from their face that their prosecution was like water off a duck's back. Wilkis was not that kind of defendant. He looked like a whipped dog. Rosner did not want to know about the federal case, but Wilkis wanted to talk.

"Let me tell you what happened to me, Brian. I'm not going to make any excuses for what I did. It was a crime, and I thought I could get away with it. I'm scared of prison. I'll tell you that, too. But I wouldn't do what those damn federal prosecutors wanted me to. They didn't care about my guilt. They just wanted to use me to trap other people. I know what I am, I'm a felon, and I'll do my time. But I'm not a rat. I'm not going to trap others to make my time easier."

"I understand, Bob. You don't . . ."

"No, I want you to hear this. I wouldn't be a Nazi, and that's how I got really jammed up. I could have walked on this crime. But the Feds wanted me to tape other people. I wouldn't. I warned the others. I called Dennis Levine. But the son-of-a-bitch was taping me! Now he's walked into the Feds. He's going to get a deal. Him, the main player and center of the whole thing. He's getting a deal for giving me up to the Feds!" Wilkis held his face in his hands in disbelief.

On Tuesday, October 21, less than a week before the scheduled trial, Fleming called Rosner.

"Let John plea in New York after pleading federally in El Paso."

"We've already been around that track," Rosner replied, and the conversation ended.

But he'll probably be going to Morgenthau, again, the assistant thought. He mentioned his concern to Moscow, who had conferred with the District Attorney that morning.

"Yes, and no," Moscow said.

"What?"

" 'Yes,' Fleming tried going to Morgenthau, and 'no', after the other crimes, the bureau has free rein to ask for the kind of time and prison we think is necessary."

Rosner worked on the questions he would ask during voir dire, the process during which potential members of the trial jury were questioned by counsel and selected to serve. He scheduled Wednesday morning the 29th as the likely time for his opening.

CHAPTER 21

ACTIVE IN COLUMBUS

On October 24, 1986, the Friday before the scheduled trial, Fleming called Rosner.

"John's going to plead on Monday."

The assistant canceled the weekend flights of his witnesses.

When Rosner arrived in court on Monday morning, October 27, Grambling was already there with Fleming and Alan Kaufman, Grambling's trial attorney. Another former federal prosecutor, Kaufman was a restrained, but powerful, court presence. He ferreted out weaknesses in a prosecutor's case with thought and tenacity, and his firm businesslike approach was itself a persuasive factor with jurors. But Kaufman would not be displaying his trial skills in this case.

Judge Cahn assumed the bench.

"May we approach?" Fleming asked. At the bench, he explained that Grambling would plead guilty to the entire indictment, a requirement since the People refused to negotiate a lesser plea.

"We have one request," Fleming continued. "John would like a few days to break the news to his children. Could the plea be taken off the record and sealed until next Monday, November 3? That will give John time to spend with his children this weekend."

Himself a family man, the judge granted the request without a second thought.

Rosner was furious. It was obvious to him what Fleming had done. Tuesday, November 4, was the midyear congressional elections, with several important governors' races, including ones in Texas and New York. If the plea was sealed until Monday, news of the plea would be buried in election eve stories. With little or no news coverage to correct his lies, Grambling could explain away the crime to his business acquaintances and, relying on that false explanation, encourage them to write letters to the court urging leniency at sentencing, or even promising job opportunities should Grambling be sentenced to probation. The assistant kept his thoughts to himself, but did object as a general matter to Fleming's request.

The proceedings began in open court.

"All right," Judge Cahn said. "This case is on for trial this morning. Before going any further, I think I ought to make sure that defendant and his counsel are aware of the fact that his co-defendant has pleaded guilty, and that was done approximately three weeks ago, two to three weeks ago."

"We are aware of that, your Honor," Fleming said.

"Your Honor," Kaufman continued. "At this time, I would make application that we conduct this morning proceedings in the robing room and that those proceedings be done under seal."

"Your Honor," Rosner protested. "For the reasons stated at the bench, I oppose any secret proceedings in this case."

The proceedings moved to the robing room. Judge Cahn sat at the head of the table, the stenographer to his left. On one side of the table, Kaufman and Fleming sat with Grambling between them. Rosner took a seat on the opposite side.

Fleming began with a brief statement.

"Both Mr. Kaufman and I have consulted at length with Mr. Grambling with regard to all of his rights and to his right to go to trial and cross-examine witnesses, and we have given him our professional view with regard to the possible outcome of that trial. We have had, as your Honor knows, a long negotiation with the District Attorney and I have been responsible for that negotiation. We have been unable to reach agreement with the District Attorney with regard to an agreed upon sentence. Therefore, we've advised Mr. Grambling, and he has accepted our advice, that he should enter what will be called an open plea of guilty to the charges contained in the indictment with the sentence to be left with the court on a full pre-sentence report and presentations by the parties."

"What's the highest degree of crime?" Judge Cahn asked.

"D felony," the assistant said. "A seven-year crime, your Honor.

"Then, is it your application at this point . . ." Judge Cahn interrupted himself. "Who's representing Mr. Grambling at this point, Mr. Kaufman?"

"I do, your Honor," Kaufman replied.

"Mr. Kaufman, am I correct, it's your application at this time or Mr. Grambling's application to withdraw his plea of not guilty and to plead guilty on all of the counts."

"Your Honor, that is our application, in view of the prosecutor's insistence that the plea be to all the counts in the indictment." There was bitterness in Kaufman's voice. "We are going to allocute to the facts."

Judge Cahn turned to the court clerk. "Will you arraign him, please?"

"John Grambling," the clerk began, "with your attorney present and sitting next to you, do you now withdraw your previously entered plea of not guilty to indictment 2800 of '85 and do you now plead guilty to that indictment, is that your plea?"

"I do, yes," Grambling said.

"Will you swear him in please," Judge Cahn instructed the clerk.

Judge Cahn then began the allocution.

"What's your full name?"

"John Alan Grambling, Jr."

"Mr. Grambling, where do you live?"

"I live in Darien, Connecticut."

"Who's the gentleman sitting on your left?"

"Mr. Peter Fleming."

"Who's he?"

"He has been my attorney and counselor up until the time of trial from Curtis and Mallet."

"Who's the gentleman on your right?"

"Mr. Alan Kaufman."

"Who's he?"

"He has been appointed by myself as my trial counsel."

"You mean he's retained?"

"Yes, he's been retained by myself to represent me."

"How old are you?"

"Thirty-six years old."

"What's the top grade in school that you've reached?"

"I've graduated with a master's degree from the University of Pennsylvania."

"Now, I'm going to ask you a lot of questions. First of all, if there's any question you don't know the answer to, tell me simply, 'I don't know the answer.' If there's any question you don't want to answer, consult Mr. Kaufman or Mr. Fleming. I prefer you consult Mr. Kaufman at this point. Do you understand that so far?"

"Yes, sir."

"If there's any question that Mr. Kaufman tells you not to answer, just don't answer it at this point. Do you understand that?"

"Yes, sir."

"Now by pleading guilty, do you understand that you're giving up a lot of rights?"

"Yes, sir."

"I'm going to go over those rights in a few minutes. Before I do that, have you ever been addicted to any drugs?"

"No, I've never taken a drug."

"Have you ever been treated for any mental disorder?"

"I've never been treated for any mental disorder. Now, for the last year, at the request of the family, I've been seeing a counselor."

"When you say counselor, what kind of a counselor?"

"Doctor and psychiatrist from Yale University."

"When was the last time you saw this doctor?"

"I see him every week."

"You saw him last week?"

"Yes, sir."

"Now, is there anything in that or in your treatment or in the things that this doctor has prescribed for you, anything which would make it difficult for you to understand what we're doing this morning?"

"No."

Rosner made a mental note. Grambling's been sent to a psychiatrist by his attorneys. They're probably preparing a psychiatric pitch for a nonjail sentence.

"Have you had a chance to talk to Mr. Kaufman about your plea and about the rights you're giving up and the punishment that you may be facing?"

"Yes, we've gone over it in great length."

"Do you need any more time to talk to him then before you plead?"

"No," Grambling said.

As he had done with Libman, Judge Cahn explained in detail the constitutional and statutory rights that Grambling would relinquish by pleading guilty, and the burdens he would bear by being a convicted felon.

"Now, knowing all of that and knowing all of these rights that you are giving up, do you still want to give up these rights and plead guilty?"

"Yes, sir."

"Do you understand the questions, do you have any further questions so far?"

"No, I understand the questions."

"Has anybody made any threats to get you to plead guilty?"

"No threats have been made to me."

"Has anybody made any promises to get you to plead guilty?

"No, sir."

"Let me stop for a minute. Mr. Fleming, do you know of any threats made to your client or to anyone else on his behalf to get him to plead guilty?"

"No," Fleming replied.

"Do you know of any promises?"

"No, your Honor."

"Have you had a chance to discuss his rights and so on with him?"

"Yes, sir, your Honor, I have," Fleming said.

"Do you believe he's waiving his rights intelligently?"

"Yes."

Judge Cahn asked the same questions of Kaufman, who gave the same replies. Judge Cahn addressed Grambling.

"Now, Mr. Grambling, I'm now going to permit the assistant . . ."

Rosner interrupted. If Grambling was going to use the plea colloquy to weasle out of an admission of guilt, the assistant was not going to participate in the charade.

"Excuse me, your Honor, I'm not participating in this allocution. I want defense counsel to allocute. If there's inadequacies, I will ask questions."

"No, Mr. Rosner. If you don't want to participate, I'll question him and that's it. It's either you question him or I question him.

The judge does not know the details of the case well enough to catch Grambling in his lies, Rosner thought.

"I'll question him, your Honor."

"That's what I thought. Now, Mr. Grambling, in a few minutes, I'm going to permit the assistant to question you, just as soon as we finish this issue. The point is that the answers you're giving to his questions can be used against you if you change your mind and for some reason ask to withdraw your guilty plea. Do you understand that?"

"Yes, I do."

"Knowing that, do you still want to go forward?"

"Yes, sir."

"Also, you understand there have been absolutely no promises made either as far as what your sentence will be or whether the plea will be acceptable to me as to each particular count?"

"Yes, sir."

"Do you understand what I've just said? I don't mind explaining it again if you don't. Do you understand that?"

"Yes."

The court turned to Rosner. "Do you want to allocute him?"

Stick to the facts, Rosner thought. It will become plain that Grambling is a liar.

"Mr. Grambling," Rosner began, "have you read indictment 2800-85?"

Grambling looked straight across the table at the assistant. "Have I read the indictment?"

"Yes."

"Yes, I have."

"Are you familiar with the allegations alleged in the 32 counts of the indictment?"

"I've read the indictment and I'm familiar with the various counts brought against me, yes."

"Are you familiar with the various facts alleged in the indictment?"

"Yes. I couldn't quote you verbatim, but I've read them."

"Are the facts alleged correct?"

"The facts are basically correct, but they are incorrect in detail."

Where is he most likely to lie, the assistant wondered.

"Let me read to you count number 22, Mr. Grambling," the assistant said. " 'The defendant, from on or about February 28, 1985 to on or about April 2, 1985, attempted to steal property from the Security Savings and Loan Association of Jackson, Mississippi valued in excess of $1500, to wit, $10 million.' Have you heard me read this count?"

"I just heard you read it, yes."

"Are you guilty of that count, Mr. Grambling?"

Grambling glanced sideways at each of his attorneys.

"I did not attempt to steal $10 million from Security Savings and Loan. What did I attempt, I've been asked . . ."

Grambling turned from Rosner, and focused on Judge Cahn. "What I did was I attempted to buy time because I knew that I could not borrow that money from them."

Judge Cahn was startled.

"Mr. Grambling," Judge Cahn asked. "Did you apply to Security Savings for a loan of $10 million?"

"Did I apply to them for a loan? Yes."

"Ten million dollars?" Judge Cahn continued.

"Yes, sir."

"Did you in connection with that application . . . was that application made in writing or orally?"

"It was made in writing and orally."

"And was it your intention that they loan you the money, was that what you were trying to do, get them to loan the money?"

"No, the attempt was to buy time. Colorado National was putting me in bankruptcy."

"Your attempt was not to borrow the money?" Judge Cahn asked incredulously. Kaufman and Fleming shuffled uncomfortable in their chairs.

"My intent was not to borrow because I knew from the beginning that we could not take the money out. I was just trying to buy time. Two, three weeks, because of the 90-day preference rule in bankruptcy. I knew that we could not borrow the money. I filed the forms."

Rosner relaxed in his chair. I'll let Judge Cahn do it, he thought.

"Let me ask you a question," Judge Cahn said to Grambling. "You filed forms asking for a $10 million loan?"

"Yes, sir."

"And was the information contained in those forms true?"

"No. Information on some of the forms was correct, some of it was incorrect."

The evasion annoyed Judge Cahn.

"Was it incorrect information on those forms?"

"Yes, sir."

"As to the information that was incorrect on those forms, were you aware that it was incorrect when you filed them?"

"Yes."

"You prepared the forms?"

"Yes, sir."

"You signed and filed or submitted those forms knowing that the information was incorrect?"

"Right."

Judge Cahn nodded to Rosner. It was a sign to continue.

"What were you going to do with the $10 million, Mr. Grambling?" the assistant continued.

Grambling turned in the assistant's direction.

"Well, I never thought that I would receive the $10 million. The purpose of the application was just to buy time so they would tell Colorado National that there was an application made to them."

Kaufman tried to throw a life preserver to his client.

"Your Honor, if I may just interject for your Honor's benefit, this transaction chronologically is the last of the transactions, last transaction that the indictment deals with. The 'buying time' that Mr. Grambling is referring to is in reference to some of the prior bank loans . . ."

"I understand that," Judge Cahn said.

". . . which are in issue," Kaufman continued. "By directing Mr. Grambling's attention to this transaction initially, when in fact it is the chronologically last transaction, the questioning makes it somewhat more difficult to explain to your Honor."

"You don't have to explain," Judge Cahn said crisply. "Believe me, I understand exactly what the District Attorney has done. I also understand exactly what you said, but that doesn't change it."

The judge turned to the prosecutor. For the first time in the proceedings, Rosner saw that the judge understood why the prosecutor had not budged from his firm position during the plea discussions.

"All right," the judge instructed Rosner. "Why don't you move in any order you want."

The assistant nodded in acknowledgment and turned to Grambling.

"Why don't we move to an earlier transaction, count number two. 'The defendants, in the County of New York, from on or about December 7, 1984 to on or about December 31, 1984, stole property from the bank in excess of $1500 to wit, $7.5 million.' Are you guilty of that charge, Mr. Grambling?"

"I borrowed from the Bank of Montreal $7.5 million which I intended to repay through the Husky/R.M.T. property in the United States. I'm guilty of supplying the Bank of Montreal with false financial information in order to obtain that money." Grambling had denied an intent to steal, a critical element of the crime. If his statement was true, he was innocent of the charge.

The judge had enough.

"Let me stop you right here. It seems to me that what Mr. Grambling is doing is that he's denying one of the elements here. Am I correct?" The judge looked at counsel.

"I believe so, your Honor," Rosner said quietly. Judge Cahn continued.

"Now, whether or not a jury would find him guilty, I think the four of us who are practicing lawyers all probably have some feeling about that, and I suspect it's all the same feeling, but that's a dirty question. He's leaving open a very specific element here as a jury question—which is a jury question, element of fact, what his intent was."

"Your Honor, if I may . . . ," Kaufman began.

"Would you rather go off the record?" Judge Cahn offered. "Or do you want to stay on the record."

"Let's go off the record for a minute," Kaufman said.

"Why don't we ask Mr. Grambling to go outside," the assistant suggested.

"Off the record and Mr. Grambling step outside," the judge said.

The stenographer's hands fell to his side.

Rosner began after Grambling had left the room. "It's obvious that Grambling can't plead guilty. He wants the benefits of avoiding a trial, but he wants to be able to walk out of this courtroom and say that he didn't commit a crime."

Fleming and Kaufman spoke at the same time.

"The assistant isn't letting Grambling say what he did," Fleming said. His face reddened. "Just because the assistant doesn't want a plea . . .

Judge Cahn shook his head from side to side, and interrupted. If a defendant believed that he would be convicted after a trial, despite his innocence, the Constitution allowed him to plead guilty while proclaiming his innocence. It was called an Alford plea, after the United States Supreme Court case in which it was first allowed.

"Mr. Rosner," Judge Cahn asked. "Would your Office consider an Alford plea?"

"Absolutely not, your Honor. The District Attorney's Office doesn't take pleas from innocent men."

Fleming and Kaufman began to argue. "That's not so . . ."

"And even if I could take an Alford plea," Rosner said firmly. "I wouldn't with this man."

Looking directly at the judge, Rosner softened his tone.

"Your Honor, at some point Grambling is going to reenter the business community, if he's ever really left it. He's going to have to explain why he was convicted. I am not going to allow an allocution where he can deny his guilt, where he can claim that he never intended to steal or to defraud, where he can point to actual language in a transcript, a transcript accepted by the court, that he really meant no harm and it was all this Office's misunderstanding of the business world that made this into a criminal case instead of a civil one. I'm not going to lose this case on the plea, Judge Cahn. If Grambling wants a transcript that he's innocent, let him go to trial and be acquitted."

Judge Cahn leaned toward the assistant and said in his gentle voice, "Mr. Rosner, I think you misunderstand how much Grambling can explain away by a plea.

"But that's neither here nor there, gentlemen," Judge Cahn said to all the attorneys as he leaned back. "I don't like Alford pleas, either. My suggestion is that we continue. If Mr. Grambling can allocute, that's that. If not, I have a few court matters that will take an hour or two, and then we can call for a jury panel."

"Your Honor, perhaps you can participate more in the allocution," Kaufman suggested.

"I'm not sure if that's for better or worse," Judge Cahn said as he nodded to the clerk, who rose and opened the door for Grambling to reenter. Grambling's face was placid, as he again sat between Kaufman and Fleming. The attorneys' faces were rigid.

"Mr. Grambling," Judge Cahn began. Grambling turned to face the judge.

"Let's keep talking about this second count which accuses you of grand larceny, stealing $7.5 million from the Bank of Montreal. First of all, am I correct that some of the documents that you submitted in support of that loan were not accurate documents, were fraudulent documents?"

"Yes."

"What documents?"

"There were documents involved with the assignment of certain securities. There were . . ."

He has to be pinned down to facts, Rosner thought.

"Which securities?" the assistant asked.

"Dr Pepper securities which were nonexistent," Grambling answered. He moved in his chair as he turned to answer whoever was asking the question.

"Is that the Lazard, Freres Consent and Agreement that was forged?" Judge Cahn asked.

"Yes, sir."

"Who forged that?" Judge Cahn inquired.

"I did, sir."

"Did you know it was forged when you submitted it?"

"Yes, sir."

"Now, did you have any reason to believe that the Bank of Montreal would have given you the loan, if the bank knew that document was forged?"

"If the bank knew?"

"If the bank knew it was forged, if they had known it was forged, would they have given you the loan?"

"Not on that condition, no, sir."

"In fact, did you feel that submitting that document to the bank was necessary to obtain the loan?"

"Yes, sir."

"Now, you said a moment ago before you left the room that you thought that if the Husky deal went through, you could repay it?"

"Yes, sir."

"Tell me, what is the Husky deal?"

"I set up a corporation to purchase assets, U.S. assets of Husky. Husky is an oil company located in Calgary, Canada."

"And how were you going to pay for those Husky assets?"

"I have to step you back and tell you a little about what happened. When the transaction was brought to me, I was provided various documents and I bought the company based on those documents. As we proceeded through the acquisition of Husky, first thing we learned was the background information that Husky had put together that had been provided to us, was totally unorganized and incorrect. General Electric Credit, through their audit people and through their particular diligence, helped me decipher what was there to see if it was worth pursuing, which I did. As we moved forward with the Husky group and got into the transaction more, it came to light that the transaction that was presented to me was $20 million overpriced. I had people that I hired going into this new company to analyze the situation, and I had the gentlemen from Arthur Andersen analyze the situation. I had four of the top senior partners working from Andersen to help us out. I'm just hitting highlights, I'm not going into details."

"But at some point, General Electric pulled back as the lender?" Judge Cahn asked.

"As of Thanksgiving day of 1984, General Electric was forced out of the picture by Husky who said, 'Mr. Grambling you do not have a banker, you have to have a banker, we have to have this transaction closed by December 31.'"

"So General Electric is now off the deal?"

"Right. Husky says, however, they take me into this other room while we're at General Electric Credit, Husky says 'we will ask our banker, who is our lead bank, Bank of Montreal, to provide the financing to you and . . .'"

"Husky introduced you to the Bank of Montreal?" Judge Cahn asked.

"Yes, they introduced me to the Bank of Montreal."

Rosner listened. Fleming and Kaufman had prepared Grambling for trial. His monologue on the prelude to the Bank of Montreal crimes had the earmarks of the inverse morality of the white-collar defense; Husky had tricked Grambling into a bad deal with a short timetable, and then Husky had forced its own bank on Grambling. It was Husky's conspiracy against this defendant that forced him to commit the crimes.

Judge Cahn allowed Grambling to ramble on some more before focusing him on what was key in the judge's mind: Did Grambling have an honest, realistic source of funds to repay the money taken. If not, he had the intent to deprive permanently under the law, no matter how much he talked about wanting to pay back the swindled funds. At a pause in Grambling's narrative, Judge Cahn asked the critical question.

"How were you going to pay back the Bank of Montreal?"

"The company itself in the leverage buyout," Grambling answered. "They will pay off its own debt and in fact they had enough, given us . . ."

Judge Cahn was annoyed. "Was Husky aware of the facts that you were submitting forged documents?"

"No. This was still after the fact. We're at the very tail end of the transaction. There were no forged documents submitted to Husky."

"Was the Bank of Montreal loan for the Husky buyout approved?"

"Yes, it was."

"Were all the documents submitted to the Bank of Montreal on the Husky loan honest?"

"They were honest."

Time to intervene, Rosner thought. Judge Cahn had not read the Grand Jury transcript for months. There was no reason for him to remember Libman's fraudulent guarantee and bogus balance sheet, which had induced Husky to loan Grambling the deposit on the buyout.

Rosner held up his hand, so that Judge Cahn could see that a question was coming.

"How about the Bob Libman balance sheet?" the assistant asked.

"That's correct." Grambling faced Rosner. "Robert Libman bank sheet, the personal balance sheet that he supplied, was inaccurate."

Judge Cahn remembered.

"It wasn't only inaccurate, it was false," the Judge said.

"False, yes."

"Forged, too," Rosner added.

Grambling turned back and forth between Judge Cahn and the assistant.

"Was it forged?" Grambling asked. He thought over the question.

"The assistant's question may call for a legal conclusion," Judge Cahn noted. "Let me ask. Mr. Grambling, did you prepare the balance sheet or did Libman prepare it?"

"I prepared it with his approval."

"You physically prepared it?"

"And who signed it?" Judge Cahn asked.

"I can't remember. I think I did."

"What name did you sign on it?"

"I would have signed his name to it."

"And the figures on that balance sheet were not correct?"

"They were not correct."

"They overstated Libman's net worth?"

"Yes, sir."

"Were you aware of that," Judge Cahn asked, "when you submitted it to the Bank of Montreal?"

"Yes, I was."

Judge Cahn asked his sum-up question to conclude the point that Grambling had no honest source of funds to repay the Bank of Montreal personal loan.

"So, the truth of the matter is that, on the Husky transaction, you had reason to believe the Bank of Montreal would never have gone through with it if they knew the truth?"

A "yes" answer would be an admission of the crime.

"No," Grambling said blandly. "I think the bank would have gone through with the transaction anyway."

Judge Cahn was stunned. Fleming and Kaufman sank in their chairs.

"Even though the bank knew that you falsified the balance sheet overstating Libman's assets?" Judge Cahn asked.

Grambling was taken aback by the sharpness of Judge Cahn's question. He looked to his counsel, and saw their eyes turn away. You could have tried that line with the jury, the assistant thought. But you can't get it by a judge.

Grambling appeared to think for a moment.

"No, sir, I can't say that the bank would have."

"As a matter of fact," Judge Cahn continued, "you know that they would not have?"

"If it would have been false, yes," Grambling said.

"It was false," Rosner interjected.

"It was false, yes," Grambling conceded.

Judge Cahn saw how Grambling wavered on the issue.

"Let me step back," Judge Cahn said. "You're not inexperienced in business?"

"No, I'm experienced."

"You know how banks think and how lenders think?"

"Yes, sir."

"And you've done transactions before?"

"Yes, sir."

"You knew pretty well that if the bank knew you had prepared a false fraudulent balance sheet for Libman overstating his net worth, the bank would have not gone through with the loan?"

"If the bank had sold a line of credit, they had to close," Grambling insisted. He could not bring himself to admit that there would have been no loan but for his falsehoods.

Judge Cahn was equally persistent.

"Let me ask you a question. What do you think that the Bank of Montreal would have done if they knew that the person they were about to lend a substantial amount of money to had prepared a fraudulent balance sheet? Do you think they would have gone through with the loan?"

"No, sir."

"So, you were aware that the Husky deal was based on a fraudulent balance sheet, am I correct?"

"The Husky transaction was not based on that solely," Grambing replied. "You're talking about a very small part of the transaction."

"It was based on the fact that the bank didn't know that you had prepared that fraudulent balance sheet?"

"Yes, sir."

If the bank was aware that you had previously submitted to them a fraudulent balance sheet, knowing it was false and fraudulent, do you have any reason to believe they would have gone through with a $7.5 million loan?"

"No, they would not have."

That's it, Rosner thought. The final admission.

Judge Cahn then asked one question too many.

"So, Mr. Grambling, if the Bank of Montreal in December 1984 was aware that you had prepared and submitted a fraudulent balance sheet for Libman, overstating Libman's balances in a different transaction, do you think that the bank would have lent you $7.5 million?"

"No, sir, not to my knowledge."

The qualification angered Judge Cahn.

"Do you really believe that the bank would have loaned $7.5 million to someone who had submitted fraudulent papers to them?"

Grambling shook his head to indicate "yes," and he explained.

"Only reason I would believe that at all is because of the timing thing, they would have to have one hell of an explanation why it would not have made the loan."

"Don't you think that submitting a fraudulent balance sheet for Libman and forged documents would have been explanation enough for the bank? You're aware that the bank would have never gone through with the loan, aren't you?"

Grambling began to backtrack.

"I was aware of it, but I was concentrating on the conclusion."

"I understand. But you were aware of it?" Judge Cahn persisted.

"Yes."

"You're not a dummy. You know business. So you are aware of it then. If the bank would have known that these documents were fraudulent, the bank would have never made that $7.5 million loan?"

"Yes, sir."

Judge Cahn was satisfied. It turned to the prosecutor. "Is this allocution on this count satisfactory?"

"Yes, it is, your Honor."

The assistant proceeded to allocute Grambling on the Richard Crawford forgeries and the Colorado National theft. With Colorado National, Grambling fell back to his defense that the victim had not relied on the false documents.

"You knew that Colorado National would rely on those altered terms of the Term Sheet in making its decision to extend the loan, didn't you?" Rosner asked.

"I knew after the fact," Grambling insisted. "They asked me about these things after the loan had been accepted. Then I supplied the documents."

He's so prepped up with his trial defense, Rosner thought, he can't allocute. But Judge Cahn would not accept the evasions.

"Mr. Grambling," Judge Cahn asked, "had the Colorado National loan money been disbursed prior to the bank's receipt of the Term Sheet?"

"No," Grambling had to admit.

"And you knew, didn't you," Judge Cahn continued, "that if you didn't supply the Term Sheet, the document that said that the Bank of Montreal would pay back the Colorado National loan, if you didn't supply that document, the loan would not have been made."

Grambling tried to avoid a response.

"They were part of the closing documents."

"And if you supplied the Term Sheet, Mr. Grambling, the money would be paid?"

Grambling could not evade Judge Cahn's inquiry.

"Right," he said.

The plea proceeded through the attempted theft from First Interstate Bank in Denver and First Security in Salt Lake. Reluctantly, Grambling admitted what could not be denied—the forgeries—while fighting any admission as to the element of the crime for which he had the best evidence—his state of mind. He admitted forging the certificates of deposit and Coronado documents submitted to Jackson Savings and Loan, but denied that his purpose was to induce the bank to make a loan.

"They were submitted to buy time," he protested. "I never thought that they would make the loan. I always knew that I would have to purchase the real CDs. No, I applied for the loan to buy time. From the very first day, I knew they would want the real CDs. I knew that from the outset."

"Isn't it a fact," Rosner asked, "that you attempted to induce the Mississippi Bank to make the loan without the original CDs?"

"No," Grambing said firmly.

Glancing at the judge, the assistant saw that Judge Cahn was frustrated and disbelieving. Enough is enough, Rosner thought.

"Your Honor," the assistant said. "The People represent that, were we to go to trial, we would prove beyond a reasonable doubt that, at the commencement of this loan, Mr. Grambling attempted to induce the Mississippi bankers to grant the loan without the physical possession of the certificates."

Last, Rosner asked Grambling about the conspiracy count. He admitted that Libman had made various impersonations to, in Grambling's phrase, make "the transaction work." Libman had done "Peter Corcoran," and the Continental Illinois bank officer, as well as "Scott Hean" when speaking with Foncannon on January 25, and "Blair Mullin" when talking to the Salt Lake bankers that same day.

That leaves one impersonation unaccounted for, the assistant thought: The January 25 impersonation of Ron Keenan for the Salt Lake bankers.

"That same day," the assistant asked, "who in El Paso impersonated Ron Keenan?"

"It wasn't an impersonation," Grambling said. "It was the real Ron Keenan."

Lying bastard, Rosner thought. If Keenan was an accomplice, why send the Mississippi packages to Keenan, "c/o Signet Securities" in Dallas? No, Keenan was no accomplice. Grambling knew that Keenan had testified against him in the Grand Jury, and was just evening the score, as well as protecting his unknown accomplice in Texas.

"Your Honor, the plea to the indictment is satisfactory to the People," the assistant said.

Judge Cahn gave Grambling the opportunity to reconsider his answers. After conferring with counsel, Grambling declined.

The proceeding was sealed until November 3, and adjourned until January 6, 1987 for sentencing.

For the assistant, the case was next to over. Grambling had pleaded guilty. Immediately after the plea, the assistant explained the proceeding to Moscow.

"It couldn't have gone better," Rosner said. "Grambling lied and evaded. The judge shouldn't have a shred of doubt left that Grambling is remorseless."

"But can Judge Cahn sentence?" Moscow asked.

"We'll see," Rosner said. "We have the usual scheduling arrangement. The defense will submit a memo and dozens of letters from Grambling's relatives and friends, all attesting to how honest he is and how the crimes were an aberration. We'll get to make our pitch for state prison in our reply papers."

Two days later, October 29, Libman was sentenced to six months in prison, as promised. Goldman tried to talk the judge out of imposing the sentence which had been agreed on.

"In the 21st century," Goldman argued, "people will wonder how a civilized society allowed a place like Riker's Island to exist. That's why I ask your Honor to consider not sending a 57-year-old, middle-class man to that hellhole. It is inhuman. I ask your Honor not to sentence him to prison."

"Judge Cahn," Rosner pointed out, "when we discussed plea alternatives in this case, I had offered the defendant a choice: one to three years of state prison or its equivalent on Riker's Island, which I'd consider to be six to nine months. The defense made the choice—the lower time on Riker's. It's a little late in the game to complain, unless Libman wants to give the plea back and go to state prison."

"There's a plea bargain here," Judge Cahn concluded. "Six months."

Outside the courtroom, after he had separated from his client, Goldman motioned to the assistant to come over.

"Brian, Bob didn't do it."

"Didn't do what?"

"Didn't impersonate Corcoran." Although Rosner did not want to believe Grambling on anything, Grambling had confirmed the impersonation two days before.

"Does Libman want his plea back," the assistant asked.

"No, I'm not saying that you couldn't prove his guilt beyond a reasonable doubt."

"So who impersonated Corcoran, Larry?"

"It was a real estate guy who was renting space in Bob's office. He was another of the Grambling helpers."

The assistant thought back to the March 1985 Libman interview. What had he said about an office renter?

"Don't bother about reindicting," Goldman motioned. "He's dead. Shot himself."

Rosner rolled his eyes.

"No, I'm not saying Bob is innocent. He knew that the call was coming in, and what was said on the call. But, you see, you think you know how things occurred just because you can prove them. It's not so."

Goldman had stated a truism, the assistant thought. He recalled his first murder trial, a case based on circumstantial evidence, including a kitchen calendar with dates crossed out by the victim. This was proof, it had been argued, of the date of the murder—the date the crossing-out had stopped. He and Moscow had tried the case together, and had made much of that point on summation, only to later realize that the killing had occurred on a different date from that they had convinced the jury to accept. The assistant had been distressed enough to consult a senior homicide attorney, whose nickname reflected his gray hair and his number of years in the District Attorney's Office. "Brian, you spent too much time in appeals," Smokey said. "Here in the real world, we just try to convict the guilty on whatever theory we can come up with. Forget the details. Is the guy you and Moscow put away guilty of the crime?" Yes, the assistant had nodded. "Then," Smokey concluded, "fuck him if he can't take a joke."

"Larry, are you telling me that Libman is guilty of the crime?" the assistant asked.

Yes, Goldman nodded, and the conversation ended.

There was a group of people that Rosner did not want to forget—the victim bank officers whose careers had been jeopardized. After the pleas and Libman sentence, the assistant wrote a letter to the Chairman of the Board of each victim bank: "Since Grambling has pleaded guilty, there will be no trial in this case. In one way, this is unfortunate. Whenever a bank is deceived in this manner, suspicion focuses on the bank officer who made the loan. Were they accomplices? Were they negligent? The material already public in this case should make plain the degree to which responsibility for this crime is solely Mr. Grambling's. He thoroughly conned officers as prudent and careful as those at your institution, as indeed, Mr. Grambling conned bank officers equally prudent at several banks in the United States. A public trial would have made even plainer that the crime was the result solely of Mr. Grambling's cunning, not any lack of prudence by the bank or its officers."

Rosner thought of the bankers at the Bank of Montreal and Colorado National. He liked them, and felt sorry for them. Maybe this will do them some good, he hoped.

Grambling's deadline for his presentencing submissions was in November. He missed it. Kaufman appeared in Part 48 to ask for an extension.

"He's writing a letter to the court explaining how those crimes occurred," Kaufman said. "And he's still collecting the letters to be submitted on his behalf at sentencing."

A sentencing delay is fine with me, the assistant thought. He had placed the Grambling case in the rear of his file cabinet. The case was over.

The case was adjourned to Monday, January 6, 1987.

December is party time at the District Attorney's Office. Every bureau has a holiday party, as do the detectives, the investigators, the accountants, and the Front Office, and every party is scheduled for a different day. December 22 was the District Attorney's Office Squad party, traditionally one of the best. The detectives deducted a sum from each paycheck towards the party fund, a catered affair in Little Italy. Attendance was by invitation only.

Prior to going to the DAOS party, Rosner checked his message box. A call had come in "re Grambling." Despite the defense counsel efforts, the Grambling plea had received extensive newspaper coverage, both in New York and nationwide. The judge's sealing of the proceeding for a week only increased the story's newsworthiness. Texan swindler sentenced in secret proceedings, the press had said. Several reporters had suggested in conversations with the assistant that the judge was on the take. "You guys are crazy," Rosner had said. "Cahn's the sweetest guy around. He sealed the record for that bum because defense counsel made a pitch based on sympathy for the defendant's family." Numerous reporters requested the indictment, plea minutes, and news of the case, as had several bankers who had had dealings with Grambling in the past.

Rosner looked at the "re Grambling" message. Another reporter or banker with a Grambling story, the assistant thought. He crumpled up the message and threw it in the garbage. I've spent enough time on this case.

He went to the DAOS party. Eddie Collins and Ronnie Moss were at the party, as were the detectives with whom he had worked his first murder case, and others with whom Rosner had worked his first frauds case. They traded war stories, mostly the same old ones, with a few new entries, such as Grambling, tossed in. "Tell me again," they laughed, "what you told Libman when you and Eddie walked in." And, as the evening progressed, they always returned to the common denomination in their careers—their sense of service to the community.

Back in his office later that evening, the assistant fished through his garbage. Mr. Hogan returned his phone calls,

Rosner thought. He wiped off the coffee and uncrumpled the paper. "Howard Linscott, F.B.I.—Columbus, Ohio."

"They work weird hours, maybe I'll catch him in."

Special Agent Linscott answered the phone.

"I tracked you down through the press," he explained, "and our office in Manhattan. You're the guy who prosecuted Grambling?"

"Yeah," Rosner said, trying to control the drunkenness in his voice.

"Grambling's been active in Columbus," the F.B.I. agent said. "Get out a pen and paper. I have some numbers you want to call."

CHAPTER 22

MAKING UP FOR PAST MISTAKES

The next morning, Tuesday, December 23, 1986, Rosner followed Special Agent Linscott's advice and called Clark Wideman, special counsel to Jefferson Savings Bank, a small savings and loan in West Jefferson, Ohio.

"We're located in a little town in the central part of the state, Mr. Rosner," Wideman began. "I'll speak with you since John tried to hurt the bank, but I can't send documents without a subpoena."

John, the use of the first name, the assistant thought. The telltale mark of sympathy. Rosner stored the detail in his memory.

"Jefferson Savings is a small institution, $42 million in assets, about $8 million liquid. It's for sale. In early October, John contacted us after learning from a broker that the bank was for sale."

Prior to his plea, Rosner thought.

"John said that he was the broker for a partnership headed by Clemens Titzck, a multimillionaire from Arizona. John gave us Titzck's financial statement. Almost $18 million net, and over 90 percent of his assets in blue-chip securities and treasury notes. Supposedly married to an heiress of the Bache family, as in Bache Securities, John told us."

Is it Libman all over again, Rosner wondered.

"The board considered the proposal. Never really said no, though it wasn't eager either. The buyout involved a trust for the four grandchildren of a William White, Jr., a director of Colonial Savings Bank and Trust Company in Chicago. The deal was confusing."

White, the assistant recalled, was Grambling's father-in-law.

"A strange thing happened while we're considering the Titzck proposal. Towards the end of October, beginning of November, John casually mentions that Jefferson might learn of a 'John A. Grambling, Jr.' who's in trouble with the law. But we shouldn't let that concern us, he says. He wasn't that John A. Grambling, Jr."

Wideman emphasized the word *that*.

"That John A. Grambling, Jr. was his cousin, a John in El Paso. Anyway, middle of November, while the bank was still considering the buyout, John proposes another transaction."

Middle of November, the assistant thought. Grambling's already pleaded guilty.

"John says that a company that he and Titzck own, Western Education Enterprises, has a $350,000 loan from Colonial Savings in Chicago, that's where White, Titzck's partner, is a director. John tells me that the Colonial loan was to buy a Chicago area building for a school, but the purchase was not made, and Colonial wants the loan recollateralized.

"He asked Jefferson Savings to issue a letter of credit, on Colonial's behalf, secured by some of Titzck's blue-chip securities. And we get a letter from Signet Securities, a Phoenix brokerage firm, saying that Titzck has authorized the hypothecation of 20,000 shares of his Rockwell International shares to collateralize the letter of credit.

"John was in West Jefferson this past Tuesday. He 'fessed up that he was the 'John A. Grambling, Jr.' that we might be reading about in the papers. He said that, as part of the Husky transaction, he submitted a financial statement in which he had made some mistakes. It was an accident. An 'innocent victim,' he called himself. But because of those 'honest mistakes' he had to plead guilty. But he was collecting 200 letters attesting to his character, including one from a federal judge. John told me that the judge in New York was going to give him probation.

"John's point was that Jefferson Savings shouldn't let the New York misunderstanding obstruct Jefferson's issuance of the $250,000 letter of credit. To convince the bank to approve the credit, John gave me two documents. I had suspicions about them. One document was Titzck's assignment of the 20,000 Rockwell shares, signed by Titzck, and notarized by Mary Adams. The other was a copy of a similar Signet Security assignment which, John said, had recently been accepted by a Connecticut bank in making a loan to a Titzck company. I had the signatures checked by a local law enforcement agency and then called the F.B.I."

Rosner interrupted Wideman's narrative.

"Clark, you haven't got a subpoena yet. But could you locate that letter for me now and read the name of the Connecticut bank."

"I thought you would want that one. Citytrust. Norwalk, Connecticut. The letter is dated August 29, 1986, allegedly on the stationery of Signet Securities, Phoenix."

"Allegedly?" the assistant asked.

"I know John's game by now. It's no secret. I liked him at one time and considered him my friend. My wife and I had John over for dinner at our home. I took his boys to an Ohio State game. He's a charming man. If he hadn't tried to hurt my client, I wouldn't be talking to you now."

"I appreciate that, Clark."

"Last Thursday, I get a call from Rocky Saxbe, a friend who's a local attorney and one of John's fraternity brothers from SMU. After John gave me the documents last Thursday, John had lunch with Rocky. He must have told Rocky what he was doing in town. After lunch, Rocky calls me. He said that he had spoken to some of his fraternity brothers in Texas. He was calling to warn me. Rocky even sent me some clippings from the *El Paso Times*. I don't have to tell you. John's mistakes were more than adding numbers together wrong in a financial statement.

"The documents John gave me last Tuesday had already been professionally examined by the time Rocky called me. The handwriting of Charles Rawles, the Signet Vice President who signed the Signet letter, is the same as that of the 'Clemens Titzck' on the notarized assignment for the Rockwell shares. It's also apparent that the Signet logo was transposed from a printed document onto the Signet stationery that John handed to me."

Wideman paused.

"John gave me that assignment and the Signet letter to Citytrust at the same time that he was telling me how he didn't really commit a crime in New York."

Though separated by hundreds of miles, and connected only by their voices, Rosner clearly perceived in Wideman's voice the pain Wideman felt at having been deceived by a man he had thought to be his friend.

"He even gave me a line about how Signet was a subsidiary of the Virginia National Bank with an office in Phoenix. By the way, I called the Phoenix number listed on the stationery. It was an answering service. Came back 'Biltmore Estates Offices.' "

Damn, I've heard that name. Of course, the assistant thought. The September 1985 check-kite. That's where Grambling put down a deposit on a $2 million mansion. Remember to call Mason, the developer. Find out what's happening with Grambling's payments.

"Have you told Grambling that the bank isn't making the $250,000 loan?" Rosner asked.

"No, the F.B.I. asked us not to. John's still calling us."

Good for the case, the assistant thought. Only one's imagination could limit what Grambling might say to Wideman.

"I don't necessarily think poorly of a person just because he's charged with a crime," Wideman began again. "Prosecutors aren't infallible."

There was a pause.

"I was charged with a crime a few years back. I was Superintendent of Savings and Loans prior to the Home State, E.M.S. Securities disaster. A Special Prosecutor was appointed. He accused me in a misdemeanor complaint of violating the revolving door statute for state officers; I had done some uncompensated work for the new Superintendent and Home State after I had left office. The judge dismissed the charge in the middle of the trial because of prosecutorial misconduct. The judge also polled the jury. They were unanimous for my acquittal."

After a moment, Wideman continued.

"It's not an experience I look back on with pleasure."

In the conversation with Wideman, Rosner had detected a touch of empathy for Grambling, and now the assistant understood: Wideman appreciated what it was to be charged with a crime.

Rosner thanked Wideman for his candor and asked him to call if there were further developments. Meanwhile, the assistant had leads to pursue. Wideman's information suggested that Grambling had defrauded two new victims, Colonial Savings Bank and Trust Company in Chicago and Citytrust in Connecticut. Perhaps other crimes were in progress. Hopefully, Rosner thought, nothing would be done until after Christmas and New Year's Day.

He began to make his calls.

On Wednesday, December 24, the assistant reached Robert Hahn, the Senior Vice President of Colonial Savings in Chicago. He explained how Grambling had obtained a loan based on collateral which proved to be nonexistent.

"Grambling was introduced to the bank in June by William White, his father-in-law. He's one of the bank's stockholders and a member of the Board of Directors. Grambling applied for a $350,000 loan for his educational company, Western Development. The idea was to build a school in the Chicago area."

"Not a very hard loan to approve," Rosner said dryly.

"You said it," Hahn agreed. "White and the bank president walked Grambling into my office to make the introduction. They never said, 'approve this loan,' but what was I to think?

"Not that I'm making excuses. We researched and documented the application. For collateral, Grambling offered shares of stock held by Mary Adams, a company officer. They came to Chicago to sign the loan documents, including her assignment of the stock. It was blue-chip securities. American Brands stock worth over $600,000."

"Did she give you the physical shares?"

"No, not at the time. The stock was held, was held allegedly, in a trust account managed by a brokerage firm, Signet Securities. There was to be a slight delay in transferring the physical shares to us because of the trust arrangement, so, as an expedient, we accepted a signed hypothecation agreement from Signet Securities.

"Based on Adams' notarized assignment, and the Signet hypothecation, the bank advanced $250,000 of the funds. But we never received the American Brands shares, so we withheld the last $100,000 pending receipt. After Grambling failed to come up with a good explanation for where the stock was, the bank made a demand on the transfer agent for the stock. Finally, we learned that the stock didn't exist.

"While we were researching whether the American Brands stock existed, Grambling was promising to repay Colonial from various sources, Fidelity Bank in Philadelphia, Jefferson Savings in Ohio. That's how you reached us. His latest promise is that his father is going to make the bank whole by next week, December 30."

"When did you find out that the Signet materials were fakes, that the stock didn't exist."

"A couple of weeks ago."

"Did you report the crime to the authorities?" the assistant asked.

Hahn hesitated.

"We have now. Grambling was always just about to pay the money back. Repayment always seemed to be just around the corner, so . . . we're a small bank, and recovering the money is what's most important to us."

The conversation reassured Rosner. That Grambling was looking to Jefferson Savings or his father to repay Colonial suggested that he had exhausted his bank introductions. The assistant subpoenaed Colonial and, after advising in-house counsel that the bank had been victimized, Citytrust. It was time to wait for something to happen.

Grambling did not make the assistant wait long. While the assistant was talking to Hahn in Chicago, Grambling was visiting with his in-laws in Chicago.

The arrest had troubled William White. Grambling had told him that the charges were a misunderstanding, blown out of proportion only because other people wanted to steal the Husky deal. To get his son-in-law back on his feet, White had introduced Grambling to a Colonial lending officer that summer. It was just an introduction, not an order to make a loan.

As 1986 ended, White looked back on the year with disappointment. In the fall, Grambling had asked White to accompany him on business trips "for credibility." Now, White feared, the Colonial loan would be a loss.

To try to make sense of what was happening, the Whites had flown their daughter, grandsons and son-in-law to Chicago for the Christmas holidays. Although the family was staying through the New Year, Grambling excused himself to leave early on a business trip. As White drove his son-in-law to the airport after Christmas, White thought it would be a good time to talk about the problems.

Grambling was candid.

"I've made some past errors," he told his father-in-law. "But I'm sorry for them. My lawyers have had me visit two psychiatrists for some months now. They've cured me. I understand myself now. I'm on the right track again. And I'm going to make up for my past mistakes."

Reassured, White left Grambling at the airport and drove home through the Chicago winter. Grambling boarded his flight to San Diego.

The next morning, Grambling went to the bank headquarters. While passing through the lobby, he picked up a promotional brochure: "We care—customers are the reason we exist." Smiling, he went to his meeting.

"Hello, Janet," he said to the loan officer. "Let me explain Mr. Titzck's needs."

CHAPTER 23

LITTLE PEOPLE

On Tuesday, December 30, Hahn called Rosner to report that Grambling's father would not pay his son's debt to Colonial Savings, and that the Colonial documents were being packaged for shipment to the prosecutor. Wideman of Jefferson Savings also called that Tuesday.

"Grambling called this morning," Wideman said. "He told me that he didn't need the $350,000 loan. He got the money from a Connecticut bank. He even gave me the phone number. I called, but it comes back to a permanent busy signal. A broken answering machine in Connecticut, the operator told me."

Probably nonsense that a Connecticut bank lent to Grambling, the assistant thought. But you can't take chances. He telephoned Kathy Kelly, an in-house attorney at the Hartford headquarters of Connecticut Bank and Trust, one of the largest banks in Connecticut, and, Rosner thought, a likely victim. He explained Grambling's style of fraud to her.

Grambling next appeared in Part 48 on January 6, 1987, the first Tuesday of the New Year. As Rosner walked through the hallway on the morning of the 6th, he passed Grambling in the phone booth located 40 feet down the corridor from the courtroom. Grambling was making a call. In a few minutes, he joined Kaufman in court.

With the palm of his hand, the clerk banged his desk three times.

"All rise," he shouted as the judge entered.

Kaufman rose to address Judge Cahn.

"Your Honor, John is still collecting the letters regarding his background and character for submission to the court.

There are other materials not ready yet. John is being treated by a psychiatrist who will be submitting a report regarding the impact that a prison sentence will have on John's rehabilitation. Lastly, John himself is preparing a statement for the court."

Head bent slightly forward, eyes downcast, Grambling nodded. He was the model of remorse.

"Many things have been said about the transactions which led to these crimes." Kaufman threw an unfriendly glance at Rosner. "John wants the court to read his own explanation for the events. So that we can get in those submissions to you, we request an adjournment of the sentencing until February 4."

Judge Cahn looked to the prosecutor. Rosner shrugged.

"February 4 for sentencing," Judge Cahn said.

Rosner and Grambling rode the same elevator to the ground floor. As the assistant hurried across Centre Street to his office, Grambling hailed a cab. "La Guardia," he told the driver. The taxi raced to make the flight to San Diego.

In his message box in the Frauds Bureau, the assistant found a note: "Call Frank Estes, counsel, Citytrust." Rosner walked quickly to his office, and without taking off his overcoat, dialed Estes' number.

"I found the loan for that August 1986 letter you sent me," Estes began. "We made a $450,000 loan to a Western Education Enterprises this past October, to buy a business school in Stamford. A Robert E. Smith, Jr., an investment banker with a firm in Stamford, brought the deal to the bank. I've been told that he's a guy in his mid-30s, medium height, and build. He negotiated the transaction and signed on behalf of the principals."

Grambling, the assistant thought. The bankers would confirm this conclusion when he sent them Grambling's photograph.

"The loan," Estes continued "was a temporary facility to be taken out by a permanent Citytrust credit. It was guaranteed by one of the three principals, a multimillionaire from Phoenix named Clemens Titzck. The other two principals are listed as Mary Adams and Patricia White."

Rosner knew that Patricia White was the maiden name of Grambling's wife.

Estes continued his explanation.

"This Titzck allegedly had his stock at Signet Securities in Phoenix. In addition to that August letter you sent me, there were several other communications with Signet. Signet sent the bank a computer print-out account statement for Titzck and a September 3 follow-up letter. The letter confirmed that Titzck's stock—J. P. Morgan, Standard Oil, IBM, General Motors, only the best—was unencumbered and available to be pledged.

"Our bank officer spoke to Titzck over the phone last August. He confirmed that his net worth was over $17 million and that he had signed powers-of-attorney, also presented to the bank, authorizing Adams and 'Smith' to sign the loan documents."

"Could you give me the number your officer called to speak with Titzck?"

Estes read the Phoenix telephone number and continued with his explanation.

"Titzck even gave a bank reference to the officer who called him. He was told to call a Joyce Lappin at Valley National Bank in Phoenix. It's a real number, and she's a real officer. Our banker called. Lappin confirmed that Titzck was a relationship, and that the bank had lent on a secured basis in the moderate six figures and an unsecured basis in the low five figures. The relationship was described as 'satisfactory.' You know, Brian, the usual bank reference."

There was a pause as Estes shifted through the documents.

"The loan was collateralized. As agent for Titzck, Adams signed a pledge of Titzck's stock, some huge amount of Standard Oil and J. P. Morgan. 'Smith' signed the hypothecation agreement as 'attorney of fact for Titzck.' Is Grambling an attorney, too?" Estes asked, and then continued.

"The idea was that, pending the establishment of the permanent facility, the bank would accept the pledge and hypothecation as an expedient, with the actual stock to be transferred to Citytrust at the time of the permanent loan.

"The originating officer, and his superior and the loan committee, approved the facility on that basis. They really thought that it was the beginning of a major relationship. Let me read you the committee memo. 'Strong potential for comprehensive banking relationship. Strong potential for additional referrals from guarantor and investment banking firm.' Sold them a real bill of goods. Well, you can guess the rest.

"The stock was never produced, and Grambling . . . excuse me, 'Smith' made various promises for several weeks that he was getting new collateral or another bank to take out the loan.

"The loan was a demand note. We demanded repayment last Friday, January 2. Yesterday, 'Smith' called. He said he was out of town on business, but he was getting a new facility to pay us off."

"Where did he say he was?" the assistant asked.

"California. He said that he and Titzck were working with a bank in San Diego."

That afternoon, Kathy Kelly and Dolores Wach, a Connecticut Bank and Trust lending officer, called Rosner.

"Brian, we found the loan application you were talking about," Kelly began. "Nothing ever came of it. But I'll let Dolores explain."

"A 'Robert Smith,' an investment banker, made an application to our Private Banking Division in New Canaan," she began. "He was a shabbily dressed guy in his 30s."

Rosner would send a photo of Grambling to the Connecticut Bank & Trust officers who, as expected, would identify the photo as that of 'Smith.'

" 'Smith' contacted the bank first week in November," Wach continued.

Right after the unsealing of his plea transcript and the consequent publicity, the assistant thought. It had been front-page news in the Connecticut papers: Good reason to use an alias.

The transaction explained by Wach was familiar: "Smith" as agent for Titzck; Titzck's financials; $450,000 loan; to be collaterized by stock held at Signet; Titzck's assignment to the bank.

"Was the assignment notarized?" Rosner asked.

"Of course," the officer answered. "Here, I'll read it. It's a form dated December 15, 1986 with the names and signatures filled in. 'Personally appeared before me, Clemens Titzck, known to me to be the signer of the foregoing instrument, signed, Mary Adams.' "

"How was the collateral to be assigned to the bank?" Rosner asked.

"It never got that far, " Wach responded. " 'Smith' had sent us Titzck's tax returns for 1984 and 1985, along with a bank reference in Phoenix, a Joyce Lappin at Valley National. We were suspicious about this application by this point. One of our officers had called 'Smith' at the New York phone number on his letterhead. The phone was answered in a different company name, and the receptionist said that she had never heard of 'Robert Smith'.

"So we were alert to a possible scam when we called Lappin at Valley National. It began as the usual bank reference call. 'Yes, Titzck is a client, long-term satisfactory relationship.'

"But our officer didn't leave it at that. He told Lappin that he had been given the joint tax return of Titzck and his wife Jeanne. It turned out that Valley National also had Titzck's 1985 return. But, Lappin told our officer, on the Valley National return, the wife's name was not Jeanne. Lappin went on to say that the social security number of the wife was different on her return from that on our return, and that there was a major difference in income."

"Bet I can guess whose return showed the higher income," the assistant commented.

" 'Smith' wrote the bank to set up a meeting between our officers, Titzck, and him on December 4," Wach went on. "But we just told him we weren't interested."

"And I guess we made the right decision," Kelly interjected with a laugh.

"We never reported the incident to the authorities," Wach continued, "because we didn't think there was enough there."

"We can't get prosecutors here to do a fraud case even when we lose money." Kelly added. "They make their careers doing drug and murder cases."

Rosner thanked the bankers, who promised to mail him the documents.

The fortuity of events, the assistant thought. Bankers at Citytrust and Connecticut Bank and Trust make their calls to verify the collateral. With the Citytrust banker, Grambling gets his phone numbers straight and has the appropriate people answer the calls. With the Connecticut Bank & Trust banker, Grambling fouls up, thus alerting the banker to a possible fraud. When both bankers call the same bank reference in Arizona, they came away with totally different results. The Citytrust officer asks the usual reference questions, gets the usual answers, and is satisfied. The Connecticut Bank & Trust banker talks a little more, and confirms that he has a dummy tax return. That guy's lucky, and saves his employer $450,000. The Citytrust officer isn't lucky, and loses $450,000. Skill and intellect, other than Grambling's in setting up the crimes, played no role.

As Rosner was to learn, $450,000 was a large and embarrassing loss for Citytrust. Within a month, the loan officer lacking in luck would be gone from the bank.

After speaking with the Connecticut Bank and Trust officers, Rosner walked through the Frauds Bureau reception area and saw that he had received a package postmarked "Chicago," the long-awaited Colonial Savings documents.

"Exceedingly impressive," the assistant thought, as page by page, he read the materials: Several forged letters from Signet, a printed Signet hypothecation form, bogus Mary Adams financial statement and "Trust Agreement." Rosner appreciated professionalism, and this was a good set of papers.

Rosner pulled his scratch pad towards him, and did some figuring: Six counts forgery, six possession forged instrument, one grand larceny second degree. All seven years apiece.

He leaned back in his chair and looked at the papers spread over his desk. If Grambling had committed the Chicago crime in New York, the Grand Jury could have indicted for another 13 felonies. A maximum consecutive sentence of 91 years on those 13 alone. All for a crime he committed in June, right after Fleming convinced Judge Cahn not to remand him, as I had asked.

The assistant sat forward and reached for the Colonial documents he had not yet examined. He found the disbursement information. This solves the mystery that occurred last summer he realized.

In June 1986, an attorney from Nassau County, New York had called Rosner with a complaint. "My client sold a trade school to Grambling in exchange for notes," the attorney had said frantically. "The business came with a $100,000 cash account that Grambling's draining for personal expenses. The business is going bust, and the notes given to my client will be worthless." Within a week, the attorney had lost interest in pressing a case because the money had been restored. "Grambling probably ripped off a bank to repay his Nassau County victim," Rosner had joked with Moscow.

The joke had been correct. Grambling had robbed Colonial in June 1986, just when he had repaid his Nassau County victim to silence that complaint.

The assistant continued to read the Colonial materials. The memoranda documented how and when the Colonial bankers realized that they had been swindled. Frustrated that they had not received the American Brands stock, the bankers demanded alternative collateral, and, in September 1986, Grambling promised a letter of credit from Fidelity Bank in Philadelphia. A Colonial officer spoke with a Fidelity officer, who confirmed that a letter of credit was in preparation. Two weeks later, the Colonial officer again spoke to the Fidelity officer, only to be told that they had never spoken before and that there would be no letter issued. "Something is not right," the Colonial officer wrote in his internal memo.

Rosner laughed, and continued reading.

In October, a Fidelity officer, a real one this time, told Colonial that Fidelity would issue a letter of credit because it was "comfortable with Mr. Titzck as guarantor." Early in November, however, a Fidelity banker told his Colonial counterpart that "Mr. Grambling had been indicted and admitted to defrauding two banks." The letter of credit was never issued.

Confirms what I learned from Fidelity this morning, Rosner thought. Fidelity had loaned money to Grambling in 1985 and, after threatening suit, had been repaid the last $100,000 in September 1986. There were several aborted loan attempts in 1986, including a bizarre incident in which Fidelity received letters of credit from an Arizona bank, only to have the bank ask for their return. After their return, the Fidelity officers learned that the Arizona banker who had issued the letters had been fired.

The assistant reached the last Colonial Bank document, a one-page memo dated December 31, 1986. The memo noted that the F.B.I. had been informed of the crime and the Supreme Court of the State of New York had subpoenaed Colonial's records.

The last paragraph read, "In conclusion, John called today purporting to be at the Great American First Savings Bank of San Diego. He is to provide a female officer of that institution sufficient shares of Morgan Guaranty Trust stock for a $250,000 loan. The proceeds are to be posted to Colonial today. He continues to amaze!"

Rosner read the paragraph again, and then checked his calendar. The 31st was last Wednesday, less than a week ago. Estes of Citytrust had been lead to believe that Grambling had been in San Diego on Friday of the past week.

The assistant looked at his watch. Although the bank day was over in New York, it was not in California. He dialed San Diego information, and, within minutes, was speaking with Darwin Olsen, Chief Counsel to the Great American First Savings Bank.

Rosner explained the situation. It was a smallish loan he was looking for, $250,000 or so. The names were Grambling and Titzck, and the collateral would be Morgan Guaranty stock, or some other blue-chip stock. The loan would be at an advanced stage, he advised Olsen.

The concern was evident in Olsen's voice.

"Is it your information that the loan has already been approved?" he asked.

"Perhaps. I'm not sure, but it might be approved, or close to it," Rosner replied.

"I'll check," Olsen continued. "But I'm not sure that there's anything we can do to stop an approved loan."

"I haven't explained this right," the assistant said. He repeated that Grambling had been convicted for defrauding banks.

"I hear you," Olsen said. "But this is southern California. If the bank doesn't make a loan after it's been approved, the borrower can sue us, both for the amount of the loan and any consequential damage he can convince a jury to imagine."

"It's late in the day here in New York, and I must not be speaking correctly," Rosner said. He wished he could reach across the country and shake the in-house counsel by his lapels. The assistant spoke very slowly. "Grambling is a convicted bank swindler . . ."

"But the Bank of America just lost that case," Olsen said. "You think I'm crazy. But you don't know what's happening here in lender liability cases. In the case I'm talking about, the bank refused to lend after uncovering evidence of fraud. It became a jury question, and the jury socked the bank for millions in damages, many more times the amount of the loan."

"What?"

"We'll check this Grambling name out," Olsen continued. "Maybe there is no loan. But if there is, we still have to look at the law to see if we can decline to lend."

There was a meeting of loan officers scheduled for that afternoon, Olsen explained, and he would inquire about a Grambling loan.

After the call, the assistant went to Moscow's office.

"Assuming there's a crime about to be committed in San Diego, what do we do, John? We can have the locals make an arrest. Or we can advance the case on Judge Cahn's calendar. Maybe we can have Judge Cahn remand Grambling before the crime goes down in San Diego."

"How's your luck been with convincing Judge Cahn to remand Grambling?" Moscow asked.

"Not too good. But the crimes I reported to him last summer were attempts. Now I have two hits, banks in Chicago and Connecticut, and an attempt in San Diego the very week he gets an extension so that his psychiatrist can report how rehabilitated he is."

"But Grambling hasn't been charged with any of these crimes, has he?"

"No." Rosner thought out loud. "And Kaufman will be able to stand up in court and get into one of those defense counsel rages, 'How dare you accuse my client of such-and-such when he hasn't been charged with a crime.'"

"How confident are you on the time that Judge Cahn is going to give Grambling?" Moscow asked.

Rosner was silent. The lack of a response had decided the issue.

"Okay, if there's a crime going down, we'll get Grambling arrested in San Diego," Rosner said. "Then we'll tell the judge."

Meanwhile, in San Diego, Olsen and Cynthia Fatica, a colleague in the legal department, attended the loan officers' meeting. The attorneys asked the loan officers whether there was a recent or pending loan of the type described by the assistant. The officers looked at one another. No one had such a loan. The lawyers were relieved.

After the meeting, Carol Cortez, one of the loan officers in the corporate loan department, returned to her office. She was met by a distraught secretary.

"Could you take a call for Janet?" the secretary asked. Janet, another loan officer, was absent that day. Cortez looked toward the secretary's desk and saw a stack of phone messages for her absent colleague.

"He's been calling all morning," the secretary continued. "He says that it's urgent. Janet approved a loan, and he's ready to close. He's been demanding . . ."

Her explanation was interrupted by the ringing of the phone. Putting on a cheerful voice, the secretary picked up the receiver. "Good afternoon, Great American Bank."

Her smile disappeared. She covered the receiver and whispered, "It's him, Carol. Please . . ."

Cortez nodded and took the line. The speaker, a male, identified himself and launched into a description of the loan which had been approved and was ready to close. It is important that it close this week, he urged. Cortez promised to pull the file and get back to him.

After the call, she walked to the loan department record file and withdrew the papers on the loan. It was a corporate loan, in the low six figures, to be collaterized by blue-chip stock. The name of the man with whom she had spoken was not on the documents. He was just an agent for the true borrower, he had explained, but the name stuck in Cortez's mind. She called Fatica.

"Cindy, the name that was mentioned in the meeting, was it Grambling?"

Yes, Fatica responded.

"Well, it's not Morgan Guaranty stock which he's using to collateralize the loan," Cortez said. "It's 6,000 shares of I.B.M. Grambling's been calling all day. He wants to know when he can come in for the money."

Cortez went to Fatica's office, and the attorney studied the documents. The next morning, Wednesday February 7, Fatica called the assistant.

"We've approved a $350,000 loan for a Clemens Titzck. He's claiming to be a Phoenix multimillionaire who owns something called 'Robert Scott Financial Services' in Phoenix."

Rosner made another connection. The Mary Adams trust document submitted to Colonial Savings was on "Robert Scott" stationery.

"The application was made by Grambling as Titzck's agent," Fatica said. "Grambling gave us Titzck's tax returns and financials. The financials showed several investments in the San Diego area, and we approved the loan based in part on the interest Titzck had in the area. The loan's to be collateralized by $900,000 of IBM stock, Certificate AK3445. After receiving your call, we called IBM. There's no such certificate."

"At this point, the bank has decided not to make the loan. Even with California law being what it is, we think we can avoid civil liability for not lending the money. Grambling, by the way, has been calling repeatedly. He's expecting to come in right away to get the money. We don't know what to tell him."

The feds are probably better equipped to handle this than the locals, Rosner thought.

"Don't tell Grambling you're on to him. Continue to talk to him. Build up the record on the loan he's trying to get," the assistant said. "And call the F.B.I. They'll tell you what you have to do. Make sure you give them my name and number."

A few hours later, Douglas Clark, the Special Agent in charge of the F.B.I.'s white-collar crime unit in San Diego, called Rosner, who gave Clark the names and numbers of the El Paso, Chicago, and New York agents working the case.

"Set up a sting," the assistant suggested.

"That's what we plan to do," the agent replied.

While the F.B.I. prepared for the arrest, Grambling went to the bank and insisted on speaking to Cortez. She was alarmed. Is he dangerous, she wondered, but she acceded to the meeting. F.B.I. agents were in the bank to protect her.

Meeting with Grambling, Cortez played her role perfectly. Acting as if the loan would be made, she negotiated loan terms. She suggested an increase in the interest rate, and Grambling put her down. "Come on woman," he said in frustration as what he perceived to be her obvious inexperience. Then they argued about collateral.

"No," Cortez insisted. "If stock is the collateral, the bank wants the IBM shares."

"But Carol, Mr. Titzck's shares are in Pheonix. You have the hypothecation agreement from Signet. You don't need the shares."

"I'm sorry, John. We can't close without the physical shares. Why don't we put this off for a few days, and you and Mr. Titzck can bring the shares to us."

Flustered, Grambling left.

He was back in her office the next day.

"Carol, I just came from Mr. Titzck's lawyer. Here's the certificate. We were able to have it delivered from Pheonix."

Cortez took the certificate.

"John, Mr. Titzck will have to assign the shares to the bank at the closing. When is he available to come?"

"Clemens won't be able to make it, Carol. He has an ear infection so he can't fly. But we'll have a notarized assignment for the closing. Can we schedule it for tomorrow?"

Cortez was not certain if the F.B.I. would be prepared to make the arrest by then. She suggested that, were Grambling to call her later that day, she would know whether the loan could close the next day, Friday, January 9. They rose, and she escorted him to the door.

"John, you've put a lot of work into Mr. Titzck's loan, doing the application, getting the collateral, coming to the bank. I'm curious. What are you getting out of this?"

"Just a finder's fee, Carol." Grambling laughed. "Just a fee. But, believe me, Carol. I'm not getting what I should."

Grambling called later that day, and Cortez, as instructed by the F.B.I., told Grambling that the closing would be the next morning, Friday, January 9. When Grambling came to the bank on the 9th, Cortez escorted him to a small conference room overlooking the bay and the Bay Bridge. She introduced the two "bankers," the F.B.I. agents, who would be "closing" the loan. In response to the agents' inquiries, Grambling crisply restated the elements of the transaction: He had provided the bank with the Titzck documents and the I.B.M. certificate; as agreed, he would be authorized to receive the proceeds and wire them out to Colonial Savings. The microphone to the tape recorder was hidden, attached by masking tape, underneath the table directly in front of Grambling. After the crime was recorded, the agents arrested Grambling. He was cuffed, and hustled off to the local prison without the niceties of his New York arrests.

The San Diego bankers were relieved. Alerted by Rosner, their institution would not be defrauded of $350,000, and their careers not blotted by the loss. The Colonial bankers, who had called Great American Savings to ask when they would be receiving the loan proceeds, were not so fortuitous. A Grambling in jail would find no new victim to make Colonial whole. The $250,000 loss was unrecoverable money, and the bank was unforgiving. Within weeks, the responsible lending officer would be at a new job.

Informed immediately of the San Diego arrest, the assistant advanced the Grambling court proceeding from February 4 to Monday, January 12. At the bench, Rosner told the court of the arrest in San Diego, and the crimes in Chicago and Connecticut.

By allowing Grambling to remain at liberty on bail, Judge Cahn had trusted Grambling, and that trust had been betrayed, with the loss of property and jobs.

The attorneys returned to their tables. Kaufman spoke first.

"Your Honor, I was notified mid-day Friday that Mr. Grambling was under arrest by the F.B.I. in San Diego, California on a charge of bank fraud."

"What was he doing in San Diego?" Judge Cahn asked crisply.

"I am not certain," Kaufman replied.

"Why did he remove himself that far from our jurisdiction?"

"It was in connection with his business," Kaufman said.

Judge Cahn looked directly at the assistant.

"Application?"

The assistant rose. He asked that a warrant be issued for Grambling's arrest, so that, should Grambling be released on bail in San Diego, he would be returned immediately to New York.

On the record, Rosner summarized Grambling's newly-discovered crimes—Colonial in Chicago, Jefferson Savings in Ohio, Citytrust and Connecticut Bank and Trust in Connecticut, Great American in San Diego—every one committed after the assistant had argued in May, unsuccessfully, that Grambling be remanded.

Judge Cahn stopped the assistant. "I think you've said enough." Turning to Kaufman, the judge continued. "I am sure that you knew nothing of his activities."

"I knew nothing," Kaufman said. Then he responded to the prosecutor's litany of crimes. "My only comment is that at least John returned to the jurisdiction after each of these forays out of the state."

Yeah, the assistant thought. Like a wolf returning to its lair.

"And," Kaufman added, "John's been remanded to the Metropolitan Correctional Center (MCC) in San Diego. As of my last conversation with John's San Diego attorney, they are not going to contest the detention hearings. He will remain in the federal detention center."

"I am going to revoke bail, put Grambling on remand status, and issue a warrant," Judge Cahn ruled.

He reached for a paper on the bench. "Also, I received a letter regarding Grambling's operation of the schools run by Biosystems."

In anticipation of the sympathy letters Grambling intended to generate, Rosner had initiated a letter writing campaign from Grambling's victims.

"It was a very angry letter," Judge Cahn said. "It accuses Mr. Grambling of looting Biosystems and causing severe financial loss to a large number of students. Mr. Kaufman, you are invited to review the letter."

The proceeding ended.

Connecticut papers reported Grambling's San Diego arrest and imprisonment. Pamela Ficarrela, the Grambling employee and sister-in-law who had distributed a forged Touche Ross financial for Grambling in 1986, read of the arrest in her local paper.

"Thank God, he's behind bars," she thought. "The little people he's hurt. He's not going to be able to hurt anybody now."

She picked up the phone and began to dial the Manhattan number. She replaced the receiver. Grambling had jeopardized her life savings. But she could not call the prosecutor, yet.

CHAPTER 24

LESS TIME IN NEW YORK

Wideman, the Jefferson Savings attorney, called Rosner on Tuesday, January 13.

"I haven't told John that Jefferson won't be making the $350,000 loan. We're still getting calls on his behalf, and I thought I'd let you know. Mary Adams called this morning. She said that John had been 'detained' in California, but that the delay shouldn't prevent Jefferson from finishing the loan. She asked if I'd accept a collect call from John so that we could conclude the transaction."

"What'd you say?"

"Well, why not. I said that I would."

Wideman continued in his even voice.

"Also, last week I called someone claiming to be an attorney in Cleveland. Fellow named Ginsberg. He gave me a character reference for John."

"Did Grambling ask you to call Ginsberg so that Jefferson would be convinced to make the loan?" the assistant asked.

"Yeah," Wideman agreed. "Ginsberg told me that Grambling had put his problems behind him. Said that he had sent defense counsel a three-page letter for him to give to your judge in New York, let him know how John has been reformed."

"I don't think that I'll be seeing that letter. Unless they re-date it. Thanks for the call, Clark."

Rosner sat back in his chair, and turned to look out the window at the Tombs. He thought about the process represented by the Ginsberg letter, a process designed to keep Grambling out of prison.

Letter writing was a ritual of all sentencing. Rosner had first seen it as a young prosecutor working street-crime cases. The kid just convicted of armed robbery or rape could always produce a few letters on his behalf. They were never convincing. The standard letter came from the local minister, who said invariably that the boy's mother was a good churchgoing woman. Perhaps, the kid could even come up with a letter that he had been employed for a week or two.

Defense counsel for white-collar criminals have elevated the letter-writing ritual to an art form. The treatises on defense practice explain how to solicit such letters, and what to induce the writers to say. The purpose of the letter writing is to convince the court that the defendant's misconduct was an aberration, prompted by social, emotional, or financial stress, anything other than inherent amorality or evil. When the crazed street criminal says at sentencing, "The devil made me do it," the court, stifling its chuckles in its gown, treats the explanation for what it is—an excuse to evade responsibility (or an actual statement of insanity, that results in the defendant being committed to an asylum, an institution as lacking in freedom as a prison).

The white-collar defense counsel presents the "devil made me do it" excuse in a polished form—letters written by attorneys, doctors, business people, politicians, and clergymen of more established denominations than street churches. As Rosner had seen, a court must take notice of such letters. When the well-dressed, middle-class criminal appears before him, few judges can avoid, however fleetingly, the thought that "There, but for the grace of God, go I." Raping and killing were inexcusable, and the street punk perpetrator will feel the stern measure of the court's justice. But a little legerdermain in a financial statement? Who hasn't been tempted? And the defendant's friends, the letter writers, are so much like a judge's own.

Damn, the assistant thought. If I were a judge I wouldn't ignore pleas for mercy from someone who's observed the defendant for years, and claims that he's a caring husband and father. All judges teetered between harshness and leniency at sentencing, and Rosner fully understood how the loving words of the letter writers could tug the judge to one side.

The accepted practice, as Ginsberg had mentioned in his call to Wideman, was to send the letter to defense counsel ostensibly to allow him to submit the letters as a group to the judge. The real reason to send the letter to counsel was to let him act as a censor. A letter writer could commit few greater errors, and the treatises warn against it, than to discuss the facts of the crime. Invariably, the writer has received his facts from the defendant, and invariably the defendant lies, telling the writer that he was framed, or convicted of an insignficant offense. Such statements in a letter—"the defendant has told me that he's innocent"—are like slaps to the judge's face. He might not know about a defendant's family life, but he surely knows that the felon is guilty.

Whatever letters Grambling had obtained would probably be useless. Letters invariably claim that the defendant is reformed: The message to the court is that a prison sentence is not necessary. The Grambling letters would make the "reformation" argument, and they would all be dated prior to the San Diego arrest.

An opinion as solid as ice in a summer sun, the assistant thought. Obviously, Grambling was not reformed, and any letter writer who said so stood naked as a terrible judge of character. If the writer's character assessment was wrong on reformation, the judge might think, maybe the writer wasn't so sharp in his observations of the loving family relationship.

The afternoon of January 13, Rosner called Judith Feigin, the San Diego Assistant United States Attorney prosecuting the Great American case. He explained the problem created for the New York prosecution by the San Diego arrest. Sentences imposed in separate jurisdictions can be made to run concurrently with one another (at the same time) or to run consecutively (one after the other). Under New York State law, a state sentence runs concurrent with a previously imposed federal sentence unless the state judge specifically states that the sentences are to run consecutively. For months, the assistant and his colleagues had feared that Judge Cahn was too kindhearted a man to impose substantial state prison. Now, unless they could convince him to say "consecutive" at sentencing, it was possible that all of Grambling's time would be served in a resort-like federal facility, just as Grambling had wanted.

"Judy, he's going to plead guilty in your case, and refuse to return to New York until he's sentenced first in San Diego. Then he'll come to court before my judge and say that he's been sentenced to enough time."

Rosner and Feigin also discussed Clemens Titzck.

"I've had the F.B.I. interview Titzck in Phoenix," Feigin explained. "He lives in a very modest home, not the place of a millionaire with $17 million.

"He told the agents that he was a friend of Grambling's father. John, Jr. recently asked him for a favor. 'I received some IBM stock recently from my dad, and I want to use it to collaterize a loan. But no bank will deal with me because of my problems.' "

Rosner anticipated Titzck's explanation.

"So Grambling asked Titzck to front for him," the assistant said.

"Yes," Feigin continued. "Grambling asked Titzck to say that the stock was his, if anyone asked. And Titzck agreed."

"There're problems with that story, Judy, aside from its unbelievability. Titzck, or someone claiming to be Titzck, appeared with Grambling at a Citytrust meeting in Connecticut. With Grambling physically at his side, posing at the time as a 'Robert Smith,' Titzck verified his $17 million statement."

"Do you have any proof that the Titzck in Phoenix was the Titzck in Connecticut?" Feigin asked.

"No, I'm not doing the case. That crime and yours are outside my jurisdiction."

"I'm not sure if Titzck is indictable in San Diego, even if he is lying," Feigin added. "No Titzck, real or otherwise, appeared at Great American. So I'm just going to leave it. Grambling is the defendant, and that's who we'll indict."

With his subsequent inquiries, the assistant confirmed the wisdom of Feigin's choice. Shortly after the conversation with Feigin, Rosner made a request of his state law enforcement colleagues in Phoenix: Could you determine the location of the telephone called by the Citytrust bank officer when that officer thought he was calling Titzck at home? The Arizona police traced the telephone to Biltmore Estates, the mansion on which Grambling had put a down payment with this 1985 check-kite proceeds. After obtaining Titzck's true home phone number from directory assistance, Rosner called Titzck, who insisted that the "Titzck" documents used in the various loan schemes were not real and were not used with his permission. As the F.B.I. had determined, Titzck had tried to help Grambling obtain a loan, but Titzck had not intended to commit a crime, or to help anyone else commit a crime with his name, as was done by Grambling and others in San Diego and elsewhere. Titzck had thought that he would assist Grambling to a limited degree. Titzck had failed to realize that, once the assistance was given, he could put no limits on how Grambling would distort that assistance for his own purposes.

Events in San Diego proceeded as the assistant had predicted. The federal judge set Grambling's bail at $2 million, a bail Grambling could not make. The federal Grand Jury indicted Grambling for bank fraud and, on February 2, he pleaded guilty. The plea was a summary courtroom proceeding, over in 10 minutes.

"Do you realize that the Great American First Savings Bank is a federally insured corporation?" the judge asked.

"Yes, your Honor," Grambling said.

"And back in late December and early January, did you try to get a $250,000 loan from that bank?"

"Yes, your Honor."

"Secured by a fraudulent 6,000 share stock certificate from IBM?"

"Yes, I did."

"Alright," the judge concluded. "The court finds the plea to be free and voluntary and to have a factual basis. It's ordered entered."

The San Diego proceedings were followed closely in New York.

"When's Mr. Grambling coming back to New York?" Judge Cahn asked counsel at the February 4 court proceeding, the adjourned date for Grambling's New York sentence.

"John is scheduled to be sentenced in federal court on March 23," Kaufman said. Outside Judge Cahn's presence, Rosner had suggested to Kaufman that Grambling be brought back to be sentenced prior to March 23. Kaufman had opposed the suggestion.

"Why should the State of New York waste taxpayers' money by flying John to New York, only to have to return him to San Diego to be sentenced. Let him be sentenced federally," Kaufman said. "Then you'll only have to fly him here and back once."

"We're happy to pick up the tab," Rosner said.

"No," Kaufman had replied. He promised that he would use every legal device to oppose a transfer to New York for a sentencing prior to the federal sentencing.

And he'll succeed in delaying it, the assistant thought. It would be an unwinnable fight.

"John will be brought to New York on March 25," Kaufman continued in front of Judge Cahn. "Immediately after the federal sentencing."

"What's the rule on state sentencing after federal sentencing?" the judge asked.

"The state time is concurrent unless you say it is to run consecutive," the assistant said.

Kaufman jumped into the opening. "Your Honor, it would ease my client's mind if you could indicate where you are going regarding the running of the sentences."

"I don't know what the sentence will be," the judge said placidly. "I'll read your sentencing submissions, and the assistant's."

Good, Rosner thought. He's not committing himself to concurrent time.

"However, I will tell you, Mr. Kaufman," Judge Cahn continued. "I have received some more very disturbing letters regarding the trade schools that your client owned."

"Biosystems," the prosecutor interjected.

"Yes, Biosystems is one," Judge Cahn said. "You may stop by my chambers and copy the letters. Very disturbing. They talked about students who have lost their tuition because your client allegedly bankrupted the school by draining it of funds."

Rosner reported the developments to Moscow.

"Today it sounds like the judge is going to sentence consecutively. I think he's disturbed by the letters I've asked the victims to write him."

Moscow nodded.

"Speaking of letters, John," the assistant continued. "The Office has been asked to write one."

"Wilkis?"

"Yes. He's coming up for sentencing next week. We owe him, John. I don't know anything about his insider-trading case . . ."

"Except that he didn't tell you about it when the Office was immunizing him in the Grand Jury," Moscow said sharply.

". . . but," the assistant continued, "he's always told the truth about the Bank of Montreal case. He came in to testify, and to be prepped for trial, even after his indictment. That's all that Naftalis wants us to say."

"I know. He's been calling me too." Gary Naftalis, a former federal prosecutor and one of the most skilled litigators in New York City, was Wilkis' lawyer.

"John, why shouldn't we say something? How many sentences have you and I stood up at? How much crap have we listened to? About how this defendant is remorseful for this, and that one is remorseful for that. And it's all bullshit. The only thing the defendant is remorseful about is how much money and time he's wasted by his court appearances. I've seen Wilkis, John. He's like a whipped dog. He's humiliated and contrite. Never going to commit another crime in his life."

Rosner remembered the first interview with Wilkis: How filled with bitterness he was, but how his face had softened when talking about his daughter's visit to his office. It was the only time that he had seen Wilkis happy. When they had last spoken, Wilkis had talked about his children.

"I'm writing the letter, John. When the Office needed Wilkis as a witness, he did right by us. And we should do the same for him."

Moscow tapped his fingers on his desk. "Keep it simple and to the facts. He was subpoenaed, he testified truthfully. Period."

"And he's contrite," the assistant added.

"Make it just that short. 'Contrite.' No adverbs." Moscow thought for a moment.

"And let me see it before it goes out."

Rosner delivered the letter to Judge Peter Leisure, the federal judge sentencing Wilkis, that day. On the stationery of the Office of the District Attorney, New York County, and over the assistant's signature, the letter was short and factual.

"I do not know what crimes Mr. Wilkis has pleaded guilty to or committed," the letter read. "In dealing with this Office, however, he has been a truthful witness." The letter described Wilkis as "genuinely contrite."

In a week, Wilkis was sentenced; one year and a day, to be served in the minimum security prison.

Grambling was sentenced in San Diego on March 23. Neither he nor his counsel made a statement prior to sentencing. They knew that every year imposed federally was, if the state sentence was concurrent, a year he would not serve in state prison. The maximum permissible sentence was five years, and Judge Nielsen imposed a sentence of four years.

On March 23, Detectives Collins and Moss were in San Diego to pick Grambling up and return him to New York. As they sat on the plane returning to New York, Collins and Grambling spoke.

"Thanks for the trip to San Diego, John. It was a nice town," Collins said.

Grambling looked perplexed.

"I was thinking of leaving the country. Would you have come after me?"

Collins laughed.

"Sure, John, I've brought people back from Spain." Collins had been on a team which had extradited from Spain an arms merchant who had sold weapons in New York to undercover detectives claiming to be terrorists. "Just don't go to some ugly country, okay, John?"

"I didn't think you'd come after me if I left the country."

Grambling thought for a few moments and shrugged.

"Four years," he told the detectives. "I'll probably have to serve only 25 months before I'm paroled, and I already have three months credit for what I've served since January. And that's without moving for a sentence reduction."

He looks fit and calm, the detectives thought.

"We're sorry that the federal sentence was so short," Grambling continued as he relaxed in the plane back to New York. "The more time I serve federally, the less I serve in a New York prison."

CHAPTER 25

FOR HIS SPOUSE
AND THE CHILDREN

On March 12, Grambling submitted to Judge Cahn his long-awaited sentencing material: a memorandum by Kaufman, an appendix of letters, and a report from a psychiatrist. Kaufman would submit a report from a second psychiatrist on March 19. The lengthiest document submitted on the 12th was Grambling's 32-page, single-spaced letter explaining his conduct. Rosner took the material to his office and closed the door. He would spend the day reading them.

"I have attempted and intend to lead an honest and productive life," Grambling's letter, dated March 6, began. "This letter and those accompanying it should never have been written. I sincerely apologize to you and to those supporters who have taken the time to provide their testimony."

Proceedings in the criminal justice system are a contest between trust and falsity. The contest is never over. Whether or how a crime was committed will be disputed prior to indictment, at trial, at sentencing, on appeal, and in post-appeal habeas corpus proceedings that occur, and reoccur, years after events. In the Appeals Bureau, Rosner had defended the legality of murder convictions (it was only the murderers who would still be in prison) 15 years after the homicide. The legal issues being reviewed are rehashes of arguments from years before. What is new is the judge and the renewed opportunity for the defendant to undo what earlier judges had done.

Grambling's March 6 statement, articulate, reasoned, was a tissue of lies designed to deceive Judge Cahn and, if not him, the future judges who would pass on the reasonableness of the sentence Judge Cahn had imposed. Grambling admitted the facts that could not be denied, and lied about the rest. Yes, he admitted, he had submitted a false Lazard, Freres consent. But he had been forced into it by Husky's dishonest negotiating tactics, and the pressures Husky had created. "Closing the Husky deal had become my entire existence. . . I broke down mentally and morally, I lost my self-control and panicked," he wrote. "In desperation, I . . . offered the Bank of Montreal $8 million of non-existent Dr Pepper stock."

To a person unfamiliar with the nuances of the case, Grambling's letter spoke persuasively. Crime by crime, Grambling had searched for gaps in the evidence, and, whenever plausible, shifted the blame for the crimes to the victims. But Grambling did not realize that Rosner had not disclosed all his evidence in court. In his ignorance, Grambling confidently wrote Judge Cahn that submitting the false Robert Libman statement to Husky in November 1984 was his first criminal act. "This was the start of John's descent down the slippery slope of misrepresentation," Kaufman eloquently put it in his own memorandum.

The assistant was astonished.

I'm going to be able to prove that he submitted the Libman statement on several prior occasions, Rosner thought. And look at what he says about U.S. Shelter. He writes as if the deal was legitimate. He doesn't know I have the documents.

The assistant took extensive notes. He would write a detailed refutation of every lie, a memorandum to accompany Grambling through the court system over the next decades.

Facts about the crimes I can correct, the assistant thought. But how do I confront the dilemma of the family?

"For over two years I have been punished severely," Grambling wrote. "I am now bankrupt . . . my home was sold in August, 1986 . . . I cannot say enough about the direct and indirect damage and humiliation to my wife, children. . . The only income for my wife to survive on is from my parents.

"In my case, incarceration is severely hurting my wife and four sons who have no home, no income, no friends to speak of, and only my family in Texas. Putting me in jail does punish me to a degree by restricting my time which is a key factor. But more important is the welfare of at least five other innocent human beings."

Incarcerate me, and harm a family: Grambling had eloquently raised the obstacle Judge Cahn would have to overcome if he was to impose a consecutive sentence. Rosner finished the letter, and read the rest of the package.

There was a letter from his wife, as well as a report from a psychiatrist with, Kaufman promised, a second psychiatrist's report to be submitted on the 19th. Only two, the assistant wondered. He flipped through the pages of Grambling's letter and found what he was looking for. "I have at my parents' request seen five psychiatrists and analysts since the Husky transaction occurred." Interesting, Rosner thought: Saw five, but got only two to submit reports. Means that he had to shop around for shrinks willing to write for sentencing.

The Grambling letter created a dispute in court on March 12. Judge Cahn treated the submitted sentencing materials as sealed. Rosner wanted to send the letter to the business people whose conduct was mentioned so that they could tell the judge how Grambling had lied. Kaufman vigorously opposed the request: Truth is rarely an ally of the defense. Judge Cahn ruled that the assistant could send business people the paragraphs that discussed their conduct.

"But no more, and they must keep confidential what you send them," Judge Cahn admonished. "And they must send the paragraphs back to you when their examination is done."

Before he could begin to send out the relevant paragraphs, Rosner was flooded with new information that proved how often Grambling had placed his own interests ahead of those of his victims. On Friday, March 20, the assistant received the call that Pam Ficarella had put off for weeks.

"This is Pamela Ficarella," a meek voice began. "You probably think of me as one of John's crooks, but I'm not. And, oh God," her voice broke, "my son and I are going to lose our house because of him."

Rosner consoled Ficarella and coaxed her to tell her story. It was like comforting assault victims in the Complaint Room.

"John had me sign some notes. It was last summer. He said it was a limited partnership he had invested in. He wanted me to get some of the money. He knows I needed it. I didn't want to sign. I shouldn't have. But I did. I asked him, 'If I sign here, am I going to go to jail?' But he told me it was legitimate.

"Now I'm getting letters from a mortgage company in Phoenix. I'm delinquent on my $5 million loan, they say, and if I don't pay soon, they're going to start foreclosure proceedings. My little house in Westport is all my son and I own. I don't know what they're talking about—property in Arizona, a $5 million loan."

She broke into tears. "God, you can't imagine the relief I felt when I knew he was finally behind bars."

The assistant elicited the basic information. The company in Phoenix was Valentine Mortgage. Ficarella also told him about a loan application at Gateway Savings in South Norwalk. "They accused me of trying to swindle them of a $250,000 loan. I never went to that bank."

Rosner asked her about the time she gave a forged Touche Ross financial statement to the realtor, the incident that, before Judge Cahn in May 1986, Grambling's counsel had explained as an instance of Pam Ficarella acting on her own.

"John had told me to give the statement to the realtor. When I gave it to the fellow, he asked me, 'Who's the Touche Ross accountant?' 'Bob Zobel,' I say, and the realtor says, 'Oh Bob, I know him.' I told this to John, and he told me immediately to get the statement back. 'Why,' I asked, and he says 'We're going to use a different company for the transaction.' But I thought the statement was honest."

Rosner suggested that they meet, but arranging a time was a problem. Ficarella worked at the Connecticut secretarial school in whose name Grambling had defrauded $450,000 from Citytrust. She also held two other jobs, including waitressing on weekends. They arranged a time for the coming week. The delay gave Rosner the opportunity to gather the relevant documents.

First he called John Milici, an attorney used by Gateway Bank in South Norwalk, Connecticut. Milici recalled the incident with Ficarella.

"Sure I know Grambling. In '85, before I came to Gateway, I did some contract work for people who intended to do a deal with Grambling. 'Big gun from Texas, Daddy owns most of the state,' was how he was described to me. When I met him, he told me some story about how he had been screwed by Husky Oil. 'Those sons of bitches,' he was complaining. 'We were going to buy the North Slope but they beat us out.' He goes on about how he was litigating in Denver against Husky and his lawyers had told him that he could expect to recover a 'very large sum of money.'

"At the time, I was impressed with the fellow. I understood that his corporation would forward the seed money to put together the current deal. Unfortunately, the money never came, and the deal I'm working on goes nowhere. Then I came here, and last year Ray Bogert, a lending officer, calls me and says, 'I have a funny file. This guy comes in with false financial documents.' 'What's the name?' I ask, and when Bogart says 'Grambling,' I realize that I know the guy.

"I'll get you the papers and put you in touch with Ray Bogert."

A few days after this talk with Milici, Ray Bogert, the bank officer, called Rosner.

"Grambling came in to obtain a $250,000 loan for his business school. It was to be guaranteed by Pamela Ficarella and Mary Adams. They never came into the bank."

"What kind of documents did Grambling give you?" Rosner asked.

"He gave us Ficarella's 1984 tax return. It showed an income of $2.5 million with the bulk, almost $2 million, coming from the dividend income for her stocks, IBM, J. P. Morgan, Standard Oil, blue-chip every one. He also submitted Mary Adams' signed financials, net $2,767,877. For the school, he gave us a 1985 statement from an accounting firm.

"That's where we caught them. The balance sheet and operating statement didn't seem to make sense for a school of this nature. I called the number shown on the accountant's letterhead, 'Phillip Porte, C.P.A., Arlington, Virginia.' I needed some explanation for the figures plus a rationale for a Washington accountant handling the books of a western corporation. Well, the letter Porte wrote says what he told me on the phone. We sent you the letter, didn't we?"

The assistant looked at the letter on the stationery of "Phillip Porte and Associates, Inc., Washington Based Healthcare Consultants, Government Relations/Communication." The address and phone had been lifted off Porte's real stationery and reproduced on the "accounting firm" letter sent to Gateway. Porte's June 17, 1986 letter to Bogert read:

I am writing to you to reiterate our telephone conversation of this morning, June 17. First, I must emphasize that Phillip Porte & Associates, Inc. is not a certified public accounting firm, nor have we ever represented the firm as such. We are incorporated in the Commonwealth of Virginia as a consulting/lobbying firm which works primarily in the health care field. . . I am extremely distressed that the Gateway Bank has received documents that reference me personally as well as the address and telephone number of my firm as an accounting firm. . . I can assure you that Porte & Associates will move quickly to remove itself from any business relationship it may have with clients who have acted in any illegal or unethical capacity. As you can imagine, our credibility is vital to our ability to work with the legislative and executive branches of government, and any compromise of that ability cannot be tolerated.

This is a story I've got to hear, Rosner thought, as he dialed the number on Porte's stationery. Porte answered, and was joined on the phone by his partner, Michael Stafford. They wanted to set the record straight.

"I met Grambling in November 1985 at an Association for Respiratory Therapy Convention, a client of ours," Porte began. "Grambling wanted to start a foundation for the elderly, the AGE Foundation. The idea was to provide the elderly with broad-based services, such as continuing education. He struck me as being articulate, and really of a common mold, not pretentious like other men with his kind of wealth.

"Mike and I liked him, and went to work immediately. We prepared IRS materials, and worked our contacts with the American Association of Retired Persons, the Senate Aging Committee, and others. We talked to Senator Heinz's staff about hearings for an appropriation, $50 million for the Foundation's first year of work. We even reserved the Speaker's Room at the Capitol for a public relations reception to announce the Foundation's establishment. It was set for June 1986.

"What didn't occur," Porte continued, "is that we never got paid. Finally, in early June, Grambling gave us a check. It bounced. Then, on June 17, I got a call from Ray Bogert from the Gateway Bank asking me about a financial statement we had allegedly prepared."

"I can't tell you how good we had felt about Grambling when he first came in," Stafford added. "Here's a guy, we thought, wanting to do something really decent. And when I think back to how he created the aura of wealth, dropping names like Morgan Fairchild or Armand Hammer, acquaintances of his who would be available to help the Foundation. He made you proud to be working with him.

"But we should have seen it coming. Remember, Phil, the story about the phones?"

"Oh, yes," Porte said.

"In May 1986 or so," Stafford continued, "Grambling asked us if we had any available phone lines in the office. He needed a line to answer 'Signet Securities' for him. He just wanted us to take a message and then tell him who had called. Well, we agreed to take messages, and several calls came in. I recall one from Arizona. We always told the caller who we were, and passed the message to Grambling."

"I feel like a fool," Stafford said. "We've worked the Hill for years. We've dealt with Senators, Congress people. When it comes to smooth and trust-inspiring, Grambling was right up there. He's the best con man I've ever seen."

"But now I can see what he was doing," Porte concluded. "He knew that he would have a sentencing coming up, and he was setting himself up for a leniency pitch. If we got the funding, he could have pointed out to the court that he was a philanthropist."

Rosner asked Porte to write Judge Cahn a letter stating just what he had said in their phone call.

Next, the assistant called Nancy Owen of Valentine Mortgage in Phoenix.

"I'm not surprised that you're calling," Owen began. "Ms. Ficarella bought the 63 acres of property last May. We loaned her the $4.5 million. The money all went to pay prior liens on the property and fees."

"Was there a brokerage fee?" the assistant asked.

"Yes. Ms. Ficarella was introduced to the transaction by a Wayne Sellness, a broker. She never visited the property, and we never met her. Sellness was the agent. His fee was $253,000. It was paid at the closing."

That's where Grambling made his profit, the assistant thought. He split the fee with Sellness.

"We never met Ficarella," Owen continued, "although we received her financial material. There were several letters from a Theodore Etten, a senior vice-president at Signet Securities in Chicago. He verified Ms. Ficarella's assets, both her stock and her money market account. There was a signed copy of her financial statement, and her 1984 tax return, as well as a copy of the letter establishing the trust by which she inherited the bulk of her $18 million net worth."

"Did your account officer verify the Signet materials?"

"Of course. He called the Signet number in Illinois, 1-312-480-9820."

Ficarella came to the District Attorney's Office after Grambling's federal sentence had been imposed on March 23. In her early 40s, thin with large eyes and light hair, she was a single parent with a 17-year-old son.

"He's enjoyed the publicity. He calls himself the 'JR of the Northeast.' After all the publicity, he said that someone should make a movie of his life."

Ficarella explained that a friend had obtained an attorney for her in Arizona. The friend would guarantee the attorney's payment, "and I'll pay back my friend. I'll be paying for a long time. But it's the only way to save my house."

She knew nothing of the financial statements and tax returns that Grambling had submitted to Valentine Mortgage on her behalf.

"I've sent Nancy Owen my real financial statement. I think there's a chance that Valentine Mortgage won't come after me even if the property sells for less than the mortgage at the foreclosure sale. But," and she began to sob. "The attorneys have told me that they're just my civil attorneys, not my criminal attorneys. If the F.B.I. calls, they said, I should remain silent. Am I going to be indicted?"

The assistant had shared various public information regarding Grambling's crimes with Owen. Her company was inclined, and Rosner was pushing them in that direction, to treat Ficarella as a victim, and not proceed against her. He told Ficarella that when the F.B.I. calls, she should have them call him. She regained her composure.

"Have you heard of Wayne Sellness?" Rosner asked.

"Of course. Sellness would call at the business number in Connecticut and leave messages for John. He was some kind of broker, like John. I told you, didn't I? John acted as the broker in Phoenix. He said that he received a cash commission of, I forget, $70,000, $140,000, something like that."

Grambling had harmed other members of her family, Ficarella said.

"He's lied to me, so how do you think he's treated Trish? She doesn't know what's going on. And as for Kathy, my sister in Chicago, he tried to get her to guarantee the Citytrust loan. He sent her forged documents to convince her. Thank God, she didn't get involved. And you know what happened in bankruptcy court, don't you? It came out that John forged Trish's name to take her stock to collateralize a loan, Bank of New York I think. He's harmed the entire family. My father is devastated."

After the talk with Ficarella, the assistant did something he had never done before. He contacted a defendant's family member, Grambling's father-in-law.

It's painful, Rosner told White, but unless the court knows the havoc Grambling has wrought on your family, the judge may accept what Grambling is saying as true, that he's a good family man, and that his incarceration would harm your daughter and grandsons. White understood what he had to do. In sorrow and anger, he wrote to the court to let it know the depth of the damage Grambling had done.

The information provided by Ficarella answered another question raised by the documents in Rosner's files. In one of his many attempted frauds against Fidelity Bank in Philadelphia, Grambling had tried to obtain a loan to be guaranteed by his alleged partner, Ed Mason of Phoenix, Arizona. Mason was the builder of the mansion in Biltmore Estates, for which Grambling had made a down payment with his September 1985 kite money.

After Ficarella's call in March, Rosner called Mason to ask about the mansion and the Fidelity Bank guarantee.

"We evicted him in 1986," Mason said. "I'd have to check with my lawyers to make certain. But between the house, and the commercial building my partner and I renovated for him, which he never paid for, we're out about, oh, $900,000 easy."

The assistant asked about the Fidelity Bank loan, and the representation made by Grambling that he and Mason were partners. Mason laughed.

"Me? Partners with that crook? But I know about that Fidelity affair. Back in 1986, I learned that Grambling had instructed a local fellow, a Wayne Sellness, to impersonate me. I saw the letter."

Rosner thought back two years to his March 1985 interview with Libman. "Grambling would give written instructions to his accomplices on who they were to impersonate, and what they were to say," was what Libman had said.

"I put a stop to it," Mason concluded.

And I guess he did, the assistant thought. The forged Mason documents submitted to Fidelity in January 1986 were the only instance known to Rosner of anyone trying to impersonate Mason. What's the guy's secret?

"Well, Ed?" Rosner asked. "How did you put a stop to it?"

"I made sure I saw Grambling next time he was in Phoenix," Mason said in his even, western drawl. "And I told him that, if he didn't cut this crap out, I'd beat him to a pulp."

And who said white-collar crime couldn't be deterred, the assistant thought.

At month's end, Rosner received a call that brought home how slightly people change over time. As with most prosecutors' offices, the Manhattan District Attorney's Office maintained good relations with reporters at several newspapers. In light of the financial crimes prosecuted by the Frauds Bureau, the assistants in that Bureau knew reporters on *The Wall Street Journal*. Rosner had given Ed Cony, one of the *Journal's* Pulitzer Prize winners, public information on the Grambling case. Cony was working the information into a story. He was an oldtimer who knew Morgenthau from his days as U.S. Attorney for the Southern District, and had written a front-page *Journal* story on another of the assistant's cases. On several occasions, Cony called Rosner to ask him to repeat information he had been told before. "It's my memory," Cony chuckled. "I'm getting old."

On March 23, the day of Grambling's federal sentencing, Cony's article appeared on the front page of *The Wall Street Journal*. Continuing on an interior page, it was a 50-paragraph analysis of the crimes Grambling had accomplished since 1984. It was Ed Cony's last story. His memory loss was not a joke. It would be diagnosed as Alzheimer's Disease. By 1988, he would retire from the *Journal* and end his journalism career.

The day after the *Journal* article, Rosner received a message that he had been called by Dr. Bryan Griffith, an orthopaedic surgeon in Baton Rouge, Louisiana. "Re *WSJ* article," the message said. Rosner returned the call.

"I've been waiting 15 years to make this call," Dr. Griffith began. "Grambling and I were frat brothers at SMU in the 1970s. He was treasurer while I was president. He embezzled thousands from the frat. Almost ended us, though his father paid off some of the money. You should talk to Ken Stevens. He succeeded me as president. He knows more about the loss."

The assistant called Stevens, an attorney in Dallas. He remembered the incident well.

"Grambling was a quiet guy. He got elected treasurer because no one else wanted the job. Besides, he was a business major, organized in ways. I remember that he prepared job descriptions for the frat officers. His description of the treasurer said that the treasurer could take out loans in the fraternity's name. 'That's no good,' I told him. 'Take it out,' which he did. And then in my role as president, I signed the descriptions to make them official.

"Round about graduation, I get a call from a Republic National Bank of Dallas officer, a frat brother. He wants to talk about the frat's problems. What problems, I ask him. Well, you know, your treasurer took out a $10,000 loan to repair the frat roof and put in new heating. He tells me, 'I got your signature on the loan documents.'

"I see the documents. Yeah, he does have my signature. And I also see, from the date, that the loan was taken out just a couple of weeks after that incident with the job descriptions."

Grambling was transposing signatures and cutting and pasting documents for small college loans, the assistant realized, just as he would be doing for million dollar loans 15 years later.

"Grambling was already off campus by the time this surfaced. I remember how he left. He had just gotten engaged. And he and his fiancee drove off in a new car. I remember thinking at the time, 'Wow, where'd he get the money to buy that baby.' " Stevens chuckled. "Guess I found out."

"What happened?" the assistant asked.

"Well, the bank was going to prosecute. But Grambling's father intervened. He was an old frat member. He told the frat that he'd pay any amount that we could prove John had taken. When Grambling's father was talking to the Republic National Bank brother, the father said that this wasn't the first time he had to get his son out of a jam. His son had done the same thing when he ran the finances for a club in high school.

"Anyway, it was summertime. Most members were away already. We could only prove that John took a few thousand, though I think the real loss, between the loan and his handling of our cash, was nearer $20,000. The frat just lived real lean the next year to pay back its debts."

"What you're telling me is like an amateur version of what he's done in recent years," the assistant said.

"Folks don't change. Grambling robbed his frat brothers," Stevens said. "And got away with it. He's just continued to do what he's always done."

At the assistant's urging, Dr. Griffith wrote a letter to Judge Cahn explaining the SMU theft. The conversation with the frat members had provided a window of insight into Grambling's mind.

"He's stolen for years," Rosner commented to Moscow. "If I had the time and resources, I bet you that I'd find proof he stole from his 4-H Club. And the kicker is that he's always gotten away with it. No wonder he thinks he can walk on water. He thinks his father will save him, or some other attorney. He's always had someone to intervene, to stand up and ward off the consequences for what he's done."

"Until now," Moscow said.

"He's not sentenced yet," Rosner added dubiously.

CHAPTER 26

GO MAN, GO!

Brian Rosner prepared the People's sentencing submissions. By pleading guilty, a defendant avoids a trial, and the detailed re-creation of his crimes. The assistant would not permit Grambling's criminal history to sink into the memory hole created by a plea.

The sentencing memorandum outlined Grambling's criminal history as it had been reconstructed at One Hogan Place. It began with the theft of fraternity funds at SMU, and continued to Dean Witter, where he had misrepresented his position (claiming to be the Director of the Mergers and Acquisition Department) and had submitted, and received credit for, fraudulent expense vouchers. Because of his threat to sue if fired, he was allowed to resign.

The memorandum continued through his bank frauds, grouped in four sections: "Grambling's crimes prior to the period covered by the New York indictment" (eleven victim banks and corporations); "Grambling's crimes from the December 1984 Bank of Montreal theft to his May 1985 arraignment" (seven victim banks); "Crimes committed between the May 1985 arraignment, and the People's May 1986 request that he be remanded for committing additional crimes" (eleven victim banks, companies, and individuals); "Crimes committed between the time that Grambling tricked the court into allowing him to remain at liberty and January 9, 1987, the San Diego fraud" (seven victim banks).

Moscow reviewed the memorandum before its submission. He came into Rosner's office and dropped the draft copy on his desk.

"It's the most prejudicial Table of Contents I've ever seen," Moscow said.

The assistant began to protest.

"No," Moscow interrupted. "I'm not saying it's unfair. I'd sentence him to life based on the Table of Contents alone. But don't you think you're being a little too hard on Judge Cahn, breaking the crimes into those before and after he didn't remand Grambling?"

"No," the assistant answered. "The judge was tricked, as was Fleming. It's a fact worth emphasizing. Were it a different judge, I might worry that he'd react to criticism by ruling against us."

To still any argument about the underlying facts, Rosner submitted, in addition to the memorandum, a 2,000 page, foot-thick appendix, containing the documentation by which Grambling had defrauded the victims identified in the memorandum. It was an encyclopedia of crime with victims in South Carolina, New York, Arizona, Texas, Kansas, Tennessee, Calgary, Colorado, Utah, Mississippi, Connecticut, Pennsylvania, Illinois, Ohio, and California. As the sentencing deadline approached, Rosner received information of a dozen additional crimes, but he didn't pursue it. I have enough to make the point, the assistant thought.

Although the search for newly discovered crimes had ended, Rosner remained in contact with his known victims. On April 9, he called Clark Wideman, counsel to Jefferson Savings, and had one of the most distressing conversations in the case.

"I'm glad you called Brian. You know that Grambling has made another offer to buy Jefferson Savings."

"He's been in a New York prison for over a week, Clark. How did he make an offer to you—postcard?"

"No, while he was in the MCC in San Diego, he called all the time."

Federal detention facilities, the assistant thought. You can't deprive detainees of their constitutional right to limitless phone calls.

"It was similar to the earlier deal, though now it was to be syndicated by a David Robisch of Diversified Financial Programs in Indianapolis. John called a few times to discuss the Letter of Intent he had express mailed to me from San Diego."

"Express mail from prison?"

"No," Wideman said. "His San Diego attorney Bob Brewer mailed it to me. Brewer also sent me John's long letter to Judge Cahn. John wanted me to know that he really never intended to hurt anyone." Wideman sounded agitated.

"It's the letter that disturbs me."

"What letter?" the assistant asked.

"You know, the long one to the judge. John sent it to me because he wanted the bank to understand how Husky had forced him into a once-in-a-lifetime mistake, but the mistake shouldn't prevent Jefferson from going ahead with the sale of the bank. I don't know how accurate John is in what he says about other things, but the paragraphs about Jefferson Savings are not even remotely correct. I've been talking to his New York attorney, Kaufman, to try to get him to correct the letter. But nothing's happening. I don't want to have to write to the judge."

"I understand," the assistant said, recalling their first conversation.

"But if I have to . . ." Wideman's voice trailed off.

Wideman express-mailed a copy of the Letter of Intent that day. Rosner saw immediately that Wideman had made a mistake in his narrative regarding the Letter of Intent. It had not been express-mailed by Brewer's firm to Jefferson Savings. It had been sent by telecopier. Each page of the five-page letter clearly bore at the top the telecopy number of Brewer's firm, and the March 19 date that the letter had been transmitted.

Rosner slammed his fist on his desk. He was furious, not because of the letter itself, but because of the circumstances. San Diego defense counsel had retained a local psychiatrist to examine Grambling when at the MCC. Counsel's purpose was to procure a psychiatric report as ammunition to argue against state incarceration on top of the federal time. In the demi-monde of white-collar crime, psychiatry is the last refuge of scoundrels. Defense counsel's sentencing argument often began with what they considered the weighty, almost unanswerable question: Why would a middle-class person, of education and wealth, with a home and a family, violate the rules of society? In counsel's view, only psychiatry could answer the question: The defendant must suffer a mental disorder. That a person was greedy, or malicious, or eminently convinced that he could benefit from crimes and get away with it, were concepts to which defense counsel often turned a blind eye. Brewer retained the psychiatrist so as to obtain the psychiatric report which counsel needed for Grambling's sentencing argument.

The report fully served counsel's purpose. According to the report, Grambling had a personality disorder similar to compulsive gambling or alcoholism. He was addicted to the tension of the "deal," the fast-lane of big money transactions. What Grambling required, the report concluded, was therapy and a strictly imposed requirement that he be prohibited from engaging in any stress-causing deal which, in this psychiatrist's professional opinion, was any transaction involving an amount in excess of $10,000. The report, and its $10,000 recommendation, had been submitted by Kaufman to Judge Cahn on March 19, the very day that Brewer's firm had telecopied to Jefferson Savings Grambling's offer to buy the $42 million bank.

Rosner reminded himself that Grambling had a skill for obtaining the trust of secretaries and receptionists. What probably happened, the assistant told himself, is that Grambling became friendly with one of Brewer's secretaries, probably the one typing his March 6 letter to Judge Cahn. He spoke with her every day from the MCC when he made corrections in his letter and, at some point, convinced her to type and telecopy the Letter of Intent to buy Jefferson Savings.

The assistant called Brewer on April 10, immediately after receiving the Letter of Intent from Wideman. As with all of Grambling's more recent counsel, Brewer was a former Assistant United States Attorney. He had served in the San Diego office. A.U.S.A. Feigin told Rosner that Brewer was a straightshooter, above board and tenacious, just like Rosner knew Kaufman and Kingham to be.

"Good morning, Bob. I'm calling about that Letter of Intent to buy Jefferson Savings."

Brewer did not indicate that he was unfamiliar with the topic of the assistant's question.

"I've been talking to Clark Wideman. He said you sent it to him. Could I ask you, did you send it to him?"

There were many ways for Brewer to answer the question. One was to say that the topic was a matter of attorney-client privilege, and couldn't be discussed. Another was to simply say "no, I don't know what you're talking about."

Brewer responded, "I don't remember."

Didn't I go through this with Libman, Rosner thought. The question to ask would have been, "You don't remember telecopying a Letter of Intent to buy a $42 million bank on behalf of an incarcerated bank swindler who, according to the psychiatric report you commissioned, should not be permitted to engage in any transaction above $10,000?" The assistant restrained himself.

Brewer's "I don't remember" was a pause for him to think. It was not every day that a former prosecutor was questioned by a present prosecutor. Brewer said that he did not do any business for Grambling, and did not know about any of Grambling's business transactions.

To the assistant's statement that the March 6 letter had been sealed, Brewer said that he did not know about the sealing. Brewer sounded genuinely embarrassed, and Rosner mercifully ended the call. Another attorney on the list of counsel misused by Grambling, the assistant thought.

Next, Rosner called Kaufman. Their relationship had become testy. There was much that a defense counsel could do for a defendant at sentencing, and Kaufman was one of the most skilled and respected attorneys in New York City. But Grambling's continuing crimes had undercut Kaufman's credibility. Having convinced Judge Cahn to prevent Rosner from disbursing the 32-page letter, Kaufman would now have to go before the judge and explain that his client had disbursed the letter anyway in an attempt to further what was undoubtedly a fraudulent business transaction.

"Al, Wideman told me that you and he discussed the 32-page letter. How do you think he got it if not from your client?"

"I thought you had sent it to him prior to the court ruling that it was sealed. I just thought I'd leave it, rather than going to Judge Cahn to demand that it be returned."

"What about doing business for Grambling?"

"Am I under investigation?" Kaufman said in an angry voice. "You don't have any right to ask me that."

Rosner said nothing. After a pause, Kaufman continued. "No, I haven't done any business for Grambling, and I told Bob Brewer not to do any either."

The assistant also called Dave Robisch, who, Wideman had said, was to syndicate the Jefferson Bank sale proposed in Grambling's latest Letter of Intent.

"I've known John for years," Robisch explained. "Our wives are childhood friends. There was some talk of a bank purchase to be syndicated by my firm, but nothing came of it. As you probably know, I wrote a letter to the court on John's behalf."

Rosner hadn't seen such a letter, so he asked Robisch to send him a copy. It was received in a few days. The letter began, "I visited with John recently and he realizes the situation he is in and regrets the mistakes he made." That's standard, the assistant thought.

"I know that he realizes mistakes were made in the Husky Oil transaction and that he regrets them very much," Robisch's letter continued. "However, these mistakes had something to do with other people involved with John, people he relied on for the proper decisions. Somewhere along the line, the mistakes were made and John fully realizes this, as the man who made the final decisions."

The basic disclaimer of guilt, the assistant thought. No wonder Kaufman didn't submit it. How many more unsubmittable letters does Kaufman have, Rosner wondered.

The Letter of Intent incident reinforced Rosner's decision to retain a psychiatric expert to evaluate Grambling. The assistant thought over the situation. Grambling has two psychiatric reports saying he was a sick man who could be rehabilitated by therapy, and that prison would serve no purpose. Kaufman is going to argue that, in light of the "scientific" evidence, Grambling does not deserve any New York prison time in addition to the federal sentence already imposed. Unless I counter this psychiatric nonsense, Rosner thought, the judge might believe it.

The District Attorney's Office, and the assistant, kept a list of regularly retained psychiatrists. They were experienced forensic experts, qualified at testifying, usually in homicide cases, that a defendant was legally sane at the time of the crime. They were also doctors willing to discount their normal fee schedule as a courtesy to the District Attorney's Office.

Law and psychiatry do not mix. The object of the penal law is to hold people responsible for their conduct. The assumption is free will, that people act as they do because they choose to. The role of psychiatry is to explain why people act as they do. It is always possible to find a psychiatrist to testify that the explanation excuses or, as Grambling's counsel sought to prove, mitigates guilt. The defense psychiatrists an assistant saw in court usually generated a disrespect obvious from an assistant's questions at trial. "Well, doctor," an assistant would ask the defense expert testifying that the killer was insane at the time he pulled the trigger, "what did he think he was pointing at the victim's head, a lollipop?" In general, assistants viewed psychiatrists as hopelessly naive. No doubt, the feeling was reciprocal.

This was a peculiar case, and Rosner decided not to go to his list of the usually retained psychiatrists. There were many victims—Biosystems students, bank officers, members of Grambling's own family—and Grambling seemed oblivious to the hurt he had caused them; or, as Rosner suspected, he actually enjoyed exercising power over other people's lives. This analysis needed a sensitivity to the effect of crime on the lives of the victims.

Although the assistant respected psychiatrists, despite his professional reservations about their use in criminal cases, he wanted a different insight in the Grambling case. The pecking order of psychiatric evaluators ran from psychiatrists (the medical school graduates) to psychologists (graduates of clinical psychology programs) to, last on the list, psychiatric social workers (graduates of social work school). It had been Rosner's experience that the psychiatric social worker often had a better feel for humanity than his psychiatrist and psychologist colleagues. The assistant did not know why. Perhaps the social worker's training exposed him or her to a broader slice of humanity, or placed more emphasis on interpersonal skills. Maybe they just had more time to be people while going through school.

Rosner knew who to retain. Over the past several months, the assistant had become acquainted with Hillel Bodek. Rosner couldn't remember how. It seemed that Bodek had just begun to appear in the assistant's office to discuss his cases, particularly the check-kite case. Bodek was the psychiatric expert most frequently appointed by criminal court judges to examine defendants, so he was often in court when Rosner's cases were argued. Maybe that's how he got to know me, the assistant thought.

That Bodek had become the judges' psychiatric expert of choice was itself a story. Bodek was a whistle-blower. In the early 1980s, he had been employed at the Bellevue Prison Ward, the criminal justice system's psychiatric facility. The ward's professional staff, including most of its doctors and Bodek, was provided by Bellevue's affiliate medical school, the New York University School of Medicine. Bodek's job was to evaluate defendants who had been observed to have potential mental problems: defendants who might be mentally unable to assist in their defense and thus incompetent to stand trial; defendants who, though competent to be tried, were insane at the time of the crime, and thus not subject to being convicted; and defendants who were just plain malingerers. Known to be efficient and reliable, with a sound judgment and superb skills with patients, Bodek's reputation among attorneys, judges and court personnel was excellent. As with many intelligent people, he could not tolerate the incompetence he saw around him.

Among the things Bodek saw was that many psychiatrists retained to work at the Bellevue Prison Ward were collecting their paychecks but not working their full hours or completing their work. Bodek reported his observations to the Department of Investigation. In retaliation, the New York University School of Medicine fired him. Of course, the school claimed that Bodek had been fired for cause. He was difficult to work with, it was alleged, and he could not follow instructions.

After being fired, several criminal court judges retained Bodek as the court's expert to continue to provide psychiatric evaluations of defendants, the very job he had performed at Belle-vue. The judges were motivated by frustration. On a daily basis, they ordered the Bellevue Prison Ward physicians to evaluate defendants, and, on an equally daily basis, the judges com-plained that the reports were not being done or were, when com-pleted, inadequate, except for Bodek's. The court appointments of Bodek mounted as the judges relied on him to do the work that the Prison Ward doctors were unable, or unwilling, to do. Bodek billed on an hourly basis for the evaluations which, prior to be-ing fired, he had performed as a salaried employee.

The prison ward doctors from New York University went into a rage. Not only had they not rid the criminal justice sys-tem of their nemesis, but Bodek was making them look bad. To the medical mind, it was unacceptable that a psychiatric social worker was being selected to do the work of a doctor. It was a professional insult, and the doctors responded by complaining to the Department of Investigation that Bodek was overbilling the city for his work.

Bodek was investigated. He produced his time records for inspection, and two things became apparent. Superficially, he was making more money on an hourly basis than he had earned as a salaried employee. But when one subtracted Bo-dek's expenses for medical coverage and other fringe benefits, previously paid by his employer, it became clear that Bodek's real income as a private practitioner was the same as his in-come as a salaried worker. And he was severely underbilling the city. To keep his accumulated bills from becoming too high, Bodek intentionally delayed submitting vouchers for about a third of his work, in essense, giving the city an interest-free loan of his services.

The investigation of Bodek ended with his exoneration. The investigation of the Bellevue doctors also ended, with the realization that there could be no crime since the doctors were allowed by contract to work elsewhere while being paid for their Bellevue service. Then the pendulum swung even farther in Bodek's direction. The Legal Aid Society Prisoners' Rights Project sued the Bellevue Ward for federal civil rights viola-tions, ultimately alleging that the New York University psychiatrists assigned to the Prison Ward were showing a deliberate indifference to patient care. As discovery proceeded in the civil lawsuit, the extent of the mismanagement at the Prison Ward became manifest. Bodek was vindicated.

But not rehired. The medical staff dug in its heels and absolutely refused to allow New York University to rehire Bodek. The District Attorney intervened on Bodek's behalf. Judges wrote letters. Bellevue would not budge. *The New York Times* ran editorials, as did other papers, asking when justice would be done for the whistle-blower. Ultimately, the issue went to Mayor Koch. City Hall refused to intervene. After a four-year struggle, Bodek was still not rehired.

"All I want is my salaried job back," he often told the assistant. "If I had it all to do over again, I never would have reported the doctors."

Rosner walked into Moscow's office the last week of March 1987.

"I'm thinking of hiring Bodek," the assistant told Moscow.

"For the Grambling case?"

The assistant nodded.

"You know what happened when Benitez hired him?" Moscow asked.

Rosner shrugged in ignorance, though he had heard the story from Benitez.

"Defendant put in same bullshit insanity claim," Moscow said. "Bodek writes this huge report. He disproves the insanity claim. But then goes on to explain how the defendant would be psychologically destroyed by incarceration, and the judge sentences her to probation."

"Well, no one can say that Bodek is our whore," the assistant replied. "That's the reason I'd like to hire him. Also, he strikes me as being sensitive to people's problems."

"Very much like Judge Cahn," Moscow commented.

"Exactly."

Moscow nodded.

"I'm going to retain him next time he comes around."

Bodek came to the assistant's office that afternoon.

"Can I use your phone, Brian?"

Bodek was frantic. Before Rosner even said "yes," Bodek had turned around the phone on the assistant's desk and was dialing. Bodek was in his mid-30s, of medium height with dark hair and the sallow complexion common to workaholics. He dressed casually, slacks with a shirt open at the collar. He was known to wear a tie and jacket, poorly matched, when testifying. He wore a beeper.

The assistant heard pieces of the conversation. Emergency admittance. Judge so-and-so. Defendant can't be in general population. With his excellent relations with the Corrections Department, Bodek could place prisoners in the necessary medical environment, or have them brought from prison, "produced" in the jargon of the court system, in an hour, when the normal bureaucratic processing took days.

After several phone calls, Bodek calmed down. Whatever the emergency, it had been remedied. Bodek hung up the receiver, and turned the phone in the direction of the assistant. He turned to leave.

"Got a minute, Hillel? The District Attorney's Office wants to retain you on a white-collar case, a bank fraud case in front of Judge Cahn."

"What is the psychiatric issue, insanity? The defendant didn't realize that the dollar bills were money?" Bodek smiled and sat down.

"It's not an insanity defense," Rosner said. "The defense has put in psychiatric reports for sympathy. You know, make the judge feel sorry for the guy. And convince him that incarceration is not appropriate."

The assistant told Bodek about the case and Dr. Kalisch's conclusion that Grambling was a stress junkie who should be restrained from all deals involving more than $10,000. He handed Bodek Dr. Kalisch's report.

"Why not $20,000, or $50,000?" Bodek asked after perusing the report for a few minutes. "There's a psychiatric basis for the $10,000 number?"

"Hillel, what do I know? That's why we're retaining you. I want a psychiatric profile on the defendant. I have no interest in what happens to him after sentencing. If he's rehabilitable, and some outpatient program is what's warranted, which is what his psychiatric reports say, great. You say it. I don't care. I just want to know it. The problem with the defense reports is that they're superficial. Lots of the jargon that's supposed to awe us laypeople, but a poverty of facts to convince you that the conclusions are right. The reports talk about Grambling and his family, the usual loving relationship, but I don't think either of the evaluators ever saw him with his wife and kids, or even think that's important. That's why I want you.

"As I said," Rosner continued, "if he's rehabilitable, let's hear it. For all I know, his shrinks are right and they just write lousy reports. On the other hand, if the defendant's just your basic manipulative son-of-a-bitch trying to weasle his way out of state prison, I want to hear that, too."

Bodek looked thoughtful.

"You know, with all his running around the country and spending money, he might have been manic at the time. And not responsible for the crimes."

The assistant looked doubtful.

"All I want is an honest opinion," the assistant replied.

Bodek accepted the retention.

"I'll need the indictment and the psychiatric reports. Also, whatever's been written in the case. All the pretrial motions." Bodek thought some more.

"To find out what's going on in the defendant's head, it helps to go over the crimes in detail. I'll want copies of documents that prove the crimes."

"You don't know what you're asking for," the assistant said, "I'm doing a memo and appendix which alone must be over 2,000 pages."

"If I'm going to do this, I'm going to do it right." Bodek was insistent. "Based on what I read, I'll decide who to interview. Of course, it will be his family and various victims. You said he has a wife and kids?"

The assistant nodded.

"After I've met him for a few hours, I'll want to see him interact with his children and wife. You said he's been in custody for awhile? He'll want to see his family. Can you arrange a room?"

Bodek began seeing Grambling within days, both in the District Attorney's Office and across the air shaft at the Tombs.

Bodek scheduled the family visit for Friday, April 3. The assistant had first seen the wife a week before, when Grambling had been returned to New York. She had been in court with Kaufman. She looked dazed and physically very much like her sister Pamela, though younger. Kaufman had commented that she had come to court by train and subway, her first time on the subway. The subway and the criminal justice system, all in one day. The assistant pitied her.

Trish Grambling brought her four boys, two, four, six and eight years old, to the Frauds Bureau on the 3rd. Since Rosner had been unable to obtain a conference room, the interview would take place in his office.

Carrying one son in her arms and prodding the other three with her free hand and cajoling words, Trish Grambling marched her boys to the room, where she met Bodek. She was in control. That morning, Rosner had bought two books for his own son: pop-up books of trains and cars. The assistant gave them to Bodek for the Grambling boys to play with, and closed the door.

As were all inmates in the Tombs, Grambling was produced at the 12th floor Bridge, where he was placed in the custody of Marty Small, a DAOS officer. Short and powerfully built, like a bull, Small had a gruff exterior, but was known to his colleagues as an officer always willing to lend a hand in a case, or go the extra mile, in order to do things right.

All produced prisoners were cuffed. Rosner had told Detective Small that Grambling was being brought down to see his children. When Grambling arrived at the Frauds Bureau, his hands were free.

The detective and the assistant spoke in the hallway outside the bureau. Rosner explained that he did not want the detective in the room during the interview.

"I'm supposed to guard this guy," Small complained, "What do you mean you don't want me in the room? What if he takes a run for the window? It's my shield."

"Marty, it's a psychiatric interview," the assistant said. "With his family. He's not going to do anything."

Mumbling cursewords, Small agreed to wait in the anteroom outside the assistant's office. He didn't like it. He and

Rosner brought Grambling to the anteroom. Small pointed at Grambling and then pointed at the assistant's closed door.

The gestures were a command, and Grambling obeyed. Dressed in his suit and tie, much as he must have looked on a work day, Grambling opened the door, and, alone, entered. From the anteroom with Small, Rosner saw and heard the reunion between Grambling and his children. There was no joy, no expressions of affection. It was cold and emotionless, as if he were a stranger, or a distant relative that the children did not know. Bodek closed the door, and Rosner left.

After an hour and a half, Rosner returned. Grambling and Detective Small were gone. Trish Grambling was there, still in control, mixing discipline and affection in managing her sons. She thanked the assistant sincerely for arranging the interview.

He wondered about her as she shook his hand. In reviewing the loan documents, Rosner had seen what purported to be her signature on various fraudulent documents. But as the investigation progressed, he realized that her signatures had been forged. She had been victimized as much as anyone else.

After she left with her sons, Bodek and the assistant were left in the office. Bodek turned dour. He looked sad, and shook his head back and forth.

"Not good," he mumbled. "Not good at all."

Detective Small entered Rosner's office.

"Romper room over? Can I get back to some real detective work now?"

He dropped a letter on the assistant's desk.

"Love letter from Grambling," he said.

The case was not making Rosner popular with the squad.

The letter was handwritten and addressed to Rosner. He picked it off his desk, and read it to himself.

"I wish to sincerely thank you for having my wife and sons in to visit me while undergoing psychiatric evaluation. We have been a very close family and I appreciate your effort to assist us. I also wish to apologize for my actions while out on bail. It was not until Mr. Robert Brewer brought home to me the significant embarrassment I caused for you, Judge Cahn and Alan Kaufman. My reasons for the incidents (foolish as they were)

were outlined in my letter to Judge Cahn of which you were provided, I believe, a copy. Thank you again for the support and consideration for my wife and sons. John A. Grambling, Jr."

" 'I wish to sincerely thank you,' " Small mimicked in a high-pitched voice.

What does Grambling think, Rosner wondered. This is the Emily Post School of dealing with prosecutors.

"Beautiful handwriting," the assistant said to Small, as he handed the note to Bodek.

Bodek glanced at it.

"Yes, totally inappropriate."

"What do you want to do with this?" Small asked. "Voucher it?"

"No, just write on the back that you received it, Marty. Date and time, and give it over." The assistant mailed a copy to Kaufman and gave a copy to Bodek.

As Rosner, Bodek, and Small read Grambling's letter, Grambling was on the Bridge, where his attitude was reinforced that, as he had written to Judge Cahn, a white-collar prisoner such as he did not deserve to be treated like a common street criminal. Detective Small had brought Grambling to the Bridge, a 12th floor hallway with elevators leading to the street, and, on the other side of the bars, the elevated passageway connecting 100 Centre Street to the Tombs. The detective had left Grambling with a corrections officer on the elevator side of the bars. It was the end of the corrections officer's tour of duty and, before returning Grambling to prison, he was relieved by a new officer. The recently arrived officer did not know who Grambling was. But he could guess: white man in suit and tie.

"Counselor," the officer spat out. Correction officers hated defense counsel, always complaining about how their clients were treated. Officers couldn't curse counsel directly, so they did it by intonation. "Counselor," they addressed attorneys, in a tone applicable to saying "viper" or "spider."

"Counselor!" The officer grabbled Grambling by the arm. "You know you're not supposed to be up here. No attorneys on the Bridge."

The officer pulled Grambling towards the elevators.

"You don't understand," Grambling began in his soft voice.

The usually soporific prisoners on the barred side of the hallway rose from their benches and stuck their faces to the bars.

"Go man, go," the first shouted.

"Go motherfucker," others joined in. They shook and climbed the bars as they screamed.

"Go motherfucker! Go!"

Startled, the officer dragging Grambling to the elevator stopped. He was torn between two dislikes, defense attorneys and their clients.

"Go man, go," the prisoners laughed and screamed.

The officer who had been relieved entered the hallway from the locker room. He saw what was occurring.

"No, man," he said to his colleague who had pushed Grambling to an elevator and pressed the call button.

"He belongs in here." The first officer grabbed Grambling by the arm and pushed him through the cell door.

Even the officers know, Grambling thought, that I'm not like the people who are in prison.

CHAPTER 27

FOR MY BOYS

The assistant finished his memorandum. He went to Moscow's office to discuss the sentencing recommendation. For years, prosecutors had complained to the New York State Legislature that the penalties for white-collar theft were too low. Whether one stole $1,500, the minimum amount that qualified as Grand Larceny, or $1 million, the maximum sentence was seven years. In 1986, Rosner had drafted corrective legislation as part of the yearly package of statutory changes proposed by the New York State District Attorneys' Association. The association recommended a larceny statute in which the punishment increased with the amount stolen: seven years for sums less than $50,000, up to 15 years for sums up to $1 million, and up to 25 years for sums over $1 million.

Governor Cuomo adopted the legislation as one of his own proposals. The bill was passed unanimously by both houses of the legislature and signed into law by the governor. The statute's effective date was November 1, 1986, prior to Grambling's sentencing. Due to the constitution's ex post facto clause, however, the sentencing change could not apply to Grambling's crimes, which had been committed before the statute's enactment. Nonetheless, the change in the law was a powerful argument that society's view of the white-collar criminal had hardened. Were the new law applicable, Grambling could have been sentenced for up to 25 years on each of the two successful thefts, those from Bank of Montreal and Colorado National.

The assistants' sentencing recommendation reflected society's diminished tolerance for business fraud: the District Attorney's Office decided that it would ask for the maximum sentence on each count, seven years for the larcenies and forgeries, and four for the attempts, to run consecutively. The sentencing statutes capped such consecutive sentences at 20 years, with a mandatory minimum of half that. The Office's request would be 10 to 20 years, consecutive to the federal time. If imposed, it would be the heaviest white-collar sentence ever in New York State.

"John, I'm trying to figure out a characterization of Grambling, something that would put in a nutshell what he's like. He has the usual personality disorders for anyone who wanted to make as much money as he did. But above all, he used people. They were just objects for his gratification."

Leaning back in his chair, Moscow looked toward the ceiling and thought for a minute.

"He reminds me of the rapists I've tried. They were never interested in women for the sex. They never are."

Rosner thought back to his rape cases.

"It's the exercise of power," Moscow continued. "The power to humiliate, the power to say, 'I'm in control.' Here's a guy who couldn't be his father: He couldn't get into a top law school. So he was going to one-up dad, and all the attorneys, and the business people. Bankers thought he was sort of slow—no great mover and shaker. But he showed them. He took their money, and he took their jobs."

The assistant incorporated Moscow's observations into the People's sentencing material, which was submitted in Part 48 on April 22. At that day's court proceeding, Rosner asked for a sentencing adjournment.

"Judge Cahn, Mr. Bodek has completed his examination of the defendant, and he needs time to write the report."

"Does that mean that John is going to go to Rikers' now instead of being kept at the Tombs?" Kaufman complained. "He's in a routine at the Tombs. He's in charge of a work crew. At Rikers', he'll be thrown into a general pen area with street criminals who don't know him. It's a major risk to his safety, and I will not consent to an adjournment unless he's protected."

"I agree with Mr. Kaufman," Judge Cahn said. "If the Tombs are safer for him, keep him there."

"Your Honor, I have no control over where Corrections . . .," Rosner began.

"Keep him there," Judge Cahn said. "Your Office and Mr. Bodek have more control with the Department of Corrections than you give yourself credit for. You know, your sentencing material was submitted late. I could sentence Grambling today without reading it. I don't want to do that."

"I'll use every effort, your Honor," the assistant said.

Judge Cahn adjourned sentencing to May.

After the proceeding, Rosner returned to his office where he met Bodek and related Judge Cahn's message.

"I can't do it," Bodek complained. "Corrections kept Grambling at the Tombs as an accommodation to me so that I wouldn't have to go to Rikers' to interview him. And Kaufman's all wrong, anyway. Rikers' is safer than the Tombs."

"Hillel, keep him there," the assistant insisted.

The next day, Rosner was called by Judge Cahn.

"Please disregard my prior order on keeping Grambling at the Tombs. You treat him as you would any other prisoner, no more, no less. He's to receive no special treatment because of anything I say."

That day, the assistant related the conversation to Bodek.

"Good," Bodek said. "As it turns out, Corrections kept Grambling at the Tombs overnight. Now they're ready to put him in a special segregated area on Rikers'. It's the safest place on the island."

Rosner was not listening.

"You know, Hillel," he said. "I think the judge began to read my sentencing memorandum."

While waiting for Bodek's report, the assistant kept in contact with witnesses and the extended Grambling family. On Wednesday, May 4, Pam Ficarella called.

"My mother was in Connecticut recently to help Trish with the kids," Ficarella said. "Mom showed me a letter John had sent her. He wrote my mother that he's going to probably serve his time in Danbury."

Danbury was a minimum security federal prison in Connecticut.

"He's trying to get someone from the White family to write Judge Cahn. He thinks he's going to get off with no state prison time because the judge is a family man who doesn't sentence white-collar criminals to prison. So he asked my mom to write the judge and say what a good father and husband he is, how important he is to the family."

"Is your mother going to write?" the assistant asked.

"Of course not. She thinks that John is a real charmer, but an awful father. He's just using the boys as a pawn to sway the judge."

Rosner relayed Ficarella's comments to Bodek, and suggested that he talk to both Ficarella and the mother-in-law in preparing his report. Bodek had already spoken to both.

On May 7, Bodek submitted his 353 page report to Judge Cahn. He had spent over 200 hours preparing the report: in interviews alone, Bodek had spent 40 hours with Grambling, and another 40 with two dozen family members, victims, and other witnesses. Neither the assistant nor his colleagues had ever seen a more comprehensive analysis of the white-collar criminal mind: the relentless drive to accumulate wealth; the use of people to obtain that end; the abandonment of all emotion and human attachment other than self-love. Easy prison time in a federal facility was just what such a narcissist believed to be his entitlement. Bodek's prognosis for meaningful treatment was dismal; and, founded on the extensive factual analysis of Grambling's life and crimes, the conclusions reached by Bodek were convincing.

Rosner spent a day reading the report. As he finished Bodek's conclusions, he was exhausted. Bodek had placed Grambling under a microscope. Removed from society, no longer a loose cannon destroying careers and businesses, Grambling had been reduced to a subject of study, even pity. It was difficult to imagine that Grambling had ever sat across a business table from a banker, and that, in such a setting, Grambling had been perceived to be nothing other than any other business person, not a bomb ready to explode the banker's career. It was difficult to imagine, the assistant thought, just as it was difficult to accept that hundreds of Gramblings sit at business meetings in America everyday.

With the submission of the Bodek report, the sentencing submissions were complete.

Meanwhile, one letter writer was in torment—Patricia Grambling. A letter to Judge Cahn had already been submitted over her name. It was the classic spousal submission: Her husband was a loyal and devoted father, and so on. In it, Patricia Grambling asked Judge Cahn to sentence Grambling to concurrent time so that he could serve his time in a federal facility in Texas where she planned to move with her sons. Let him be near the family, the letter pleaded: We need him.

It was a moving and articulate submission designed to appeal to Judge Cahn's feelings as a husband and father.

And it was a lie. Grambling had asked her to submit a letter. The letter itself had been written by defense counsel. She had little choice but to accede to its submission. Trish and her sons were living on money provided by the Grambling family. She feared that if she withheld approval of the letter written for her, or complained about its inaccuracy, the funds would be terminated. She did not discuss her fear with defense counsel, or even try to tell him her true emotions. Trish approved the letter to be submitted in her name.

But as sentencing approached, she had a fear greater than the Grambling family's termination of funds. She had a fear for her boys. Grambling had always been a poor father, emotionless and never available. He had lied to his sons about his crimes, just as he had lied to anyone who asked. And he had lied to her, about too many things to be counted. But those lies did not matter anymore. Trish was seeing something worse.

The boys were becoming like the father. Not that she begrudged him. He needed help, and she only hoped that he could find it in prison. Not from the sort of psychiatrists he manipulated so well, but from someone like Bodek. She trusted Bodek. He was the only psychiatrist in the criminal justice process who had shown any concern for her and the boys, any feeling for what they were suffering. And, after the interview at the District Attorney's Office, she had sought his advice and help. He had always been available.

Her husband's arrest in San Diego had been a liberating experience. She could stand back and measure the damage Grambling had done to the boys, the warping he had already caused in their characters. Perhaps, after many years, he could come out of prison and not be a danger to the moral development of her sons. But not now.

What could she do? Write a letter was all she could think of. But a true letter, unlike the fraudulent one submitted over her name.

But even if she wrote it, how could she get it to court? Would a letter to the judge be read by Grambling, or the family? Who could she trust to deliver such a letter? The defense attorneys were Grambling's attorneys. That was apparent and, she guessed, the way the system was supposed to work. She and the boys were just pawns for them to obtain the sentence desired. After sleepless nights, she asked the one person she trusted to convey her true letter to the judge.

The attorneys were in Part 48 on May 16 to argue an aspect of the sentencing proceeding. Judge Cahn considered the People's sentencing memorandum to be a sealed document. On the 16th, the assistant asked for permission to unseal the memorandum for the purpose of sending it to prosecutors in the several cities where Grambling had committed crimes for which he had not yet been indicted. Over Kaufman's objection, Judge Cahn granted permission and set May 21 as the sentencing date.

Prior to the argument that had brought counsel to court that day, Judge Cahn noted that "just for the record, I want you both to formally know that I have received an addendum to the Bodek report, which addendum I have sealed."

Kaufman and Rosner looked at each other. The assistant shrugged, as if to say, I don't know what it is, I just pay the guy.

"It is a personal communication for my eyes alone," Judge Cahn explained. "I have sealed it, and it will remain under seal."

CHAPTER 28

DOING JUSTICE

On Wednesday, May 20, Rosner and Moscow discussed the oral argument for the next day's sentencing.

"How old is Nick?" the assistant asked.

"Three," Moscow said. Nick was Moscow's son.

"You ever notice how much a kid has developed by three?" Rosner continued. "He has his own personality, strengths, and weaknesses. You can see what kind of boy he's going to be, and what kind of man. It's as if kids are born wired with certain skills and sensitivities, all to be developed by their upbringing. But still, born with a basic personal wiring."

Moscow nodded in agreement.

"Grambling was wired all wrong," Rosner said. "He never developed a conscience. He's obviously not a dope, and he's not a bad writer. You can see the letters he's written. But he has no inner sense of integrity, no gyroscope to direct him to do the right thing. Never did. He has no regret at the harm he caused and absolutely no ability to put himself in the shoes of the people he's hurt.

"John, we're over-educated when we come to this job. We've read *Crime and Punishment* so we expect defendants to writhe through some struggle of conscience when committing their crime. Or, at least, afterwards."

Moscow shrugged. They had each seen struggles of conscience, though rarely.

"You don't see it with Grambling," Rosner continued. "Every day of crime was just another day for him, as it has probably been since he was a kid. Grabbing at money and power over other people's lives was his definition of self, and whenever he got jammed up, he could always buy a lawyer to rescue him. Maybe even now."

"What do you think the judge will do?" Moscow asked. "He's one of the lightest sentencers in the county."

The assistant thought a minute before answering.

"I think he'll impose something heavy. He reminds me of an Old Testament judge. He feels the weight of the power he wears. He doesn't like to use it. I almost think he's afraid of it. He's so aware of his fallibility and the consequences of exercising power in error. But he knows what to do when the use of power is right. I think he knows what to do in this case."

Moscow looked skeptical.

"I got a call this morning," the assistant added. "The judge wanted to meet with the family prior to sentencing. Wanted to explain what he was going to do, I guess."

Moscow's expression changed from one of questioning to one of pain. He slammed his hand palm down on his desk.

"That's wholly inappropriate. He . . ."

Rosner cut him off.

"And then I got a second call canceling the arrangement. The judge realized that what he wanted to do was wrong. The only place where he can explain his sentence is on the record, in open court.

"He's going to sock Grambling, but he was looking for a way to insulate the family. The point is that he's thought over this sentence deeply. It's tormented him 10 times more than Grambling is tormented by his crimes."

Sentencing was 10:00 A.M. on May 21. Grambling's wife and mother arrived at Part 48 early, as did other mothers and wives. Thursday was Judge Cahn's sentencing day, and Grambling was not the only defendant awaiting judgment.

"All rise," McCormick shouted. The room came to motion as Judge Cahn took the bench.

"Let's proceed," the judge said to the clerk. McCormick nodded to the captain of the court officers.

"Grambling first," the clerk whispered.

Two officers brought Grambling, in handcuffs, through the rear door. As the guards escorted Grambling to his chair at the defense table, Grambling tried to walk freely to the bar separating the well of the courtroom from the spectator's section, where his mother and wife stood waiting to greet him. The captain of the court officers, a middle-class black man who had risen through the ranks, violently jerked Grambling back from the bar.

"You stay here," the officer barked.

The violence of the officer's action startled Rosner. Word had spread through the court system that Grambling thought himself morally superior to the minority residents of Rikers' and, by implication, the captain.

Judge Cahn saw the small act of violence, and looked disapprovingly to the clerk. McCormick nodded. He would talk to the captain.

The clerk coughed to clear his throat.

"This is number one on the sentence calendar," he announced in his public voice. "John Grambling, the defendant, is present in court as is defense counsel and the A.D.A." The clerk looked to Judge Cahn.

"Arraign the defendant, your Honor?"

"Arraign the defendant," Judge Cahn said.

"John Grambling, stand up, face the court. John Grambling, with your attorney present, standing next to you, you are being arraigned for sentence on your plea of guilty to indictment 2800 of 1985 of the following charges contained therein: Conspiracy in the fifth degree; grand larceny in the second degree, two counts; attempted grand larceny in the second degree, three counts; forgery in the second degree, 13 counts; criminal possession of a forged instrument in the second degree, 13 counts.

"Before sentencing," the clerk read from his typed form, "the court will accord the Assistant District Attorney, your counsel, and yourself an opportunity to make a statement to the court on any matter relevant to the question of sentence.

"For the People, Mr. Rosner."

The assistant rose and approached the wooden podium he had brought to the courtroom. There would be no summation in this case, no opening or testimony to explain why the District Attorney's Office had evoked its power to prosecute, or why Grambling deserved the state prison sentence that the People had proposed. This would be the assistant's only opportunity to explain.

"Your Honor, sentencing is one of the gravest parts of the judicial function. I believe that I have a sense, your Honor, of what you are going to do today. What I would like to do in the next few minutes is to explain that what you are going to do is correct, to explain why John Grambling deserves the maximum sentence that can be imposed under the law."

The room was hushed as the assistant set out exactly what he was asking Judge Cahn to do.

"The People are asking the Court to impose a sentence of two-and-one-third years to seven years on each larceny count, and on each forgery count, to run consecutive to each other. In total, that is a sentence of $69^2/3$ years to 209 years, which is reduced by statute to a sentence of 10 to 20 years. There is no doubt that he will be paroled after 10 years. Ten years for all the crimes that Mr. Grambling has done. And, I ask the court to make this 10-year sentence consecutive to the federal sentence that Mr. Grambling received for the San Diego fraud, one of the many crimes Mr. Grambling committed while on bail from this court."

Rosner heard the gasps from the spectators behind him: It's a big sentence. Never lifting his focus from the judge, the assistant explained the predicate of his argument, that white-collar crime was serious, and deserving of real prison time.

"People have a special name for the crimes that Grambling has committed. These are 'white-collar crimes.' And 'white-collar' is a phrase which, in the minds of many attorneys and judges, is meant to conjure up an image of less important crimes that do not merit prison time, and certainly do not merit state prison time.

"Judge Cahn, I have reread the larceny statute. No special subdivision says that a poor man who steals is subject to state prison, but that a wealthy, educated man who takes millions of dollars by false financial statements, by deceiving others, by betraying their trust, is to be convicted and sentenced under a special 'white-collar' provision of the Penal Law.

"Indeed, just last year, the Legislature passed a bill to raise the penalties for several so-called 'white-collar crimes.' In support of the bill, Governor Cuomo submitted a memorandum which I have here."

The assistant lifted a sheet of paper from the podium. He held it as he read:

> The premise of this bill is that the large-scale white-collar thief is as culpable and as deserving of state prison as the street youth who takes property by unsophisticated threats of force. The bill would eliminate some of the disparity between the sentencing of white-collar defendants and street criminals. This different treatment for the street criminal and the white-collar crook corrodes confidence in the fairness of the Criminal Justice System. This bill would end this unfair disparity in sentencing.

The assistant slowly returned the document to the podium and, after a pause, continued.

"Judge Cahn, those are powerful words. I wrote them for the Governor. That bill was passed by the Senate and the Assembly, unanimously. And I remember the bill's first words: 'The People of the State of New York represented in Senate and Assembly do enact.' The premise where we begin, Judge Cahn, is society's belief that the educated swindler deserves real prison time."

Rosner paused again as he glanced toward Kaufman. There was a possibility, the assistant knew, that Kaufman or the defendant would say something to reignite Judge Cahn's sympathy. I have to remind the judge, the assistant thought, that he cannot believe anything they say. He turned to the judge, and began.

"Of course, your Honor, we were not supposed to be here today. Sentencing was scheduled for January 6, 1987. On that day, the defendant appeared in this very courtroom to request an adjournment so that he could put together more sentencing material for the court. Sentencing was rescheduled for February 2, 1987.

"That sentencing did not occur. It did not occur because while on bail, pending this sentence, Grambling was arrested in an attempt to steal $350,000.

"Judge Cahn, I would like to have you imagine what would have occurred on February 4, 1987 had Grambling not been arrested. The defense would have presented the court with letters from family and friends attesting that the defendant is remorseful, that he is rehabilitated, that he will never engage in such conduct again.

"Those are the letters that you would have received on February 4, 1987, Judge Cahn. Letters from decent, well-meaning, compassionate people. But letters from people who would have been as fooled as the victims of this man have been fooled and deceived for the past three years. Indeed, the letters you would have received on February 4 are very similar to the letters that you have, in fact, received from the defense for your consideration today."

The assistant emphasized his point by tapping his finger on his podium in cadence to the rhythm of his speech. As he reached the word *defense,* he pointed at Kaufman. The assistant paused. In a low, soft voice, he began again.

"Of course, on February 4, 1987, had the defendant not been apprehended for committing additional crimes, you would also have received psychiatric reports. This is no surprise, Judge Cahn. Attorneys have written books on how to conduct a sentencing for the so-called white-collar criminal. The first thing an attorney must do is to retain a psychiatrist. Many practitioners in the psychiatric field do not believe in incarceration. It is not in their nature. They believe in any alternative other than incarceration. Again, these are decent, well-meaning people. It is easy for counsel to locate these people and have them write letters explaining how far the defendant is on the road to rehabilitation, how the defendant is remorseful, and how, whatever he has been convicted of is something far, far in his past, and is never going to occur again.

"Those were the reports you would have received on February 4, Judge Cahn. Indeed, they are very similar to the reports that the defense has submitted for your consideration today."

As he brought his comments to a crescendo, he again turned to Kaufman and pointed. He remained turned to defense counsel, inviting Judge Cahn to also look in that direction.

"Of course, also on February 4, you would have received a statement from Mr. Kaufman as to why Mr. Grambling deserves to be treated differently from a persistent mugger. It would have been an articulate statement, and a well thought out statement. Mr. Kaufman, of course, would not have known about the $350,000 San Diego theft, which would have been accomplished by February 4. Mr. Kaufman would not have known about the $450,000 theft from Citytrust in September, 1986. He would not have known about the $250,000 theft from Colonial Savings in June 1986. Mr. Grambling doesn't tell these things to his attorney. Mr. Kaufman would have been misled, as have all of Mr. Grambling's prior attorneys in this case, and in his prior business dealings. And Mr. Kaufman, with the best of intentions, would have stood up and made a pitch about remorse and rehabilitation. And it would have been totally, totally wrong."

The assistant faced Judge Cahn.

"And, of course, on February 4, Mr. Grambling would have stood up and told you, Judge Cahn, much as he is going to tell you today, how remorseful he is. How everything that he had been convicted of is the only criminal or dishonest thing he has ever engaged in. How he is on the road to recovery. And every word he would have told you, Judge Cahn, would have been a lie.

"Now that's what would have happened on February 4. There is a point to this, Judge Cahn. John A. Grambling, Jr. is the ultimate manipulator. He has tricked and deceived and used business people, educators, bankers, family members, people of experience and sophistication far greater than you or I. Frankly, Judge Cahn, in the mind of John Grambling, you and I, with all due respect, are small potatoes in the realm of the people he has successfully deceived."

And don't let him manipulate you was the assistant's message. Rosner spoke about the lies in Grambling's letters to Judge Cahn, and his lack of remorse. Then he reached the victims, the bankers who had lost their jobs or suffered personal and emotional scarring, and the others.

"There have been other people Grambling has harmed. They are mentioned in my memorandum. His sister-in-law, the many thousands of students who were put out on the street when he bankrupted the Biosystems School."

Rosner pointed at the defendant.

"He would really, really, have you believe that there are no victims to white-collar crime?"

The assistant shifted through the papers on his podium.

"Let me just read one of the letters that the court received from one of the many students whose life was damaged by the bustout of the Biosystems School. This is a letter written by an Illinois lady, one of the school's correspondent students.

" 'I was a student in Biosystems until the program shut down in May of 1986. I had a student loan out for $1,900. I'm a single parent with a six-year old daughter. I am now working two jobs and needed the extra education under my belt and can ill afford to pay their money back for services I did not get, and I am also having to pay the money back two years sooner than I expected to.' She wants to know what the court can do to help her."

"Here's a letter from a woman in Arkansas. 'I am a 51-year-old widow trying to get my education.' There are many other letters to the same effect.

"No, these victims are not major banking institutions. These are not officials at big businesses. These are little people with very modest aspirations in life, people who work two jobs a week so they can get a degree and make a few thousand dollars extra a year. And this is the school that Grambling bled to death. So don't let anybody tell you, Judge Cahn, that so-called white-collar criminals cause harm to no people."

The assistant held the letters he had just read in the air.

"Twenty-five hundred students like this spread throughout America.

"My point is this, your Honor. To John Grambling, people are objects to be used. Whether they are bank officers or family, they are just pawns to be used for his gratification."

Rosner glanced towards the defense table. Grambling was impassive. Kaufman looked troubled. Out of the corner of his eye, the assistant saw Grambling's mother and wife in the front row. Okay, Hillel, the assistant thought, here's your part.

Rosner reached the psychiatric reports. He dismissed the defense evaluations as the reports of good-natured but ill-informed evaluators.

"One point I do want to comment on, your Honor, is the absolute cynicism of this defendant in his use of psychiatry." The
assistant explained Grambling's attempt to purchase the $42
million bank at the same time that he submitted the psychiatric report proposing the $10,000 cap in his business activity.

"And with regard to the other defense psychiatrist, the one
who believes in the possibility of rehabilitation, I will note that
this psychiatrist was treating Mr. Grambling and rehabilitat-
ing him for a period of time. That psychiatrist was seeing Mr.
Grambling during the period that Grambling committed the
several dozen crimes starting on page 58 of the People's sentencing memorandum and running through page 76. If that
psychiatrist had some doubts about the prospects of rehabilitation, he has a good factual basis for his doubts."

Rosner waited for the spectators' laughter to end, and then
continued.

"The People submitted a psychiatric report, Judge Cahn.
Mr. Bodek makes a sad but true point. What you see regarding
Grambling is what he is. His criminal nature is his personality.
He is going to go into prison. I can pray, and we can all pray,
that he changes."

The assistant held up the sentencing memorandum he had
submitted.

"But this memorandum, and the facts contained in this
memorandum, is John Grambling. Prison will not change him.
But we can send a message to society by incarcerating him. We
can deter others, and we can deter him. The People ask the
court to impose maximum consecutive sentences, consecutive
to the federal sentence. Mr. Grambling has earned every single
day.

"Thank you, your Honor."

Rosner had spoken for 40 minutes. He sat down.

"Mr. Kaufman," Judge Cahn said.

Kaufman rose. He approached the assistant's podium,
which had been placed between the attorneys' tables.

What's he going to say, Rosner thought. He can't discuss
the crimes, the facts, the letters. What's left?

Kaufman immediately focused on the core difference between white-collar crime and street crime: For all his conduct,

Grambling had left no blood on the sidewalk, and as a result should not receive substantial prison.

"What in fact the prosecution is saying is that John Grambling ought to be treated as a John Hinkley or a David Berkowitz, a Charles Manson; violent-prone people, who because of their psychological makeup will likely go out and commit the same depredations against innocent people and have to be locked up for the maximum period of time. The equation that the prosecution is trying to persuade the court of is the equation of John Grambling with the most violent sadistic criminal that comes before the criminal justice system. And that is where we have our fundamental dispute with the prosecution's recommendation, your Honor."

Trial attorneys develop a sixth sense. They can tell when their arguments, or their adversaries', are having an effect. Manson, Hinkley, the assistant thought. They deserve life in prison. I'm talking about 10 years. He looked to the judge. No, no effect, yet, the assistant thought.

Kaufman reached the psychiatric reports. He had to dismiss Bodek, but not too harshly. The prior proceedings had made clear that Bodek was respected on Centre Street. Kaufman proceeded deftly.

"Doctors Kalisch and Prelinger have a different opinion, your Honor, I say most respectfully, from Mr. Bodek, who the court has known for a while and respects. Doctor Prelinger comes into this proceeding with far more qualifications and ability to render an opinion than does Mr. Bodek. Doctor Prelinger has been a clinical psychologist for 31 years, head of the Mental Health Systems at Yale University and a professor of Clinical Psychology and Psychiatry at Yale Medical Center. And, yes, Doctor Prelinger obviously, calling it as he sees it, says, yes, there is a problem with treating people like John with conditions that he has. He doesn't come out and say: Oh, I'll see him once a week and everything will be fine. Doctor Prelinger says treatment is questionable, it is difficult. And Doctor Prelinger says yes incapacitation for a period of time is probably necessary. And I am not standing up there disagreeing with that one bit, your Honor. We understand that John has to be incapacitated for a period of time. The question really is how long? A day under 10 years, or 12½ or 13 years, is considered too short as far as the prosecution is concerned.

"Doctors Prelinger and Kalisch give their opinion as to the virtues of a prolonged incarceration of that length. But your Honor, we submit that a more reasonable, rational and proportionate period of incapacitation serves the purpose of protecting society from the possibility, indeed the probability that John, if he were released today, tomorrow, or next year, would go out and resume that same type of conduct. But a period of incarceration, say, of three or four years, would serve the purpose of protecting society; would mean that at the time John is released, he would not be in a situation, he would not be reentering life with the circumstances that would permit him to resume the type of conduct that occurred in 1983 through 1986."

There, he's reached the nub, the assistant thought. Bottom line, Grambling needs a four-year sentence, just what he received in San Diego. Not a day more. Rosner stared at the judge. Judge Cahn sat stone-faced.

Kaufman continued. With one swift argument, he tried to convince Judge Cahn that he should not consider any of Grambling's more recent crimes in imposing sentence.

"Your Honor is aware that John Grambling pled guilty here, didn't insist on trial, didn't insist on the expenditure of resources that a trial would necessitate."

Yeah, thanks a lot, Rosner thought.

"He pled guilty also in San Diego and is sentenced to four years in custody by the federal judge in San Diego. Your Honor has been provided with a copy of the transcript of the sentencing minutes in San Diego, and your Honor knows that Judge Nielsen in California was aware of many of the transactions which the assistant has informed your Honor about. The judge specifically mentioned obviously not only the San Diego transaction and the Husky transaction, but the Chicago bank transaction and the Connecticut bank transaction, as well as the Phoenix real estate transaction. The judge indicated on the record that the sentence that he was imposing was a reflection of the fact that John was committing crimes while he was out on bail from the New York court. Those crimes have been taken into account in one sentencing proceeding. To take them into account again and to impose maximum sentence, I think, your Honor, is unfair and improper."

Kaufman wound down his argument and sat down. He was a brilliant orator. But Rosner had seen not a flicker of sympathy from the judge.

"All right, Mr. Grambling, do you want to say anything?" Judge Cahn asked.

"Yes, sir."

Grambling rose from his chair and began to approach the podium which had been used by Rosner and Kaufman. Kaufman tensed. Rosner's mouth dropped. The court guards approached Grambling with arms outstretched and hands ready to grab him: Felons were not to wander from their chair.

The room was dead silent. Startled, Grambling stopped. With his jaws clenched, the captain of the court officers pointed to Grambling's chair. Confused, Grambling retraced his steps, and, standing at the table, clutched a wad of yellow sheets in his hands.

This is it, Rosner thought. The transition from freedom. He doesn't grasp what just happened to him.

"All right." Judge Cahn nodded.

Grambling began.

"Thank you, your Honor, for the opportunity to speak before the court. I normally speak without notes but because of this very important hearing I would like to read most of the text that I have written.

"During the last three-and-a-half years of my life I have exhibited a business conduct which at best could be called abominable. I stand here lacking little, if any, credibility. I do wish to thank my wife, mother, and friends who have come here to show continued support and I will try to prove myself to them in the future.

"I have now had four-and-a-half months in jail to reflect on my actions and the problems and the hurt that I've caused. I do hurt for the institutions that I damaged and the many individuals whose lives I have disrupted and I'm truly ashamed of my behavior.

"I had a dream in 1983 of building my own financial services company to specialize in mergers, acquisitions and corporate finance. And I had hoped to generate revenues from fees generated by representing companies as well as from management fees from companies we acquired . . ."

In his flat, toneless style, Grambling droned on. He talked about his business and its problems. He used words that had an emotional connotation, but he drained them of feeling, and meaning. His legendary charm, his charisma, had been lost. Rosner looked between Grambling and the judge: nothing, no emotional connection, no scintilla of belief.

"After being arrested and convicted for the last attempt at a loan in San Diego, I have had four and a half months to reflect on the last three and a half devastating years. I realized beyond a shadow of a doubt the seriousness of the crimes, and absolute lack of judgment I showed in handling these problems. Having to obtain loans and then continually refinance the loans, made it appear as if I had a series of bad loans outstanding, but it was one continuous problem from the initial capitalization of the company. I tried very hard to correct the deficiency which took up all my time.

"During the four and a half months in custody, I gained a firsthand knowledge of what serious crimes I committed. I understand not only what I've done to hurt several banks, various family members, and myself, but what it means to break the law and be in jail. The realization of being incarcerated and living in a violent prison world is eye-opening and devastating. Under no circumstances will I ever put my family, friends, or myself through the pain and suffering I have created during the last three-and-a-half years. Under no circumstances do I wish to ever set foot in a jail after serving my sentence for these crimes. I will always have to live with the hurt I've caused to every one emotionally and financially.

"During the course of my incarceration I have been examined by the State's representative, a social worker, to determine my mental health."

Rosner looked straight at Grambling. During the interviews with Bodek, Grambling had tried to manipulate Bodek into making a recommendation of probation, and Grambling had thought that he was succeeding. How was he going to explain away the devastating report Bodek had written?

"I am a personality type where it is hard for me to open up and tell my life's problems to complete strangers, someone I don't know, someone who is not a medical doctor and may not have doctor-client privilege, and who is, in fact, the state's expert witness. It is hard for me to be open and express my emotions in front of an individual who asked me to dictate an interview to him when he takes it down on a lap computer and I'm sitting in the District Attorney's office or in a holding cell at the detective's office. It is hard for me to answer them and be open as I found it hard for the interviewer to take down my comments accurately."

The bastard hasn't lost his ability to lie or blame others, the assistant thought.

"I am a very feeling person. I don't show it immediately to every person. I may not outwardly show my feelings. I do feel and I do hurt.

"I do have remorse for what I've done. I know how much I've hurt my family; every time I talk to them and talk to my little boys and they ask me to come home. And I hear that they've been acting up and have been harsh to my wife while I've been away. I know that I hurt my wife very much, who put a financial and emotional trust in me."

Grambling read the words with the emotions of someone reading a corporation's annual report. The lack of affection was chilling.

"I have caused our home to be sold. We are now wondering where the next income comes from. I know that I've hurt my father and mother. They wonder, he wonders what the hell I did, why I did it. I didn't have to. There is no need for any of the criminal conduct that I've mentioned. I've wasted his fortune in legal bills and repaying my debts. I know I've hurt my sister-in-law and my father-in-law who I love and respect, involving their personal funds and integrity in my business pride. I know that I've hurt many fine businessmen who trusted, liked, and respected me, where I've used their trust and disrupted their lives by having to deal with my problems."

Rosner moved his eyes from Grambling. He could no longer look at him. The words were correct, the sentences were grammatical, the sentiments were proper. But every word was devoid of belief.

"I hope in your sentencing today that you'll give strong consideration to my immediate family. I have been lacking as a father and husband for years. And I know in my heart I can be a kind and giving person and I love my wife. I can be a trusted and hard-working husband. I love my boys and they need to grow up with a father. I wish very badly for my family problems to work out. But for me to be accepted, for me to be considered by my family as a credible person, I know I have to prove it to my wife and my boys, and my father and mother beyond the shadow of a doubt. It is a matter of trust and self-control and putting morals back in perspective.

"I never had a legal problem in any job I held prior to 1983, be it related to finance or any other field. I'm very willing to change careers to a salaried position. I'm very willing to undertake extensive rehabilitative mental health treatment in a serious manner in a genuine effort. During the last two years with a number of illegal loans outstanding, there was no way for me to give therapy a chance to be effective. I was focusing 100 percent on correcting the deficiencies and the loans. I didn't want to go to jail or extend my sentence, and I believe I'm ready for treatment.

"Thank you, your Honor."

This was the time that the assistant hated. The investigation, the solving of the crime, thrilled him, as did the satisfaction of convicting the guilty. But he was never happy at sentencings, not even of the killers. Resolution was the only emotional state.

If only it could have been different, he thought. If only we who enforce the law had an alternative other than the one the defendant forced on us. I've done what my oath of office required. Now, it's up to the judge.

"We've heard a lot of things, a lot of comments this morning," Judge Cahn began. "And sometimes, listening to Mr. Rosner, Mr. Kaufman, Mr. Grambling, you think you are not talking about the same person. But we are.

"Let me see if I can't first pull it together a little bit and then make some very specific comments, Mr. Grambling, about your sentence. Mr. Rosner makes the point that there should not be a discrepancy between white-collar crime and blue-collar crime, and of course, in principle, he is right. There should not be. But in practice, there is a difference between a crime against a person and a crime against property. There is a difference between someone who rapes you, or threatens to rape, or threatens to kill or threatens to maim, and someone who may cause just as much damage with a fountain pen, but there is that difference.

"Mr. Grambling, you've hurt, as you yourself said, every single person who you came in contact with. You've hurt yourself most of all. You've hurt your parents, your wife, your children. You have hurt numerous people who came in contact with you in a business way, and whose careers were damaged, or ruined. You've hurt numerous students.

"In my mind, what I've seen running through this, both in the crimes to which you've pleaded guilty in this indictment, and the numerous crimes set forth in the People's sentencing memorandum, is a general disregard, simple disregard, of truth. Documents have been prepared, and submitted to banks, and they have had absolutely no relevance to reality. Documents which banks rely on, and which banks are expected to rely on, have been manufactured, photocopies have been manufactured, have been made up, signatures have been forged, other people's names have been signed. People have been told to make telephone calls, and lo and behold at the other end of the wire, there is someone who says I'm Mr. so-and-so from a financial institution, and it is somebody you've put up to it.

"The thing that runs through this completely is an absolute lack of respect for truth to anyone. And I must tell you, you've made a statement here, a somewhat similar statement was made by you in your letters to me, which I have read and taken into account, and I must tell you, with all due respect to you, I must tell you straight out, I have very, very serious doubts in my own mind that I can believe any of what you say. And I say this to you because every other thing that you've done, at least that I have seen that you have done, has been untruthful. And all the things that I have mentioned have been untruthful.

"Let me say, starting off with the sentence, it is going to be a long sentence. It is going to be a long sentence simply because I think that the people, the people of the State of New York, are entitled to a certain amount of protection. I think the actions that you've done are extremely dangerous; they are dangerous to the financial system; they are dangerous, as I said, to everyone you've come in contact with. I don't believe you should be punished more because you come from a privileged background, but, having said that, you've used the knowledge you obtained in your privileged background to make it possible to commit these crimes.

"There has been this constant disregard for truth which has characterized everything you've done. You've said this started in approximately 1983. I don't believe it had. I believe it started earlier. I believe it started when you were working for the institutions that you were working for. I believe it started, it shows in the circumstances under which you left those institutions, which has been brought to my attention.

"In view of that, I, as judge, cannot take it on my responsibility simply to say, well, let's hope that treatment will rehabilitate you. It is a responsibility that I cannot take. I think the public is entitled to protection from this kind of thing, whether that public is made up of bankers, whether that public is made up of students in trade schools, or that public is made up of family, or friends whose names have been signed without their knowledge, or whose signature has been obtained without telling them exactly what they are signing to and who therefore now have a problem.

"I know your sons and wife specifically are going to be terribly, terribly hurt by this, as they already have been. It is a harm that I've given lots and lots of thought to. I have given a lot of thought to the hurt that your parents have. But when it comes right down to it, I don't know, frankly. I don't know how to lessen the harm and hurt other than to do something which I feel simply I can't live with in this situation, because of your record of actions in this situation.

"I hope, and I know that your mother and your wife are sitting in the back, and I hope that with your parents' help over this lengthy and very difficult period that you are going into, you will be able to rehabilitate yourself. I hope that they themselves will be able to come to grips with the difficult period they are going into, seeing and knowing that their husband and son is going to be in this situation. But with all of that, I still have to say to you it is something you have brought on yourself. But more than that, it is something that I cannot take the responsibility of taking a chance that it is going to happen again."

Judge Cahn picked up a sheet of paper. The sentences, Rosner thought. He moved his pen to his scratch pad.

"As to count two, grand larceny in the second degree, I am going to sentence you now to a term of imprisonment of seven years, a minimum to be served of two-and-a-third years before you are eligible for parole. That is consecutive to the federal sentence and to any other sentences that will be imposed.

"As to count three, four, five, six, seven, and eight, I sentence you to a term of imprisonment of seven years on each count, a minimum to be served of two-and-a-third years on each count, with each sentence concurrent with the sentence on count two. All of these counts are basically the Bank of Montreal crimes.

"As to the Colorado Bank transactions, count nine, grand larceny in the second degree, I sentence you to a term of imprisonment of seven years, with a minimum of two-and-a-third years before you are eligible for parole. This sentence is consecutive to every other sentence I have imposed, and consecutive to the federal sentence."

The assistant understood the pattern. Judge Cahn was imposing the maximum sentence on each count. For the crimes committed against any one bank, the sentences were to merge, to run concurrent. However, the merged sentences for each bank were to run consecutive to one another, and consecutive to the federal sentence.

The assistant quickly did his arithmetic: seven years apiece for the two complete larcenies, four years each for the three attempts, and a minimum of one third on the total sentance. The final sentence would have a maximum of 23 years, reduced by statute to 20 years. Seven and two thirds to 20, consecutive to the federal sentence in San Diego. Even with parole, Grambling would be in prison until the 21st century. It was the longest sentence ever imposed in New York State for white-collar crime.

Rosner looked at Grambling. He was emotionless, as he had been throughout the day. Not a tear, not a grimace.

Judge Cahn completed his sentencing on each of the 32 counts.

"I have a number of other things that I want to say. You had a co-defendant in this case."

"Yes, your Honor."

"Your co-defendant pleaded guilty, and frankly was sentenced to a much lesser term of imprisonment. I say now, although he is not in front of us anymore—I believe he has already served his term of imprisonment—I say now, if I had known at that time all of the machinations and all of the ways that this has been done, and the actions that he did, the way he was involved, I would not have sentenced him to the comparatively small amount of sentence that I did. I would have taken a much more strenuous position, and insisted on a much more serious sentence than I did.

"I have two final things to say. I hope that this sentence sends a message out to the community as a whole. We in New York live, after all, in the financial capital of this country. I hope the message is clear to other people in this city, in this state, indeed in this country, that white-collar people who commit white-collar crimes are subject to serious punishment, are subject to incarceration, are subject to incarceration in the same way, and in the same places as other people are. That's one."

"Second of all, on a more personal level to you Mr. Grambling, you are going into a very difficult time. I hope that you mean sincerely the things that you've said to me this morning. I'm sure that your mother and your wife will do everything they can to help you rebuild your life. I hope you mean it. I hope that you are at some future time able to rebuild your life."

The judge leaned back in his chair. The burden of his oath had been discharged.

The clerk of the court handed a slip of paper to Grambling.

"Let the record note," McCormick shouted, "that the defendant has been handed a written notice of his right to appeal."

"Your Honor, one request," Kaufman said. "Especially with respect to John's mother, who has come up from El Paso for this. We would ask if it is possible, consistent with security arrangements, if the two Mrs. Gramblings could visit with John in a juryroom for a few minutes."

The court officers looked at the judge in disbelief. The judge looked at the spectators' gallery in the courtroom. He could see the dark-skinned faces of the young mothers and wives in court to witness the incarceration of their loved ones. For those prisoners, the visits with the family would occur in court, at the wooden barrier separating the spectators from counsels' tables.

"No," Judge Cahn said. "I think that what is done, as a practical matter, which can be done here, is that each of the Gramblings can have a visit, separately with him here in the courtroom."

"In the courtroom?" Kaufman was startled.

"Yes," the judge said. "That's the usual procedure."

Rosner quickly left the courtroom. Burdened with his folders and podium, he stumbled to the main corridor and saw Bodek, who had just completed a court appearance in another courtroom. Taking the podium, Bodek helped the assistant carry his courtroom paraphernalia. As they walked, the assistant explained what had occurred in Part 48.

Bodek mumbled numbers as they reached the elevator bank.

"Twenty-four months federally. Seven and two-thirds, probably more . . . No, Brian, not enough. By the time Grambling's out . . ."

Bodek mumbled some more numbers.

"Nope, youngest boy will be 14. Grambling could still have an influence on him. You got to do something more to protect the children. The youngest needs another two, three years."

Rosner shook his head. "It's up to the feds in Chicago or Connecticut."

"Do you think they can get the kids another two or three years?" Bodek looked distressed. "It might not be enough."

An elevator arrived; its doors opened. The assistant stepped in and held the door open with his foot. Bodek looked around and realized that he had left his attache case in the courtroom. He began to talk as he walked away.

"Brian, didn't he do any other New York crimes? You got to . . ."

"No, Hillel," the assistant said firmly. "You can only do what you can do. And I'm done."

Rosner let the elevator door close. He returned to One Hogan Place to work on his other cases.

EPILOGUE

ABUSE OF TRUST

On February 2, 1989, the New York State Appellate Division, First Department, heard Grambling's appeal. The argument occurred in the court's magnificent hundred-year old courtroom. Facing the walls of marble, richly veined in chocolate and burnt orange hues, the five justices sat on a dark oak, heavily carved bench where, from their elevated antique chairs, they gazed down upon the carved chairs and podium of the attorneys appearing before them. Above the bench and the podium is the lighted glass cupola, ringed with tiles naming the great judges who, from this very room, have rendered the law of New York State.

For the appeal, Grambling had retained Roger Bennet Adler, a former Assistant District Attorney in Kings County. Adler had argued many precedent-making cases in this and other New York State courtrooms. His argument on February 2 was simple: Grambling was a first-time offender and family man, who had engaged in one criminal transaction involving the various acts related to the Husky deal. As a consequence of the limited nature of the crime, and the length of his other sentences—for the Colonial Savings theft in Chicago, Grambling had been convicted in Chicago federal court and sentenced to four years of federal time consecutive to the San Diego four years—it was argued that, without harming society, the New York State sentence could be reduced to nine years from the 20 years imposed. To a large degree, counsel attributed the length of the state sentence to the Bodek report. Both orally and in his brief, Adler launched a bitter assault on this mere social worker. Bodek lacked "the therapeutic background" of Grambling's psychiatric experts, Adler argued, and, Adler continued,"Bodek with a straight face, convinced a Judge that a 36-year-old businessman in trouble with the law for the first time is not only beyond help, but must be given the 'maximum incapacitative sentence' to 'protect' his wife and children."

"What do the justices think of this 'mere social worker' argument?" I wondered as I sat in the audience. I knew that one of the five justices was married to a social worker, as was I. A second justice had presided over a racially charged homicide case in which Bodek had testified convincingly.

My reflections were interrupted by Assistant District Attorney Doreen Klein's approach to the podium. Petite and attractive, Klein was a young assistant in the Appeals Bureau, as I once was. At this, the first post-sentencing proceeding, it was her job to ensure that the justices knew the facts and did not, from ignorance, undo what Judge Cahn had done. Working long hours and weekends, she had written a brief refuting in detail the mistaken premises of the defense argument.

As they demonstrated in their comments to counsel, the justices knew the facts. Swiftly, they swatted down the argument that Grambling was a first offender. The white-collar criminal usually comes to us as a first offender, one justice noted. "The whole pattern of his life" has been one of dishonesty, another justice said. He even stole from his fraternity, observed a third; he has "littered" the community with victims. The court heard Adler's argument that Grambling was afflicted with the disease of "doing the deal": The justices were unmoved. The court's concern was the protection of society, and the only assurance of protection appeared to be the sentence imposed. In his last argument in Grambling's defense, Adler emphasized that Grambling had received the Husky deal from investment bankers, who had misstated the numbers and thus inserted Grambling into the disaster. "Maybe they should be in jail too," a justice shot back. The argument ended.

On February 16, 1989, the Appellate Division unanimously affirmed Grambling's conviction and sentence. Subsequently, the Court of Appeals, New York State's highest court, refused to hear an appeal from the Appellate Division's decision. The New York State appeals are at an end.

When I was interviewed by Mr. Morgenthau for my position as an assistant, he asked me how certain I could be in my judgment when I decided to pursue a case or seek a sentence. I did not know what I was expected to say so I answered truthfully. I doubted that I could always be certain in my actions, but expected that I would reflect on my conduct and, by a process of continuing reexamination, reach some comfortable level of certainty, secure in the knowledge that I could always be convinced that I was wrong and act accordingly. Insofar as that can be a philosophy, it is one to which many assistants adhere: Continuous reflection on the wisdom of one's acts. I have questioned myself about this case.

In hindsight, the reader might ask, as I have, "How did Grambling ever expect to succeed?" Grambling's various defense counsel have also asked that question. They think that the asking is exculpatory. They presume the answer to be that Grambling did not expect to succeed. Accordingly, they conclude, Grambling's conduct was indicative of self-destructive, diseased behavior warranting psychiatric care and not prison. The reader is familiar with the logic.

"How did Grambling ever expect to succeed?" is, I think, the wrong question. Until January 1985, Grambling did succeed. Within the business community, he had a reputation of integrity and creditworthiness. He had defrauded a half-dozen banks and businesses with such perfection that the victims did not even know that they had been swindled. He had stolen $7.5 million from the Bank of Montreal and $6 million from Colorado National. He was about to obtain the $100 million necessary for him to enter the oil and gas business. He was successful beyond his wildest dreams. For John Grambling, crime paid handsome rewards.

That success would have continued but for Scott Hean's innocuous remark to Ivor Hopkyns, "Isn't it about time that we should be getting the Dr Pepper stock proceeds on that personal loan?" The remark led to the January 15 phone call to Lazard, Freres, and the cascade of events that brought Grambling down. What would have happened had Hopkyns not spoken to the real Corcoran on January 15? The $100 million loan would have been made. There would have been adjustments because of the guarantee problem, but adjustments are in the nature of banking. The deal would have been done, and Grambling would have owned the oil company, with its millions in assets and cash flow. With funds from his most current victim, he would have papered over his prior crimes. But he would not have changed his character. The lack of integrity he had brought to his prior business affairs would have been applied to his future dealings as the owner of Grambling Energy. It is just an opinion, but I have no doubt that his ownership of Grambling Energy would have been the platform for future and larger frauds. The unraveling of the schemes began with Hean's off-hand remark to Hopkyns. As Napolean is said to have remarked of his generals, I want men who are capable, and lucky.

There is a moral in the events. The business of this country proceeds on trust. Of course, bankers and other people check documents and backgrounds. But there comes a point at which the checking stops, at which the parties accept what is said or written because of a basic presumption of honesty. Grambling understood where the checking ended and the trust began. He abused that knowledge, and he abused the trust that people hold based on that ultimate assumption of honesty. I do not know whether the ratio of John Gramblings to honest business people is one to a thousand, or one to 50 thousand, or far less. Bankers are trained to evaluate credentials and assets. They are not instructed how to exercise a psychiatric insight into the customer. Perhaps they should be so instructed, and perhaps this book is, to its limited degree, the beginning of the training they need. No banker should ever forget that he could be dealing with a person whose moral universe is not his own.

It is traditional in an epilogue to make the reader current on the major actors and entities discussed in the book.

After his retirement from Colorado National, Bruce Rockwell assumed the presidency of Colorado Trust, a philanthropy with $250 million in assets. Designed to improve the lives of Colorado residents in health and medical areas, the Trust, supervised by Rockwell, extends grants of $40 million a year. Tom Foncannon, still at Colorado National, is a senior lending officer in the oil and gas division. He thinks of this fraud weekly. It's like having been raped, he says. It does not go away. As to the bank itself, in the Grambling bankruptcy proceeding, it recovered $1,850,000 of its $6 million loss.

At the Bank of Montreal, a larger institution for whom the loss was proportionately smaller, events have been kinder to the officers. Ivor Hopkins continued as a lending officer in the Corporate and Government Group in Calgary; in January 1990, he was promoted to a position at the bank's Toronto headquarters. In late 1985, Mullin was transferred to Houston, where he assumed responsibility for a portfolio that grew from $500 million to $800 million under his stewardship: He has left the bank and presently is a general manager of a food manufacturing company in Vancouver, British Columbia. Hean is also in Vancouver. In November 1989, he was appointed Senior Vice President in charge of the bank's Corporate and Government Group in British Columbia. As to the institution, in November 1989, the bank won its costly five-year struggle with its insurer. In a settlement, the bank recovered the remaining principal on the Grambling loan ($150,000 had been recovered in the bankruptcy proceeding), as well as a substantial portion of the accrued interest and costs of recovery, mostly attorneys' fees.

Regarding Husky Oil, two events of note have occurred. In December 1985, Husky sold R.M.T. for an amount almost identical to what Grambling was to have paid a year earlier. The buyer was a resident of Brigham City, Utah, and the leveraged financing was provided by a local bank fully familiar with Husky's American operations; The First Security Bank of Utah. Husky, incidentally, is again a client of the Bank of Montreal. What turns around, comes around.

Among the attorneys, the following has occurred. Leaving Shearman & Sterling, James Busuttil returned to the federal government as a special attorney for environmental matters. He then reentered private practice: He joined several Shearman & Sterling colleagues at a newly formed Manhattan firm, Porter & Travers. He has remained active as an advocate of international human rights. Jon Greenblatt became a partner of Shearman & Sterling in January 1989: He has since worked on other major fraud cases. Martin Flumenbaum, among his subsequent cases, represented the insider-trader Dennis Levine; currently, Flumenbaum is counsel to Michael Milken, the Drexel Burnham trader who pleaded guilty to securities fraud and who is a defendant in multiple civil suits. In that same criminal case, Peter Fleming represented Milken's company, Drexel Burnham. Among Alan Kaufman's more recent cases was his representation of a defendant in the federal racketeering trial arising from the corruption-plagued Wedtech Corporation. Unlike the Grambling prosecution, in the Wedtech case, Kaufman had the opportunity to show his trial skills: His was the only defendant acquitted by the jury of all charges.

As to the accomplices, unwitting or not, I last saw Libman at the time of his October 1986 sentencing. As he was being led from court in handcuffs, he motioned to me. I approached and he said that he had "no ill feelings." Libman served six difficult months on Rikers' Island: He has written a manuscript about his experience. He is presently a real estate consultant. Robert Wilkis, having served his year and a day in Danbury Prison Camp, an Allenwood-like prison in Connecticut, has started his own business in Manhattan.

Grambling is in federal prison. The federal prosecutor in Denver has pursued charges arising from the collapse of the Biosystems trade school and the defrauding of its students. Grambling is presently trying to negotiate a plea to the Denver charges, as well as a reduction of the eight-year federal sentence imposed in Chicago and San Diego. Once his federal time is at an end, he will be transferred to New York State to begin his 20-year state sentence.

He appears to have learned little from prison. In September 1988, I received information that he was "at it again," sending packages through friends in an attempt to obtain bank funding.

He has also continued his ill effect on his sons. In one letter, he told the boys a parable of his life. Goldilocks had gone to the Three Bears' house and, having eaten the porridge and broken the furniture, left. Then the Big Bad Wolf came in and fell asleep on a bed. When the Three Bears returned, they saw the wolf and, falsely accusing him of the damage, beat him up. The message to the children is that the father is an innocent man, unjustly accused. His once-a-week phone calls send a similar message. He's in jail, he tells them, only because he made some "mistakes." The sons are growing up thinking that you go to jail when you make a mistake; they are terrified of making any mistakes, however trivial. Grambling cannot explain to his sons the moral context of his "mistakes" since he has yet to admit to himself that he violated a moral code. The wife currently pre-reads all letters to the children, and listens to all phone calls. She has not yet made the decision to end contacts between the boys and their natural father.

Trish Grambling has remade her life. She remarried recently and is living in a New England state. She never knew her husband: "It's as if I went to bed with a boy scout, and woke up with Jack the Ripper." She was as deceived as anyone. She has said that she wishes she had just been raped. Then it would be over with. But now she has to live with raising her sons in the hope that they will not become like the father. One friend, thinking he was being sympathetic, told her that he could not understand why Grambling's sentence was so high for "just a white-collar crime." She could have ripped out the friend's throat. The "just a white-collar crime" is something that she lives with everyday. At least the courts have given her sons time to develop somewhat free of their natural father's influence.

As to those in the court system, this is what has occurred.

Hillel Bodek is still being retained by counsel and the courts. In one of my last fraud cases, I was disturbed by the lack of rationality to the defendant's conduct. I asked Bodek to examine the defendant. With his usual perception, he discovered organic brain damage that diminished the defendant's ability to control her impulses. The injury was treatable by drugs, and the treatment has allowed the defendant to enter the successful course of rehabilitation and probation that I and Bodek had urged on the court. The injustice of Bodek's treatment at the Bellevue Prison Ward has not been rectified.

Among the prosecutors, Kindler and Moscow are, fortunately for New York County, still at the District Attorney's Office. They handle that Office's most difficult cases. In 1988,

Mayor Koch appointed Benitez to the position of Coordinator of Criminal Justice in New York City, a post Benitez resigned on the election of the new mayor in November 1989. The following month, Benitez was appointed a judge of the New York City Criminal Court. In that same November 1989 election, the voters of New York County reelected Robert M. Morgenthau to his fifth term as District Attorney; he was unopposed.

As he was in 1985 through 1987, Herman Cahn is a Civil Court judge appointed to sit as an Acting Supreme Court Justice. He is currently assigned to Civil Term.

After the Grambling case, I remained in the District Attorney's Office for 18 months: I had other matters to complete. My last trial was a case I inherited from John Moscow (and a case in which I received invaluable assistance from U.S. Attorney Giuliani). I tried a former New York City Deputy Mayor who, in order to obtain a military contract for his company, had bribed a General of the New York Army National Guard. It was one of the most difficult and important trials of my career. It was lost until summations. But with the People's summation, the day was won; and on November 18, 1988, after making my sentencing argument in that case, I resigned my appointment.

It was hard to leave the District Attorney's Office. The 1980s was an unusual time to be in public service. When I graduated from Columbia Law School, money was of little concern to me and to people who were my friends. I could pay for food, rent, and books, and most everything else was unneeded luxury. Public service was an adventure and, as one of my mentors advised, its own reward. Then I married, and we had children. When our Manhattan rental apartment was converted into a co-op, and my wife and I did not have the money to buy our home, I realized that perhaps I could no longer afford to stay in the Office. I am grateful for having had attorneys such as Kindler, Moscow, Benitez, and Morgenthau as my teachers, and I look with unabashed envy at the young assistants who have succeeded me.